THE END OF AN EPOCH

THE END OF AN EPOCH

Aline,
Countess of Romanones

Copyright © 2015 by: Fundación Aline Condesa vda. De Romanones
All rights reserved.

ISBN: 1508630968
ISBN-13: 978-1508630968

*To my dear grandson,
Juan Figueroa Sayn-Wittgenstein*

CONTENTS

1	Leaving New York City................................	9
2	Arrival Madrid 1944....................................	19
3	Bullfights and Danger..................................	33
4	Paris 1946...	44
5	Return to Madrid..	49
6	Marriage..	61
7	The Wedding...	68
8	The Honeymoon...	71
9	Capri, Venice, Rome....................................	75
10	Ocean liner, Pearl River, New York................	79
11	New York City..	86
12	Madrid 1948..	93
13	Married Life, Luis's Office & Jose Silva...........	102
14	Extremadura..	109
15	Luis & The Civil War....................................	119
16	Ambassador Lodge, Changes........................	128
17	The Medinaceli Palace Madrid......................	134
18	Pascualete, Shepherds.................................	141
19	Pillete & Pepe...	155
20	Family Life and Servants..............................	161
21	First Trip to Las Dueñas................................	182
22	Primitivo Comes to Madrid, Maria and Chickens.....	192
23	Tyrone Power, American Stars in Madrid...........	204
24	Puppy, Felipe 2, Eboli...................................	212
25	Roman Origins of Pascualete.........................	228
26	The Windsors...	238
27	The Children..	257
28	Ferrieres & Rothschild..................................	260
29	Jaen, The Shoot & Franco.............................	273
30	Lawrence of Arabia.....................................	284
31	Paleography, Canilleros, Tia Carmen...............	288
32	The Four Sisters..	296

33	Jackie Kennedy at Dueñas.............................	304
34	History of Las Dueñas..................................	314
35	Cordoba, Monasterio de San Jeronimo...............	317
36	The Jews and Pedro Golfin............................	327
37	Windsor and Franco Shoot.............................	339
38	Glamourous New York.................................	355
39	The Windsors again....................................	361
40	Marbella and The Arabs...............................	373
41	Marcos – Trips to Filipinas............................	381
42	Tea with Old Ladies...................................	408
43	Marriages..	418
44	To Granada with Audrey..............................	424
45	European Summers.....................................	432
46	Morocco...	436
47	Franco's Death, Black Ambassador, Elections 1977...	473
48	Windsor Three..	481
49	President Nixon..	489
50	Lectures...	493
51	Meeting Reagan..	498
52	Intelligence...	503
53	International Women...................................	505
54	Duchess of Windsor Four.............................	512
55	Changes...	515

CHAPTER ONE

LEAVING NEW YORK CITY

Little did I realize as I waited for the telephone call that night in the hotel room in New York that my life from then on was going to be so radically different. I was prepared for the danger because I had volunteered for "hazardous duty " and had received intensive training for whatever risks espionage might entail - it was 1943, the middle of World War Two and I was barely twenty one years old. The wait for news of the departure of my first airplane flight to Europe in a Pan American Clipper might take several days. I had never been more than a few miles away from the town of my birth or later on from my university . But at the moment my main interest was to take an active part in the war, where my brothers and men friends were already risking their lives.

After two days anxiously next to the telephone, on the second night the call came. Top secrecy was strictly maintained for all Pan American Clipper departures – only a month before enemy agents in the United States had advised their allies abroad of the clipper departure resulting in a crash landing in the bay of Lisbon which had killed Allied officials and some movie stars on their way to entertain our troops. Ten minutes later there was a knock on my door - two men stood there ready to drive me to the wharf from where I would be taken to the Clipper. On the short trip to the dock the men were silent – so was I - but the anticipation and joy I was feeling kept me trembling. The night was black and a cold wind was blowing when we arrived at the pier. As I descended from the car, a man in a heavy military overcoat reached out and led me across the wharf and down dark steps into a motor boat. Without a word he indicated a bench and an empty spot next to two other men also in uniform. As I took my seat immediately the boat was put into motion – only the sound of the motors broke the night's silence as we bounced across the waves toward a shadowy outline of the huge plane floating on the sea.

I had never been in a plane nor near one before and the sight of the huge Clipper in the dark shadows beyond made my pulse quicken. Soon we reached the plane where another stairway led up into it; meanwhile large waves were making the gangplank bounce. I found it difficult to grab my hat and keep my balance in the strong wind until a strong gentle hand helped me until I was inside the plane. I had no time to look around - someone took my arm and led me to a large comfortable armchair nearby and before I could see anything else, the same person was securing straps on the arms of my chair. Nearby several men were seated on a wide sofa, another in an armchair facing mine. Evidently we had been the last passengers to arrive because almost immediately the roar of the huge motors resounded and soon the plane began to move. Now I glanced around and could see that my surroundings were similar to the transatlantic ocean liners I had seen in movies- the seats were not in rows – this part of the interior of the plane was like a large salon. As I looked about me, we were skimming across the sea, the tremble of the big plane over the water and the jerks made by the booming motors caused my chair to shake violently. I grasped the chair arms, my body bouncing with the plane's movements as it took off. The huge motors now throbbed stronger – and stronger - making the plane move still more violently - the jolting movements and sounds increased my joy – it was a moment I would never forget. The violent trembling continued, my body following the plane's shuddering movements as I basked in the delight of knowing that finally I was on my way and would soon be taking part in the Great War.

I sensed that we were rising – gradually the shaking stopped – the plane became stable, only a low hum of the motors – yes we were on our way. Through the window next to my chair not one light was visible - New York City was in its usual wartime black-out.

A voice on the loud speaker informed that we would refuel in three hours and a half in Bermuda and from there continue on to Lisbon. The attractive man sitting in the armchair facing me now leaned forward – "Perhaps you are unaware that you are the only woman on board. We are thirty-two passengers in all- the clipper doesn't take more." Then very kindly he began to explain details of the plane. "We travel in luxury – wait till you see the dining room on the floor above".

He was certainly correct – when dinner was announced one of the passengers led me up a curved stairway to a large room with sparkling white damask clothed tables where we were served as in an elegant restaurant. There for the first time since I had met him three months before in the hotel Biltmore in New York, I recognized one of my first OSS contacts, Larry Mellon. I was unaware then that he and the man sitting next to him, Jim McMillan would both be working with me in Madrid where I was to be the new Secret Intelligence agent.

In Bermuda the swells of the waves were too big for the plane to take off for several days- so we arrived days later than planned at our destination- Portugal and Spain – the two neutral countries in war-torn Europe. It was nighttime when I had my first view of Europe. Lisbon lay below like a dazzling diamond horseshoe of flickering lights. It appeared to me as if we were arriving at a gigantic party in full swing - gaiety seemed to beckon in the velvet night from the shimmering bay. Perhaps it was the contrast with the blackout in the United States or that this was my first plane trip, but I was spellbound. Just then a steward came to my armchair and told me that the captain invited me to view the landing from the cockpit – thus I had a special stimulating view of the bay and the water as I stood next to the captain's seat. AS the clipper settled down on the sea splitting the waves into peaks of creamy froth, the plane spurted ahead, high sprays of sea water bathing the glass cover of the cockpit. The sight was unforgettable and the sensation was exhilarating. Then I saw many small rowboats nearby and asked the captain what they were.

"Those boats!" indicated the captain as he pointed to them. "Look at them well, they are the enemy, the Japanese. Their intelligence center operates out of Lisbon and Madrid. When our Clipper crashed a month ago, the Japs were cruising the wreckage before anyone could get to the scene - they picked up pouches destined for Allied embassies, leaving wounded passengers to drown while salvaging top-secret documents. Beware," he said, seriously. "Under Lisbon's frivolity lurks a city of deadly intrigue."

My two companion OSS agents, William "Larry" Mellon and James MacMillan told me as we climbed from the boat which had taken us from the clipper to the dock that they would take me to my destination, the Hotel Palacio in Estoril, which was about half an hour away along the coastal highway.

While the reception clerk thumbed through our passports , I enjoyed looking around at the luxury of the old hotel, the ornate carpet, the antique furnishings, the baroque wall clock – this was my first awareness of the beauty and elegance of old world- Europe and it was fascinating me already.

Larry Mellon glanced at his watch. "Can you change into evening clothes in twenty minutes? I must go to the casino, and you should come, too. We may meet one of our agents there."

The idea of seeing a casino thrilled me - I was ready and dressed in fifteen minutes flat. The gambling palace's bronze-embossed mahogany entrance doors were attended by footmen in livery. Inside the scene was breathtaking, because of the sheer scale of its opulence. From cavernous ceilings, crystal chandeliers were suspended on ropes of bronze poised above a bank of game tables. Enormous arched windows were cloaked with fringed burgundy velvet; red carpeting absorbed our steps. The clatter of chips and whirr of roulette wheels could be heard as we entered.

"Prenez voux places. Rien ne va plus," the croupiers shouted. Muffled voices spoke in many tongues. Larry pointed to the Japanese milling about. "Aline, watch those fellows. Here in Lisbon they receive information about troop departures from seaports on our West and East coasts, which they relay to Tokyo and Berlin. The Japanese have an excellent worldwide espionage network. They're contacting agents here in the casino, picking up messages, including dates and hours transmitted by the numbers played at the roulette table—right under our noses."

My colleagues wanted to discover to which agents the Japanese were transmitting information at those roulette tables and asked me if I could make heads or tails of the number code they were using. One of my specialities at the spy school had been deciphering all types of codes which I seemed to excel in - coding was going to be part of my job in Madrid along with many other tricks of the trade for which I had been prepared. But that night in the casino I was unable to help although I enjoyed the novelty of testing my abilities in a gambling casino filled with Germans, Japanese and other Axis enemies.

Eventually we moved on to a "chemin de fer" table, where eight players were seated and over twenty stood watching - many in evening dress, nobody was shabbily clothed.

"Never speak audibly near a game table," whispered Larry. "Gamblers are superstitious, especially when the stakes are high. There are over ten thousand dollars in escudos and chips on that table right now."

A plump lady in red lace with a diamond-and-ruby brooch pinned above her monumental bosom was about to pull cards from a wooden box in front of her. A red-nailed finger slid card after card over the green felt surface, facedown—two for her opponents and two for herself.

"A gut-grabbing game," Larry murmured. "Not to be compared to roulette. The winner is the one whose cards add nearest to nine, not more. Kings, queens, and jacks count zero. Aces, one. Look, she's turned up one of her two cards—a three. Now the opponent has the chance of deciding if he wants a third card." A hush engulfed the group. "Ah, he's having difficulty making up his mind." Larry's whisper was getting louder. "He probably has five, maybe even six." The player gave a minute negative shake of his head. "See, I was right. He doesn't want to take the chance. Another card may raise his count over nine." I watched as the lady pulled a third card for herself.

"That's Madame Lubescu and the jewels she is wearing represent all that is left of an enormous fortune given her by King Karol of Romania. If she loses tonight--!"

My eyes were glued to the pile of chips. Would she win? After a split second, she flung the cards down on the green felt with an obvious sigh of relief—echoed by the surrounding crowd. Her opponent got up without a word, and she waited until the croupier shovelled the chips and bills into a neat mound in the center of the table and placed them before her. Her hand wavered over the box for a moment. She was tempted to try again. If she won she could double her money. Slowly she began to slide the chips into her purse, followed by the bills. We all watched. She stood up and left.

We wandered through the game rooms for a while, Mellon scanning the faces. Then he guided me down a wide corridor to the WonderBar, the nightclub "famous," he said, "for its cuisine." At midnight the crowd was at its peak and every table was taken; the floor was filled with couples moving to the music of a rumba band.

After a few minutes at the long crystal bar, we were seated near the dance floor: Larry leaned close. "The man dancing with the lady in the silver dress. You'll be seeing a lot of him in the future. That's Top Hat, one of the best agents we've got."

My first impression was: Top Hat the cat. He was sleek and feline; thick eyebrows and a narrow moustache gave him a slippery air. His glamorous partner was obviously enjoying his conversation.

"One of Mr. Top Hat's attributes, obviously, is his charm for women," I commented.

"Charm?" Larry returned dryly. "He doesn't just charm them—he slays them."

After dinner, we strolled back toward the game rooms through the high-ceilinged hall, chatting about the contrasts with life at home. Suddenly the piercing shriek of a terrified woman resounded through the wide corridor. In an instant the scene before us became a bedlam of people running. Larry sprinted ahead, and I followed just as fast. By the time we reached the end of the long passageway, a crowd was gathering around something on the red-carpeted floor. I stared down at the crumpled body of a man lying face down. Larry, who was just to my right, gripped my arm. Then I saw why. A knife protruded from the center of the man's black dinner jacket! We remained frozen. More screams from behind us. A woman fainted. Kneeling down, Larry felt the man's pulse while the crowd pushed and shoved to get a better look. It had happened too fast for me to digest its meaning—the scene had the unreality of opera. Then my companion turned the body over, just enough to see the face.

The ashen countenance of the stricken man confronted me. Already color had faded from a big nose and jowls. Mellon appeared struck by a revelation. I knew in that moment that Larry recognized the man on the floor.

What snapped, there and then? What delusion of mine? This was the difference between textbook medicine and the operating room. The contorted face, frozen in pain, awoke me to the reality of what I was in for. Blood now was staining the thick carpeting, beading my black satin pumps with tiny droplets. When I looked up, a mass of bewildered faces—ladies in jewels, some of the uniformed staff, and a few croupiers—were staring.

Straightening, Mellon braced his hands on my shoulders and pivoted me around, propelling me with an energetic stride through the crowded hall toward the entrance.

"Is he dead?"

"Very much so."

"Do you know him?"

"Of course not. Come on, we can't get involved."

"How can we not get involved? Won't we be questioned?"

"Aline, where do you think we are? Wake up—this is Lisbon. The only thing anybody in there cares about is getting rid of the body so they can get back to the tables. Some of those gamblers may look opulent, but most of them are betting tomorrow's breakfast."

On the ride back, each in our own world, we barely spoke. I was thinking how fast death can come. The sumptuous hotel lobby was deserted, and the ancient clock above the concierge's desk ticking its steady monotone marked three-thirty. Mellon left me at my door. "Try to put it out of your mind, Aline—get some sleep. Wait for my call in the morning."

I nodded.

In my room I opened the balcony doors and listened to the ocean splash in the distance, a few straggling lights were blinking like beached stars. The cold moonless night brought me back days before to the Brooklyn pier. Already my universe had changed. I had tasted the excitement, but also the horror. Nevertheless, I was able to sleep soon afterwards. Was it fatigue or a new callousness?

The next day Larry avoided any reference to the night before as we careened along the rugged ocean highway to the city of Lisbon.

Soon the road sprouted tributaries—we followed the snaky narrow streets that braided the steep hills of pink and dusty-beige Lisbon. In a cobblestoned square near the docks, fishermen and their wives were selling shiny codfish from crude stands of wooden crates, the men in baggy black corduroy trousers and blouselike jackets, the women in ankle length skirts, fringed black shawls, and black head scarves. A few cars circulated, but many people thronged the streets on foot, and a small red trolley rattled by.

Just in front of a fortress rising in craggy splendor above the bay, Larry told the taxi driver to stop. Paying him, we got down and walked toward a side street. He pointed to the large structure above us. "That was one of the few buildings to withstand the earthquake of 1755. Voltaire was here then and described the holocaust in his story, "Candide". Remember?"

The street was narrow and steep, bordered by old gray apartment houses with balconies where clothes hung to dry and waved in the salty sea wind. At number 16, Larry opened a door and led me through the small patio, then down an ancient stone staircase- obviously he had been here before.

The cellar room, windowless except for one grated aperture up high, was engulfed in clouds of the cigarette smoke created by the ten men who sat in a circle. I recognized Bill Casey and Russ Forgan from the plane; otherwise, the assortment was a melting pot.

One looked like an academic, another was a Mediterranean type, another with a British accent offered me a chair.

Larry went to the center of the circle. The group, reseated, shifted collectively in their chairs. The damp cellar room became silent.

"The news stinks," Mellon announced in his slow drawl. "The head of one of our MO teams was captured and our transmitter reports the Krauts began the torture by pulling out his fingernails one by one."

I did my best to hide my revulsion. MO agents were those behind enemy lines, spreading psychological warfare in southern France, sometimes blowing up bridges and sabotaging enemy routes. He went on, "One of our colleagues in France dropped in the Pau area was picked up on arrival. Pretty bad, eh? That might indicate a double agent someplace." Mellon waited a few moments to let his information sink in. "If so," he continued, "Operation Anvil is being sabotaged from within."

"How about our agent bumped off last night in the casino'" asked a skinny young American called Jack seated next to me.

"Forget that incident," Mellon advised sharply.

So the corpse had been one of us. That made the scene I had witnessed still more appalling. While Larry was relaying technical data, I decided the best thing I could do was to hope no one would become aware of the depths of my insecurity at this moment. Last night had been a warning of situations we might face in the future. And what I had heard this morning was proof that our business would necessitate more skills than those taught at "The Farm".

CHAPTER TWO

ARRIVAL MADRID 1944

The lush green valleys of Portugal were left behind. Soon I was gazing down on the barren fields of Castile - a gray chilly looking sprawl - and the snow-covered peaks of the Guadarrama Mountains. None of the usual Castilian sparkle in winter of sun warming the untilled orange and red fields or the customary splendor of a deep blue sky that I had read about. The view matched the state of the world at war and my precarious job as the new espionage agent. But scanning the austere countryside below I sensed a mystery, a sort of magic, not unlike the feelings mentioned by Merrimee or Gautier in their books or any of the other foreigners arriving a century before in stagecoaches or on horseback. Spain during the past century and even before had attracted courageous visitors looking for adventure in this country so unique and unlike the rest of Europe. The land below now revealed rolling prairies ploughed in symmetrical stripes of reds, browns, greys. The plane descended in a birdlike arc along the course of a sinuous river on a high plateau. Where were the people? Only a tiny village now and then with little houses squeezed together dotted the checkered landscape. So this was my destination? As I gazed down, I prayed that I would be worthy of the mission which had been entrusted to me.

As I stepped down from the small Iberia plane, the chilly winter wind whipped my skirts and I had to grab my hat so it wouldn't blow off. Larry Mellon and Jim McMillan had remained in Lisbon – as I had been informed, I was supposed to arrive alone. The flight over Portugal had covered endless green lush terrain, but here there seemed to be neither people nor life of any kind. I buckled against the wind and ran across the empty air field, only one plane was in sight, and as I rushed past it, a huge black Swastika painted on the wing seemed to glare at me – so I was finally in a war area. That German Lufthansa was ominous and made me realize that here in Madrid I was really getting into the war. But I was exhilarated and happy, finally I was stepping foot on Spain, the destination for which I had been trained. A shiver of excitement ran up my spine and the nearness of adventure in this exotic ancient country filled me with joy.

In the garage like room that composed the entire air terminal, two customs officials, Civil Guards in strange hats and ankle-length olive capes, greeted me with smiles. "Buenos días, señorita." After stamping my passport and briefly inspecting my luggage, they kindly escorted me to a taxi. Some enemy, I thought, but then I remembered the scene in the Lisbon casino and realized I shouldn't be overly confident. Yet it was difficult not to smile back. These Spaniards were friendly and kind – it showed in their warm brown eyes and every gesture.

The taxi bounced through the outskirts of Madrid on a pitted dirt road with scarcely any traffic other than two carts pulled by donkeys, then we passed a spectacular red brick building, huge and round, even I could realize that was a bullring, then a few streets lined by shabby buildings. A few minutes later we arrived at a boulevard where well-dressed children played under the vigilance of governesses in picturesque plaid skirts, fringed woollen shawls, and large globe-shaped gilt earrings.

"La Castellan," the driver announced proudly.

Like Lisbon, the city was almost bereft of autos; a few bicycles, some dilapidated carriages drawn by bony horses— no policemen or traffic signals at all. At one point, the driver sideswiped an approaching taxi, whereupon both drivers rolled down their windows and shouted "Idiota!" Spanish wasn't going to be difficult to learn – I had had only one month intensive training in the language in Washington. Every few blocks we passed a plaza with barren trees and waterless fountains adorned by gigantic statues; bordering the boulevard were granite palaces, their iron-grilled walls enclosing gardens. The peaceful wide avenue with its surrounding residences had an air of old-fashioned opulence and dignity.

We turned into the curved drive of the stately Palace Hotel about eleven o´clock in the morning where a fancily dressed doorman took my bags and led me up the steps and to the reception desk where my passport was requested. This was the moment planned in Washington for me to meet, in a seemingly accidental manner, the agent who would assist me "on the outside," Shepardson had said.

As I turned around, a man emerged from behind a marble column, striding toward me exactly according to the predetermined arrangements. The feline gait registered even before the exotic, high-cheekboned face. Top Hat!

At the same moment, something else happened. Behind Top Hat, a good-looking young man was approaching also. Which was my contact? When I dropped my handbag as had been planned in Washington, both men darted for it. This created a problem for me - I looked from one to the other- which was my contact? Then Top Hat, with a polite "excuse me" to the younger man, picked up my purse and handed it to me.

"The historical way to meet a lady." His words, although the correct code, were pronounced with the affected air of a bad actor. At close range, his features appeared tinged with a slightly sinister cast; maybe it was the gangster´s moustache over the seductive smirk of his mouth. He had thick black hair shiny with brilliantine, graceful fingers, and extremely white teeth.

"Edmundo Lassalle´s my name. Would you do me the honor of joining me for a drink in the bar this evening?"

Now I answered with the previously planned sentence: "How kind of you to invite me."

We exchanged a few more words before I put my hand out to say good-bye. Top Hat bowed slightly, kissing my hand, his air still theatrical.

When I reached the elevator I was surprised to find the same handsome young man awaiting me with my two suitcases in his hands. His presence as we ascended made me nervous. He was well-dressed, tall and blonde, certainly not a bellboy- his English was perfect as he spoke to me in the elevator asking for my room number. Could this be a German agent –could I have been uncovered so soon? I was relieved when the door of my room closed behind me.

I looked around. The oak flooring was only partly covered by a tattered red carpet, yet the apartment was spacious, high-ceilinged, with mahogany scroll-worked furnishings and armoires instead of closets. I pumped the long round bolster on the bed, so different from pillows in America and hard as a rock. Next I went to the windows and parted the heavy red velour, then the lace curtains. In front, an imposing edifice with two carved stone lions adorning the wide steps; over the entrance was inscribed "Las Cortes"—the Spanish Parliament, no less.

One taxi beetled around the plaza to the right, where a statue of Neptune decorated another dry fountain; a yellow trolley rattled by. On the sidewalk below, an old man waved pieces of paper. "Lotería," he squawked in a rasping voice. Lottery and all, the city possessed a slow, pacific rhythm, light-years away from the commotion of Manhattan.

That night as I entered the bar of the hotel at nine-thirty dressed in my most elegant black dinner outfit - Edmundo Lassalle raised my hand to his lips while bestowing a stunning smile and then led me to a banquette. Having modeled during summer vacations and during the months since I graduated for the best haute couture house in New York City, I had an excellent wardrobe, but I had never been in a bar in my life.

My parents had obliged me to commute back and forth to my home town daily when I worked in New York the summer vacation and from September to June for the last four years I had been living in a catholic women's University run by nuns.

Once we were seated he asked, "What will you have? Here everybody takes dry sherry or a gin fizz."

"I don't drink."

"Divina," he purred. "Better for your work, my dear." His smile still embraced me.

"Do you have any idea who that good-looking young man was in the lobby this afternoon?" I inquired.

He shrugged. "Just an admirer, I presume. Your entry caused quite a sensation."

I looked at him dubiously. "Do you know, he took my bags up to my room, and when I offered him a tip, he wouldn't accept. He spoke perfect English. I suppose he could just as well be German?"

"Don't worry about it. You're new. You will be under observation for a while."

"Since we will be working together, don't you think I should know what your cover is?"

"My cover is that I am a Mexican." I tried not to laugh. What else could he have been?

"The representative of Walt Disney in Spain. This gives me the possibility of appearing neutral and enables me to see people of both sides. The plan is to take you to a reception given by the Marquesa of Torrejón, where you'll meet Spaniards—foreign ambassadors, a few enemy spies, also rich, beautiful titled women from other countries. Only women with influence today can obtain exit permits from the countries at war. Madrid is considered the paradise of Europe right now. This will be the ideal opportunity to introduce you to the social world of the city, so your special work can begin immediately."

A short plump man accompanied by a blond woman stopped at the table to speak to Edmundo. My companion stood up, mumbling a few words to the man, and quickly sat down again. "A friend of mine from the secret police. Couldn't introduce you because he's with his mistress. Mistresses and respectable women have no contact here," he explained.

I took another look at the lady, wondering how I would ever distinguish the difference.

"My dear, you're going to adore this city," he began. "Everyone here is worth taking note of. Over there," he indicated with a nod, "are the Italians. Next to them the Germans. Just behind, Rumanians, Poles, and Bulgarians. The Japanese stay in that corner."

"Are some enemy spies?" I asked.

"Some?" he laughed. "They're *all* spies. Not a reliable person in the place."

"Does that include you?" I smiled.

"Absolutely not." Again a flash of teeth. Something about the sly smirk, his poise, the squeaky giggle, made me feel he was as shady as anyone he had pointed out.

"Who is the Marquesa of Torrejón?

"She is the most popular social leader, and her gatherings the spiciest. I hope you have a wardrobe to meet the demands of Madrid's social life. If not, I recommend a visit to Balenciaga, he is best designer in Europe- but he is Spanish and has a fashion house in Paris and here as well. Women in Madrid are especially chic, but the American Ambassador Hayes's wife is, frankly, dowdy, while the German ambassador's wife has a flair that makes her most popular.

The majority of Spaniards are pro-Allies, politically. But darling, much as I love the Americans—and work for them—their social graces don't hold a candle to the Europeans." His eyes darted from one end of the room to the other. Each newcomer was closely appraised, but Top Hat's glib conversation never stopped.

He crunched a potato chip as he spoke, seldom waiting for me to respond. His foreign accent made everything he said sound alluring. "Lent is a letdown. They play a lot of cards in their chilly palaces. You know, there is a lack of coal. That's why most of Balenciaga's dresses are of wool and with long sleeves. During Lent the ladies have tea and say the rosary a lot; the men gamble and brag about their *conquistas,* their seductions. Franco outlawed public casinos. Probably a good thing. Spaniards are natural-born gamblers. Betting is permitted at the jai-alai court on Calle Hermosilla. You've got to see with what speed the bookies take the bets and then stuff their betting slips into slit tennis balls and toss them up to the stands. Jai-alai is the fastest ball game in the world, you know. The players are usually Basque. With any luck, Lent will be pepped up by some romantic scandal. There is no divorce, and adultery is an inevitable game."

Edmundo arose again, this time to bow to a particularly attractive woman who proceeded to the table behind us. "The *guapísima* Marquesa of Córdoba," he muttered to me as he sat down. But even she had not distracted him from his determination to inform me totally on life in Spain. He continued his diatribe more or less where he had left off.

"The grandees rarely go to their country estates, although they possess enormous properties. The ration of petrol is thirty liters a month, so most travel by train when they are obliged to make a visit to their farms and ranches. Their partridge shoots are very grand. The banquet tables are set up out in the field with silver and crystal, served by white-gloved men in livery. But they all prefer the gaiety of the capital to the country—unless there is a shoot, of course. Rural life in Spain is hard. No electricity, no plumbing, no heating, not even decent roads. The civil war didn't help that situation, either."

" When the shooting season ends, carnival begins, with the masked balls and parties. The whole city used to go masked in the streets, but Franco put an end to that. A pity. It would have been so useful for our business. I love disguises, don't you?"

Edmundo gesticulated frequently with his graceful fingers. Often his voice rose in a squeaky crescedo at the end of a sentence. I couldn't make out yet what kind of person my new colleague was, but he was bizarre.

"A formal dinner invitation reads ten-thirty, but you may not get served until an hour later. But then the Gypsies for the entertainment don't arrive until two, so why begin earlier? Anyhow, no one awakes at dawn. And remember, it's bad manners to telephone a lady before noon."

He asked for another gin fizz.

"After Lent and Holy Week comes the Fair in Sevilla in April. What magnificent carriages and horses—the harnesses are always decorated with pompons and bells! The sound of castanets and dancing in the streets night and day for one whole week! And, my dear, Spaniards are really democratic people. The most. The Gypsies, the poor, the rich, the Grandees, the shepherds and the cow herders all dance and drink together whenever they are celebrating a holiday. They are proud and individualistic. No inclination for regimentation, like the Germans. They envy each other but would die for a friend. Hate to obey the laws and are completely ungovernable. They enjoy especially complaining about their government, whatever it might be—monarchy, republic, democracy, and they've had them all."

He ceased talking for a second while he searched his pockets for another pack of cigarettes. "Really, Aline, you will have to make me a gift of some of those cartons you have available in the office to help make friends. These black Spanish *cigarillos* smell terrible." He waved to a waiter, gesturing expressively with his hand to his mouth to indicate what he wanted, and then turned his attention again to me.

"May is the month of the Fair of San Isidro, patron saint of Madrid. Bullfights for seventeen days straight. When June rolls around, the wives and children are packed off to the north. The husbands stay here, presumably to work, but the offer of the day is to play—with their girlfriends, of course. The weather in Madrid is dry and hot but never unbearable in the summer."

The waiter appeared with an assortment of cigarettes and cigars. The transaction absorbed the attention of my colleague for a full five mintues. At last he seemed satisfied and returned to his self-imposed task of making me the best-informed newcomer in Madrid.

"There will be a smattering of Axis and Spanish personalities at the Marquesa's. Concentrate on the women, the only way to get invited inside a Spanish home. The idea that Spanish women are submissive is ridiculous." He pulled a gold chain and watch out of his vest pocket. "You must be starved. We have a reservation at Edelweiss."

"A German restaurant?"

"Yes- not the best but you will see more of the enemy. Edelweiss is a favorite of German diplomats and sympathizers."

A crowd was waiting inside the door, but Edmundo and I were led to a table immediately. The room was unpretentious, overcrowded, and buzzing with voices. I watched the waiter fluttering around Edmundo. If he's on the payroll, he's overdoing it, I thought. "Would Señor Lassalle care for some pickled herring just flown in from Berlin? Tonight we have wiener schnitzel or venison." I felt like laughing. Here I was already feasting on provisions from the enemy's capital.

Edmundo lit a long, thin cigarette. "You must understand the quality and pace of the world you are entering. Right now we are in the shooting season. Partridge and wild boar, my dear. You rarely get anything else when you dine at the home of an aristocrat. Especially at the dinners given by one of the grandees who are the cream of the nobility. They live in splendor, but they certainly don't squander. Not one peseta! They shoot four days a week and eat the fruit of their efforts seven. Work is always secondary to enjoying life in this country. That goes for all levels of society."

By the time I was back in my hotel I realized that I was deep in the world of the enemy and enjoying it and feeling warm towards the people - all against the advice I had received in the spy school. Not only Edmundo had just warned me but during that secret intelligence training, I had been instructed to beware of all Spaniards- Spain although playing neutral was in reality favorable to the Nazis, its leader was a dictator called Franco who was something termed "fascist", not compatible with our American way of thinking.

Yet there was attractiveness wherever I looked. The waiters- the taxi driver -could these Spaniards really be such dangerous adversaries as my instructors believed. I was reminded of the words in Alexander Dumas' book which I had brought with me – he wrote concerning his visit to Spain in 1846: "Spanish coachmen are more accommodating than their French counterparts, and after ten minutes conversation with animated gestures of explanation, everything is satisfactorily arranged."

Today exactly one hundred years later the same seemed to have been the case in the rickety ancient taxi this morning. The driver who had been sitting at a higher level in front making the taxi resemble more a carriage than a car, had been smiling and making conversation as I was driven towards the city. We had bounced along the dirt road with holes but he continued to speak to me even if I could not understand him. Only three years before the Spanish Civil war had ended and despite those terrible years of violence and poverty, everyone I had seen since I arrived seemed to be happy and friendly.

My Spanish was limited to one month of classes after hours in the spy school and I had been warned that if I did not speak it fluently within three months of my arrival I would be sent back to Washington. Fortunately already I had learned that Spanish was going to be easy.

What Edmundo told me that first night on the banquette of the bar of the hotel Palace and the next evening at Horcher's, the famous Berlin restaurant, facilitated my understanding of many necessary Madrid social customs. He had also mentioned that the elegant Restaurant Horcher had been transplanted from Berlin to Madrid after two bombings and now was considered the best in the city of Madrid. Edmundo in his detailed conversations might well have been reading out of a crystal ball, describing my future. But as he sketched the habits and customs of the Spanish people, most particularly the grandee's—the highest society—I listened with rapt attention so that I could enter this world as I had been instructed and accomplish what I'd been sent to do.

For the next several weeks, Edmundo was invaluable, arranging meetings which enabled me to begin my undercover work and penetrate Spanish society. At that time we were only twelve trained espionage American agents in the country working under the cover of the American Oil Mission. Even with the nationals we recruited we were very few in comparison to six hundred axis spies scattered all over the Iberian Peninsula. Therefore our work was intense.

Among my obligations was recruiting native women to form chains to follow and investigate suspects, and finding myself an apartment where I could hide women agents who crossed the frontier bringing us information on German troop movements. After having volunteered for "hazardous duty" I felt guilty to be enjoying a life of peace and graciousness in Madrid while a war was going on in the rest of Europe. The only foreigners were those attached to the different embassies, which was also the usual cover for many intelligence agents. There were no tourists, a few foreign businessmen-no Americans; the city was almost exclusively made up of nationals whose courtesy and kindness was captivating. One day I asked an elderly couple where I could find the museum of the Prado and they insisted upon accompanying me five long blocks until we arrived at the wide steps of the famous building built during the reign of Charles the third in 1770. In the street men had the habit of tipping their hats to friends passing by; always men offered their seats in the trolley to any woman. If it happened to be a cold windy day, many men wore huge capes which they slung over one shoulder and covered their mouths. When I enquired about so many people with scarves wrapped over mouths, I was told that the wind from the nearby Guadarrama Mountains "would not put out a candle, but could kill a man".

When I found an apartment about two weeks later, my "portera", who usually was sitting in front of the building door when I left for work in the morning, bragged to me daily of her communist allegiances, but at the same time she saluted politely a neighbor, the Duke of Silvela, who must have been on the opposite side during the civil war, with a "buenos dias Senor Duque" when he passed by. He in turn would incline his head and tip his hat to her, replying "Buenos dias to you, Dona Antonia." Sometimes she would be bare breasted nursing her latest child, and the Duke would pause to compliment the baby. The city was peaceful and it was an unexpected delight to live amongst people with such good manners and who had been able to recuperate from the horrors of their recent war.

Every chance I had, I went walking along the avenues and the narrow side streets to enjoy the sights. Many natives wore quaint costumes which were a delight to see. Priests with huge oval brimmed hats, often so wide they had to turn sideward's to enter a store, nuns in a fascinating variety of habits, the most spectacular being those with wide white stiffly starched coifs—they always walked three together and their headdresses took up the entire width of the sidewalk. Barbers, bakers, blacksmiths, shepherds-all had their own special costume or uniform which added to the charm and attractiveness of the thoroughfare. Most of the working women wore black bandanas on their heads and long cotton skirts with aprons, now and then a woman in black with a lace mantilla would appear coming out of a church.

The American Embassy offices occupied a large two floor apartment on the Calle Miguel Angel where all American diplomats, plus the OSS Counter Espionage section, and native employees were located. However we, who were in S.I. (Secret Intelligence) section of OSS, were operating from a small apartment in the Calle Alcala Galiano, 4 – we were not allowed to go to the embassy offices which were only twelve blocks away. We had been told that embassy employees did not have the same security training as we did and that we should avoid contacts with them to eliminate questions or curiosity about our cover in the American Oil Office. In the same vein we had been advised to use communists as agents since Spanish communists had been allied in their civil war with the Russians who were now our allies. We soon realized that this was an error - in most cases pro-ally Spanish nationalists who were strongly anti-communist were equally reliable so we used both indiscriminately. Nevertheless the women I recruited as agents for my Cell became my friends - all of them were communists. As incomprehensible as their political beliefs were to me, their loyalty and kindness was as outstanding as that of the aristocrats from whom I was attempting to get another type of information. From the beginning it seemed to me that all Spaniards shared the same characteristics of respect for each other, a tendency to criticize the dictator, General Franco, to make jokes about everything, and the men all bragged about their valor.

The first Sunday I was free from work I took a walk dressed in slacks - the shocked stares of men and women made me realize that I'd better not wear them again. In the streets men had a curious custom of murmuring compliments to every woman, old or young, beautiful or not, who passed by unaccompanied by a man. In the beginning I did not know enough Spanish to understand what they were saying until Edmundo explained that this was a charming Spanish custom, that these remarks were called "piropos" they were supposed to flatter and to be humorous, the woman was not expected to acknowledge them. Evidently this custom was considered chivalrous.

My maid Angustias was tall, bony, black-haired and possessed two prominent gold teeth which somehow indicated her social status as above that of the portera who she treated with disdain. Her brothers had been killed during the civil war. One had been in Madrid and obliged to fight with the Republicans, the other had been in Burgos and obliged to enlist with the Nationalists. Angustias said she had no idea what the war had been about and had no preference for either side. Despite the fact that everyone was poor due to the ravages of the Civil War, the people in the streets were neatly dressed, and women usually in black, many men and women wore rope-soled shoes called alpargatas which were comfortable and cheap.

My portera's husband was usually drunk and had a vile temper. His wife, Dona Antonia, ignored his vociferous insults and spent hours sitting on the street in front of our door. Even on the coldest mornings, she continued to feed her baby at her bare breast. As soon as I took residence in the building, she informed me that she was pleased to have "una Americana" in the building, because not even wealthy Spaniards could obtain sugar or flour or other staples, but that the "Americanos' had everything. Obviously I would have to provide a few little packages. Angustias startled me by declaring that I would have to have another servant. When I complained, she stretched herself to her full height, declaring almost indignantly. "Una senorita Americana must have at least two servants". I dared not protest and soon learned to relax and enjoy my unexpected luxury of a maid and a cook; they spoiled me forever after.

CHAPTER THREE

BULLFIGHTS AND DANGER

At night when I returned home from the many social events Edmundo introduced me to – usually at least at one a.m. or much later, the "Serrano" who I soon learned was the name given to the night watch-men who protected the residential streets of the city, would open my large metal door for me..The "serreno" of my area fascinated me. No matter the hour or who dropped me at my door he was nearby - I usually exchanged a few words with him before entering and going up to my second floor apartment. I learned not to carry a key -no one in Madrid did – the custom was to call out "Serrr e e no" as loud as possible – very soon out of the dark night would appear a man wearing a loose shabby jacket with a great mass of keys jangling from a belt at his waist which made a welcoming sound as he approached banging his wooden stick on the cement sidewalk.

I liked him from the first moment; his kind face was creased and wrinkled, always smiling. Every night on arriving at my door I soon learned to copy the Madrid custom of calling out loudly and then Ramiro's rap-rap-of his wooden stick would echo on the cement sidewalk followed by a long drawn out "Voooy-Voy". It was a delightful way of ending my evening.

One night as Edmundo's taxi pulled away from the curb, Ramiro walked closer whispering something in my ear. When he saw that I did not understand, he spoke more clearly,"the senorita must be careful – a German in the number 22 of this street was asking me the hour the senorita usually returns at night. "No me fio en el" I don't trust him –he is not a good person. Be careful, Senorita."

Gradually Ramiro began to offer interesting tidbits about that particular German and about others as well, one of whom was a member of the German secret service, the Abwehr. "Since the Senorita is Americana and your countries are at war, I want to protect her."

Apart from my interesting work in the code room and my constant contact with my women's cell, just wandering around the city was a delight. Urchins with huge brown eyes and long eyelashes appeared to open taxi doors, putting out their little hands for money, One day when I was sitting on a bench in the Plaza Santa Ana, a bootblack pulled up a stool and began to shine my shoes with no invitation on my part- he said that this was a favor but that the tip would be whatever I wished to give. Who could refuse such politeness?

Almost from the first day a mysterious admirer began to smother me with flowers and chocolates and barrera seats for the bullfights—the admirer turned out to be one of the top bullfighters, Juanito Belmonte who had seen me in a restaurant dining the first night with Edmundo Lassalle. The day after his "Mozo de Espadas", man of swords, had appeared at my door in the hotel with two assistants carrying huge boxes of carnations and two sparkling embroidered garments, explaining that these were all gifts of Don Juan Belmonte.

"If you please, "I asked who is Belmonte?" The short grey-haired man in a black suit, white shirt and no tie was shocked that I did not know the name of the most famous bullfighter in Spain and when I refused to accept the matador's "traje de luces", - pink satin pants and jacket beautifully embroidered with gold threads and sequins- the man could not believe it. When after many calls and flowers I met Belmonte, I was astounded. I had expected a matador would be tall and strong, like a football player. Juanito Belmonte was short, skinny, not good-looking but with large brown eyes, dark hair and a pleasant smile, In those days a bullfighter was a national idol, today the soccer players have taken their place, but in the nineteen forties there were still no football stadiums in Madrid, nor were there microphones so no popular singers were available for the masses either - bullfighting was the one and only popular spectacle for people all over the country.

Juanito became a good and useful friend for my espionage activities, although he was unaware of that. Since gasoline became harder to obtain, I had to struggle to maintain my cover as Juanito could not understand how I worked so many hours in the American Oil Mission, and yet no oil was forthcoming for the country.

Edmundo Lassalle enabled me to meet some girls my age whose fathers in one way or another were connected with the government or areas useful for information about Germans in Madrid – it was hoped that I could establish friendships with them and obtain general enemy war information. Thus soon I had two close Spanish girlfriends, Cristina and Casella plus other Spanish friends who became instrumental in taking me into the social life of the city.

One night they invited me with a group of friends to the local country club of Puerta de Hierro, for a large dance and dinner – golf prizes were to be given that evening. Therefore I invited the group to my apartment for cocktails before going to the club. Since everyone in Spain had difficulty in obtaining whiskey and cigarettes, I explained I had plenty of both and they were delighted to come, soon my apartment became a popular rendezvous for a large group of young Spaniards of families convenient for my work. They were especially impressed with my apartment because I had transformed one small salon into an American type bar with stools and benches. One evening about twelve friends appeared with Cristina and Casella –saying that more would arrive soon and then we would all go to the dance in the country club later on. .

When the doorbell rang since the entrance to my apartment was near, I opened the door- two men were standing there - one was tall dark and slim, but the one who attracted my attention was blonde, very sunburned, dressed in a beige trench coat, and very good looking. His name was Luis. From then on he invited me often to dine and to go to bullfights - but since I had been warned while in training that if I had a romantic relationship with any man in Spain, I would be sent back to Washington, I avoided seeing him too often. An OSS woman agent in Lisbon had fallen in love with a Portuguese employee with whom she had created such a serious security error that she had committed suicide. Therefore my boss was very vigilant and I was cautious about maintaining unknown my enthrallment with Luis.

One day Juanito called to say he was sending me four barrera seats for the bullfight on Sunday where he would be one of the matadors. This would be my first bullfight – I invited my new Spanish girl friends to accompany me – they were impressed to learn that I had ringside seats -"the most expensive affair in Madrid is the bullfight." The bullfight was going to enhance my relationship with my new Spanish contacts.

Just entering the huge circular red brick building was a significant experience for me – as we mingled with the mob at one of the large entrances, I remembered observing this impressive building as I passed it on my way into the city that first day when I arrived from Lisbon . Today masses of excited spectators waited in lines at the various entrances to the building. Inside people rushed to buy cushions which my friends told me were indispensable to soften the hour and a half seated on the hard cement benches . Once inside the ring we were led to the center front ringside seats , the best of all and the closest to the fight. My colleagues were ecstatic-they had never dreamed of being in these, the choice seats in the plaza - "Madrid has the most important bullring in the entire country", they informed me. My friends were trembling with anticipation, I was fascinated with the glorious sight of the round ring, the arches and boxes above , the rumble of excited voices, and in front of me the huge empty ring of yellow sand – all around the ring it appeared that not one seat was vacant.

    Right on the dot of five-thirty the blaring of trumpets announced the fight was about to begin. Everyone sat down, while a large band on one side of the spectator's area struck a *pasodoble. Then* the doors on the opposite side of the arena opened, and a parade appeared of *bullfighters, picadores, banderilleros,* and *peones*—all dressed in shiny brightly colored satin suits embroidered with beads and sequins— the show had begun!.

At first I didn't know where my bullfighter friend was, then Casilda pulled my arm.

"Look at Juanito! Maybe he will place his cape on our railing."

    Then I saw him, walking front-line with two other matadors – Juanito had his heavily embroidered cape over one shoulder and partly wrapped around his body while clutched with one hand at the waist, evidently the classic style – it was sparkling brightly in the sun, the exotic black matador's *montera,* hat, was placed straight over his black eyebrows, the face was dead serious. The three matadors, front line stepped forward across the golden sand in unison, shocking-pink stockings moving in time to the music, walking straight to the president's box just above us, adjacent to that in the next box

Casilda pointed out to me ""that's General Franco, he doesn't come often. We're lucky today to see him."

Juan bowed deeply, saluting the president of the ring, bowing with hat in hand, as did the others. Then he turned to one of his fancy dressed fellows who had followed him, Casilda said this was one of his *peones- then Juanito,* handed him his glittering green cape, and nodded in our direction. In a minute, the cape was spread out in front of our seats. My friends were beside themselves with joy and stupid, ignorant me, a nobody from a small town in the USA was still unaware that I was providing these girls from the best families in Spain with a treat that I did not even understand.

The matadors executed a few test swirls with their yellow-and-, red capes, then the trumpets announced that the first bull was to be released, and then I happened to turn my head around and was startled to see a face that had often been shown me in the OSS training school - the head of intelligence in Germany, Schulenburg. Unfortunately this distracted my attention from the fight, but only for a few moments.. But in my excitement I missed the dramatic moment of the entrance of the first bull which was to be for another Matador called MANOLETE. My girlfriends could not understand why I was not more attentive to the ring, I controlled myself and made an effort to return my gaze

The great Manolete was slim, haggard, gray-faced, and he did not impress me with his first bull. In fact, I decided bullfights were cruel and disagreeable. I would never go again. Casilda explained that the bull had been bad. Manolete had had to kill quickly, which did not allow time for passes which would show his skill and courage. We stood up, as did most of the crowd, while the carcass of the dead bull was dragged out of the ring by two horses urged on by red-bloused men snapping long whips, and *monosabios*—"wise monkeys.". "Wise enough not to fight a bull," explained Casilda. I looked around the ring. This time I saw that

Schellenberg was talking to a woman I knew who was in the German Embassy with whom he appeared to be sharing a joke. I had to advise my boss as soon as possible, but that was going to be impossible for now. Who would dream there was a war going on?

When the trumpets rang forth the next time, it was Juanito who we going to fight. This time I struggled not to look for the SS officer. A gigantic black-and-white bull roared into the ring. I could hear him snort like a locomotive as he stormed past our seats. Only the empty arena and that wild, ferocious beast racing around looking for a victim. Then dramatically Juanito appeared from behind a small enclosure, lifting his bright red cape high in the air, swaying it to attract the bull's attention and shouting, *"Eh, toro, toro."* Maybe it was the fact that I had missed the sight of the first bull as it entered the plaza, but this time my attention was glued to the ring. The crowd was like one person-breathless with anticipation. So was I. Now the bull attacked - it was easily four times the size and ten times the weight of my skinny friend.

I held my breath, horrified, not knowing what to expect. To me it appeared that the animal would plow right into Juanito. It was headed straight for him, alone in the huge ring. Then, *swish –the bull* the bull just barely missed him, racing through the cape, raising it in the air as if it were chiffon. But in one split second, the animal whipped around and was after his victim again, more ferocious, more determined to tear him to bits. I forgot the SS officer, the war, my mission. Here was excitement as I had never imagined it - intense, compelling, hypnotizing—a death struggle enacted before my eyes. And the certain victim was a friend! I was horrified, terrified. How long would it take? Again the bull lurched for the man. This time he was certain to rip him to pieces. Juanito pulled the cape closer to his body, and just as the beast reached the heavy cloth, Juan twisted, wrapping the cape around his body, leaving the animal plunging into open air. The crowd roared in one voice, "Ole!" I relaxed. But only for a second. Juan bluffed the bull several times more, the horns just grazing his body, all that weight, those long horns stabbing and thundering into the cape harmlessly, Juanito moving gracefully, with ease, as in slow motion, moving at just the perfect moment to avoid the sharp needle points of the huge ivory-colored horns.

Then the inevitable happened. The bull as he passed the matador hooked with one horn, just slightly, but Juanito was thrown into the air. The *peones* rushed into the ring, three of them at once, waving and tossing their capes. Juan lay inert on the ground. I was sure he was dead. My hands clenched the iron rail. Men groaned, women screamed. The strength of the bull was such that one flick of his left horn had thrown Juan like a rag doll. One of Juanito's black bullfighter's slippers was lying on the sand.

Then, to my amazement, Juanito jumped to his feet. A trickle of blood ran down his embroidered green satin pants, an open tear split his sparkling jacket. But he was running toward the bull again with the red cape in hand as if nothing had happened, with more determination than before. With a gesture of insolence and indignation, he taunted the bull while directing the *peones* to disappear. This time when the bull attacked, Juan was ready. He knew now that the animal hooked on his left side, so Juanito pulled him close, very close, to the right. The crowd rolled out an agonizing "Aaa-ahhh", until the animal had stormed through the cape, then they all let loose, screaming, jumping to their feet in a delirium of joy. I remained seated, exhausted. What I had witnessed was unbelievable. I had even forgotten that one of our known most dangerous German enemies was somewhere in this plaza.

The *picadores* on their padded horses now entered the ring. Juan's man of swords, the one who had appeared at my door that first day, rushed to his side to investigate the cut under the jacket. Juan brushed him away and entered the ring. After the bull had been picked, and had thrown down two horses and their riders, and the banderilleros had plunged three pairs of spiked sticks decorated in colorful crepe paper into the beast's neck, Juan took the red woollen cape and approached the animal for the important part of the *faena*.

Again he drew the bull close to his body, in a circle so small that the animal was almost bent in half, drawn around the man's waist like a towel, the horns no more than an inch away. Every movement was a delight of elegance, lightness, precision. Now and then, Juanito directed the animal with a swing of the cape away from his body, and then stalked toward the audience, his back to the bull in an arrogant display of fearless disdain. Each time the mass roared their delight. Then he killed the animal with one stab of the long silvery sword.

After as Juan paraded around the ring, his *peones followed* behind him throwing back the flowers, hats, cigars which the enthusiastic public tossed at him. When he reached our setas he stepped in front of me to throw me the ear he had been given as his prize. His gesture was so unexpected I almost missed catching the horrible thing.

"What luck, Aline—to have a famous bullfighter throws you an ear at your first bullfight!"

I looked at the ghastly prize in my hand, amused. Yes, I was lucky. I had always been lucky.

That night I managed to advise my boss that I had seen the important Abwehr agent in the bullfight. We never learned just what transaction brought Schellenberg to Madrid but I had learned to keep my eyes open no matter where I was in the country – it seemed that no one else of our small group had seen him.

From that time on I had a greater respect for Juanito and often went to parties with him and other bullfighters - often during these evenings I met famous flamenco stars who were also present. However during the bullfighting season, Juanito had little time to be in Madrid since he was fighting almost daily all over the country.

The spectacle itself is ancient- the colorful satin "trajes de luces" suits of lights, embroidered in gold, the tight pants, the deep pink socks, the way the matadors stride into the ring, the plumed hats and black velvet knee breeches of the aguacils seated on their horses during the "paseo", parade, all has been the same from the times of Felipe the Second. The "corrida" itself is scary, men are killed and maimed every season; if the bull is really strong, the horses can get thrown in the air, the "picador", the rider with the sharp pole, can end underneath the horse. Those moments of intense emotion cannot be seen in any other spectacle. The first bullfight in '44 overwhelmed me, I could not look at parts of it, I was shocked and determined never to return, but by the time the next Sunday rolled around, I couldn't resist the temptation of taking part in that incredible exhibition again, because everyone takes part in the fight. What is happening in front of you absorbs your entire being. The intense fear, then the exhilaration that follows when a matador brings the enormous beast swirling around him, the sharp horns barely grazing his body, the magic of man's power to face death with valor and grace. And the beauty and strength of the medieval atmosphere with its color and excitement pulls many of us back again and again to another and yet another bullfight.

More good bullfights are found in Madrid than in any other part of Spain; the month of May due to the Feria of San Isidro in Madrid offers a fight every day and for the rest of the year the bullfight season is longer than anyplace else, beginning in March and lasting through October. Matadors' reputations depend much upon the Madrid public who understand the art of bullfighting; they make their greatest efforts there since the bullfighter's future depends in great part on how well he fights in the Madrid ring.

Juanito was no longer fighting by the middle 1950's. When his colleague Manolete was killed by a bull in 1947, he was very affected - also by then he was a rich man and had no need to face a bull in the ring. But Juanito had begun his life in very humble circumstances which story he told me soon after we met. He had been an illegitimate child of the most famous matador of all times, the reknown Juan Belmonte, and looked so much like his father in appearance that people recognized Juanito as his son even when he was a young boy in Sevilla. The comments became so general that when Juanito was ten, his father legally recognized him and in this way he gained his father's name. His famous father had been fighting in Peru when Juanito was born and married there - it was only when he returned to Spain did he learn that he had a son. In the meantime Juanito's mother had to work however she could, as a seamstress, as a maid, in order to take care of him when he was small. Juanito told me that he began bullfighting in order to support his mother although he hated it and was frightened every time he entered the ring. In those days a good matador could become rich quickly. – Juanito wanted to be able to give his mother the comforts she had missed. I met his mother several times and was always impressed by her dignity and dedication to him. Eventually Juanito married a lovely girl of Spanish society who bore him three children. Years later in the sixties, I heard on the radio that he had died suddenly of a heart attack. He was not yet fifty. It was a sad shock for me. Juanito had been one of my first real friends in Spain and had introduced me to many of the country's pleasures. He had not only been extremely brave in the ring—but he was also kind to everyone and generous. With his sense of honor and dignity he represented those characteristics I admire in Spaniards.

But the handsome Luis continued to impress me and I realized he was also useful for my meeting key people in the government , however I was usually very busy in the evenings with plans Edmundo had made where we would be trailing one or another of the enemy agents ,usually in a restaurant or in a nightclub.

As the season ended Juanito left Spain to fulfill his yearly contracts for bullfights in Mexico, Columbia and Peru. But I had continued to see bullfights with Luis who also took me to the best barrera seats, so I was quickly becoming a real fan. Luis was also very fond of flamenco and through him I came to know more gypsy singers and dancers- the elderly Pastora Imperio and the new sensation, Lola Flores. Madrid's social world was dominated by flamenco and bullfights.

Meanwhile my espionage work kept me busy –at nine every morning I would enter the American Oil Mission offices, and usually I would leave the office about eight P.M., the normal Madrid office working hours. Nevertheless I had also to arrange time regularly during the day for the women's cell, and also for meetings with my Spanish agent inside the Japanese Legation, but since another part of my work included meeting people in the social world who were suspected of being pro-German, I seemed to be busy during the day and also until two or three every night..

CHAPTER FOUR

PARIS 1946

At the end of the war I was the only Madrid OSS agent to be chosen to continue espionage under a new cover in Paris where I worked with Jack Okie, an OSS colleague from the Lisbon office. Jack was an attractive young man of about thirty who had been considered the top agent in that office – he had also come to Madrid several times during the war.

I was not unaware then nor was it generally known later that when OSS was terminated by President Truman in August 1946, General Donovan created a super secret intelligence group with its central office in Paris to preserve the agents and expertise built up by OSS during the war. Until September 1947 when the CIA was founded, this interim group operated under the cover of "World Commerce" with offices in the Hotel Plaza Athenee in Paris – it was financed by several of Donovan´s wealthy OSS colleagues through the New York "Bache and Company". Before World War Two, the United States had no foreign intelligence service ,only the American State Department had been responsible for collecting intelligence. While I was working in this Paris office, Frank Ryan, who had been the OSS officer in Washington in charge of Portugal and Spain during the War, was the person who directed our activities. We renewed contacts with agents in Czechoslovakia, Switzerland, West and East Germany and the Scandinavian countries. The Cold War was already underway and we were contacting agents and preserving experience that had been built up during the war.

Paris during those post-war years was a city in a constant state of celebration. The nightclubs were the most elegant in Europe enhanced by excellent often famous Jewish musicians similar to the atmosphere that had existed in Madrid during the war. It was customary at night in the most popular restaurants and nightclubs for women to wear long elegant gowns often with large velvet hats with plumes as well. I used to wonder how I was going to dance with such a large hat but since I seemed to do just that almost every night gradually it became quite simple. Since in the winter months the heating was not yet sufficient, most of the velvet or satin dresses had long sleeves.

Elegant clothes had always been a necessary asset for me. Paris was still more glamorous than Madrid during those post war years and often my dates were men interesting to us in our intelligence work. Meeting key personalities convenient for our investigations was easy and for me clothes were a necessary asset. Often if Frank Ryan needed information from any special group or person, he would take me to dinner with them – explaining beforehand exactly what information he wanted me to uncover. He was aware that I had learned in Madrid that men could not touch certain subjects without creating suspicion, but that a woman pretending ignorance and innocence could ask almost anything. Among these personalities I met many political leaders, ex-kings, and business personalities.

 Soon I realized I had to get more new clothes so I went to Balenciaga - although I had ordered many outfits in Madrid, his most important salon was in Paris. After seeing the collection, I ordered two dresses – now my salary did not include such additions as it had in Madrid during the war - I needed the dresses urgently so I requested the fittings as soon as possible. In all haute couture houses worldwide, three fittings were then obligatory. When I appeared for the second fitting the vendeuse told me that I was going to have the honor of Monsieur Balenciaga himself doing my fitting. This did not impress me - when I was modeling for Hattie Carnegie, owner of the top haute couture salon in New York, since I was then her head model, she had done most of my fittings herself. Balenciaga soon appeared and after politely saluting me, started his work - he was tall and slim and obviously shy - he hardly spoke. But when the fitting ended he asked me quietly if I would be willing to be photographed for the American Vogue magazine in the dresses I had ordered. I well knew that Vogue was the epitome of publicity for all dress salons. At first I was reluctant – I had done photographs often and had been highly paid for it – a few photographs in Vogue meant nothing to me, but I could not tell him this. Noticing my reticence he added in his low voice "Of course, Senorita, we will have your name mentioned under each photograph." I knew that my name did not add to the importance of his clothes and that he was merely trying to be polite, so I accepted.

As the months rolled on Luis would call although long distance was difficult and the line was always noisy, he wanted to come to Paris but could not obtain the necessary "exit permit" but he did write me regularly, usually asking what I was doing and with whom. One day he managed to get a call through to me at the office. "I've been reading the Paris newspapers .What was you doing at Maxim's with the King of Yugoslavia? I played golf with him and he's not only a bad golfer, but he's also a big bore." I was delighted to realize that Luis was jealous.

My Balenciaga dresses were a great advantage and when I went to order another, the vendeuse told me that Monsieur Balenciaga had said he would lend me any of the evening gowns I might need from his collections since all of them fit me. Therefore when I had a ball or an important black tie evening affair I always had one of the best gowns in the room. Meanwhile Luis had put me in touch with some friends, the Ybarra sisters who lived in a palace at 16 Place Etats Unis, where often I was invited to dinners followed by dancing. Also the wealthy, socially prominent Charles Beistegui, half Spanish , half Mexican, who I had met in Madrid during one of my OSS most dangerous weekends invited me to his large house party weekends at his famous chateau on the outskirts of Paris. For all these occasions, the proper attire was an indispensable ingredient.

Our intelligence office on the second floor of the new and yet unfinished Hotel Plaza Athenee was close to the small hotel St. Regis where I lived. My companion and boss in the office, Jack Oakie, did not have to maintain the hectic nightlife. During the daytime we were the only two employees, with the exception of a French ex- resistance agent who acted as secretary in the office to accomplish the enormous job of reuniting wartime agents from all over Europe. We were also obtaining information on suspected Russian KGB agents who were employees in certain French businesses. Our office name, World Commerce, and a cotton import-export company, covered our activities with a Czechoslovakia company exporting cotton fiber to Denmark. During this time another ex OSS European agent, Hans Czernin of the famous Czernin family from Prague, came in now and then to help us locate agents who had worked with him during the war- we were always very very busy.

    Frank Ryan, the man who had recruited me for OSS appeared frequently to direct our work and to put me in contact with social groups where KGB agents might be entrenched. Although we were very few agents, our obligations multiplied and soon it became obvious that we needed an office in Zurich.

    When I told Luis that my office was sending me to Zurich where I would be for the following months, he became indignant. "What kind of crazy work do you do? First you are in Madrid in the oil business, then in Paris where you seem to go out with every exiled king. "

    In Zurich Frank Ryan had made reservations for me in the Hotel Baur-au-lac, the luxury hotel of the city, but on my own I had to look for a small office where I could receive the agents we were contacting. Life became more complicated when I met a very attractive German girl, Helga Nehring – she was down and out and begged me to help her. I discovered almost immediately that she could be an excellent means to uncover German Nazis in Switzerland – some were trying to escape the pending Neuremburg trials. After getting permission from Frank Ryan, I gave assistance to Helga and she became an important asset in my work. She had been a well known beauty in Germany and close to Hitler and some of the main officials of his government. In fact she had been involved in one of the many attempts to assassinate him, but had escaped.

    Helga was able to provide me with names and bank numbers of German accounts covering money robbed from

Jews during the war. She introduced me to the Argentine Ambassador, Benito Llambi who had befriended many German Nazis who had escaped to Argentina. Through Helga and carefully using our contacts with the argentine embassy, we were able to uncover ex-Nazis now escaping to Mexico and to Argentina. Our work became dangerous and we both realized that exiled Germans in Switzerland were trying to discover who was uncovering their identities. Benito used to come to Zurich from his embassy residence in Bern to take me to dinner as often as I would see him. When I went with Helga to St. Moritz, he also went skiing with me. But his attentions became too insistent. Without my being aware Benito had written to my father asking permission to marry me. My father immediately telephoned me from Pearl River – I told him Benito was crazy and that I had no interest in him at all. Just about this time I was given my first vacation in three years and left for Madrid to see Luis.

CHAPTER FIVE

RETURN TO MADRID

It must have been about end of April 1947 when an ancient war-torn train took me from Zurich to Paris where I changed for another to the Spanish frontier. Because of the difference in the width of railroad tracks, French trains could not enter Spain, a precaution that had been taken when railroads were first installed to make invasion from France into Spain more difficult. All passengers had to plod over the bridge, tired from the journey and eager to reach Irun, where I would catch the night express to Madrid. Halfway across the bridge I stopped and leaned over the railing, gazing down into the water. For a few moments I thought about the many critical political meetings that had taken place in this precise spot over the centuries between French and Spanish monarchies. Also I recalled the meeting only a few years before in 1940 between Hitler and Franco, when fortunately for the Allies, Franco had managed to keep the Axis forces on the French frontier and did not permit their entry into Spain to reach Gibraltar and close the Mediterranean to the Allies.

It was nearly dusk. Below a small motorboat chugged by - several fishermen were casting their lines at different points along the banks. I wondered what awaited me in Madrid. Like a homing pigeon I only knew I had to go. What would it seem like to be in Spain on vacation? No need for a revolver, no worry about who was following me, no secrets to be unraveled. I laughed to myself. Secrets! Just to find out where Luis was and where he spent his time would be work enough in the beginning. And how would I feel when I saw him again? Was I really as in love with him as I'd been imaging? I thought of my mother's last letter telling me about the wedding of two of my best friends and reminding me that I was twenty- four, an age when a girl should be thinking about getting married instead of a career. I wondered if there would be a good bullfight in Madrid on Sunday. But most of all I wondered about Luis. I was happier than I had been in a long time.

The next morning when I awoke in my old-fashioned wagon-lit sleeping compartment, quickly I rose to my knees on top of the bed, separated the wine-colored plush drapes and the lace window curtains, and raised the shade. We were just pulling into the small station of El Escorial. Passengers were descending and others were boarding. Packages were being lifted onto the train, mail sacks thown up to the conductor. The whistle blew forlornly two or three times and slowly the train crept out of the station. I stayed glued to the window. The four towers of the monastery Phillip the Second had built rose over the little village like an upside-down parasol. My heart beat faster. Madrid was only one hour away.

The train clicked along, swaying pleasantly through a world of rugged gigantic rock formations, pine forests, and multicolored open fields. I took a deep breath as I looked out at the austere beauty of sun-drenched Castile. Everything I saw reminded me of Luis. Never had the Spanish countryside looked more appealing, the little whitewashed houses with their worn rust-colored tile roofs, the austere lemon toned-stone walls of the ancient buildings. Sometimes a barren field was broken by stretches of undulating fields of waving green wheat. Under clumps of live oak trees, cows and donkeys shared the meager shade. Earth, red as brick, moved by my window, to give way to pearl-gray expanses, then dark brown turf with stripes of bright orange. The view from a distance looked like a mosaic whose design and color had been invented to please my eye alone.

The magical country seduced me. I was in love with Spain. Would I still be in love with Luis when I saw him?

The night train arrived early in the morning in Madrid's Estacion del Norte. Luis was there waiting for me. The minute I saw him I realized my feelings had not changed, despite the months in Paris and the difficult ones in Zurich. My feelings about Luis and Madrid were the same.

Now every day after I arrived for several weeks, Luis appeared in his Cord convertible with the top down in front of my building. As I looked out the window of my second floor apartment I felt a thrill just to see him there. What was going to happen to me? Falling in love with a foreigner was taboo since I was still an espionage agent. That was the order in those days. Therefore I had never allowed myself to trust anyone. But now the war was over, I realized I was helpless to resist Luis' charm. His attentions, I was certain, could not be some sort of trap. One glance at his clear green eyes and honorable countenance dispelled such notions. Nevertheless, for me this situation had to lead to marriage or I would have to leave. I had only three weeks vacation. My orders were to return to Washington for a brief "fresh up" course and then on to Czechoslovakia.

Yet I knew that Spaniards took a long time to decide upon marriage; divorce was not possible in those days, in fact divorce did not become legal until 1981. Back in the forties once married there was no way out. Not only that impediment existed but it was highly improbable that a Spaniard belonging to an old aristocratic family would marry a foreign girl from an unknown family – even for a girl to work and live alone was considered shocking for the those families. Standards concerning a girl's reputation were rigid in all levels of society; above all her reputation had to be irreprochable. It was not considered proper for a woman to go unaccompanied by a man to any bar, restaurant or night club. Girls who worked as models were not considered respectable either, so I had concealed that part of my background. There were all kinds of limitations on a woman's respectability that I had abided by - from the first moment I had made every effort to maintain a behavior that would give little grounds for criticism. My strict mother and father had made that effort quite easy for me.

Often Luis had mentioned that he intended to marry me; he made a point of introducing me to his father and step-mother and most of our dates were accompanied by one of his married sisters, all these indicated that he was serious, but no definite wedding date was made, and my vacation time was each day shorter. We usually spent our days at the country club; Luis was a top golfer, playing thirty-six holes a day and I was taking lessons. The country club was in an area which had been the site of much fighting during the Civil war when the clubhouse had been destroyed. In its place an attractive red brick building had been built which they called the "chalet". The view was lovely, high on a slope looking out at the blue Guadarrama Mountains. We had late lunches there and sometimes at night there would be dances when golf trophies were awarded. On June 23rd, Saint Juan's day, the dance also included a huge bonfire which brave young couples would race through the burning embers as that saint had done centuries before.

One day we went to a friend's "finca", ranch, where young bulls were bred and prepared for the ring. The testing of the bulls and the females for their usefulness for the fights is called a "tienta". These private properties have small bullrings, the season's top bullfighters had been invited to test the bravery of the bulls, and after a few bulls had been "tested" often some of the guests are invited to try their skill. Since I had seen many bullfights and knew most of the top matadors who along with Juanito Belmonte had often explained how to handle a bull, I thought I knew much about the game and decided that now was my chance to show off in front of Luis - so I stood up and offered to go into the ring. Luis was horrified – he tried to stop me, but I was determined.

At first I passed the young bull well enough two or three times, - the crowd applauded. But then I made the mistake of looking up to see if Luis was watching me. At that moment one of the bull's horns caught the corner of my jacket and threw me in the air. As I hit the ground, I was blinded by the sand of the arena, at the same time, capes were being tossed by the bullfighters nearby to distract the bull and take him away from me. Then I felt hands pulling me by one leg off the field out of danger. Through the fog of dust I recognized it was Luis. I was mortified - what a spectacle I must be. Then amidst the confusion, the voices, and the clouds of sand, I heard him mumble, "It's about time you stop doing these foolish "Americanadas", American tricks, and marry me." Luis' words were more than worth the fright I'd been through. But another week passed and still he did not make a date. As the days went by my happiness faded.

The last day of my vacation Luis appeared as usual in my apartment to pick me up for our daily session of golf. With an expression of disbelief he stared at the trunks and suitcases in my entrance hall. Evidently until then he had not taken me seriously when I had reminded him frequently that my vacation was ending; only now did he finally realize that I was really leaving. He begged me to change my plans, but I told him that was not possible, that I would lose my job and that in fact today I was not even going to have lunch with him-that a friend of his, Raimundo Lanza, an Italian Prince who had been asking me for a date for weeks was waiting for me at Jockey, the "in" restaurant of those days. With a composure I was far from feeling, I grabbed my hat and gloves and rushed down the stairs. Luis ran after me, but in that moment I saw a taxi passing by and left him standing bewildered in the street as I jumped into the taxi and disappeared.

About an hour later Raimundo and I were just beginning dessert when Luis appeared in front of our table in the restaurant. Despite his usual tan, he looked pale. "Aline, "he said, "I would like to speak with you. Alone."

I asked Raimundo to excuse me, Luis and I crossed the room to a secluded corner table. He began immediately. "My father is waiting for you right now, our family priest is with him. Everything is set."

"Luis, what do you mean, everything is set?" "Naturally my father has to talk to you. And since you didn't believe that I was going to marry you, how else can I prove to you that I'm serious?"

"Are you telling me that you asked your father if you could marry me?"

"No, I told him that I was going to marry you. But in this country one's parents must be properly informed and the family priest must make the preparations. Please come and see for yourself. My father and the priest are waiting. We'll be married one month from today. That's the quickest I can arrange the papers, I'm told. Now you can send a cable to your company and say that you will not be returning. Ever."

Forgetting Raimundo we both ran out to jump into Luis' car and hastened to the house where indeed his father and a tall black frocked priest were waiting. Luis' father did not sound pleased but after a long conversation with him and the priest, his father suggested we proceed on to Luis' grandfather's house. He said he had telephoned and the old count was expecting us. The grandfather's palace was on the Castellana across from the American Embassy residence where I had spent the last months of the War on the top floor in our OSS code room. I had admired the turn-of-the century mansion which had been the center of Spain's political and cultural life before the Spanish civil war, but I never dreamed that one day I would be part of that family. I didn't know that Luis' grandfather was the famous Count of Romanones since Luis' title was Quintanilla. I still found it confusing that members of the same family all seemed to have different names or titles – there was no way I could know who was related to whom. Since so many Spanish customs were different to what I had been accustomed I merely 'considered this one more difference between Americans and Spaniards.

The wide iron gates of the Romanones palace were opened by a uniformed guard and we swept up the short curved drive to a side door. I glanced quickly at the garden, recognizing the two sycamores on either side of the front entrance which I had seen many times looking from the window of our OSS office just across street.

Luis seemed tense as he opened the door and pushed me inside."Look, Aline", he said, "do not be frightened by el Abuelo, my grandfather. He is overpowering, but if he doesn't like you at first, he will eventually. He can be affectionate and his sense of humor is famous." This is all Luis told me of his very famous grandfather – I was entirely unaware that he had been elected prime minister three times, that he had been the youngest mayor of Madrid at age 21, that he had held every important political office in the government at one time or another, and that he had started obligatory public education or that he was the most popular and famous man in the country- his name known even in the most remote small town..

By this time we were in a large entrance hall with a ceiling three stories high - a wide curving stairway led to the floor above. At the foot of the stairs on either side were suits of armor. I would have liked to raise the visors on the metal helmets and take a peep inside, but Luis pulled me on .. As I walked up the stairs. I sensed that this meeting was crucial. No matter what Luis had said, I was now aware that the marriage could not take place without the approval of the family - evidently the Abuelo was the most important member. The enormous house was so silent, it almost gave the feeling of being uninhabited. Upstairs, thick carpets supressed the sound of our steps as Luis led me through one room after another.

Luis continued to explain. "My grandfather is accustomed to getting his own way. Everyone in the family is frightened of him."

"Luis," I whispered, "are you afraid of your own grandfather?"

"Absolutely. Though I wasn't when I was small. He used to take us children out shooting. Sometimes there would be as many as six of us, between eight and twelve years old. he had the courage to place us in butts on either side of him, a dangerous position because children with shotguns are apt to make mistakes." Luis smiled. "We obviously didn't kill my grandfather, but he has lots of buckshot in his body as reminders of our mistakes. He did teach us all how to shoot though and how to handle firearms safely. But more important he taught us a love and appreciation of country life. But when we grew up, his attitude toward us changed. In fact in a book of his proverbs he gives an idea of his point of view about children and grownups. One proverb goes something like this. "Children when they are little are like asparagus, nice and tender, and one would like to eat them, but when they grow up, they become tough and one can't swallow them." Well el abuelo certainly acts that way with all of us. But don't worry. I am gong to marry you, no matter what he says."

The Count of Romanones, former Prime Minister of Spain, friend of the exiled King, author, businessman, the most famous and respected man in the country, was sitting in an armchair with a plaid blanket over his legs, staring at me with piercing bright blue eyes. He had a prominent chin, a big nose, and a nice face. He rubbed his hands, one inside the other, as he continued to observe me in silence. He was eighty-four years old, but his expression was alert and there was an air of vitality about him. He then peered into my eyes and fascinated I stared back unblinking. Those eyes as blue as the spanish sky became warm and inviting. His mouth crinkled into a smile. I liked him immediately.

Finally the old man said, "Bueno, so you want to marry my grandson, "mi primogenito" (heir) - since Luis was the eldest son of his eldest son, Luis would inherit his titles – I was unaware of these details. "Tell me what do you see in him? Frankly I don't see anything." And with that he chuckled and indicated I sit in the chair in front of him.

Looking around, I saw that Luis had sneaked out, but his absence did not detract from that first meeting being thoroughly enjoyable for me. When Luis dared to appear twenty minutes later, his grandfather was in a good mood, "Well Luis, You have my approval for your marriage – this young lady has just the kind of new blood that this family needs."

We, the abuelo and I were close friends from then on.

Nevertheless despite El Abuelo's warm approval, which obliged the entire family to accept the wedding, marriage was still not easy. The family was adamant that the wedding take place in Madrid. Exit permits were obligatory for natives and difficult to obtain, also there was no way el Abuelo and the rest of the family could make a trip to the United States with the lack of air travel and few ships. It would be easier for my parents to come to Spain since Americans did not have difficultly now in obtaining visas.

The first thing I did was to inform the office in Paris that I would not be going on to my next assignment , therefore would not be taking the boat and using the ticket they had sent me. I made clear that I would not be able to go to Washington because I was going to stay in Madrid to marry the Count of Quintanilla.

It wasn't easy to marry a Spaniard - old aristocratic families like Luis's took marriage very seriously, and added to that an American girl of an unknown family was not considered a reliable wife , but Luis was as in love as I was and faced up to the difficulties. Fortunately his all-important grandfather had decided that I was not a dangerous choice and we made a definite date for the large wedding obligatory in his family.

After sending my notice to Washington , before twenty-four hours had passed I received a call saying someone would arrive to finalize matters with me. To my surprise Frank Ryan himself showed up at my apartment only two days later. There were no regular commercial plane flights in those days, he must have already been someplace in Europe and travelled immediately to Madrid by train.

Frank was usually healthy looking and calm but that day when he entered my apartment he was pale and nervous. Maybe it was the warm weather, his forehead was covered with persperation one kiss on my cheek left a few drops. With a minimum of the usual greetings, he walked into my salon – he had never been in my apartment before and looked for a place to sit down. Always polite, once there, before sitting down himself, he indicated that I take one of the two chairs , then he sat down facing me.

"Aline, he began, " I have come here to discuss this idea of your impending marriage. I want to make you understand there are important reasons for you to postpone this marriage for the good of your country. This is not the time for a patriotic girl such as yourself to leave the "company". He continued and I dared not say a word. "For a long time we have been working together forming a team of intelligence experts. You are now an officer –you received your indoctrination in our country´s first school of international espionage and have served three years in wartime activity, plus this past year in Paris and Zurich as you contributed to reorganizing agents all over Europe – you cannot let us down now. We need you. We have great plans for you. We have planned a "fresh-up" course for you in Washington. Then we will send you to new areas with a new top cover."

He reached out, grabbing my hand, the sun was shinning through the window illuminating his earnest tense features. Many important events had occurred in the small salon in this apartment on Monte Esquinza, but I realized this was one of the most critical for my future. As he spoke I was suffering also. I admired Frank, I felt a definite affection for him, I felt comfortable in my work and disliked intensely creating a problem or disappointing him. The sincerity of his words was more obvious due to the persperation now covering most of his face. Abruptly he let go of my hand and reached into his pocket, extracting an envelope which he handed to me. "Here is your ticket back on THE FRANCE, the best ocean liner crossing the Atlantic nowadays, it leaves in six days. You have plenty of time to catch it. Do not abandon us now, we are at a crucial moment. You can postpone your wedding for a year at least."

His intensity surprised me. Never had I considered myself so important or indispensable – I had been fervently involved in all I did and I liked my work, the intricacies, the mystery, the secrecy, the danger. Also I was very fond of Frank, but I was in love with Luis and my boss's pleas did not change my mind.

When he realized that I was not going to cave in, Frank shook his head, an expression of despair reflected in his face as he leaned back in the chair. "Of course you are young, you are unaware of the plans we have for World Commerce. We considered it prudent that you and others not be informed of the current changes. But I can assure you that you will miss a very exciting adventure. You are perfect for the role we had chosen for you, " He wiped his face, and the loss of lives have all been involved in your education and experience for this work."

While Frank was talking to me in Madrid I was unaware that changes were occurring in Washington. In fact I was always under the impression that World Commerce was merely a cover for OSS as the American Oil Mission had been a cover in Madrid. I had been doing the same kind of espionage activity - using the same know-how to keep abreast of the activities of the Russian KGB. I had been paid my usual salary in the usual manner. For me nothing had changed. I still didn't know that I had been working for a super secret interim agency while OSS was changing its name to CIA. My colleague, Jack Oakie, had probably not known about these changes either or he would have told me.

Years later I learned that the future of USA intelligence was being determined in Washington just during those days while Frank was with me in Madrid. General Donovan and his intimate group of financiers managed to preserve the intelligence expertise which functioned during World War Two until CIA was created in September 1947. Most of colleagues in the Madrid OSS office had returned to their pre-war work and a few had joined the new CIA.

CHAPTER SIX

MARRIAGE

My happiness conflicted with worries of how I could afford the large wedding Luis had said was required. We of the Madrid Secret Intelligence part of O.S.S. had received an order from Washington to pay back a certain percentage of our past year's wages to the government. I never understood why, but I paid it immediately. This left me with less money in my savings account. Later I learned that noone else of our group had paid this because they considered it unfair. At any rate my financial problems were partly solved when Luis told me that since my family lived abroad that he was going to pay all wedding expenses. Then he said that he wanted me to have a wedding gown just like his mothers. She had been killed in an automobile accident when he was eight; he showed me a photograph of her dress of meters of white satin damask covered with fine lace, a chain of orange blossoms suspended from the waist reaching to the floor, an enormous skirt ending in a long train. The cost of something similar horrified me but I was again relieved when Luis told me it was customary in his family for the groom to choose and pay for the wedding dress. What a nice custom.

    Luis drove me to Balenciaga on the Gran via, the main thoroughfare - in those days there were few automobiles and we parked right in front of the shop. Balenciaga's salon was considered the best in Madrid. There seemed to be much excitement as the entire collection of evening dresses was paraded before us, but Luis insisted that he preferred a dress similar to the one his mother wore at her wedding – he brought out a picture which he had been carrying in a large envelope. Then we proceeded to select the material, the length of the train and such details. As we stood ready to leave, the head vendeuse approached saying she had just spoken to Balenciaga in Paris telling him about our wedding and that the bride was the same American girl as in the Vogue photographs of his last collection. She said Balenciaga was very impressed that I was marrying the "primogenito" of the Count of Romanones - that he had suspected that American girl was going to become "somebody", but he was especially delighted to learn she would carry such an important title of his own country.

After leaving Balenciaga's salon, Luis began to explain. "We have several customs in our families for weddings - customs that the man has to comply with and some for the woman as well. Not only is it customary for the groom to pay the wedding dress, but also he gives the bride a diamond bracelet."

"But, Luis, I'd like a ring. In America, the custom is a diamond ring."

"Well, maybe I'll give you a ring, too, but you must have a diamond bracelet, that is our custom."

Customs in Spain, I had already learned from his sister, had remained unchanged for generations. She had told me that before their Civil War a bride normally received a whole trunk of gifts –it was usually an ancient Japanese small trunk of inlaid mother of pearl filled with family gifts - two mantillas, an ancient veil of old Brussels lace, at least two tiaras or more and of course the engagement diamond bracelet.

"Luis, what about the woman's gift to the groom? What am at I expected to give?"

"You must buy me a gold cigarette case. I've already chosen the one I want at my family's jeweler, Paco Sanz, on the Gran Via. When you go there, he will show it to you."

That evening, Luis took me to dinner at Jockey and brought out of his pockets a mass of glittering jewels that left me staggering. One was a large ruby set in a brooch with two huge diamonds. "this belonged to my Mother", he explained. Then he handed me a gleaming pearl necklace with a large diamond brooch as clip which he made me put on, showing me that the clip was supposed to be in front not the back as is usual. Then he took out of another pocket the pearl and diamond earrings to match. I had never owned nor longed for valuable jewels. On receiving all these, more than pleasure I fear that I displayed only amazement. With each jewel I became more aware how necessary it was that I get Luis the correct customary woman's wedding gift for him.

Paco Sanz was the most expensive jeweler in Madrid. I went there the next afternoon. "I'm the novia of the Conde de Quintanilla," I began.

"Ahhhh, si, senorita. I recognized you. El Senor Conde has selected the loveliest cigarette case that we have."

It was also the most expensive. The cost made me dizzy, but I thought of the jewels Luis had given me, and I smiled at the salesman. "It's perfect."

I had planned on buying a few dresses at Balenciaga and getting myself some nice lingerie, but I now decided to find an inexpensive way of obtainaing a proper a trousseau. Luis had already rented a house in Capri for our summer and intended to take me on an extensive honeymoon afterwards throughout Europe and then to America- " we will decide later how long we stay in each place", he had said. Luis was longing to see the USA which he only knew through the movies. Obviously I would need a large wardrobe for the long honeymoon he was planning..

Fortunately in those days there were many inexpensive dressmakers in Spain. I had been recommended to Angelita by my "portera" and in fact she had been useful for me during one of my espionage operations two years before. First I went to Zorilla on the calle Serrano, Madrid's leading store for material. Then l bought the latest French fashion magazines and with Angelita's excellent handiwork, managed to obtain a beautiful trousseau which looked like Balenciaga but cost one tenth as much.

Luis decided that the wedding would take place in his eldest sister's house which was in the center of Madrid and next to the church where everyone in his family had been married for generations. Since this sister at the moment was in her large ranch in Cordoba, he suggested we go there so I could meet her and discuss wedding plans. "The trip will be a treat for you. Cordoba is one of the most attractive cities in this country. My great grandfather was from Cordoba and I inherited his famous palace in the middle of the city. But Isabel inherited his large finca."

I was delighted to have the opportunity of visiting a place I had read so much about. Cordoba seemed to have been one of the cities Europeans looking for adventure and those brave enough to face sudden perils and discomfort had frequently chosen when making a visit to Spain. The books stated that Cordoba maintained the strongest Arabic influence of any Andalusian city and that the famous Mezquita of Cordoba, a myriad of columns and arches, was one of the ten wonders of the world – in the tenth century the calif of Cordoba had been recognized as head of all Arab leaders in southern Spain and the calif's `palace in Cordoba had been even more luxurious than the palace of the Alhambra in Granada. Again I was intrigued by the fascination of this ancient country that was soon going to be mine. When I first arrived in Spain in 1944 Europeans I met often said "Europe ends in the Pyrennees"- evidently the seven centuries of Arabic control over the Iberian peninsula had left the country very different from the rest of Europe. Also among the many books I had read by tourists visiting Spain in the nineteenth century were those of an englishman named Borrow who came to catholic spain to sell bibles - he fell in love with the gypsies and the people in the country areas and returned many times. It seems that in the

1840's other famous authors visited Spain - Ford and Merimee, and Gautier, and Alexander Dumas – all had been fascinated by the exotic atmosphere and the differences in customs. Dumas' description of Cordoba in 1846 described its charismatic ancient atmosphere – "like stepping into another country, more remote in time as when the calif of Cordoba was reigning there and all powerful in the arab world."

In other books I had read that travelers to Cordoba could be waylaid on the roads and that there were bandits in the mountains. I certainly never expected to encounter such difficulties on the gloriuous May day Luis and I started our trip. I still remember the beauty of miles and miles of rolling fields covered with wild red poppies like a huge flame silhouetted against the Sierra Morena mountains and the blue sky. We skirted the city and climbed into the mountains through hills and fields where not a village nor a shack was visible.

As we were driving through the rough country, Luis told me that he had just sold his palace in Cordoba only two months before. " If I had realized then that I was going to marry so soon, I might have kept it, it was very ancient but I never passed even one night in the place although I inherited it many years ago. Evidently my great grandfather, Perez de Guzman el Bueno, was a very important person in Cordoba. The palace is unusual – it was built so the owner could go up to the second floor on horseback- I would have liked that."

"Oh Luis what a pity you sold such a unique family home."

"What could we do with a house in Cordoba? One has to maintain guards to keep it up and we can always visit my Uncle Peps Merito when we want to come to Cordoba. His home, San Jeronimo, is much more luxurious than any other. Wait till you see it. We don't have time on this trip , but as soon as we are married and come back from our trip abroad, I'll take you there. There's no place that can compare to it."

.   By this time I realized that for Luis what I considered the marvels and mystery of Spain -the old palaces and castles were run-of-the mill. Finally about four kilometers beyond the city which we did not have time to enter since we were arriving late,   we finally arrived at the remote property, deep in a mountainous area. Now we followed a seemingly endless dirt country road until we arrived at the rustic white washed house that Luis' mother had used as a shooting lodge and where his eldest sister Isabel and her husband lived during the Spring months. I had not met Isabel but I liked her immediately and her husband was especially attractive and charming. The next day when I told him I liked to ride, he ordered two horses to be brought to the house and proceeded to take me for a long excursion through the wild countryside. Then partly to entertain me and partly because the entire family loved to shoot, he arranged a wild boar shoot for the following day.

    We started out before daylight taking a dirt path that led up into the mountains; first we travelled in jeeps and then we mounted horses. About three hours later when the sun was out strong, we were in Indian file climbing a narrow path as silently as possible – we had been warned not to utter a sound so that the boars we hoped to kill would not hear us and be scared away. We were getting close to the place chosen for the first drive which was near the house of one of Luis´sister´´s shepherds. Suddenly our head guard startled us with a frantic gesture, indicating that we should stop. As I remained on my horse, I saw the other guard jump off his horse and run towards a clump a trees where two donkeys were calmly nibbling at the grass. The scene didn't mean anything to me nor did it appear slightly threatening but everyone else seemed to realize that we were in danger. My brother in -law motioned to us urgently to turn about face. I didn't understand why but realized that we had to get away as quickly as possible.

Meanwhile the head guard and two other aides grabbed the rifles which were strapped to our horses, and raced up into the mountain. I did not know then that dangerous bandits lived hidden higher up in the mountain and made raids regularly on farms to steal foodstuffs. The sight of the donkeys tied to a tree loaded with sacks of sugar and flour had alerted our guards to the fact that bandits were nearby and that they might return to recover their stolen goods and would certainly attack us .

Later that day when we were all safely back at the house, the guards returned telling us that the shepherd who inhabited the small guard's house in that part of the property where we had been, had been killed when the bandits robbed him. This attack had occurred just a short time before we arrived. The bandits had heard us arriving and had left their booty in order to escape faster. Two civil guards were now looking for the bandits – they told us that indeed we had been lucky not to have been shot. These bandits are called "maquis"and for many centuries came down from the mountains to rob when they needed food and money. What most amazed me was that noone seemed especially surprised that such a shocking tragedy had occurred in these modern times – to me this sounded like stories of one hundred years ago. I wondered how my sister-in-law and her husband would find another sheppard willing to accept such a dangerous job in this wild part of the mountains.

Luis told me on the way back to Madrid that the opera "Carmen", based on a story written by Prosper Merimee tells the story of these same maquis coming down into precisely this part of the southern mountains - that the plot of the famous opera contains this same type of occurrence we had just experienced. But Merimee heard and wrote about these stories in 1847 and I was living through them in 1947!

CHAPTER SEVEN

THE WEDDING

A few days before my parents were due to leave Pearl River for the wedding, my brother Tom had a serious automobile accident, so they sent my nineteen year old brother Bill in their place. He arrived a day before the wedding and had never been to Europe before. The wedding party at Luis' sister's house was to be at nine o'clock at night following the wedding in the church where Luis' parents had been married. Our wedding was going to be the social affair of the season in Madrid.

My brother Bill and I stood side by side in the back of the church while the bells chimed, waiting for the signal to enter. I was attired in an enormous veil which coverd not only my face but reached to my waist and Balenciaga's replica of Luis' mother's wedding dress with a damask satin train a mile long, my brother was in a rented morning coat, striped pants, and gray stock, which Luis' valet had knotted for him. As we stood there, Bill was calm, but I knew he was in shock. He didn't know anyone, nor did he speak a word of Spanish. As I placed my arm in his, I thought I was calm but my brother told me years later that my arm had been trembling. I knew that in front of us were Luis' many relatives, some exiled kings and queens, a lot of grandees and the Abuelo Romanones in the front pew. The church was packed, most of the guests I had never met. The only ones I felt I had on my team were Luis, my brother, and *El Abuelo*. As yet I was completely ignorant about Spain's aristocracy – it seemed to me that everyone Luis knew had a title so I was no longer impressed by such details. All I knew was that Luis was the most exciting man I had ever met and by some miracle he was marrying me.

"Bill," I whispered, "we must walk very, very, slowly. Just keep in step with me."

There are no wedding rehearsals in Spain, so this was it, our only chance, and it had to be perfect. The organ sounded the first chords, a strange sort of Arabic music it seemed to me, and we started down that long, long aisle. I'd been the bride in many fashion shows, so actually I had rehearsed this moment many times. It was eight o'clock at night as I walked down the wide aisle of the huge church - I looked up at the distant altar and prayed that I looked like the wife Luis wanted his family to see.

The ceremony was different from those in America. Ten men, some dressed in morning coat, others in military uniform, formed a semicircle near us on either side of the altar. These were witnesses, a group composed of close friends, and distinguished members of the family. Then Luis' sister Isabel and my brother Bill, taking the place of Luis'" mother and my father, as was usual in Spanish weddings, stood each at one side of us on the altar. At one point Luis placed, piece by piece, twenty-five glittering gold coins into the priest's hands. I wondered if this was a holdover from medieval times, when dowries were paid, or when wives were bought. The ring went on the right hand instead of the left. As the ceremony proceeded, I passed from one surpise to another.

Although Luis and I had been totally unaware , a note of suspended danger had occurred as the church was filling up before the ceremony. The Argentine Ambassador to Switzerland, Benito Llambi, who had pursued me so persistently in Zurich had learned about the wedding, had come to Madrid. That day he must have been deranged - although I always suspected him to be slightly unstable, but I never dreamed he would carry his exaggerations so far. He appeared in the chapel in the midst of a line of guests and was in a pew with a pistol in his pocket. Fortunately he sat down next to two of Luis' friends who noticed that he was fingering a revolver. He was nervously taking it in and out of his pocket. When they spoke to him, he told them he was not going to allow Luis to marry me, that he was the man Aline should marry. Somehow these two friends managed to remove him from the church and get him in their car and far away from the celebration. We did not learn about this until much later. Benito Llambi was also an Argentine military officer and had been a close friend of Preisdent Peron who had named him Ambassador to Switzerland in 1946. I had met him through Helga Nehring – she was very attractive and had an admirer in the Argentine Embassy. The Peron Government had been a useful ally to Hitler during the war and this Ambassador had befriended many Nazis on their way to Argentina. As Helga and I were able to discern, the Argentine Embassy had detailed information concerning bank accounts of the many Nazis they were helping to escape to Argentina. Towards the end of my months in Zurich, Benito had written my father without mentioning it to me, asking permission to marry me. My father immediately contacted me by phone from Pearl River - I told him Benito was crazy and that I had no interest in him at all. The last days I was in Switzerland, I tried to avoid him and when I arrived in Spain I had entirely forgotten everything related to Benito Llambi.

But back to the wedding – when it was over, after signing many documents in the church, Luis suggested, "Before we go to the big party at my sister's house, let's slip out and make a visit to see *El Abuelo*. He will not be able to come to the party and we'll never have time before we leave for Rome tomorrow morning."

Luis' grandfather was not strong enough to withstand a dinner for 250 people and looked up in surprise when he saw us walk in. I was still in my wedding dress. The old Count took both my hands, smiling at me.

"Aline, I have attended many weddings in my life. I have seen many people of different station joined in matrimony, but I want you to know that today I was very proud of you. You walked down the aisle like... . like a queen."

I looked up at Luis and saw that he was as moved as I was.

CHAPTER EIGHT

THE HONEYMOON

The next day as we began our honeymoon, who should be seated across from us in the almost empty first class cabin of the Iberia plane to Rome but Eva Peron. Eva Duarte, originally an entertainer in a Buenos Aires nightclub had become famous when she married Juan Peron, the powerful charismatic President of Argentina. Peron had been a known ally of Hitler who it was believed had provided him with financiation to assist in his election. Beautiful self-assured Eva had also been useful to Peron due to her popularity with the working classes and together they had led a much publized political life. Eva as the representative of a foreign head of state who had aided spain that year with much needed wheat,was feted by everyone and I met her frequently during the weeks before my wedding at cocktails in many houses in Madrid and in Argentine Embassy dinners.

Today as usual her dyed blond hair was pulled back in a huge chignon, her eyes outlined in thick black mascara. But her skin, despite the dollops of red on the cheeks, was luminous. A mink stole, which had become famous in Madrid because she flaunted it at all the official receptions despite the warm June weather, was draped over the arm of her seat. A pink straw hat adorned with feathers crowned the bulging blond hairdo, and a black veil floated over the highly painted brown eyes. When Luis got up to talk to someone in the back of the plane, Eva moved across the aisle to the seat he had left. In her hand she held the *ABC* newspaper, which carried a picture of Luis and me on the front page. Pointing to it, she asked who had made my wedding dress. Then she chatted for a while about the difference between Balenciaga in Madrid and dress houses in Rome. She explained that she was obliged to give much importance to her attire and coiffure because she was expected to create a sensation each time she appeared in public. "Mis *descamisados* would be let down if any woman outdid me." She paused and, with an arrogant toss of her head setting the feathers on her hat aflutter, added: "But I manage to be sure that no woman ever does."

Although I knew Luis would not like me to get involved in espionage again, and although I had told Jupiter that I was *cortando la coleta*, a bullfighting expression meaning "giving up the fight", temptation beckoned as she continued to talk. Her bodyguards were now in conversation with my new husband and, it appeared, would be for some time.

Deftly, I thought, I thanked her for her wedding present, a lovely Ming vase, and directed the conversation gently around to the unfound art works looted by the Nazis during the war and shipped to Argentina. I was taking advantage of knowledge I had obtained a few years before while working for OSS in Madrid. Then I referred to the Nazi money sent to Argentina. Eva looked at me severely. I had obviously hit upon a delicate topic. Her silence was ominous. Her expression changed -a feeling of tension arose between us. When finally she spoke, the words came out with such venom that I feared Luis would hear.

"Querida," she said with that Argentine intonation, "take my advice. If you want to live long enough to enjoy your honeymoon and the life of a grandee countess, do not ever talk about such things. It can be very dangerous. *Comprende?*"

And she moved back across the aisle to her seat.

But that was not the end to a calm plane trip for Eva. As the plane was taxing across the tarmac in the Rome airport, Luis nudged my arm and pointed out the window. There a huge sign with large black letters held by four persons displayed the welcome in Italy for Eva. "PUTANA GO HOME". We did not see her again, nor did I learn what she did after that arrival. The Italians were aware that Peron when he had been Argentine ambassador to Italy just before World War Two had been Hitler´s good friend and had encouraged Mussolini to join forces with the Germans. The Italians had no love for Peron or for his wife.

  Prince Raimundo Lanza, met us at the airport, - this was the same friend I had lunch with the day Luis finalized our marriage. The crowded road from the airport was a far cry from the orderly traffic in Madrid or even Paris. Rome was more crowded and much less orderly than Paris also but Raimundo managed to drive through the hectic traffic zigzagging in between the lines of busses and cars into the center of the city, finally depositing us at the Grande Hotel.

 While Luis spoke to the concierge and gave him our passports I was standing at a slight distance just behind him – I saw the concierge return the passports and shake his head negatively. Evidently he would not allow us to share the same suite- my passport was in my maiden name and there was no indication that we were married. Luis insisted. Then I clearly heard the concierge say that he did not believe we were married. This was an extremely uncomfortable moment – I had never shared a room in a hotel with a man – in those days such behavior was not accepted. People nearby were listening to the problem – the situation was becoming more embarrassing by the moment. Although I could hear Luis explaining that we had been married yesterday, the concierge refused our passports . I could now hear him clearly. – "you must show proof , I cannot allow you to share the same suite. Suddenly Luis turned around and asked me to hand him the Madrid newspaper of that morning that was under my arm. He opened it and pointed to the first page –fortunately there was the photograph of both of us coming out of the Church yesterday. The concierge smiled and we were much relieved.

My new clothes were perfect for our busy life in Rome, although I barely had enough evening gowns for the many dinners. We remained in Rome for over a week attending the numerous invitations in our honor that Luis' father and abuelo had arranged for us with their many friends.

First the Spanish Ambassador Sangroniz gave a large black tie dinner in our honor. I had already met him in Paris during the eight months there the year before while working for OSS. The Ambassador, as I entered that night, presented me with a beautiful passport carrying my new names and title -I was now Spanish and the Countess of Quintanilla. The palace that had harbored the Spanish Embassy for many years was impressive and beautiful. The next day, the Prince and Princess of Torlonia gave another dinner for us- the Princess was a sister of our King Juan in exile in Portugal.

There was also a dinner in the fabulous French Embassy- a magnificent palace – superior to any I had yet seen. When we entered the huge salon, I was amazed and especially pleased to recognize the ambassador – a friend whom I had worked with during the war in Madrid when he was head of Free French intelligence. Luis was startled and impressed as the Ambassador greeted me - "What a pleasure to have my beautiful friend Aline in this embassy". We had seen each other often while I was working for OSS and we had also lived through a drama one night when after dining in a madrid restaurant, one of our companions was murdered. It was exciting for me to see him again and a special treat to realize that I already knew this important personality. The palaces in Rome were overwhelming, more impressive than those I had seen in Paris – the entire city of Rome overwhelmed me although I barely had time to enjoy sight-seeing. Too many invitations arrived and Luis was as anxious as I to get to Capri, so we made excuses and left on a train for Naples and from there took the ferry to Capri.

CHAPTER NINE

CAPRI, VENICE, ROME

Capri was a delight that summer of 1947. Luis seemed to have friends everywhere and those friends introduced us to more . The house that had been rented for us by Raimundo Lanza was on the beach where everyone met in the morning to go out in a boat to swim. Since we had the entire second floor of the huge palacio which included an enormous terrace just above the beach looking out to the sea almost immediately we started to invite people after boating and swimming to lunch with us.

Below us lived Princesa Caraciollo, an attractive spanish woman who Luis knew from Madrid -she had married the top prince of Naples who had been one of the Italian pilots fighting in Spain with Luis during the Civil war. Also Fulco Verdura, who had not yet become the famous jeweler of later years, was in another smaller apartment. Then in the largest space below was Princess Manona Pignatelli, an elderly excentric personality with an appearance that fascinated me - her face covered with thick white makeup, her arms laden with large gold bracelets from her wrists to her upper arm – she explained that she had put her fortune in gold during the war so as not be robbed, She was cohabitating with a much younger sturdy fisherman – which would have been shocking in Madrid but here in Capri Spanish social restrictions seemed not to exist.

At night we usually went up the hill to the town in a horse drawn carriage since automobiles were not allowed on Capri. Everyone met for cocktails up in the plaza- it was also customary to shop before and after dinner – the shops were always open at night – we immediately bought the classic velvet cordoroy slacks that seemed to be a uniform for Capri evenings in the nightclubs.

Every morning we went down to the small beach below our house to wait for our friends to appear – among them was usually Eva Mussolini, daughter of the Italian dictator and widow of Count Ciano. I was astounded when I met her, remembering that her father had ordered the execution of Ciano, her husband and father of her children, because he had objected to Mussolini's aligning Italy with Hitler. Also Gianni Agnelli, who was to become president of FIAT, was often there with Pamela Churchill , now separated from Winston Churchill's son.

When friends' boats appeared we went out a short distance for a swim – the beaches were very rocky. After a swim sometimes we continued in the boats to visit the different grottos – the most popular was the Blue Grotto which was beautiful and enchanting - so large, so silent, so blue blue. Almost every day we spent time deep diving looking for "erizios" a kind of round black shell fish covered with a prickly crust which when opened provided a delicacy which Luis particularlly liked to eat.

One day we were in someone's larger boat and decided to visit the opposite side of the island and go ashore there to lunch. When we arrived in front of the restaurant we all jumped into the water to swim to the beach. On my way while swimming , I turned my head back looking for Luis – to my horror I saw that he was having great difficulty – in fact he was going under, floundering, and gasping desperately for breath . I managed to swim back and grab him - then others came to help. I had never seen Luis swim before – so far in Capri he had remained in the boat while I was under the water looking for the erizos he liked to eat. The Italians, like myself were surprised to realize that he couldn't swim since he was a top athlete in so many sports. Later when we were alone I questioned him about this unusual problem.

"When we were children during our summers in Biarritz our governesses never allowed us in the water for more than a few moments and even then just far enough to get our legs wet, then they obliged us to take five drops of quinine which was supposed to protect us from getting a cold. I never had the chance to learn how to swim-not even when I was older - the beach we went to in Biarritz was considered dangerous and few people went in far enough to actually swim."

It had surprised me that there seemed to be few people who liked to swim among my friends in Spain – there were no swimming pools and in San Sebastian on the beach in the summer people merely went in the water for a few minutes to cool off. Swimming was not a sport anyone seemed to give importance to. Police in San Sebastian patrolled the beach to ascertain that men wore tops on their suits and women were obliged to wear suits with skirts but there were no lifeguards.

"Poor Luis", I thought, all those governesses – "they probably didn''t know how to swim themselves."

How lucky I was not to have had even one governess! Luis´ bringing up had been so different from my happy childhood in Pearl River. I was learning surprising things I had not known about Luis every day.

On the twenty-seventh of August we received the news that our friend Manolete, the best bullfighter of all the past decades and our favorite, had been killed in a fight in Talavera de la Reina. The Italians were amazed to see how upset we were. We had even changed the date of our wedding to be able to see Manolete fight - he was not only a friend but a hero as he also was for most Spaniards- We saw in the newspaper that all Spain was sharing our sorrow.

From Capri we went to Venice for the month of August. My awareness of the beauties of Europe grew with the magnificence and exotic beauty of that city. At night we went in gondolas to balls in palaces illuminated by large torches – the huge flames covered the façades. Although most of the guests were Italian, the person who was to become the most important for us was a famous American social columnist, Elsa Maxwell. She soon became very fond of Luis- he was always a success - his wit, his amusing conversation and his facility in all languages. Luis never seemed to make an effort to make friends – in fact when he first started to talk to Elsa Maxwell it was to criticize a statement she had made about the Spanish Civil War. "what you are saying is absolutely incorrect" I heard Luis say, "you had better ask me since I was in that war." A half hour later I noticed that they were chatting together like old friends . She was a particularly unattractive middle-aged woman – fat, not an attractive face either but peppy with a good sense of humor. When she left at the end of a week she took the date of our arrival and I heard her addressing my husband. " I will make a reservation in the hotel Carlyle for you as as soon as I arrive in New York. Luis, you can't stay anyplace else and you will have a party in your honor the next day. You said you were arriving on November 11th. Call me." - she gave him a card and telephone number.

After over two months in Italy, we interrupted our honeymoon to return to Madrid to prepare our luggage for the trip to other European cities and the longer one to the United States . Luis went to the Balenciaga collection with me. It was 1947, the year of the "new look" which created a sensation in the world of fashion – Balenciaga and a new designer called Dior had shown collections with hemlines dropping almost to the floor – up until that date hemlines had not varied each year more than a few centimeters below the knee . I would need an enormous wardrobe since Luis had planned on spending October in Paris and London and then to New York in November - he insisted on buying me almost the entire collection. I complained – I didn´t look forward to the many hours of fittings – I had spent too much time fitting clothes while modeling in New York and would have preferred only a few special outfits but Luis insisted that I would have a large wardrobe for the many invitations he had already received for affairs in Paris and London.

Our weeks in Paris were quite different from the year I had been working there in intelligence – at least the daytimes were different, although we spent our evenings in the same nightclubs. At least here I already knew the city better than luis did and most of the glamorous places. After several weeks of partying and shopping, we left for Claridges in London- Luis knew this area well -again we enjoyed many invitations which had been prepared for us beforehand by his father or grandfather. Luis never bragged about anything, nor did he seem impressed that in London and in Paris as soon as we arrived the Spanish Ambassador in each country gave a dinner in our honor with key people of the city. In London we also spent much time in the National Art Gallery which interested Luis since he was an artist and hoping to make a career of painting. In Paris Luis convinced me to accompany him to antique shops on the west bank which fascinated him – we did the same in London, thus I began to learn about art and antique furniture – a necessary part of my education - Luis was opening many new worlds for me.

CHAPTER TEN

OCEAN LINER, NEW YORK, PEARL RIVER

We embarked on the new transatlantic liner Queen Elizabeth for New York in November - Luis wanted to meet my parents and see the country –he had never been to the USA – and no one of his family had been there since before the Spanish civil war. The crossing was my first of many transatlantic ship voyages later on. The boat was beautiful, the most modern and luxurious of those days with a lavish dining room and a great band for dancing - the Captain invited us to his table every evening. Our companions at table were among the most important passengers on board, but they were all older and we wanted to be free to enjoy other parts of the ship-the voyage took almost five days- years later when we started travelling to the USA in the Constellations that at first stopped in Madeira and took only 24 hours the short trip was impressive but even when the flight time was reduced much more we still missed the glamour and luxury of those great ocean liners.

We took advantage of all the games and amusements - not only the dancing but paddle tennis, swimming , deck games, and a new American game called Bingo. Luis insisted on trying everything. He also attended some special lectures providing information for foreigners who were going to the United States for the first time while I went to the hairdresser instead. Luis won a prize in bridge and another in Backgammon – he was good at every game but I knew nothing about any of them.

On the last day I happened to be on deck when the Statue of Liberty came into view – I was thrilled. I had never seen it before -although I had worked in the city I had never gone down to the end of Manhattan to view the famous statue. For me this was an important moment - I wanted Luis to share the thrill so I ran back to our suite where he was packing some last minute things.

"Luis, Luis, come quickly you must see the Statue of Liberty . It's a wonderful sight". But he didn't appear to be interested. I couldn´t understand. "Luis, hurry. Come come."

By now I was already going back towards the door. Luis turned around and merely looked at me, "I do not intend to go to look at the Statue of Liberty." I was astounded. He went on. "I will tell you why. For five days now all I have been listening to in the lectures for foreigners has been "the country with the biggest bridges, the tallest buildings, the fastest cars, the prettiest women …. All I intend to do is to meet your mother and your father and get back to my own country where people are not bragging all the time."

This was a discouraging beginning for our arrival, but more was to come. When we arrived at the customs port of entry - the official stood back observing for a few moments my multiple suitcases of luxurious matching suede , all expensive wedding gifts . The official asked Luis for the keys. When Luis could not find them, the man proceeded to break them open. We were both shocked watching him destroy our new deluxe luggage, superior to any I had ever seen. But when the customs man opened the suitcases and saw my glittering embroidered evening gowns, he looked up at Luis amazed.

"What is your wife, a movie star? And what are you, a banker? "

Luis was horrified - in Spain no official would dare to speak in such a manner. This disappointing reception on the part of the customs's official made Luis still more skeptical about the great USA. I was becoming despondent – the customs official had been rough and discourteous - this time I realized that Luis had every reason to be disenchanted with my wonderful country.

But as it was to turn out Luis´ displeasure during our arrival soon changed, thanks to the friend we had made in Venice during the summer - Elsa Maxwell. We soon learned that she was the most important organizer for social affairs in New York city - she also had a power and influence with the press that destroyed some and glamorized others – her articles were read by everyone from society leaders to business men and politicans. When we arrived at the hotel, we found an invitation from her for a party in our honor for the following evening . The next night that party seemed planned especially to entertain Luis. Elsa seated him next to Grace Kelly, the most famous movie star of the moment. We met many key people of the USA .and Luis was charmed with their friendliness and lack of formality - he became especially friendly with the famous Hollywood producer, Jack Warner - they both liked to play poker and they made a date for a game soon after. Hattie Carnegie was one of the players - I had modeled for her only four years before. Elsa herself was also another member of the poker group.

During the party that first night in New York Anne and Jack Warner invited us to visit them in California . Luis decided immediately that as soon as we had time it would be fun to buy a car and drive across the country - Hollywood was a magic word for Spaniards.

At another of Elsa's parties we met the Duke and Duchess of Windsor and became friends from that moment on. We also met interesting personalities from New Orleans, Chicago and Palm Beach. Many became friends and hosted us at parties during our long drive across the country months later - many Americans came to New York in November to take part in that popular social season – we also became familiar with the famous nightclubs – El Morocco –The Stork Club- those same places that my colleagues in the model room had gone to every night but that I had never known. Many of the new acquaintances we met in these parties later came to visit us in Spain and became lifelong friends. We seemed to be invited by everyone we met –Luis said, "Americans are generous and hospitable, much more so than Europeans" . We were among the first Spaniards outside of Salvador Dali to arrive in America after World War Two. People wanted to learn what was now going on in Spain with a dictator in charge - many had erroneous opinions of what had happened during the Spanish Civil War due to the reports in the newspapaers.

PEARL RIVER

But the experience that established forever Luis´ affection for my country was his week in my hometown of Pearl River. Never again did he mention the bragging lectures he had attended on board the Queen Elizbeth. My father came to drive us the hour trip across the George Washington bridge along the Palisades parkway up the Hudson River to Pearl

River. I had been worrying about what Luis would think of my birthplace. Our town was still small and picturesque in those days, typical of the ideal American small town - I had always been very proud of it. In the center of the town was the square with the names of those who had died in the first World War. The railroad station divided the town in half – one train left each morning taking those who worked in New York to the big City- and it returned with the same people at night. Next to the station was the Dexter Folder Company, the big factory founded by my grandfather Dexter and his elder brother where the majority of the men in the town were employed. In fact the town had been started by my grandfather and his brother who had chosen this site as the best place because of the railroad connection which was necessary for shipping their printing presses to New York and to ports for export to Europe.

We lived on a hill up above the town - our house was not large, nor did my grandfather have a large house- his older brother who had been the founder and owner of the business was the wealthy one in our family and possessed advantages we did not enjoy. As we neared our house I looked at Luis worried about his opinion, but he was smiling.

"Just what I have always imagined a real American house would look like", he said as we entered the circular drive.

Allthough my parents had met Luis the day of our arrival, the problems with the customs official had spoiled our dinner with them in the hotel- Luis kept mentioning the rudeness of the customs official so my parents did not become aware of his charm and sense of humor. But from the first moment Luis was in our home, he and my mother got along so well that I saw him rarely after that. He was fascinated with the modern American kitchen – Spanish kitchens had no modern equipment at all – there wer no frigidaires in spain, only ice-boxes. Then he wanted to try to show my mother how to make certain Spanish dishes – of course he had no idea , I don´t think he had ever been in a kitchen but it amused him to cook with so many electrical attachments. Soon he was asking us to eat in the kitchen where a table was next to the large window looking out to the garden and then apple orchard which I had raced through so often on my way to the bus to go to New York when I was modeling.

The local newspaper had published an article stating that a real European Count was in town –it was also mentioned that he might be wearing a crown – all of which revealed what a really "hick" town Pearl River had been in those days. Luis was amused and we all had good laughs about the mention of the crown. Soon Luis began to take walks in the town along Central Avenue and Main street obviously enjoying everything he saw - people began to approach him saying they knew me or my parents and wanted to welcome him. He was delighted with their friendliness and cordiality.

When he returned that first day , he told my mother. "There is a barber shop. I saw the sign and would really like to go. How does one make an appointment?"

"You don't need a haircut, Luis and you don´t need an appointment, " said my mother.

"No, but I want a haircut anyhow because I've never been in a barber shop in my life. In Spain the barber comes to the house. That's no fun. "

Soon one of Luis's new friends in Pearl River became Mr. Preziosso, the only barber in town. He was the father of twelve children, one was Maria, a girl who had been in my class in school.

One day I took Luis to see our school house in the middle of the town - a long rectangular red-brick building facing a large football field. Football was the favorite sport of our town – two Pearl River students had become famous football heros when they attended universities. I had always been proud of our school and it gave me a thrill just to stand there looking at it, but I realized that for Luis accustomed to the impressive ancient buildings in Spain, this edifice must appear very drab. As we stood on the football field looking up at the school building, I pointed to the lower right hand corner, and told Luis that at age four I had begun school there and had graduated at age sixteen from that room on left corner of the top floor – that I had spent one year in every room in that building - I pointed to the windows of each class as I spoke.

For what was an embarrassing long minute , he said nothing – just looked around at the bulding, at the green field, at the flag waving above the center window of the principal's office.

Then he turned to me. "You really spent a year in each of those rooms.?"

"Yes, I started in the kindergarten in that lower corner and finished in that room just above it on the top floor.

"Aline , how lucky you have been. All my life I wanted to go to a school, a real school. But my father and grandparents would not permit it . Instead the professors came to us . Never was I able to know what it was like to go to school to play games with other boys. And just when I was about to go abroad to begin the university, the Civil War broke out – by the time it ended I was too old to go. My parents and grandparents thought we would have a better education with private teachers, so I missed all the companionship you have had - I was even obliged to learn sports with private trainers. Yes I learned polo, tennis and golf but never had the chance to play football on a field like that. I always wanted to play football. You are so lucky to have had all those years in such a perfectly marvelous school – this is all like seeing a movie for me."

On that first trip to Pearl River with Luis, he was as entranced with all he saw in my country as I had been when I arrived in Spain. Also I realized that I had been the fortunate one - not him with his family's many titles and wealth. Little by little I was learning about my husband''s upbringing and his family's customs – everything about his background was so different from mine that I realized it was only a miracle that had brought us together. Yes, although Luis was better educated that I in many ways – he spoke and wrote perfectly five languages – he had a familiarity with art and antiques and music that I did not have, but he did not have the preparation for life that I had received as part of a middle class American family. I wondered how Luis's sisters felt about their education. Did they also regret never having attended a school or University? That day as we stood on the football field I realized that family wealth and special priviledges do not provide children with better opportunities for life than my simple American education and backgrount had done for me.. We had been six children in a small house with one maid who usually slept in my room. Luis had been brought up in a huge palace with 60 servants and three governesses , French, German and English , all living in his home at the same time. His youth sounded grand but actually it had been pitiful because he had not been given the opportunity to compete with others his age nor to join in their sports and studies. I decided then and there to bring up the children we might have as near to the middle class American manner as possible and I imagine Luis was making the same decision. Indeed I had been the fortunate one.

CHAPTER ELEVEN

NEW YORK CITY

During that first visit Luis spent much time walking along Fifth Avenue shopping and looking in the windows. Since he enjoyed it, he walked slowly and everyone passed him by. "I do not understand," he comented to me " Americans are always running as if they were going to a fire. What are they hurrying for? Nobody walks fast like that in Madrid." It was true, we lived at an entirely different pace in Spain, but by now I had become accustomed to the Spaniards slow stroll along the streets. Luis was especiallly attracted by the window decors of the big department stores and often returned from his "paseo" describing dresses he had seen that he thought would be nice for me. In Madrid, his tailor, shirtmaker, and shoemaker all came to the house, so he had never spent time looking at shops. In those days in Madrid large department stores were unknown –and there were no shop windows slightly like those along Fifth avenue.

One day on returning from his window shopping , he said, "you will have to get rid of that Balenciaga dress with the big ruffle and bow on the skirt."

"But I love that one."

"I used to, but not any more. I started seeing a copy of that dress at Bergdorf Goodman, it was exactly the same, but the ruffle and bow were smaller. In Saks, the same dress was in the window, but the ruffle was still smaller and the bow, too. By the time I got down to the bottom of Fifth Avenue, that bow was so small that you could hardly see it. That's it, you cannot wear that dress anymore. Where is the best dressmaker in New York?

"The very best is your poker partner, Hattie Carnegie. In America she is the equal of Balenciaga in Paris."

So we went to Hattie Carnegie's salon which I certainly knew well – it was a nice feeling for me. Luis saw the collection with much interest and intended to buy me the entire line despite the large amount of Balenciaga outfits I already had, but when he saw the prices, he changed his mind. The difference with Spanish prices was unbelievable in those days. That day Hattie was observing me carefully.

"Aline," she said, "you can't wear that long hair wrapped in a braid around your head. You must have it cut."

So when I went back to Spain, I was the first to have short, curly hair. Spain was still years behind, even in hair styles.

In February Luis bought a convertible car for the trip and we began the long journey, starting slowly down the eastern seacoast, then through the southern states and finally stopping at New Orleans for Mardi Gras. We had already been invited to all the Balls and also the horse races before we left New York. Luis' father then was president of all Spanish racing and the president of the New Orleans races had become aware of that and invited us to his box. Then he took us down to the finishing line for the end of the most important race. I was wearing Balenciaga's most sensational woolen tweed suit with a long full skirt almost reaching my ankles - probably due to the weight of the thick wool, the skirt suddenly fell from my waist to the ground. Next to us were all the photographers waiting to catch a shot of the winner, and behind us were rows of spectators. The jackets that year were especially short so there I stood all of a sudden almost naked from the waist down, The glance of horror on Luis' face as I leaned down to pull up my skirt shocked me -I looked for a manner to hook the heavy skirt at my waist but the hook had broken . I staggered with my two hands grabbing my skirt as we both turned and rushed to our car.. Luis mumbled, "After that scene you have just made we'd better leave this city immediately," He didn't mind leaving New Orleans because he had not enjoyed it at all - in the balls every night , only the men who were members of the clubs were allowed to dance with the ladies –Luis was indignant being obliged to sit in a balcony above the dance floor and watch me dance with one New Orleans man after another. Already he had found the American custom of cutting-in very rude in dances in New York and Washington, but for him this Mardi Gras New Orleans custom was the limit. As we drove out of the city he declared with solemnity that he would never go back to New

Orleans and we never did although in my opinion it is one of the most attractive city in the USA.

The trip by car to California seemed endless – but Luis did not mind, he was fascinated with the diners along the highways where he ate hamburgers for the first time and played the slot machines – – these things did not exist in Spain. Everything in America was new for Luis, just as everything in Spain had been new for me. Nevertheless the view during the long long drive was monotonous - every city and town was similar- the architecture of the buildings the same as the place we had left a day before, all the towns had the same Central Avenue and Main street just like Pearl River. And here in this enormous space there were only endless flat highways with no curves, no hills , no valleys, nothing interesting to look at. The central part of the USA provides enormous agricultural wealth but lacks the beauty of the ancient small villages of Europe. The trip also took many more days than we had calculated - often it seemed we were in the same town as three days before – the towns and houses were so much the same.

Finally we arrived at the impressive Hollywood house of Jack and Anne Warner which was a delightful relief. A large garden surrounded the house where we discovered a bridge which by pushing a button would go up or come down – we could never understand the purpose. All the guests at his large dinners were famous movie stars – most of them seemed to be afraid of him – at least they treated him with a respect that amazed us since he was always cozy and down to earth with us . Anne Warner never appeared at all, Jack merely said she was "traveling". Several times he organized a poker game which seemed to be his greatest relaxation even though he seldom won.

Over a large fireplace in the main salon was a Dali portrait of Anne Warner. The face was beautiful but the body was surrounded by little snakes. Guests were expected to spend some time admiring it. Luis and I had already seen another strange Dali portrait in Mrs. Harrison William's home - she was one of the most beautiful women of those days in New York. Dali had painted her lower body in rags while above she was dressed in an elegant gown and exquisite jewels. Over a year later in Madrid at a dinner in our house we mentioned these paintings to Salvador – Luis and Salvador had fun discussing the differences between New York and Madrid. Salvador had been in New YOrk several years before we arrived. Laughingly he explained, "the way to impress Americans is to shock them. That portrait of Mrs. Williams was the result of gossip I had picked up in her dinner party. One of her close friends told me that she had been born in Chicago, the daughter of a groom of race horses, that until she married the rich Harrison Williams she had lived obscurely. I had unlimited requests to do more of my wild shop windows . Americans are not like Europeans , no – no - not at all. But I had a good time there. I arrived without a penny and left with plenty."

After a few days in his house Jack Warner suggested we go to his studio where he had arranged a luncheon in our honor.

"It will be at twelve o´clock noon, so please be prompt. After the luncheon I will take you around the studio where you can see some interesting films now in production."

When we arrived at the gate, well before twelve, it was as difficult to get into the studio as entering a munitions factory had been when I was training in OSS in war time. We explained to the official that we were luncheon guests of Mr.Warner but he did not believe us, finally another employee appeared and we repeated our reason for coming – this man also shook his head insisting that Mr. Warner did not lunch with anyone. Nevertheless since we refused to leave eventually he informed us that he would be our guide and show us the studio. This man took us through many different sets - in one we met Lauren Bacall and Humphrey Bogart who were filming "Key Largo". Then we were escorted into a dining room filled with more famous stars. We were delighted with all we were seeing, but disappointed that we hadn't seen Jack – we told our guide again that we were certain we were supposed to have lunch with Mr. Warner. The guide just waved our suggestion aside, as he accompanied us to a table. "Impossible. Mr. Warner is a very busy man."

We didn't mind- and went to the buffet, chose our lunch and proceeded to eat. Actually we were elated to be among so many important movie stars, our eyes were popping. It was March 1948, and Hollywood's heyday.

I had just taken a cold chicken leg in my fingers and was about to put it in my mouth when our guide came back from a telephone call to our table shouting and raising his hands in the air.

"Stop! Stop!"

The tone of his voice was so full of fear, my fingers maintained the chicken-leg in mid air. This must be poisoned, was my first thought.

"A terrible mistake has been made!" He screamed. "An absolutely terrible mistake. Mr. Warner is raging. There's a luncheon in your honor and you are supposed to be there and not here."

"Yes, we told you that."

The man literally lifted us from our chairs and pushed us out of the dining room. Now we were both reluctant to leave, -our companion was so frightened that he pushed us both down the hall. "Run, please run. I am going to be in terrible trouble. I may lose my job."

In a pompous official dining room about eight executives of the studio sat surrounding Jack at a large rectangular table. They were all men and none of them were movie stars. It looked most boring.

"Jack", said I, "we were on time. You told us to be here at twelve, and we were at the gate before that. The guide took us around and then to a lovely dining room."

As we finished desert, the butler passed around a silver tray full of packages of cigarettes, chewing gum, and boxes of chicklets. We had never seen this done before. Jack Warner turned to me and said, "What brand do you smoke?"

I was embarrassed by his question but since he insisted I indicated one.

"Ah, Philip Morris? Well, have some." And, he began to take packages of Phillip Morris and stuffed them into my pockets, he even took my handbag, opened it, and put two packs in there.

We were both very surprised. He must have read someplace that cigarettes were hard to get in Spain - we just couldn´t understand his strange gesture. Later, on our way back to Warner's home, Luis said " I certainly think this is the best country in the world, but your compatriots have unusual manners and tastes. " then he went on "And furthermore I guess I just don't catch on to this American sense of humor. Did you notice how they were all laughing at everything Jack said at table- I didn't hear him say anything particularly funny, did you?"

The house of the Warners surprised us more every day. Everything was controlled by electric buttons - the roof in our bedroom rolled back by touching an electric switch. There were special electric switches that moved walls and ceilings. We became terrified to touch any switch –once Luis entered a bathroom on the first floor during a large dinner – steam started to pour out of the walls and Luis emerged covered with sweat, his clothes soaked. He learned that a sauna was installed in that room.

Jack invited his studio stars for dinner at his home. I was impressed, but Luis was fascinated. Some of those stars became lifelong friends. In the sixties when Spain became a popular place to film for American producers due to the low cost and the sunny climate, we had the opportunity to respond to their kindnesses -Tyrone Power, Frank Sinatra, Lauren Bacall, Clark Gable-Ava Gardner, Deborah Kerr etc.

Repeatedly during our visit Jack Warner tried to convince me to do a film-test, but I had no slight interest in changing my life as a Spanish Countess for an American movie star. I was in love and enjoying life with my husband too much to even consider such a future.

From L. A. we went to San Francisco to visit Dororthy Spreckles of the famous sugar family. I had met her while doing espionage in Paris in 1946, but Jack kept telephoning to Dorothy's house pleading with us to return to L.A. - for an important dinner or for an opening. Thus we returned to Los Angeles and spent another week with Jack.

CHAPTER TWELVE

MADRID 1948

Our trip back toSpain on a Spanish merchant marine belonging to the Aznar family of Bilbao, was a far cry from the luxurious Queen Elizabeth from London to New York but it was a fascinating experience although it took twenty one days. The owner of the shipping line was a close friend of my father-in-law and this return trip had been a wedding present, making it possible for us to bring back to Spain all the things we had bought in the USA – our new automobile, frigidaire, vacuum cleaner, washing-machine plus many domestic electrical articles - all things that were not available in Spain.

On the only deck five cows were tied up - they provided meat for us and the crew during the long crossing from to Bilbao. There were only two other passengers, so our only companions were them, the captain and the cows. The crew lived below deck and we rarely saw any of them . When one morning I saw a cow missing and learned the reason, I dreaded arriving on deck each day after that – the animals had become like household pets but every fourth day, more or less, there would be another cow less. I got accustomed to petting the cows as I would a dog and complained to the Captain who was by then almost our best friend in the world, but to no avail – the cows continued to disappear regularly. I ceased eating meat and have never enjoyed it since.

Finally we arrived in Spain on June 21st – almost exactly one year after we had left on our honeymoon. As soon as our life together began in Madrid I was astounded by the amount of things I still had to learn about Spanish customs. When I married I had been unaware that my wonderful husband belonged to such a famous family. I did not know he was a Grandee nor what that meant, nor could I understand how most of the people I met with him at shoots, dinners or balls were now all relatives. It took time to learn that many titled people were related – that for centuries these Grandee families had intermarried and remained close together.

At first we moved into Luis' bachelor apartment, but since I was now pregnant we needed something larger. Only apartments seemed to be available in the growing city but I found something unique, a newly built medium sized house with a garden and a swimming pool, only about ten blocks from the Abuelo's house. The area was considered to be on the outskirts in those days and Luis declared that he could not afford it. When I suggested that he get a bank loan, he was aghast. "In my family we don't ask for loans". His strange answer surprised me, but I was still determined. "What about borrowing the money from your grandfather" Luis was even more horrified. "No one would dare ask the Abuelo for a loan". Everyone else in the family –his father and his aunts seemed to agree with him, I realized for the first time that they were all terrified of " el Abuelo". I still knew very little about the Abuelo's importance. Noone had ever told me that Romanones had been the most outstanding Prime Minister of King Alfonso X111th – in fact I had never heard the name Romanones before the day we went to his house to get his approval for our marriage, nor did I yet understand anything about titles. My year and a half in the country before my marriage had been dedicated exclusively to espionage - my social life had been organized to uncover Nazi sympathizers - none of my spanish friends had informed me that Luis 'family was especially wealthy or famous. Neither I nor anyone else knew I was going to marry Luis until a month before the wedding – there had not been time for someone to tell me about his family. I had met many people with titles so I thought titles in Spain were especially abundant and merely another strange custom. Now looking back at those times, I realize that since Romanones at that time was one of the most famous names in the country, probably people took it for granted that I had to be aware of what was public knowledge. But for me el Abuelo was like any other grandfather , maybe a bit nicer and I certainly was not afraid of him.

    I went to speak to the Abuelo about buying the house - after a short conversation explaining that I was certain it would be a good investment - that I believed Madrid had to expand in that direction during the next years, as I had hoped, he agreed to make us the loan for the amount Luis lacked- which was about four hundred thousand pesetas (don't remember how much that was in dollars). He made clear that this was a serious business matter and that the money would have to be repaid. Luis had already told me I could offer the Abuelo two of his Goya paintings as collateral if I obtained the loan which he doubted. The abuelo did not accept the collateral but insisted that the money was merely a loan. I only discovered that he had always intended it as a gift when he died four years later. We still live in the same house sixty years later, in what is now considered the center of the city.

Despite my previous years in Spain and my small variety of Spanish friends - bullfighters, flamenco stars, "rojos" reds, and a scattering of aristocrats, I was still a foreigner in 1948 - every day I was confronted with strange customs. There was still much to learn.

Usually while still in Luis' apartment, I awoke earlier than him and would ring for my breakfast which I began to consume as quietly as possible so as not to disturb him who was right next to me in the bed. I had become accustomed to breakfast in bed in my wartime apartment by my two indulgent maids who insisted that " an american senorita must have breakfast in bed". One of those first mornings as I was enjoying my usual orange juice , pancakes, bacon, and tea, Luis' sleepy voice interrupted me. "This is impossible".

I hadn't realized he was awake. I kissed him good morning. "What's that Luis?"

Groggily he raised himself on one elbow. "That's what I want to know. What is that?"

He was staring at my tray and at the same time touching his cheek where my lips had evidently left a bit of sticky syrup.

"Aline, I really can't stand this. You must change your breakfast habits or I'll have to move into another room."

"I'll change anything. Anything you say. Just tell me what's wrong..."

"These smells, those repulsive things you Americans eat at this hour!" He looked at the clock and moaned. "Eight-thirty! No Spanish lady is awake so early. It's not fair to the sevants. They can't serve our dinner at ten-thirty at night and then breakfast so early. You should sleep until eleven." He rolled his eyes. "And this food! Aline, you don't have to fortify yourself to work in a field all day."

"But what does a Spanish woman eat?"

"For breakfast, a cup of tea and a small piece of toast or a croissant with a bit of marmalade, but that's all."

I wasn't going to risk my husband for any breakfast. So from then on I stuck to that Spanish lady's breakfast, merely adding a glass of orange juice..

But that was only the beginning. The next day during lunch, another problem surfaced. He was shaking his head.

"Luis", I choked. "I can't eat any faster."
"It's not that. It's your left hand under the table. That's not attractive. In fact, it's very bad manners."

"But I was taught to eat like that. My mother made us have the left hand on the lap under the table when not using it.".

"Well, perhaps in America, but that's not the way here. Also you need both hands to eat properly. You hold the bread in one when it is free. Americans push with their fingers; here we push with a fork in the left hand or with a small piece of bread. And that American custom of cutting the meat, then putting the knife down, changing the fork over into your right hand, then putting your left hand in your lap! Aline, I get dizzy watching you. Why go to all that trouble? Try it our way. The fork in your left hand, the knife in your right and keep them that way. And," he went on, I wouldn't want anyone to suspect that you had your hand on the man's leg next to you at a dinner party."

I looked at him, horrified.
"Oh, yes. That's just what they might think. So no more hand in your lap, please."

The late Spanish night hours had long since become natural for me. Everything began two hours or more later than in the USA - I found that having a snack between meals solved the hunger problem. Learning to calculate in pesetas instead of dollars still did not come naturally nor changing from miles to kilometers, or pounds to kilos, or farenheit to centrigrade. But the weather was glorious, winters were sunny with deep blue skies, not cold enough to snow and according to Luis never enough rain.

Luis liked to entertain and I did also , so we began to organize dinners which in those days were black tie for the men and long evening dresses for the women.- the invitations were always for ten-thirty at night and one sat down at table about eleven –fifteen. After the first dinner party to which we invited about twenty people, the majority older than us , mostly Luis's relatives that I had met since our marriage, I received a telephone call from Luis's cousin, the Duchess of Sueca, an extremely elegant lady of the generation of Luis' father. "Aline, began Belen Sueca, "since I suspect you and Luis will be often inviting people to dine at your house in the future, and since you are a foreigner you will have to learn how to seat the tables correctly according to our protocol."

Of course I was still the small- town American girl and had not the slightest idea of how to seat any table according to protocol – they had not taught me such details in the intelligence school , much less a table with royal highnesses and Grandees. Several deposed kings came to Spain often whom we met at Luis' father's house and then invited them to dine in ours. I realized that I must have made some grave mistakes in that first large dinner and understood that Belen, the Duchess of Sueca was being extremely kind to offer to teach me Spanish protocol. Now that I was aware of my ignorance, I wanted to learn how to comply with these obligations better than anyone and listened with much attention to her advice. Spanish protocol , as the Duke of Windsor told me years later is the strictest in Europe.

One of the greatest pleasures of my married life was being able to own riding horses and to ride every day. Since Pearl River was in the midst of open country there had been an excellent riding school and riding had become one of my favorite sports. During those war years in OSS I realized that my Spanish girlfriends had many more social attributes than I. But apart from their proficiency in various languages and ability in tennis and golf, none of them had ever been to a university - that type of education was considered superfluous for women and not attractive for a well brought up girl . The only time I seemed to make up for my deficiencies was when I dove from a high board into the only pool in the city. They were all impressed. I was amazed - in America many girls I knew could have done the same thing.

When my first child was born, a son, the Abuelo was delighted. Since he was so famous his visit to see me and his principal heir created great excitement in the little British-American hospital. There was much bustle as a specially comfortable chair was placed for him next to my bed.

"Bueno, bueno," he said as he investigated the baby. "We need new blood in this family. He looks strong. And oh, I see he has inherited my nose. That's a good sign".

I wasn't too happy about the nose, but I pretended to have the same opinion.

"What name are you giving the child," he asked.
"Oh, naturally Luis like his father."
"Bosh," cried out the Abuelo banging his walking stick on the floor. "That's impossible. "this child is my "primo-genito" and will carry my title one day. He must be called Alvaro like me."

Whatever the abuelo said was law, I knew that already , so I dared not make any complaint. My child became Alvaro from that moment on. We continued to chat for a few more minutes and then the nurse appeared to say that it was the hour for the baby to be fed.

"Bueno, bueno, feed him," insisted the Abuelo. The nurse looked questioningly at me since I was breast feeding the baby. She stood there waiting, understanding that I wanted the Abuelo to leave before baring my breast. But he did not budge, and finally he looked up to her demanding why she did not go ahead with the feeding. The nurse explained. "it's that the Countess has to feed him personally."

"Oh, I don't mind, go right ahead."

"No, Abuelo, I can't do that."

Shaking his head in disgust at my prudishness. He stood up, came closer again to the baby, poked his finger for a few moments into the baby's mouth, gave me a kiss on the cheek and then left. Being accustomed to our American idea of cleanliness, his finger in my baby's mouth worried me.

Luis arrived a few minutes later. I told him we would have to change the baby's name because his grandfather wanted it named after him.

"Don't worry. We have to name the baby after so many relatives that he will have many names."

"But I don't like complicated long names."

"Don't be silly, Aline, It's the first name that counts. We will have to start with Maria... to honor your mother..... then Alvaro for my grandfather."

"Horrors, Maria's a woman's name."

"Not necessarily so here. It's a religious name. And anyhow we'll call him Alvaro."

"But I don't like that "Maria" coming first."

"Don't be silly, Aline. there are thousands of men named Maria something or other, like "Jose Maria". You know that and vice versa."

"I know.....I know....but.."

"And this will just be on paper. How else can we honor your mother?"

"Luis...believe me....my mother would prefer to miss the honor than to have a grandson named Maria...."

"You're really being silly."

"I refuse to have a son named Maria. I thought I'd become very Spanish, but I'm not that spanish yet...."

So we honored Luis' great grandfather instead of my mother and various other grandfathers as well, for which I'm sure they were all grateful. Our first son became Alvaro Luis Enrique Guillermo Alfonso Jacobo Figueroa Griffith. All Spaniards had to carry the name of the father and the mother.

Two weeks later, acccording to Luis the baby had to be baptised. Since by then I was riding again and doing my normal life, he warned me that I would have to get back into bed to receive the guests, that I would have to put on the new lacy satin bedjacket he had bought me for the occasion, and he told the maid to make up the bed with the fanciest hand embroidered sheets as well...

> "But how can I go to the church if I have to be in bed?. I asked.
> "The mother doesn't go to the church."

Since by now I was well aware that there was no use in my trying to change ancient spanish customs, I removed my riding clothes, put on the bedjacket and jumped into bed just before the family and guests began to arrive after the baptism which had taken place in the church. Alvaro and I received our guests in grand style in my bedroom –we were both dressed in lace and satin. Alvaro outdid me in his inherited long baptism gown of cream colored satin and lace which reached to the floor, while I was propped up in bed on lace pillows in a special silk beribboned bedjacket- Luis' gift for the occasion was beautiful.

There were so many spanish customs I had to learn- life married to Luis was a world of discoveries for me – everything was new and different but I was in love and it was delightful – I was becoming little by little as Spanish as if I had been born in the country.

CHAPTER THIRTEEN

MARRIED LIFE, LUIS'S OFFICE & JOSE SILVA

Spaniards still spoke frequently of their recent civil war of 1936 to '39 in which one million had been killed of the 27 million population of that time. Those three terrible years were hard to forget for people of both sides. But now they were learning to work side by side and were rebuilding an impoverished country.

For me it was a surprise to discover that living in a dictatorship did not seem very different from life in the United States. A peaceful orderly atmosphere reigned throughout the country. Although censorship of the press existed, those who cared to criticize the government and General Franco seemed to do so as loudly and as often as the spirit moved them in social gatherings and in the streets. My father-in-law, president of the Grandees of Spain, represented the opinion of most members of the aristocracy – he was in opposition to Franco and looked upon him as a dictator unjustly usurping the rights of the King Don Juan, who was in exile in Portugal.

But I began to admire Franco – throughout the World War he had not been intimidated by the Nazi troops threateningly located on Spain's northern border. After the war ended, Franco's government was pro-American, and created special laws to encourage American investment. As a result private industry for the first time was commencing in the country which created a multitude of jobs. Also many schools were being created throughout the country - although there was still poverty, living conditions for everyone had improved, especially for the poor. And the most important development of Franco's leadership was that for the first time in its history Spain was developing a large middle class. The rationing of the war years had disappeared and the entire country was beginning to enjoy a few modern advancements. Nevertheless carts drawn by donkeys filled with produce were still coming into Madrid from the country and sometimes flocks of sheep would fill the Castellana on their way to market. Frankly I was charmed by these scenes, so unusual in my own country. Automobiles still had to be imported, as yet none were manufactured in Spain.

Although in those days I appreciated the delightful life I was leading, I was still unaware of many details about my new family & I was gradually getting accustomed to the advantages it gave me. All the members of Luis large family were outstanding in their liberal views, their lack of snobbishness and their individuality. They not only accepted me but thanks to the Abuelo they embraced me with affection which added to my happiness.

Daily I went riding in the Club del Campo, a large public property on the outskirts of the city, about fifteen minutes by car from my house. Often we had guests at home for lunch or dinner or went to a formal affair in an embassy or a private home. Luis suggested that it would be nice if I would visit his grandmother in the afternoons around tea time now and then - he added that women of the family were expected to do that. So I did go several tiimes to the big house on the Castellana – the routine was especially boring, we would say the rosary, then have a cup of tea and chat. The Abuelo was never present at these afternoon affairs and I missed him. Despite my four years living in a catholic women's university I only attended these affairs a few times, I did not have enough religious spirit to give up my horseback riding at that hour. While the Abuelo Romanones was alive, I sometimes went in the morning with baby Alvaro to visit him. Very soon I was able to name another son Luis after my husband, but Alvaro continued to be the favorite with the Abuelo and the one I took with me when I went to visit. One day the Abuelo convinced me to leave the baby there "for a few hours only". The few hours grew to three days and desperate I reclaimed my baby threatening the Abuelo not to visit him again.

However a short time later when I was pregnant with my third son, the Abuelo died. That previous summer he had come to visit me in Zarauz, a beautiful resort next to San Sebastian on the northern coast where we were spending the summer in a rented house. The abuelo despite not being in good health wanted especially to see Alvaro, his "primogenito" who had always been a fascination for him despite his many other grandchildren. When Luis telephoned from Madrid with the sad news, I was stricken and wanted to leave immediately to attend the funeral but Luis insisted I remain with the children in Zarauz. I still regret not having been present at that famous extraordinary funeral. When I saw the reports and photos in the press I finally realized for the first time the Abuelo's national importance and his popularity. The entire wide central avenue of the Castellana was closed from one end to the other with masses of people who remained for hours waiting for the funeral procession to pass. The radio and newspapers declared that Madrid had never experienced a funeral of such magnitude with so much popular acclaim and support. Masses of citizens from all over Spain had come to Madrid and followed the hearse throughout the city - afterwards many followed the procession by car as the hearse proceeded to the burial in Guadalajara - the Romanones birthplace about forty minutes from Madrid. There again an enormous tribute by the entire populace took place. During the weeks that followed, the press published articles daily about the advantages and benefits Romanones had obtained for the people and the country. Many were the columnists who commented on Romanones' dazzling speeches in parliament, his brilliance as an orator in the congress, his wit, his innovations. Today still eulogies of Romanones appear frequently in the newspapers - his many brilliant political comments are frequentlly quoted and used as headings in the press.

During these years I had tried to comply with the obligations I sensed were expected of Luis' wife – I assisted several charitable organizations which the family supported, often adding a few American methods of obtaining contributions. Luis and our lives also revolved around visits to various family shoots in the nearby countryside. Apart from my daily horse back rides, I took golf lessons – hoping to be able to accompany Luis who held a low `handicap - something I never managed to do. But what surprised me was that Luis never went to an office. Sometimes men he referred to as "administrators" and a secretary came to the house and he would spend a few hours with them but he never mentioned his business matters to me, nor explained exactly what kind of affairs he was involved in. I was worried, wondering where our money came from , but when I questioned him about this, at first I received only vague answers - finally he told me that women in Spain did not take part in men's business affairs and that seemed to end the matter.

One day shortly after the abuelo´s death while watching Luis play golf, a friend happened to comment, "Aline you are so lucky. I've just come from a trip to Extremadura. That southwestern province is the most wonderful part of Spain—so wild , so romantic, so old-fashioned. The last vestige of what Spain was like hundreds of years ago! You are indeed fortunate."

"Fortunate?" I asked. "But what does all that have to do with me?"

"Don't tell me you didn't know that Luis owns some of the best properties, "fincas", in that part of the country?"

No, I hadn't known. I had no idea that Luis was a landowner, large or small. He not only never mentioned anything about his work or business but absolutely nothing about anything he owned. I thought he had enough money to get along on from some kind of family business but I never had the feeling that he had much. He was far from a spendthrift. I knew his father had large properties properties for partridge shoots. Other times we went to fincas of friends further away in the mountainous sections of the country for big game shoots of wild bore and deer, but never had Luis mentioned properties of his own. When I asked him about our friend's comments, and said I would like to see his fincas, he scoffed, "Why, the man is insane. Extremadura is the poorest, most backward part of Spain. And what is more, I no longer have so many fincas there. This Franco government has just expropriated five of my largest properties, supposedly to provide work for the poor, and what I have left are located in isolated areas with no roads. Napoleon's troops destroyed everything in that part of the country at the beginning of the last century. You would have to travel part way on a donkey to reach any of them. Impossible."

Of course, that made his fincas sound more enticing to me. but he also added that his mother from whom he had inherited these properties had never visited them and he saw no reason for me to do so. I pointed out that perhaps in the past years roads might have been built, but he assured me it was unlikely in those parts. After several weeks of my nagging, finally, his patience hanging by a shred, he agreed,"Very well, if you insist on this mad idea, then go to my office and speak to my farm administrator, Jose Silva. It will give him quite a shock as he has been working for our family for forty years and I doubt he has dealt with a woman about such things. But he is patient and will give you whatever information you want."

Thus I appeared the next morning in the dusty dim offices where an elderly, owl-eyed plump little man was awaiting me. Don Jose immediately fell into the stilted third person used by subordinates in those days.

"What an honour to have the Senora Condesa gracing our offices!" He beamed and smiled as he directed me to a chair in front of his worn mahogany desk. "What can I do for the Senora Condesa? I am at her service."

"I would like some information Don Jose, about my husband's fincas. I want to visit one in Extremadura."

Don Jose's face changed dramatically. He leaned forward. "But is something wrong? Does the Senora Condesa not have confidence in my management?"

"Oh, heavens no, Don Jose," I said quickly, "Don't misunderstand. It's just that American women usually are interested in our husband's business affairs, even if it is only to give an occasional opinion."

He shook his head from side to side. Then he stood up and went to a filing cupboard where he pulled from the shelves a large stack of papers and then returned to where I was sitting.

"The Senor Conde," he began, "has several very nice properties in Extremadura, the cattle and sheep raising district of Spain."

"Where exactly is this?" I asked.

"Well, I would say it is about half way between Madrid and Lisbon in the southwest. To go there one takes the main road to Portugal."

"Tell me, which of these properties could I visit?"

"Let me see. Well, the fincas in the province of Badajoz have no town near enough to provide comfortable accommodation, and they are too far away anyhow. Undoubtedly, the finca near Trujillo called Pascualete would be the nearest. It is about one hundred and fifty miles from here. This one your husband inherited in 1936 from his maternal grandfather, the Conde de Torre Arias, Marques de Santa Marta, probably the largest landowner in Extremadura."

At the risk of seeming disloyal to my husband, I muttered something about not understanding why Luis had not taken more interest in these properties.

At that Don Jose's expression changed again, this time to a look of infinite sadness and gentleness.

"After all, the Senora Condesa must realize that the Senor Conde was only eight years old when his mother died, and although he then inherited from her his title of Quintanilla along with some properties, he obviously was not of an age when he could take care of them. And these properties actually were not finally settled until several years ago—so they have not been his for very long."

"Then later when he inherited fincas from his grandfather, Torre Arias, who was shot down by the Reds in the streets of Madrid during those first dreadful days of our Civil War, the Senor Conde was only seventeen years old. That was the last time I saw the Senor Conde until after the war. He escaped from Madrid to the northern part of Spain where he joined the Nationalist troops. Being under age, he enlisted using an assumed name, he lay many months, horribly wounded in an improvised hospital near the front line trenches of Bilbao, without his family being aware. He had enlisted as a private and by the age of eighteen he was a first lieutenant.

"Do not think that our Spanish boys are lazy and uninterested in their country's welfare. Remember that as children they were exposed to the atrocities of a bitter Civil War. Nineteen men of your husband's famly were killed in that war, some as young as your husband and others older," he concluded sadly.

However, I wanted to get back to the subject at hand. I informed Don Jose that I would like to visit the ranch he suggested—the one called Pascualete.

"Of course," he replied. "As the Senora Condesa wishes, but I feel it is my duty to warn the Senora Condesa that this is the most isolated section of Spain. There are no comfortable places for you to stay overnight and the inns in these country towns provide miserable food—everything is cooked with rancid olive oil. It is not an area where a lady such as the Senora Condesa should travel."

I had heard all this before from Luis, who had gone further, saying there were no bathrooms, and that my bed was likely to be filled with rats, bedbugs, and cockroaches. Don Jose's warning did not impress me at all.

"Don't worry, Don Jose, I'll manage somehow."

"Then I will advise someone from Pascualete to come to Trujillo which is the city nearest to the finca to meet you. However, it will take at least four or five days for my letter to arrive and another week to receive an answer."

"But I don't want to wait that long. Why not send a telegram?"

"Senora Condesa, a telegram and a letter are one and the same thing in that part of Spain. Either one would have to be delivered by donkey."

Luis, who was easy-going and always willing to give in to me, finally decided to make the best of it. "I suppose I should have realized when I married an American that my life would be turned upside down."

By then I had already learned that being an American was a tremendous advantage in tradition-bound Spain. Any unorthodox notion was immediately attributed to this unfortunate acccident of birth.

CHAPTER FOURTEEN

EXTREMADURA

The trip was fascinating, leaving Madrid on the road to Extremadura and lisbon – we travelled in two cars, one belonged to a couple from the Bazilian Embassy, in our car we were acompanied by a Catalan friend who lived in Madrid, and a beautiful French woman, Annabella, who had been a famous movie star. We were introduced to her first by her ex-husband, Tyrone Power, an american actor we had met during our visit to Jack Warner's house in Hollywood. By the time we left Madrid everybody was enthusiastic about visiting this remote province.

We knew there were few gasoline stations along the route, so we had filled the tanks and taken additional gallons in the trunks of the cars. Although the road was only a two lane highway, it was almost void of traffic and in quite good condition, being the main route to Portugal. We were in a green Studebaker which we had bought during our honeymoon in the United States - the Brazilians were driving a black Embassy Packard. Since there were so few cars in Spain, our cars caused a sensation whenever we passed through a small town. "Americanos, Americanos" the people shouted in the streets as we passed by.

When about 73 kms. out of Madrid, we saw on the side of the road the majestic castle of Maqueda, reminiscent of knights in armour, Luis informed us that it had belonged to the Duke of Osuna before the war but he had lost it in a poker game. "one of the reasons," Luis went on , " why Franco outlawed gambling, I suppose. Spaniards have always been reckless gamblers." Then about 70 kms further on we arrived at the equally romantic looking castle of Oropesa perched high on a hill, its turrets and crenelated walls outlined against the clear blue sky. Luis told us that it belonged to our friend Pepe Frias and had been in his family since the fifteenth century. The Duke of Frias was a handsome fellow and a great shot. . Years later Pepe sold this castle to the government and it is now an excellent government "parador". hotel.

About 30 kms further, high on a hill were the ruins of another medieval castle, the castle of Monroy. All the way down on our right were the glorious Guadarrama mountains which in winter and Spring are snow-covered. Our route wound through many small whitewashed villages where the people always waved to us, thrilled to have the view of a car passing by. There were endless fields of green wheat and in others flocks of sheep or dark brown cattle grazing on the winter pastures, and sometimes a field of olive trees in neat even rows. The sky was blue - everything seemed to glisten in the winter sun.

Then suddenly Luis pointed to the silhouette of Trujillo which appeared jutting up against the blue sky on the horizon, reigning alone over vast endless fields. Even from a distance the walled in city with turrets and thick ancient stone walls was breathtaking. It was so medieval, so reminiscent of another age, isolated from everything, high up on a hill, as Spanish castles always are. As we came closer we could see the ancient crenellated walls and the many stone towers which had protected its inhabitants for two thousand years. The castle on the top, Luis explained had been built by the Romans in the first century. Then he pointed out the parts of the wall whose crenellated stone borders had sharp points. "That is the arabic wall , constructed in the eighth century. The wall where the almenas have square tops is Roman. Two walls were constructed around the city...with a difference of many centuries. ". A thrill crept up my spine. adventure was lurking inside those walls. Now we were entering the narrow curving streets leading up to the plaza, and when we arrived, it was another sight of beauty surrounded by arches and huge fifteenth century palaces. I did not know then that I was viewing one of the most impressive ancient plazas in Spain.

We arrived in Trujillo later than calculated, but Luis' tenant farmer was awaiting us. He was my first introduction to the Extremanian country man—the Spanish version of a cowboy. He looked about fifty and wore the outfit of the Spanish farmers—a coarse, dark blue cotton smock, with full gathered sleeves and a straight-brimmed hat - grasped in both hands was a thick, home-made walking stick. An expression of tranquillity and goodness shone from his dark-lashed, clear brown eyes lighting up his weather-beaten face.

This was Juan, who Luis explained was the "arrendatario", the renter who, with his three brothers, leased and worked all the land of the finca. Juan was the one who made the yearly trek to Madrid to pay the rent, so of course he knew Luis. He used to appear in the house in Madrid with a cheese and a smoked ham in one hand and in the other two leather bags containing the years rent in cash. finca.

He took off his wide-brimmed, black felt hat, bowing deeply; Luis shook hands with him and exchanged a few pleasantries. We followed them both into a small building which had a sign "Hotel Cubano" over the door. Behind a small reception desk, stood a smiling, bespectacled man, trying hard to give the impression that customers for the Hotel Cubano appeared every moment. But the utter silence and dimness of the place made it apparent that for the time being we were the only visitors.

I heard Luis say to Juan, "Just a minute. I will take care of the rooms and order dinner and then I will be with you and introduce the rest of the party."

A look of deep concern came over Juan's face. "But Senor Conde," he said, "what is this about rooms in this miserable little Inn when the palacio of the Senores Condes is awaiting you?"

Luis turned to Juan in amazement, as if he had not heard clearly.

"What are you talking about, Juan? What palacio?"

And Juan, in truly dramatic Spanish style, replied with a flourish, "What palacio other than Pascualete, the palacio of the ancestors of the Senor Conde, the oldest country palacio in this part of Spain."

Annabella, who had some understanding of Spanish, said "What on earth is he saying, Aline? What's all this about a palace?"

Luis turned to her speaking in French, "Don't pay any attention to him. These country people call any heap of old stones a palace."

But Juan continued, "And Senor Conde, the people of Pascualete have been preparing for days for your arrival. Our women have been cooking for you and would be very disappointed."

I insisted that we go immediately and Annabella backed me up.

After ten kilometers on a road out of Trujillo , Juan told us to turn on a dirt cowpath to the right. By now it was a pitch black night, but Juan directed us around stones and trees we could not even see. Every so often we had to get out of the car and search for a way around some big rock, - all the while Luis was complaining:

"Can't you see? This is absolute madness. No one in his right mind would start off on such a trip in the black of night. The cars are going to be ruined - actually it is my fault for permitting such an absurd trip. We could just as well have waited until morning."

Finally we were told to stop. (Actually, it was only eight kilometres on the cowpath.) The headlights of the car revealed a massive stone arch and underneath many men, women and a few children. Juan, who by this time had us completely in his power, escorted me out of the car and walked along beside me.

"Juan, what are all these people doing out here in the dark of night?" I asked.

"The Senora Condesa does not realize that this is a great day for us. It must be over a hundred years since anyone of the family of the Senor Conde has ever visited this finca. These people have been here all day waiting to meet, for the first time in their lives, the owners of Pascualete, where they and their ancestors have lived and worked for many generations." He scratched his head, "Not since the damn Frenchies took Trujillo has anyone of the famly stepped foot in Pascualete."

I realized he was referring to Napoleon's conquest of Spain. I started to calculate—that was in 1808... Goodness! One hundred and forty four years ago.

Several oil lanterns lit up the crowd under the stone arch and as we approached a ray of light fell on a tall, lean man with a lined, dark, handsome face and a mop of unruly black hair. The bone structure clearly marked under the dark leathery skin and the piercing black eyes brought to mind the faces in El Greco's paintings. A crumpled hat was grasped in his hand and as we approached and were introduced, I was particularly impressed by his quiet air and dignity.

"This is Primitivo," Juan explained, "the guard of the Senores Condes. He was born here at Pascualete, as were his father and his grandfather, all of whom have been the head guard of this ranch for many, many years."

Even his name, "Primitivo", fascinated me's –he proceeded to present his wife, Maria, whose appearance, alas, was as plain as her husband's was dramatic. At first glance she seemed a coulourless, nondescript woman with mousebrown hair drawn severely back into a sparse bun. Neither fat nor thin, tall nor short, Maria wore a black baggy dress gathered at the waist by a large black apron.

Now the rest of the group came forward to be presented.

"Many of these people are shepherds, as this finca produces mostly sheep," Juan explained to me. "some live far away from the palacio in "chozos", straw huts, at the outposts of the finca. But they have been waiting today many hours to meet the Senores Condes."

One after the other , they passed in front of me and Luis, sweeping into deep low bows as they were presented. Not one person moved away until all had been presented - then we passed through the arch and found ourselves in a spacious patio – it was too dark to be able to see anything of the large stone building. We were directed up a dark twisting staircase into the house where another stairway led to a large bare stone room with whitewashed walls, a vaulted ceiling and an enormous fireplace which illuminated the room.

A great stone canopy overhung the fireplace which stretched almost the entire width of the room. Underneath, on the walls, hung many skillets and copper pots, while two stone benches flanked either side of the hearth. Two women were kneeling in front of the open fire preparing our dinner. One was turning a heavy iron spit which held two sizzling suckling pigs whose drippings she poured every now and then into a pot of beans slowly simmering in one corner of the fire. As we walked across the floor of ancient tiles, the women jumped up and then went into dips or "reverencias" as these bows are called in Spanish. I realized then that these people for centuries had maintained the same respect for the owners of large properties as had been customary for royalty, but what amazed me was to see that here in this out of the way property these century old customs were still in use.

The women indicated the only pieces of furniture in the room—a large table covered with a heavy cloth which fell to the ground and several rustic chairs. We pulled out the chairs and sat down - as I put my legs under the tablecloth I felt a delicious warmth. I lifted the heavy cloth and saw underneath the glimmering of red hot coals in a brazier—a marvellous substitute for central heating.

"This sort of table", Luis explained, "is known as a "mesa Camilla" - they are used in all kinds of country houses in Extremadura when it is cold.".

After a delicious dinner of roasted suckling pig, chicken and potatoes all cooked on the open fire and a porridge of lentils served by the two women, Juan, the "arrendatorio", appeared to ask Luis if he would like to see the bedrooms they had prepared for us. That was all the encouragement we needed. Big lanterns were brought and, guided by Juan, we went back down the same stairs we had just climbed and out to the patio again. This time we turned and entered the first floor of the same large stone building through large double wooden doors under a stone arch. As if by a miracle, helping hands appeared out of the darkness, doors were opened and shut for us and shadowy creatures flitted about to help.

We found ourselves in a large very dark area with vaulted ceilings and huge carved wooden doors below massive stone arches. Only the glimmer of the oil lamp Juan carried illuminated our path.

"This is the "zaguan", the entrance area of the palacio" Juan indicated, with a grand sweep of his hand.

The proportions were beautiful – high arched ceilings and lots of space. There was no furniture but in the dim corners were big sacks and boxes, which Juan explained contained the wool, olive oil and other produce of the finca. There were no halls in the building, but as we walked from one room to another, I noticed the interior walls between the rooms were over three feel thick and appeared to be of solid stone. Every room was on a slightly different level. We went up a few steps to one room, then down again, then up again.

In one vaulted room, I stopped to inspect the windows. Instead of being square, like most windows, they were arched and had carved wooden shutters. As I tried to open the shutters I was overwhelmed to see the depth of the window sill - it was deeper than the length of my arm, for I could just barely reach to the shutters. As I was doing this I put one of the lamps Juan was carrying down on the sill and moved my head up to undo a bolt on the shutter. Then I saw, on a huge stone slab some sort of writing carved into the stone.

"Look!," I cried, "Look what I've found!"

As more lanterns were brought, we saw very clearly a stone with inscriptions. And our Catalan friend said, "Aline, these are Latin inscriptions. I have seen them before. It looks like a Roman tombstone."

We found others as we proceeded.

On we went through this long, high building of stone, which now, we could see, had once been a large rectangular edifice with a patio in the centre. Again we went upstairs...there seemed to be no internal stairway joining the two floors... by the same outside steps we went upstairs again to another enormous room which looked like a chapel. At one end was a balcony with stairs leading up to it.

"This was once the watch tower of the house," explained Juan, "but now we store wool here."

The servants were scurrying around in different large barren rooms to arrange the beds which had amazingly thick high straw mattresses. Maria patted one "made with fresh new straw, senora condesa," she said. I realized that they imagined the thickness would provide a more luxurious bed, but they had been stuffed over three feet high - later we had great difficulty climbing up into them. The men took Annabella by the feet and the arms and had to swing her up – she fell into the deep straw mattress and disappeared from sight.

The next morning we reassembled in the room where we had dined the night before and found Maria on her knees in the fireplace preparing coffee, toast and eggs. Again we were greeted with curtsies and bright smiles and were invited to supervise the preparation of our soft-boiled eggs as they bubbled away in pots on the open fire before us. As we tooks seats at the round table , we lifted the thick cloth and again were grateful for the warmth of the hot coals underneath because there was no glass in the large balcony window in front of our table and a cold breeze was blowing in. Outside was a large cobble stoned patio and in the distance open country where sheep were grazing under olive trees – all had been shrouded in darkness the night before so we were still ignorant of our surroundings. Hurriedly we finished breakfast, impatient to get out into the sun-drenched countryside.

When we descended the winding stone stairs we emerged into the sunlit patio, and became aware that it was enclosed on both sides by ancient cowsheds of the same stone as the palacio.

"Look," said Luis, as he pushed open a half-shattered wooden door leading into one of the cowsheds. Amazed, we peered down a seemingly endless long tunnel-like room with a huge endless arch above. "This long arch," said Luis, "is something these humble people were able to construct centuries ago . It's called a Cannon Arch- this is amazing, look – it goes on and on. It is said that modern architects do not know how to build such a long arched ceiling."

At that moment Juan appeared. "Senor Conde, these stone feed-troughs are for the oxen we use for the work in the fields. About fifty oxen inhabit this building and another large number are kept in the other building. They leave early in the morning with our people to plow the fields."

I noticed that the stone feed troughs were worn, obviously from centuries of use. Everything about this palace was very very old.

As we spoke a motley collection of mules and horses were being saddled in the patio. We were graciously offered mounts to proceed for our investigation of the property. We had barely begun our ride when suddenly Luis shouted, "Primitivo, ride back to the house quickly and bring me my shotgun from the car." As he called out I saw a larg band of partridge lift from the bushes and fly off. I knew he was thrilled to see the partridge and that thanks to them we would be spending more time in Pascualete than his recent ancestors.

Winding our way down through open wheatfields and rolling groves of evergreen oaks every now and then we saw clustered on the hill-tops small round straw huts which upon closer inspection proved to be the homes of shepherds who cared for the flocks in that area. There were always three round straw huts – according to Juan one of these chozos was where the family lived, the next largest was for the donkey and the smallest was for the chickens. Finally we arrived at a high cliff which looked down into a deep gorge where the waters of a small river swirled below.

Restoring the palacio became an important part of our lives from then on.

CHAPTER FIFTEEN

LUIS AND THE CIVIL WAR

Ever since Don Jose told me that my husband had escaped from Madrid at the beginning of the Civil War to enlist when under age and later had been seriously wounded, I tried to pry from Luis more details. But my husband was not one to talk about himself - it seemed that the proper moment to get him in a mood to discuss his Civil War experiences never arrived. One day as we were driving to attend a partridge shoot in his father's "finca", property, about twenty kilometers outside Madrid, Luis finally was fed up with my nagging and started to tell me a bit of his story.

"The day the War began, July 17, 1936, I was playing golf in Puerta de Hierro. My sister, Isabel, had played golf earlier and was waiting for me to finish my game so we could go home together. For some time there had been demonstrations in the streets by communists, people in the club referred to them as "rojos". Actually they were anarchists and were making life in Madrid threatening for everyone. We were young, I was seventeen and didn't know much about politics. But I knew that a week before the police had had difficulty preventing a mob from burning a church. But despite the lack of safety my family had remained in the city because my stepmother's father was seriously ill in the hospital. Since my mother had died eight years before we had lived with my father and his second wife part of the time, although we also lived off and on in the house of our Torre Arias grandparents.

When I came into the clubhouse after finishing the 36th hole, Isabel was very upset.

"Papa has telephoned" she said. "Blanca's father's operation is over but papa says we must not go home. The house is being watched by a group of dangerous looking people. He insists we meet him at the hospital instead. There is too much unrest in the streets."

"When we arrived at the hospital, there was much confusion. An ambulance was at the side entrance despatching stretchers with wounded persons. Two nurses were struggling to transfer one large body from a stretcher to an emergency table." As Luis continued speaking, his expression became grim. "I stepped closer to help." he mumbled, "The sight was horrible. A man's bloodied body covered with black scorched flesh, his face was almost unrecognizable, his hair was singed, he was delirious and groaning with pain. Isabel stood next to me almost paralysed by the ghastly sight." He paused, obviously he was remembering the scene, then he went on. " As I helped to move the body, one of the nurses told me that the "rojos" had hung the bodies of three monks by the feet over the altar and set them on fire. "This one is still alive, she said as she tried to comfort him." She couldn't stop mumbling, "I'm afraid to see what the next one will look like when he comes in. This fellow won"t last long."

Luis continued, "About then two men from the ambulance appeared with the next stretcher, but we were pushed along the hallway by another nurse to the room where my father and his wife were supposed to be awaiting us. No more had we reached the second floor than we saw two more miserably wounded men. These were walking at least on their own two feet, but the condition of their clothes and faces showed that they had been severely beaten.

By now Luis was completely involved in his account, as if he were reliving the moments."My father was waiting for us and as we entered the room we saw that he was talking to a doctor who we knew was an old family friend. We told them about the terrible scenes we had just encountered.

"We're overrun with cases like those," Doctor Echevarria said. Then he turned to my father, "You and your children are not safe on the streets nor in your home. This is the worst yet. It might be only a reaction to the rumor that the army has said "enough" and will finally do something to bring order. But today there are dozens of gangs of "rojos' attacking homes, arresting the owners and beating up anyone who appears priviledged. Until now the police have remained cautious and frightened and merely look on. I can give you beds here in the hospital, at least for tonight. Stay. With luck if the rumor is true , the army will take over and this will be under control tomorrow."

Interrupting Luis´account , I asked, "But where was your grandfather Romanones?"

"He was already in Biarritz for the summer. Most people had left Madrid before the first week in July. It was already the eighteenth of July. Also Casi, (Luis's youngest sister) was with friends in the mountains in La Granja. so we were not worried about her. But I was wondering how my grandparents Torre Arias were managing since they were still in Madrid also. So that night from the hospital I telephoned their house. Calixto the head butler answered."

"Calixto, it's me, Luis. Let me speak to my grandparents. It's urgent."

"I'm very sorry senor, but the Senores Condes are not here."
"Then where are they?"
"In America, Senor."
"Are you mad, Calixto? I had lunch with my grandmother just a few hours ago."

"Did you senor?"
"You served it yourself. You and Guillermo. What's wrong with you?"

Calixto's voice changed tone. Suddenly he sounded relieved. "I'm so sorry. Sr. Conde. I don't hear well- I didn´t recognize your voice. I was afraid it was another trap. Los Senores Condes left hours ago. They have taken an apartment in the Hotel Palace under the name of Don Alfonso Perez and Senora. Anarchists have been here but the gates are locked, they saw the number of guards we have at the gate and went away."

By now Luis and I had almost arrived at his father's property, but I begged Luis to slow down and tell me what happened next. He continued.

"The next day was horrible, one of the worst days of my life. We went to the apartment of uncle Eduardo (his father's brother, the Count of Yebes) which would not attract as much attention as our large house. From there I managed to get my grandmother Torre Arias by phone at the hotel Palace. She was very distraught. She told me my grandfather had gone for a walk on the Castellana that morning, many hours before and had not yet returned. She had heard there was shooting going on all over the city and told me she was worried something had happened to him."

"That night I went to see my grandmother in the Hotel Palace", Luis went on, "my grandfather had still not appeared. My grandmother was beside herself with worry. She had been asking all the hotel employees to help her obtain news of my grandfather. Finally around midnight the concierge, a sympathetic older man advised us that he had been able to learn that my grandfather had been shot and killed by a group of "reds". That they had shot at random all the people they saw who appeared well-dressed along the Castellana, and that my grandfather had the bad luck to be one of the first. A bell boy from the hotel had seen them throw his body into their truck on top of others." Luis sighed and was silent for a few moments." He had often spoken to me about his grandfather Torre Arias with much affection, describing to me how he had fooled the customs officials when they asked what he had in one of his large trunks on his return from Cuba, and how he had answered, "filled with cigars, nothing else. Take a look. " how the customs laughed thinking he was making a joke and that was how his grandfather had managed to enter into Spain with hundreds of his favorite cigars.

But after a few moments Luis went on,"My grandmother of course was desperate and determined to go out herself to look for his body and give him a proper burial. But the concierge told us they would kill her too. He had heard that all the bodies had been dumped in the city public cemetery. He suggested finding someone reliable to accompany me to find the body and identify it. The concierge insisted that they would manage to have him removed and would help us bury him wherever we thought fit."

We were now in front of Luis' father's country house, but we remained in the car while Luis finished his tragic story. He was more upset than I had ever seen him - now I understood why he had never wanted to talk about his war experiences. "You can imagine how all this affected me," he murmurred. I had been brought up too protected, too isolated from the world and now at age seventeent I had to search through piles of mutilated bodies to find my own grandfather." He slouched in his seat and took out a cigarette. "the place was horrible. Stinking bodies all around. It must have been about two o'clock in the morning and I had to use a flashlight. Finally I found him, my poor grandfather, just thrown there in a heap, blood all over his face and clothes. In his upper jacket pocket was his usual white handkerchief, although now all filthy and stained with blood and dirt, and in his inside pocket in its usual place was his cigar. I can remember in my childhood watching my grandfather finish his daily "toilette", how carefully he would stuff his monogramed stiff white handkerchief in his pocket, then he would go to the table in his dressing room where there were 30 boxes for cigars. The cigars would be moved by his valet each day to a new box with a different humidy. I loved my grandfather who was gentle and kind to us and to everyone. That night was an experience I'll never forget."

 For several years I did not ask Luis to tell me more about what happened to him in the war, but one day when we were sitting in a butt in the country waiting for the partridge drive to begin, I got him to talk about it again. We were behind a thick cover of retama bushes, Luis opened the top of his shooting stick and sat looking out over the green branches in case a bird passed overhead, and I next to him seated on my leather chaps on the ground so as not to be in his way when the shooting began. The leather chaps protected me from the cold earth. On Luis' right with his back to the butt was his loader with another shotgun ready to hand over when needed. As Luis changed his gun from his arm to rest on his knees, I noticed him wince and rub his upper right arm with his free left one. "Can't hold my gun too long in the same position," he explained. "It's the arm infected with gangrene during the war and it still hurts now and then. the doctor cut out a lot of the upper half so I wouldn't lose the whole arm."

I'd often noticed Luis' terrible wound – part of his upper arm had been severely mutilated, but when I had asked him about it, he never gave more explanation than saying it had happened in the war. "Luis, why don't you tell me for once exactly how you were wounded?"

"It happened in Vitoria. I was left for dead among others in the field. It must have been late at night or early in the morning when a doctor and two nurses were looking through all the bodies scattered over the battle field. By a miracle a good friend of my sister Isabel was among the nurses and she recognized me. She looked for a doctor immediately. I was unconscious. They were just in time, I was told later. I was taken into the operating room and that doctor was able to remove entirely the gangrenous part of my arm.

But my cousin Alfonso was not so lucky. He was the son of Uncle Alfonso Torre Arias, he was exactly my age and my best friend and had been with me throughout the war. Only a few months before I got hit, he had volunteered for the airforce. On his first mission, he was shot down, not killed, but so badly burned that it took over a month for him to die—in terrible pain all the time."

"Oh, Luis, what ghastly experiences you have had, and you never told me about all this before. When you were in that war, I was still in high school far away from even imagining such dreadful things could happen to anyone."

"Exactly nineteen of the boys and men in my familly were killed in that war. Most were cousins young like me. I was the only male left of that generation in our family."

" How did you get out of Madrid? I know some of your family was imprisoned by the "reds" and executed for no reason whatsoever."

"We had to find places to hide. My father managed to get us into the Peruvian Embassy, but there was not room enough for him so he went to his good friend, the American ambassador who often had come to large dinners that he and his wife Blanca gave in their house. Do you know the ambassador did not allow him in and the reds took him there and then, on the steps of the American embassy residence, the old Montellano palace, same place where you worked during the last month of your war. While my father was begging to be allowed in, the reds came and put him in jail. Many times he was taken out into the patio of the prison to be executed and for unknown reasons, he was not shot. Probably because one of our old servants to protected him , a fellow who had been an aide to my step mother's father in the army- the Duke of Sevilla, he had been a famous general. That man was one of the guards at the jail and intervened to save my father over and over again. but some of my uncles were not so lucky."

"And your grandmother Torre Arias?"

"She was in the Peruvian Embassy with me.She was very affectionate and while we waited several weeks in the Peruvian embassy she used to talk to me for hours about family things –she recounted to me the time when I was about eight years old and reminded me that I liked to accompany her in her carriage when she delivered cards to her many friends, a custom of the society ladies of her time. Then I remembered how she would carefully turn down one corner or another of her visiting card before leaving it . Once I tried to help her. "No Luisito " she said. Let me turn down the corner of the card. A card is turned a certain way to give a cerain message to the lady it is directed to. Sometimes it means "please return my call" –other times "I will come back later" – and so forth."

I went on with my questions "Yes, but how did you get out of Madrid?"

"With a Peruvian passport. The embassy was able to find me a ride on a truck to Valencia, once there we were sneaked on to a freighter leaving that same night for Marseilles. My cousin, Antonio was with me, he's the one who became a pilot. We both arrived with no money and by a miracle we were able to go from Marseilles to Biarritz where my grandfather Romanones usually spent the summer. For two days there we were well fed and rested – the trip on the boat had been awful and we had nothing to eat on our way to Biarritz. But as soon as we could, we escaped from the house and went across the border to San Sebastian to enlist. My only thought was to avenge my grandfather Torre Arias. I lied about my age. Antonio did too and before we knew it we were both in uniform and sent to one of the front lines. If I told you some of the atrocities I saw there you would not believe it. One night some of our own men who had just taken over a village, raped a dead woman in the street. I got sick to my stomach."

"What about the young fellows on the other side - the side of the "rojos"?"

"I don't know. They must have had terrible experiences just as had. Miraculously for a few years after the war those of us who had been on opposite sides were kind to each other, all of us were so glad to have seen the end of those terrible three years, all we wanted was to forget about it. But in those first days of the war such horrors ocurred that we had all begun to hate each other, which made it easier to fight, although we were too young to know anything about politics. However, I can tell you there were plenty of foreigners in our war, most favored the other side – at the very beginning masses of Russians piled into Madrid, they draped a three story picture of Lenin over the facade of the great post office building in the Plaza de Cibeles. They also created torture centers called "chekas" - the Russians did much to incite the civil war and to divide us Spaniards. "

Suddenly the first wave of partridge flew over our butt. Luis jumped to his feet aiming his shotgun- at the same moment the sound of our neighbors shots also burst through the air. Luis became immediately involved in the shooting and his tragic tale was never mentioned again - by either of us. But his story had made me more aware of the horrors the Spaniards of both sides had gone through. Often I asked friends to tell me their experiences in that terrible war. Although it was still a topic people would refer to, they only spoke of generalities, few were willing to recount detailed personal experiences.

CHAPTER SIXTEEN

AMBASSADOR LODGE, CHANGES

Meanwhile many of Luis' extensive properties in the province of Badajoz near Llerena were being expropriated by Franco's government – the explanation was that this was being done to provide a system of reservoirs for irrigation for the farmers of that region. Soon more and greater problems surfaced with the government in relation to Luis' properties in Extremadura - many more were also expropriated by Franco's government. We were always informed that the government would pay for them, but payment took twelve years and when we finally received the money it was much less than the real value of the property. Luis lost much of his fortune during those Franco decades because it was almost impossible to fight against the government expropiations, nor did he make an effort. I was indignant and shocked that Luis accepted the government robbery of his property. His answer to me was "After the horrors of our Civil war and losing so many cousins and friends , if giving up half of my ownings will improve the country I don't intend to complain. – I would give up much more to avoid another war." All these regulations ordered by Franco helped the poor people of the country, but the large landowners suffered enormously. Nevertheless due to this and other innovations made by Franco's governement, gradually I witnessed the life style of the working class improve.

Back in Madrid we were always busy. Apart from the children and my riding every day in the Club del Campo, we had frequent formal dinners at night . All embassies were located in Madrid and we now had many friends among the foreign diplomats. In those days formal dinners were in black tie, so I also had to spend time fitting evening dresses for these occasions – there was no ready to wear clothing yet available in any store in the city.

In 1955 a carismatic American, John Davis Lodge, was named United States Ambassador to Spain. He and his beautiful wife, Francesca, moved into the small palace on the Calle Lagasca that had been the residence of the American ambassador – the present American embassy and residence on the Castellana had not yet been built.

Francesca was unusual, she possessed a great sense of humor and a good will that was obvious in every endeavor she embarked upon. Before I met her, I already had a hint of her unique personality. Shortly after their arrival the new Ambassadors were invited, as was customary, to a dinner in their honor at the Ministry of Foreign Affairs. The next morning, a friend called me. "You won't believe it, Aline." Her tone indicated she was about to communicate uncommon news. "Your ambassadress arrived at the very formal dinner last night at the Ministry clicking castanets. Can you imagine the impression she made. She was clicking them as she walked into that very formal room with the most distinguished persons present . Everybody was astounded."

Obviously the minister must have been astounded as well- until then a strict protocol reigned everywhere - especially in the foreign ministry. Francesca had an unusual daring personality. Later we learned that she had been a professional dancer and soon the news spread that the American Ambassadress was taking flamenco lessons. In those days ambassadresses did not indulge in such endeavors.

But this was just the beginning for Francesca Lodge. Shortly after we met, early one morning her voice was on the phone. "Aline, I've decided to give a women's luncheon. I want to invite the wife of the mayor and the wives of most of the ministers."

"Do you think you're doing the right thing?" I replied.

"Spanish women never have luncheons alone together. At least I've never been to one or even heard of a woman's luncheon in the twelve years I've been here."

"Well, I think that they'll have a great time. It's an american custom, and I intend to do it."

A few days later, Francesca called again. "Maybe you were right. I've been getting so many telephone calls from ladies asking if there was a mistake made on the invitation because the husbands name was not mentioned."

Nevertheless the day of the luncheon arrived. We were about twenty women including wives of government ministers, the mayor's wife, a woman lawyer and a famous author. It seemed to me that we were having a marvelous time, a racket of laughing and chatter. While coffee was served, Francesca, who was also great at making impromptu speeches, stood up with an enchanting smile and sparkling blue eyes looking around the room. "How did you like your ladies' luncheon?"

The wife of one of the ministers answered immediately, "Actually, Francesca, it's been very much like our funerals."

Francesca's face showed her dismay. "Oh, dear, and I thought you were enjoying it."

"Of course we are, but until now the only chance we women have had to get together like this and chat has been at a funeral, which we do enjoy if the deceased is not a close relative. In Spain women are not supposed to go to the cemetery - when the corpse is taken out of the house, we stay there to keep the women of the family company, usually there is a buffet for these occasions and we have the opportunity to talk for hours about eveything, just as we have done today."

The mayor's wife spoke up. "This luncheon has seemed more like a wedding to me. I kept expecting to see the bride walk in." Then another interrupted. "It's that way in Spain, Francesca, if we don't have a funeral or a wedding, we women seldom have the opportunity to get together in a large group. Your American custom of women's luncheons is great."

The beautiful American "Ambassadress" was a success from the start. She continued to do one extraordinary thing after another. She rode horseback from Lisbon Trujillo with 65 farmers from southern Spain, being the only woman in the group. When the caravan arrived at a village, people often would be lined up on either of the street, exclaiming as she rode by, "Viva los Estados Unidos! Viva la Senora Embajadora!" Francesca showed her kindness to all, she also founded the first seeing-eye dog school in Spain.

Yet she did not outshine her tall handsome husband. His warmth and humor, his hard work visiting all corners of the country won him a popularity that has never been equalled by any other United States Ambassador in Spain. Once, when I was walking with him along the Gran Via in Madrid, a taxi driver leaned out the window of his car, gesticulating wildly, calling out, "Hola Juanito!" Everybody knew him by that Spanish version of his name. His popularity reached even one of the new villages the goverment was building for laborers in southern Spain where it's inhabitants named their main street "Mister Lodge", their way of showing their affection and appreciation for a geat American ambassador. His excellent spanish was an asset in the serious matters he handled with the government, Spanish officials felt closer to him, they appreciated his good will and affection for their country. In social affairs and parties his excellent singing voice also made him a favorite. John and Francesca were unique and a big boost for the United States of America. During his appointment relationships with the Uunited States improved.

He encouraged General Franco to attract American industrialists to the country by giving them special privledges if they invested in Spain. During Ambassador Lodge's years in Spain the country started to climb out of poverty.

By 1968 Spain reached a level of competence with the rest of western Europe- such an enormous difference from 1944 when I began to live in Madrid. For the first timein its history the country was booming with industry and machinery. Those employees who used to arrive at Pascualete on donkeys from Santa Marta now came in small cars called SEATs. Spaniards began to send their children to families in the United States and Great Brittain to learn English. Traffic lights began to appear in Madrid and in other large cities. For the first time schools were founded in small villages throughout the country. These improvements were taking place with Spaniards of both sides who only a few decades before had been killing each other. Spain had become a modern country in record time.

Centuries of old-fashioned laws were also obliterated. In the fifties the frst time I went to the Directon General of Security to obtain the necessary EXIT PERMIT obligatory to leave the country, a written legal permission from my husband was requested. I was indignant with the employee and declared that I would provide no such thing – that I would complain to the USA embassy. Foolish me. Luis suffered with my independent American woman's ideas and customs – in Spain men were still given rights superior to women in the fifties. The overwhelming power men used to have legally over women made me sometimes laugh and other times indignant. Luis sympathized with me and considered these restrictions for women preposterous. Finally improvements for women's legal rights were made by Franco's government and gradually I was losing any feeling of hostility toward his dictatorship.

During a dinner in the Embassy one night tall Ambassador Lodge addressing his twenty-four Spanish guests stood up to speak, something he did especially well. "This new progress and prosperity we all observe in Spain is due in great part to the strong authority of your government and its ability to maintain peace and put people to work. I congratulate you for this. But you should also be aware of a new treaty your government has made with the United States government in which there will now be built three american air bases and two American naval bases on Spanish soil. This effort represents large sums of American money and technical skill, through which Spain is benefiting – an important proof that the goodwill and good wishes of my country are with you."

Through John Lodge's efforts the American boycott against Spain was also lifted. American industries began to take advantage of the facilities the Franco government was offering for foreign investment - American capital started to build factories all over the country. John also had friends in the film industry since he had been an actor in Hollywood during his youth - he now encouraged American producers to take advantage of Spain's low prices and good weather - this initiated many years of American film-making, which in turn created more jobs and a better foreign image. The Lodges contributed to eliminating the anti-american sentiments which were a hangover from the Spanish-American war in Cuba of 1898.

Before the Lodges term of office in Spain ended, their young daughter Beatriz married a spanish diplomat. That she would marry a Spaniard had been seen as inevitable – she was tall and blonde and beautiful and whenever she walked through the city, the men would shower her with "piropos". The perfect ending to this Spanish-American romance has been that in 1998, about thirty-eight years later, this couple became the Spanish Ambassadors to Washington D.C.

CHAPTER SEVENTEEN

THE MEDINACELI PALACE MADRID

There was ample room to park a car on any street in the city although by this time there were more automobiles, but the quaint yellow street car on the Castellana had not yet disappeared. That wide avenue still maintained the air of ancient grandeur that I had known since my arrival ten years before - it was still bordered by huge old mansions, iron grated fences and secluded gardens with tall sycamores – it was still an impressive beautiful avenue and many old palaces continued to be inhabited by their original families. The Dukes of Alburquerque still owned the palace in the Plaza de Cibeles, but soon it was sold and became the headquarters of the Bank of Spain. However other palaces were being bought by foreign governments and converted into embassies.

In the streets of Madrid in the fifties, one could still behold many of the enchanting modes of dress which formerly had fascinated me. Although priests no longer wore their spectacular wide brimmed round black hats, they still were robed in long black cassocks. The nuns continued to wear habits and coifs – the most spectacular were those with white stiffly starched headdresses like wings which in a good stiff wind appeared could blow the wearer all the way to heaven. Yet by the sixties most of the picturesque trade outfits were disappearing..

Men began to abandon the long romantic capes I had admired on chilly days. These classic capes were wrapped around the body, draped over one shoulder and sometimes even muffling the mouth – usually in navy blue or black for evening - brown or grey for daytime, with red or green or blue satin reverses. Diana Vreeland, the ruler of the world of fashion, editor-in-chief of Vogue, came to Spain especially to buy these beautiful capes. She told me "they are so elegant - no longer possible to find in any part of the world and the most chic for a man when worn with a tuxedo at night. I bought Luis severalbut he never had the habit of wearing one, I found them romantic and glamorous. I say I bought several because everytime I managed to oblige him to wear one in New York he would lose it. Often I heard the pleading voice of a friend, "Oh, Luis please give me that cape for my husband...please..." Then Luis would insist upon making a gift of the new cape I had just given him.

During the fifties in Madrid on Saturday nights we often were invited to dine and play cards at the home of Luis' uncle, the Duke of Medinaceli whose palace with its ample ground occupied an entire block in the plaza de Colon, (plaza of Christopher Columbus) which in those days was perhaps the most attractive of the three plazas on the Castellana. In the center of that plaza presided an impòsing statue of Columbus above a circular fountain and on the opposite side of the street was the ornate Palacio de la Moneda, (the Palace of the Money). Luis´uncle´s palace was surrounded by spacious gardens with high trees, bordered by the Castellana on one side and by the Calle Genova on another. In the Spring tall bushes of thick lavender and wisteria draped over the iron grated wall into the street and in the summer the perfume of jasmine vines wafted to those passing by.

As we entered the huge old palace I was always impressed. First we passed through a long hallway bordered by gilt sofas and ancient armchairs of worn red damask. Then through a salon with portraits of ancestors in white wigs, brocades and lace cuffs, after that another corridor with walls covered by tapestries depicting battle scenes with men in knickers on prancing steeds bedecked in bright jackets and plumed hats. Our footsteps made no sound on the thick red carpeting, and the silence in the endless empty rooms as we followed the man-servant that first time ,for me produced an ominous atmosphere which made the sudden sight of a large room filled with men in black tie and bejeweled ladies in long dresses still more imposing.

   Luis was an expert at every card game and his uncle was especially fond of him so I suppose that is why we were invited because one glance at the salon revealed that the other guests were much older and more important than us. The high celinged room had two huge fireplaces burning brightly , the guests were seated in different small groups where butlers in uniforms of dark blue velvet, long tails and satin vests were serving drinks.

   After greeting Luis' uncle and wife with the usual Spanish formality and then approaching each guest and going through the same formality, the men standing and kissing my hand, then my shaking each ladies hand,- ladies did not kiss on the cheek in those days, we sat down near his uncle and joined in the conversation which happened to be about the bullfight that afternoon. Luis, of course knew well all those present and explained to me as we approached each that this one was his uncle, that other one his cousin etc. I was astounded , it seemed in every party we went to the guests were always Luis´ relatives. Despite my good memory it was difficult to remember the long complicated titles but fortunately Luis had told me I could address everyone by their first name which simplified this name problem for me.

The animated conversation did not last long because soon the plump middle aged blonde hostess, Luis's uncle's second wife, indicated we should rise and go into dinner. Luis whispered to me as we stood up informing me that the dinner would be rushed through because she was a card player and did not want to waste time eating at table. When I entered the huge dinning salon, it was so beautiful, I would have liked to stand still and just gaze. The tables glittered, the five sparkling bacarra goblets at each place reflected the glowing candlelight from three huge candelabra on each of the two long tables-shiny vermeil plates, servants in white wigs, the male guests in black tie, the ladies looking for their places, their jewels blinking in the candlelight. Also the oscillating flicker of the candleabra on the walls added to the room's festive atmosphere.

Here too the walls were crammed with large paintings, the high ceiling was embellished by an arabesque border. There were too many things to observe but I had to ignore them to look for my place at the table.

Protocol in Spain had always been a serious matter – until about 1990 at formal dinners grandees in serious dinners continued to be placed ahead of everyone except foreign ambassadors and active ministers. This particular evening a certain amount of time was consumed while the thirty-two guests found their placecards. I had become aware of the disadvantage of Spanish protocol when recently married at almost every dinner I found myself sitting next to the same elderly duke. Finally one evening as that duke, another of Luis' many uncles, took his seat next to me, I commented, "I'm sorry you have me again- let's hope this will be changed next time." . He laughed "Not at all, Aline. You'll have me here for years, or if not, some other man as old as I. You have little chance of having a handsome young man next to you because we are seated according to rank of title. It just happens that your husband inherited his title early because his mother died young." Then he went on ."Anyhow don't despair we have solved this problem quite well by spending the least time possible at table, that's why coffee is served in another room where we can all sit wherever we wish."

Half of the guests at the Medinaceli palace that Saturday night and many other Saturday nights were cardplayers, the others spent the rest of the evening conversing with the Duke; usually there was a mixture of titles, a minister or two, and often a noted Madrid doctor was there who also played poker, and a writer who did not play cards but who made the Duke laugh. I wasn't interested in the conversation of these older men so I drew up a small chair behind Luis and watched the poker game.

That night the wife of General Franco was present, but I did not see her the following saturday nights – she was attractive and distinguished . "La Senora" as she was referred to, played pinacle at a separate table with three other ladies which was probably the reason she had accepted the dinner invitation. Luis and some of the other men and women were at the poker table – the favorite game for the Duchess of Medinaceli. I was thrilled to meet Mrs. Franco since I had not had the opportunity before. General Franco and his wife seldom went to private houses and I was surprised to see her. That night he was not present and I merely had the opportunity of greeting her when she entered and of saying goodnight when she left.

   I became bored watching the poker game and joined wives of the card players who were seated in a small group near the Duke's circle of men that was animated in conversation. One of the ladies complimented my black embroidered dress which had a small train and was one of Pedro Rodriguez's most outstanding that year. I had taken care to wear a gown with aconservative neckline - in those days necklines had to be discreet to keep in tone with the strict decorum. Jewels were also a necessary part of a lady's outfit so whenever I went to a formal affair I wore those Luis had given me but the jewels I saw that night at the Medinaceli palace were more impressive. When I complimented one lady's jewels , she told me that the only belongings she had been able to save from her home in Madrid when the Civil War broke out were her jewels. That remark spurred the other ladies to comment on the ordeals they had undergone during their war - people were still traumatized by the horrifying war experiences.

   At these dinners the old-fashioned maquillage of the women seemed to be what had been in style before their Civil war in 1936. Small round red circles of rouge were painted on their cheeks, and thick mascara that made their eyelashes stick together. One of the ladies must have noted my glances and asked about women´s make-up in America. I explained the principal points that differed and also told them that we did not wear boned corsets as I had seen in Madrid shop windows - that we used comfortable elastic girdles and nylon stockings rather than the silk stockings they were still wearing. The ladies were intrigued and asked if I could help them obtain these modern American marvels. Although people were now able to obtain whiskey and cigarettes which had been almost impossible during the war years, women had no awareness of modern customs of dress. Few foreign fashion magazines were available yet and the only American movies were old ones. I was amused to realize that American cosmetics and nylons could still help me make friends so many years after my OSS days.

   Through my fondness for history I had learned that centuries before my arrival other visitors had been as surprised as I, by spanish social customs. In the French Countess d 'Áulnoy´s book about her visit to Madrid in 1679 – she was astonished to see in a party in the palace of the Dukes of Alburquerque in Madrid that the ladies were seated on raised platforms on cushions arab-style while the men reclined in armchairs. She also found it strange that ladies were served a beverage of water with sugary sticks while only the men had wine.. Yet she was impressed by the ladies sumptuous embroidered gowns which she said were superior to those in Paris. When I arrived in Madrid three hundred years later the embroidered evening dresses were still impressive but in the large palaces the ladies no longer reclined on Arabic cushions.

 The last time we went to that Medinaceli palace before it was torn down was for a first communion luncheon on a warm May day. The elderly Duke's second wife had provided him with a third daughter- a surprise to all since the lady was already far over forty when they married. His two daughters by his first wife were fortunate that the child had not been a boy or the titles and the centuries old palaces and castles would have gone to him instead of to Mimi, his eldest daughter by his first marriage. Only when there are no sons does the eldest daughter inherit the titles in Spain. However in England, if there are only daughters , none of them inherit , only the nearest male relative can inherit. The luncheon was an enormous family affair with first, second and third cousins and their descendants. The starched embroidered cloths on the tables made shiny white splotches in the midst of the luxuriant greeness of the garden. Ladies all wore wide brimmed hats, the little children were dressed in ruffles and the boys in sparkling white sailor suits ran about the garden in between the many small tables .

But by the end of the fifties charismatic traditional Madrid had lost its individuality. Within one decade the propagation of television and the onslaught of tourists removed the quaint colorful garments from the streets as well as the previous customs of courtesy. Nevertheless men and women in Madrid on the streets were always better dressed than Americans in New York City at any time of day. Blue jeans had not yet taken over -appearance and clothes had always been considered an important item by spaniards, no matter the occasion or their rank.

But the first old palace on the Castellana to disappear, about 1956 , was the one sold to build the modern unattractive American embassy residence, an endeavor started by Ambassador Griffits, who was posted there just before the Lodges arrived. This edifice marked the beginning of the loss of the old world charm of that avenue. Within ten years most of the old palaces lining that avenue had undergone the same fate. Ironically the prosperity and rapid growth of the city was responsible for this great loss. The old palaces, the ancient grilled fences and gardens were replaced by office buildings of an unattractive architectural variety that destroyed completely the avenues previous grandeur. Even government buildings such as the Palacio de la Moneda, (Palace of the Money), were demolished and the entire Plaza of Colon was wiped out along with the Medinaceli palace. Poor Christopher Columbus was removed from his post in the center of the plaza to an almost invisible spot high on one side of the Avenue - now he looks so small up high on a column that he is almost invisible. The plaza also lost its previous beauty. When "Colon" presided there no one dreamed it would become just another traffic hub surrounded by modern buildings with no similarity in their design. Unfortunately Spaniards did not complain about these destructions and seemed unaware that their city was losing its beauty and charm..

CHAPTER EIGHTEEN

PASCUALETE, SHEPHERDS

For one reason or another, we were so busy in Madrid and with trips to New York and shoots that I did not return to Pascualete until well over a year later. The Abuelo Romanones had died a few months before and I was already seven months pregnant with my third child and anxious to get away from the eyes of everyone. I now was the accepted normal Spanish wife- three children in three years. Extremadura was the perfect place to be with that big stomach, so I went with my two children, a Spanish nanny and Pepe the chauffeur to spend a few weeks in the old palacio and to begin to make it liveable. This time Luis gave all assistance to my trip but was unable to accompany me – he had golf games, partridge shoots with his father near Madrid and business meetings. It was January on this visit and unusually cold. Three times we lost our way in the night darkness on the cowpath leading to the house. When we finally passed through the entrance arch the wind was hissing and wailing round the eaves of the stone building, bits of straw and dust whirled in the air before our headlights. The storm must have completely blotted out the sound of our arrival because not a person nor an animal was in sight.

Baby Luis stirred in the old nurse's arms and started to cry. Alvaro was asleep in my lap and as I leaned over to blow the horn, he awakened and also began to cry. I handed Alvaro over to the nurse and stumbled out of the car to knock on the big solid wooden door of the guard's house. This was a long thin building squeezed up against one corner of the rectangular patio which obviously had at one time been a chapel. My knuckles ached as they struck the iron nail heads on the ancient door's surface. When the upper half of the door swung open abruptly and Primitivo's face apeared, lined and darker than ever in the shadows, I was choking from the litter of dust and stray bits of straw blowing about my head. His black eyes stared at me bewildered.

"We had no word the Senora Condesa was coming. This is terrble! Nothing is prepared!"

"Didn't you receive the message the Senor Conde sent a week ago?" I asked.

"No". he shook his head. "No message arrived here, Senora Condesa"

By now Maria had appeared carrying an asortment of huge rusty iron keys. These ancient keys were so enormous that I have placed many of them on the wall as decorations. Maria was fully dressed and much more in command of the situation than her husband. Her expressionless face showed no sign of concern. Only her voice revealed that she was upset and rushed. She bowed ceremoniously and then suggested I keep the children in the car until candles had been lit and a fire started.

After a short interval Maria descended to inform me that we could enter and led the way with an oil burning lamp up the stairs into the house. I looked about. Eight new rush-bottomed chairs were piled in a corner and next to them some rough-hewn wooden slats which proved to be two dismantled beds. Luis had told me that there would be plenty of furniture, for he had ordered it .. So this was it. Not one other thing was in any of the rooms we were to occupy.

Maria understood my face of despair.

"Now, now, the Senora Condesa must not fret. I have an excellent crib for the baby. My Augustina is six years old now and too big for it anyway. Also the "mesa Camilla" (table) takes up too much room in my little house."

"But the dishes, Maria, and the sheets—there seemed to be so many things here the last time I came."

"Well, those things belonged to the wife of the "arrendatario", (the tenant farmer), and to me. We wanted the Senores Condes to be comfortable. The house has never had any furniture or belongings in my time nor in the time of Primitivo's father either. But there is no cause for worry. In ten minutes the Senora Condesa will have all that is necessary."

  And she was right. Within no time the beds were up, fresh straw mattresses appeared with clean-smelling sheets and warm wool blankets. Baby Luis was already in Tina's crib in the next room and complaining bitterly, but Alvaro was happy again running around among all the busy people. Suddenly I heard him stumble and shriek. Rushing to pick him up, I found his mouth was bleeding. He had broken his front tooth right in half—one of the few he had.

  What a disaster this trip has been, I thought, as I finally got into bed. Why did I bring the children to this isolated place? What if they get sick and no doctor for miles?

  But things are never so bad in the light of day, despite the fact that I had put Luis in bed with me and Alvaro on my other side to keep them warm. Nevertheless I cheered up as

Maria appeared telling me there was a good fire in the next room and she had already prepared our breakfast.

Now my real adventure was about to begin, I wanted to launch many projects I had in mind. Since the last visit, I had decided to make this fascinating ancient building habitable, but I wanted it to retain the appeareance of centuries past when persons with different tastes had inhabited it.

As Alvaro and baby Luis and I huddled around the table in front of the huge flaming fireplace eating breakfast in our coats, I realized the first thing I had to do was put glass in the windows. The shutters were opened to let in the daylight, but they also let in the cold January wind. I summoned Juan, who had been waiting outside in the patio.

"Juan, I have a great deal of work I want done in this house and I need many workers."

"We are at the disposal of the Senora Condesa," he said - then he disappeared. A moment later he returned with three men whom he introduced as his brothers. The four men stood silently at attention. After shaking hands with each of them, I began my orders like a drill sergeant.

"The first thing we must do is put glass in the windows."

They seemed to find this a little strange. "But Senora Condesa, we have to send to Trujillo for the glass, and I do not know if there is anyone around here who knows how to cut it. Perhaps the carpenter in Santa Marta would know how to do it," Juan added a bit dubiously.

This was the first time that I realized there was a village nearby called Santa Marta, and it brought to my mind that Luis's grandfather, the Conde de Torre Arias also had the title of Marques de Santa Marta.

"I must send a man right away, for it will take at least two hours to bring the carpenter here," he added.

"But, Juan, if the village is close by, why on earth will it take so long?"

"The Senora Condesa does not realize that there is only a cowpath to Santa Marta. We will send someone by the fastest horse we have, but even so, two, maybe even three hours is the best we can hope for. I do not dare to send the Senora Condesa's nice car for fear it would be destroyed!"

As soon as Juan disappeared, I addressed myself to the next brother.

"Now I need at least four more chairs and two more beds." I gave the measurements. The second brother grinned happily at me and continued grinning and nodding his head.

Finally another brother, Jose, said "I am sorry, Senora Condesa, but Alberto does not hear very well."

It was apparent that Alberto not only didn't hear well but didn't hear at all. However, Jose assured me about the furniture.

"It will be easy to make all the furniture the Senora Condesa desires," he said. "Gracias a Dios, Pascualete does not lack trees and we have several dead ones now that can be used." Then he rushed off.

To the fourth brother I said, "Of course, we shall need mattresses..." and I stopped. He, too, grinned foolishly, and I wondered if deafness ran in the family. But not at all. When he finally opened his mouth to speak, he was so voluble I could hardly stop him.

"Oh, Senora Condesa, if we cannot make mattresses here then there is no place in the world that can make mattresses. Here in Estremadura we have the finest wool from the Merino sheep—and the sheep at Pascualete are the best of all the Merinos. I personally will cut the wool with my own hands, I will weigh it with my own hands and then my women will wash it..." I was relieved that the mattresses did not have to be made of straw.

"Marvellous, marvellous." I finally cut off this eulogy and he left. So there I was with deaf Alberto, not knowing what to do. I began making signs of a hammer and nails, and beaming with comp rehension, he left me in the middle of my efforts and off he went.

From this day on every morning I gave the orders for the work of the day and thereafter the four brothers would appear, hats in hand, waiting for their instructions. Whenever I asked the brothers to recommend a store in the nearby town of Trujillo where we could buy some of the necessary items, they always assured me that stores were too far away and that no shop in Trujillo could provide furniture , insisting that whatever I needed could be made in Pascualete. "There is nothing we cannot make senora condesa- we and all our employees here are accustomed to fabricating all our own necessities."

Afterward watching the many busy people for a few minutes, I would go down to the patio, and from the landing on the steps I observed with fascination the frenzy of activity—painting, carpentry, cutting wood, bringing water. The entire life of Pascualete was centered in that patio. It was always filled with people and animals and from my vantage point I could observe clearly everything that was going on.

One of the things that amused me most was the morning ritual of Isidora, the fat middle-aged wife of one of the cowherds. Her first act was to comb her long dark hair, so matted with grease that the filthy broken-toothed comb could barely get through it. She combed slowly and deliberately, dipping the ugly black comb every few moments into a basin of water in her lap. After several minutes of this, she took her two able hands and slid her hair back sleekly into position, gripping the long tail and twisting it at the nape of her neck into a neat, artistic little knot.

Her beauty treatment for the day being over, Isidora bounced up from her low rush-bottomed chair, tossed the contents of the white pan over the patio wall and went into her stone house adjoining the cow stalls, emerging again with two enormous clay water jugs. At the well just outside the patio she filled both jugs, and in one smooth movement swung the first clay jug on to the top of her head and then, holding her shoulders, neck and head very stiffly, reached down and grabbed the other jug which she placed on her well-padded hip. She walked majestically back to her little door and, if I happened to be watching, she seemed to make it a point to turn her head sideways now and then so that I might see with what ease she carried her burden.

In a few minutes she again emerged, this time with a Singer sewing machine, vintage 1910, which she set up in the same sunny corner outside her door. Always singing some tuneless song, she pumped the pedal with vigour and moved quantities of old clothes back and forth under the needle.

Seeing the sewing machine that first day, I realized I had found an invaluable aid in my decorating schemes. I walked across the patio to her.

"Isidora, do you suppose you could help me make the curtains for the house?" I asked.

Her round face beamed with pleasure. "Ah, Senora Condesita, we country women take great pride in our sewing. It will be a privilege to help the Senora Condesita and we can even weave the material, if she would like."

From then on I discovered the delights of a morning conversation with Isidora. She always had a juicy or dramatic bit saved for me, generally a catastrophe of one sort or another. One day it was how her son had caught his hands while fixing the spokes of a cartwheel; another day, her sister-in-law's child had fallen down the well. And if I mentioned any ailment, she was quick to prescribe all sorts of miraculous herbs which she produced wrapped in filthy paper parcels.

Making my usual rounds one morning I noticed something new in Isidora's appearance—a pair of black-rimmed spectacles rested precariously on the tip of her nose.

"Ah, I can see the Senora Condesita is admiring my new spectacles," she said smugly.

As I came closer I could see that a dirty cord encircled her head and held the contraption in place.

"New!" I replied. "Isidora, I have never seen anything so old in my life. Where did you get them?"

"The barber in Santa Marta sold them to me for three hundred pesetas, (about two dollars). They belonged to his mother who now rests in peace."

As Isidora spoke she removed the spectacles and turned them over admiringly in her hands for a few moments and then ceremoniously, exctly as one dons a hat, she put them back in position..

"At least the Senora Condesita must admit they give one an air of importance. No one else in Pascualete has ever owned spectacles before – they are very helpful in threading small needles."

A few days after I had marshalled my army of workers, I decided to go into Trujillo to telephone Luis - I told Juan to inform the chauffeur we would leave immediately.

"Oh, no, no," said Juan shaking his head, "the Senora Condesa cannot hope to speak with Madrid today. Why it is already noon."

"Juan, I have all the afternoon," I reminded him.

"But to make a telephone call to Madrid, the Senora Condesa must rise at six in the morning and drive to Trujillo and be able to place the call before nine o'clock. Even then it might take all day to get through to the Senor Conde."

"Oh dear," I cried, "and I was so anxious to talk at once to the Senor Conde so he might send some furniture and foodstuffs down by truck. I had hoped to have these things by tomorrow night."

But again Juan was shaking his head sadly and patiently and saying, "No, no."

"Now what's the matter, Juan?"

"Perhaps the Senora Condesa does not realize that a truck cannot possibly come on the muddy cowpath to Pascualete. It has rained these past days almost every night. Of course, I will be glad to send out a cart with a team of oxen to bring whatever the Senora Condesa wants. But we must make these plans ahead of time so that the oxen can leave at four o'clock in the morning. It takes the cart five hours to get to Trujillo where they will meet the truck - then they must load everything and another five hours back. Si, si, it requires time." (Nowadays 2006 it is a trip of fifteen minutes by car or truck.)

Everything, I soon realized, required infinite amounts of time, but despite these frustrations, I was happy and so wrapped up in my work that I almost managed to forget that I was pregnant.

But for the moment I had to concern myself with a basic necessity to my American way of thinking—a bathroom. I could not go on with this system of bringing all our water up from the well and chamber pots under the beds.

When I first broached the subject with Juan I could see he had no idea what I meant. Finally, I had to use the more vulgar word for toilet.

"Now I understand," he said, a bit embarrassed. "In our houses we do not have these modern innovations. We do not find them necessary. Of course, I have heard that such apparatuses are used and I realize that perhaps a great lady such as the Senora Condesa might want one. I think sometimes they sell them in Trujillo, as I have heard there is a store that posesses one there. Of course, we shall have to send a team of oxen to fetch this aparatus, but as all the carts are out on missions for the Senora Condes, it might be several days before this can be done."

"Do you know of a plumber, Juan?"

"What exactly does a plumber do, Senora Condesa?"

I explained that he puts tubes and pipes together so that water will flow into these things and Juan said, "Well, I do not know of anyone who calls himself a plumber, but I do not see why a good bricklayer could not do the work as well."

And so, I became the plumbing engineer, with a bricklayer to carry out my ideas. We ordered a big water tank from Trujillo and put it on the roof and then with much difficulty we bored holes through the stone walls for the connecting pipes. One day, while having lunch in front of the fireplace in the large salon, it occurred to me that I also could have HOT water by putting still another tank in the wall of the chimney over the burning fire and connecting it with a pipe to the bathroom.

The workmen lent themselves to the creation of the bathroom with great enthusiasm, even though they were not certain of the end result. They made the fixtures I had described to them with cement and tiles. When finished the tub was a truly grand affair, large and square in the middle of the floor faced and lined with beautiful brilliantly coloured tiles which they had found for me easily since tiles were made in all the nearby villages. The completed tile basin for washing face and hands rested on two cement legs, wonderfully crooked .

With great pride, the workmen came to the patio one day and announced, "The 'salon de aguas' (hall of waters) of the Senora Condesa is now finished and awaiting her approval."

They looked so pleased while I investigated the details of this unusual room. But there was one slight omission. The basin for washing hands and face was a work of art with intricately designed beautiful blue and yellow tiles, but it had no hole for drainage. I explained to them that I wanted a basin that drained.

"Oh, the needs of the Senora Condesa will be taken care of immediately. Nothing is simpler!"

I went on about my work and was startled when a few minutes later I was called up to view the basin which they informed me now drained perfectly. Amazed that these simple workmen had managed to install and connect the necessary pipe for the drainage so quickly, I rushed up. There I viewed the basin which drained. They had merely cut a small hole in the center of the sink and placed underneath it on the floor below an old bucket.

Whenever I was not working—and especially in the evenings after sunset—I often took this opportunity to get to know these wonderful, simple people who now filled my life. I visited Isidora almost every evening when her three sons returned from their work in the fields and when her husband Paco had finally tucked away and fed the last cow in his shed.

However, in Extremadura no modern agricultural machinery had yet arrived so mechanized farming was unknown. The people continued using the same methods as centuries before - throughout the fifites and well into the sixties. Plowing was done by one man directing two oxen pulling an iron land breaker over the earth. The fifty oxen for this purpose occupied the long building Luis had called a Cannon Arch and other oxen were in another building nearby. Also there were many donkeys –they were used for everything, especially for travelling since there were no buses or cars. During the harvest, the men worked in pairs, one cut the wheat, the other tied it in packages and carried it. One man was bent over slicing the wheat, the stalks of which he handed to the man standing next to him - when the man doing the cutting complained that his back was too tired, the other took his place. Seeding was also done by hand and was a gesture especially beautiful to observe. Years later when giving a lecture in Topeka, Kansas I was struck to recognize that the statue of a farmer in the town square had been sculpted in the exact same position as our farmers used when seeding in Pascualete. Agricultural methods evidently had been identical worldwide before the invention of machinery.

Often I would find the four brothers seated in front of a tiny fire which Isidora made on the stone floor in one of the two rooms they inhabited. This fire consisted of a few twigs and light branches leaning against the stone wall. There was no chimney, and sometimes the smoke was so thick I could not stay very long, but at other times the fire burned brightly and the smoke seemed to disappear as if by magic through the ceiling of the building which I observed had many large holes.

A double bed almost filled their room and the ceiling was covered with strings of Spanish sausages and bright red tomatoes which glistened in the light of the small fire. (I was amazed to learn that tomatoes and grapes might be kept for many months by stringing them up in a room with good air and ventilation.)

Just outside the door two long files of oxen were tied in their open stalls, loudly munching the hay in the old stone troughs. A couple of donkeys at the further end now and then gave a kick to one of the oxen - then the cowherd would grab an oil lantern from the wall and walk up the path between the two lines of cows, his worn leather chaps swish-swashing cosily. He scolded the animals for their misbehavior, as if they were his children:

"Petra, Petra, move over and give the poor old burro room to lie down. He has carried many sacks of logs today and he deserves to sleep as well as you. If you are a good girl I will give you an extra handful of hay in the morning. You should be ashamed of yourself for always causing a fuss with your old friend."

This soft-hearted old man, the husband of Candida, was squat, with a square bewhiskered face and a thatch of wiry grey hair held down by a grubby old felt hat. I noticed that the men in Pascualete always wore a hat indoors, as well as outside. The only time any of them removed their hats was when they came to talk to me. Strangely enough they seemed to lose all their self-assurance when they had their hats off.

Sometimes when I kept some of the extra employees from Santa Marta late trying to finish the work, I felt I should drive them home in my jeep. The path to the little town was far worse than the one to the main road – it had deep holes and crevices. The first time I made the trip, I was quite relieved when the little town finally came into view. In the distance a few pale oil lamps flickered from the doors of a line of low stone houses on a street of dark stone buildings. As the car advanced I could barely make out the picturesque arched doorway of what I was proudly told was the church. Abruptly I remembered one of the family titles "Marques de Santa Marta " -It seemed to me quite surprising that something which to me had seemed so outstanding as a title of nobility could have as its basis such a miserable little village. In those days I still was unaware that the King designated the person as Marques or Count or Duke with the name of a property he owned - Santa Marta and all the property surrounding it for centuries had belonged to my husband´s ancestors. Suddenly a family of fat pigs got in our way and I had to stop. Before I could turn the car around, mothers and wives and children began to swarm about us. One of the steady helpers at Pascualete, El Barbero, so called because he was also the town barber, brought his buxom wife to be introduced.

"Would the Senora Condesa kindly honour our humble home?" she said as she indicated a small doorway at the side of the road. I expected a thoroughly miserable scene of dirt and disorder and when I entered I was amazed to find a spotlessly clean room, the red and white tiled floor sparkled in the rays of the family fire. Several copper pots gleamed decoratively on the whitewashed wall above the hearth and a small "mesa camilla" just like mine in Pascualete with several chairs surrounding it, occupied the centre of the room. Near the hearth were several little three-legged stools and in a far corner several small children were playing on the floor.

"Please take a seat," she said. "Would the Senora Condesa like to try my home-cured ham and a glass of wine?" she asked as she sliced some ample portions. I realized that El Barbero's wife was offering me the food for herself and her family for several days, but she didn´t allow me to refuse.

Later that night when I returned to Pascualete, a terrible storm broke out, which lasted for days. On the fourth night—I heard a knock on the door.

"Just a minute," I called as I jumped up and quickly threw on my dressing gown. It was Juan and his brother Jose standing side by side, twisting their hats in their hands and looking very uncomfortable.

"What is the matter?" I asked.

Juan began, then his brother Jose put in a few words, then he stopped helplessly and Juan with great difficulty and embarrassment blurted out:

"Senora Condesa, the water is rising so fast and the dirt lanes are so filled with mud that if the Senora Condesa does not leave immediately this same night, she might not be able to leave for ten days."

When I did not look particularly upset by that, Juan haltingly went on to explain that they were not very adept at helping ladies to give birth and a hospital in Madrid might be more comfortable. And considering that I was on the point of producing a child, they advised me to leave that very night.

I awakened the children and dressed them - with great reluctance I left early in the morning with the aid of a pair of oxen that managed to pull our jeep through the mud ponds. My only thought was to dispatch with this child as quickly as possible and return to my work at Pascualete. My son Miguel was born a month later.

CHAPTER NINETEEN

PILLETE & PEPE

After giving birth to Miguel, my visits to Pascualete were as frequent as possible but now I began to spend time in Trujillo on buying expeditions. But I never seemed to know where to shop for the various things we needed. Materials and wool, pots and pans, nails, paint, wire—each was sold in a different store hidden away in one of those curved narrow streets. But the day I met Pillete these problems soon evaporated.

Pepe, the chauffeur, had driven me into Trujillo that day, and we had stopped at the two petrol pumps hoping to fill our tank, but the attendants told us there was not a drop of petrol in the Trujillo area. Their pumps had been dry for ten days.

"Pepe, we haven't enough gasoline to get back to Pascualete," I pointed out to my young driver as we drove through one of the four entrances leading into the main plaza. "And look at that car. It's old but the owner must have found petrol somewhere." In the far corner of the empty spacious plaza was one shabby old black car.

It was a grey, rainy day and the main square was deserted except for that one old jalopy, more practical than one might think, for they were the type of car that could manage the bumps and ruts of the primitive country roads.

"Senora Condesa, I think I know the only man in Trujillo who could help us," Pepe said. "I am afraid to ask him myself. I am not important enough for him to do such a big favour for me, but if I introduce the Senora Condesa to him, I am sure he would help us."

"Who is this man?" I asked.

"His name is Pillete, he owns the bar over there," said Pepe, pointing to a corner of the plaza.

I looked around the arcaded plaza to where he indicated and saw a sign "Bar Imperio" written across a building which had once been a palace—all the buildings facing the plaza had probably been palaces in the sixteenth century but now the lower stories were converted into stores or restaurants or offices with living quarters up above.

As we approached the Bar Imperio on this chilly day everyone was huddled inside. As we entered I noticed the scent of coffee mingled with heavy whiffs of black tobacco smoke.

Many men dressed in the typical country outfit of worn brown cordoroy smocks and raggedy black pants were seated at several small black marble-topped iron-legged tables playing cards - several onlookers were drinking and talking and watching the card players. At the far end a young boy in a white coat stood at a long marble counter serving drinks to other weather-beaten farmers.

The men all had their hats on, but their country canes were propped neatly against a column in the centre of the room, their big black boots made scuffling sounds on the tile floor as the card-players restlessly shifted their feet.

While Pepe who was at my side looked around searching for the proprietor, I saw a short, plump man with dark skin, cheerful small black eyes and a bulbous nose waddle towards us.

"Buenos dias, Pepe," he said, "What can I do for you today?"

"I want to present you to the Senora Condesa, said Pepe. Pillete beamed at me for a few silent moments revealing a prominent gold tooth. He wore a small black beret perched over sparse greying hair, a stubble of beard covered his plump cheeks. Before shaking my outstretched hand, he rubbed his hands vigorously on his trousers.

Bowing deeply and with the same big grin he began to speak, "This is a great pleasure, Senora Condesa. We all know about the wonderful things the Senora Condesa is doing in Pascualete. What can we do to serve her? My wife and my five sons are at her disposal."

With that he snapped his fingers imperiously at the young white-coated men whom I had observed working like demons behind the bar. They stopped in their tracks and came running at his command, standing respectfully at attention like soldiers.

From a back room appeared his wife who was a feminine replica of Pillete – short, plump, the same little black eyes, the same waddle, the same round pleasant face and even the same gold tooth!

After the amenities were over, I explained,"Yes, there really is something you can do for me." I told him about the lack of gasoline for my car.

"Well, Senora Condesa, I am not rich enough to have a car myself, but I have a friend who has one and gasoline too. In fact, just over there in the corner is a man who might be able to help us—and knowing that the gasoline is necessary for the Senora Condesa, I am sure he will find all you need."

With that problem all but solved, his wife warmly invited me to sit down and have a cup of coffee, while Pillete went off to negotiate for my petrol. Delighted, I sat down, but his wife respectfully remained standing.

"Please, Candida - she had the same name as the woman with the glasses in Pascualete - do sit down with me. Perhaps you could give me some suggestions about where I might find some of these things on my shopping list."

I needed blankets, towels, material for curtains, some bedsprings, butter, vegetables...

"This is a very discouraging list," I added, as I finished reading it to her.

"No, no, Senora Condesa, everything is very simple. You sit here and relax and I will send my sons to buy everything for you.

"Juan," she cried, "go at once to Hernando's, bring several blankets for the Senora Condesa to inspect. Be sure they give you a good price and new ones, not last year's which have been sitting around collecting dampness and bugs." In an aside to me she added, "I know that the store the Senora Condesa has been using for her dry goods is very unreliable."

"And you," as she beckoned to another son, "tell Don Alfredo to send us a dozen of his best towels. Stop by the butter shop, be sure it is the freshest butter she has."

The boys disappeared in all different directions - this accomplished, Candida turned again to me, "Perhaps the Senora Condesa would like to use our telephone. We have one of the few telephones in Trujillo," she added with pride. "We have noticed that the Senora Condesa goes to the telephone company to call Madrid, many times she waits all day. Perhaps she would be more comfortable placing her calls here."

I was amused to realize that I had been so carefully observed during my previous visits, that my movements had been duly noted and discussed.

"Thank you so much," I said, "but now it is a little late to place the call."

"Perhaps not, Senora Condesa. My son's novia is the telephone operator and he may help you get it through more quickly."

So Juan placed my call to Madrid, and within an hour I was speaking with Luis! Now I realized what Pepe meant when he described Pillete as the most important man in Trujillo.

From then on the corner table at the bar Imperio became my office. It became sheer necesity for me, in order to do my shopping, to consult with Pillete and Candida while their five sons atended to my long list of items. They never allowed me to pay for one cup of coffee nor would any of the sons ever accept a tip for their many errands.

Gradually, I made friends with some of the customers of the bar, most of whom were farmers from the neighbouring countryside. There was no problem which could not be solved by a visit to Pillete's establishment, and if, for some reason, he could not handle it, one of my new-found friends was bound to come up with an answer.

I especially liked coming to town on Thursdays, the day of the weekly fair, when the Bar Imperio became the meeting place for masses of smocked cane-carrying farmers. At about eleven-thirty in the morning, with loud cries and gesticulations, they proceeded to buy and sell sheep, pigs and fodder. It resembled a real Stock Exchange, but was certainly more interesting and more colourful.

With Pillete at my side, all sorts of doors were opened for me. This energetic, clever man also owned an ice factory - was a skilful carpenter as well. He had a cabinet maker's business which he claimed produced the finest furniture in Estremadura. In business he was shrewd and although no one could ever fool him, he was popular with the entire town and known to be an honest, good, reliable man. The nuns and priests expecially adored him because he had sent them food and provisions at his own expense during the Spanish Civil War.

One day, while sitting at my table in the Bar Imperio with one of my new friends, I asked why there were so few women in Trujillo and none in the bar. The farmer graciously offered me the ingredients for rolling a cigarette, and then with what seemed to me a shy glance at my blue jeans, he answered, "It is not the custom of the 'ladies' of Trujillo to go to bars. Their days are spent in their homes, taking care of children."

My pride in having become 'one of the boys' was shattered. The black tobacco in the rolled cigarettte which I had accepted only to be polite, tasted still more bitter; and my jeans, which I thought looked practical and right for the country, suddenly seemed indecent. I realized that of course, a Spanish woman, whatever her age or figure, would never wear pants in public. After that day of awakening I found that a divided skirt was almost as practical and although I continued my visits to the Bar, I restricted my use of pants to the finca only. And I made no more efforts to roll and smoke their horrible tasting black tobacco.

Now that I considered myself practically a native of Estremadura, it was especially annoying always to find masses of children following me from store to store. They even followed me in Caceres, a city almost twice as large as Trujillo and far more cosmopolitan, where I went to do my more sophisticated shopping. One day I turned around quickly and grabbed one of the little boys who had been on my trail for the past hour.

"Tell me, little one, why are you following me? Am I so different from all the other ladies on the street?" I asked.

I had dressed very carefully in a dark skirt and suit jacket, low walking shoes and considered my costume very discreet. The child's big brown eyes, shining out of his pale little face, became round with amazement.

"But, Senora, you are wearing a hat."

So it was my old shooting hat which gave me away! After that, I tried these expeditions without a hat, but it was no use. Then I remembered how strange and different out-of-towners always looked to us in Pearl River. It did not have to be a hat or anything in particular. We just found them different.

I often threatened Pillete as he walked with me through the streets of Trujillo shooing off children, village idlers and even a few stray cats and dogs. "One day I 'm going to appear here in my guardesa's black city-going dress and wrap up my head in her old black scarf. Then maybe no one will notice me."

With that Pillete let out his deep guttural laugh—so contagious that everyone around had to laugh with him. With me especially, Pillete always seemed to be laughing because for some unknown reason he found everything I said funny.

From the first day I met Pillete, I was never permitted to walk alone in Trujillo again. He became my shadow.

CHAPTER TWENTY

FAMILY LIFE AND SERVANTS

Although my children were the most important part of my life at this time, Luis and I often were away for weekend shoots and made frequent visits to neighboring countries - but I felt secure having so many good people taking care of them. I knew Felisa, the cook loved them as she did her own, that the governess was intelligent and responsible. Pepe, the chauffeur and general man of all trades, kept his eyes on them as well and entertained them with amusing tricks, while Maria Luisa, my maid, informed me meticulously on the telephone if everyone fullfilled his or her obligations. Spaniards love children and the other three or four servants not only took an interest in them but seemed to be always delighted by them. But I soon realized too much so when on returning from a short trip, I discovered that the children had been having dinner at ten at night because Alvaro, age four, "insisted that he have his dinner at the same hour as his parents."

However, I was adamant about bringing up my children American style. For me, still, whatever was customary in America was the right way. In Pearl River I had been brought up to study seriously and to work – I agreed to have my children being educated with the same social manners as their father - he had insisted they learn perfect manners, to kiss ladies' hands, to stand up whenever a grownup came into the room...etc., But as soon as they were old enough, I forced them to take lessons in guitar, tennis, golf and riding – these lessons combined with Luis' family's favorite pastime, shooting, as time went on kept them busy. But when I tried to squeeze in lessons in arabic, Luis put his foot down. "These children are going to be the greatest bores in Spain. We're not trying to produce a new race of monsters."

Since none of these possibilities had existed in my smalltown and my parents certainly could never have afforded them anyway, I wanted my children to profit from the multiple advantages Madrid had to offer. Also everything was so inexpensive. Servants, governesses, all the different teachers for the lessons were about half the cost as in the USA. In Madrid in those days of the fifties, there were still no domestic electrical appliances, few washing machines, which meant a maid was needed only to wash, another to iron. everything in fact had to be done by hand, no electric frigidaires yet either. Also there had to be two men-servants, Luis had been acccustomed to many more , they served the table, drove the car and took care of the garden. All told there were enough extra people in the house to create a tremendous amount of quarreling, with likes and dislikes among them, which seemed to develop for the most minor reasons. I had to be cautious not to show any favoritism. Envy was one of the causes for trouble and a prominent characteristic of all spaniards, as they were quick to inform me.

Since Luis did not want his children brought up as he had been with tutors coming to the house, he insisted that we send them to school as soon as they would be accepted. We were both determined that they would be brought up like the majority of Spanish children. Also we agreed that it would be advantageous for them to visit my parents in Pearl River in the summers so their english would be fluent – french was already natural for them due to the French governess. They had been with me often visiting my parents since they were babies – now when the eldest, Alvaro, at age eight was sent alone to spend the summer with my parents, Luis advised him that he would have to work - he telephoned my mother and asked her to assign Alvaro some chore that would be a worthwhile working experience. My mother told Alvaro he could pick the vegetables in her garden and then sell them so he would make some money. Alvaro picked all he could, then filling a basket he began every day to go from house to house selling. After a week or so of this my mother complained to Alvaro that he would have to sell less vegetables because she needed some for her own use. Alvaro answered that she could not have any if she did not pay for them because his father said he had to work and learn how to make money as everyone else did.

Alvaro, Luis and Miguel lived on the third floor of our house with the french governess and a maid. Most of their meals were served there, sent up through a dumbwaiter to their playroom. One evening when I came home, I heard their voices crying loudly - I rushed upstairs. The faces of the two oldest were bathed in tears , they were sitting at a small table and absolutely screaming. Miguel was in his highchair, and the governess was having a noisy quarrel with Pepe who was serving. . Neither understood the other since she did not speak a word of spanish. But between sobs, Alvaro explained.

"Pepe cooked our goldfish," he wailed, pointing to the goldfish bowl which was empty and then to the serving dish on which there were five fried goldfish. I could not understand. Pepe was so kindhearted and he loved the children. The crying of the children was so loud that I could barely hear Pepe.

"Senora Condesa, I have only done this to save the children from a terrible catastrophe. It is because I am so fond of them that I have done it. In Spain it is very bad luck to have live goldfish in the house and the only way to take the curse away is to fry them and eat them. Therefore I took the gold fish and cooked them and they had better be eaten."

Spanish superstitions were many and new for me. Hats could not be placed on beds. Certain people were considered bearers of bad luck and when they came into the room, the others would inconspicuously make the sign of the devil's horns with two fingers and touch wood. When I asked for explanations of what the person had done to create such a fame, there was no sensible explication...other than the remark, "When that man enters a room, something bad is apt to occur."

FELISA

About this time William Larrimore Mellon, the OSS agent who had come with me in 1943 on the Pan American clipper, sent me some antibiotics to help people in poor areas of the city. In Spain neither penicillin nor any other antibiotic was yet available. I informed doctors in schools and hospitals in these parts of the city that I had penicillin available free of charge for needy cases, and in a short time I had already supplied several people with the medicine. One cold December night, as I was about the leave the house with Luis for a cocktail party, Pepe told me there were two women asking to see me at the back door. When he showed them in, they explained that the son of a relative was dying and they needed penicillin to save his life. They were obviously desperate and my heart went out to them - I felt convinced of the truth of their story. But since the doctors had warned me that others had sold my penicillin on the black market, I now had only a limited amount left , I decided to accompany them to Vallecas to see the sick child myself.

Luis was worried, "that's an isolated part of the city and could be dangerous at night. Unfortunately I can't go with you. I promised my father to take his place at this affair. But take Pepe with you and I'll telephone a "practicante" male nurse, to accompany you. Also he can give an injection, if it is necessary. You can join me later. We will be having drinks for at least forty-five minutes before the dinner, so there is time for you to arrive."

Pepe and I with the two women who had requested the penicillin got into the jeep, then we picked up the male nurse. The night was cold and windy. We drove fifteen minutes to the area they indicated on the outskirts of the city. The panorama in Vallecas in those days of the fifties was depressing. Since the end of the civil war, many destitute people from the provinces who had come to Madrid looking for work, had constructed miserable improvised shacks which housed entire families in that area next to the railroad tracks. The streets were merely muddy paths winding around near the railroad station of Mediodia. The women accompanying us said we would have to walk the rest of the way or the car would get stuck in the mud - so we got out of the car and plowed through deep ruts in the road. As we walked past the huts, the few people loitering in the narrow streets eyed me suspciously... my hat, my high heels, my Balenciaga coat. I felt uncomfortable.

"Here we are, Senora, right here", said one woman pointing to a raggedy cloth blowing in the wind in front of what appeared to be a mound of dirt. She lifted the filthy cloth door and indicated me to enter. I had to bend low in order to get in. Once inside , I could stand quite easily. There was a small fire on the floor, the smoke of which seeped out through a hole in the ceiling. A woman with long curly black hair sat on an empty orange crate next to a wide bed where one small blond child with his eyes closed lay motionless.

She jumped up, startled, as I crowded into the room with the nurse. Her face was quite beautiful, her expressive green eyes revealed suffering and fear. As I took in the scene I imagined my own torture if one of my children were in a similar situation. My heart went out to her. In silence we looked at the small child. The "practicante" pulled down the ragged blanket, touched the child's head, opened the child's eyes; then announced, "this child is already just about dead. There is no use wasting this penicillin on him."

I wanted to remove those ugly words from the air. "Of course something can be done for him.' I said and grabbed the doctor's prescription, which the mother had given him. "Two hundred thousand units of penicillin every twelve hours, " I read out loud. I looked to the practicante. "how much penicilllin do we have?"

He opened the leather case, where he had stored the box I had given him. the light from the oil lamp hanging from some part of the ceiling was evidently too weak for him to be able to read the labels, so he took his glasses out of his pocket, cleaned them slowly with his handkerchief, put them on, glanced at the box , and said, " We have here ten million units of penicillin."

I looked at the child again and at the mother. Her eyes were observing me pleadingly. "Well, we shall give him all of it."

"What ? Ten million units?"

"Yes, all of it."

"I tell you senora condesa, It's not a matter of pencillin. the child is almost dead."

I insisted and watched while the practicante made the injection, making up my mind that the next time I would know how to do it myself. I looked about the room, if it could be called such. On the floor, because there was no table, were three dishes and three tin cans which obviously were used as cups. In the heat of my indignation all sorts of thoughts ran through my head. Naturally, I reflected, there are communists and socialists in a country where people can be so poor, where women see their children die for lack of medicine, where human beings live in mud huts between railroad tracks. What kind of a monster is this Franco not to have improved conditions in the twelve years since the civil war ended.

I told the mother of the child that I would find a hospital, that we would save him, that she should not worry. Then I turned around and rushed home. I never called Luis. I had forgotten that such a thing as parties existed. First I called the British - American Hospital where my children had been born and where I knew the nurses and the director as well.

"Impossible, Countess. We cannot admit a Spaniard in the hospital who might have a contagious disease."

"But he does not have a contagious disease. the doctor's report says he has tubercular meningitis."

But there was no way I could get any hospital to accept the child. I called the obvious ones all over the city and always got the same answer. No matter what I offered to pay they would not take the child. Finally I went personally to the large hospital of San Carlos, they agreed to admit him. The next problem was an ambulance. In those days, there were few ambulances in Madrid. Neither the Red Cross nor any hospital had an ambulance available. Finally I decided to take the child myself. Somehow we managed to get the jeep to the door of the hut. I was terrified the child would die on the way - he remained unconscious bundled up in a dirty wool blanket in his mother's arms.

On arrival at the hospital, the doctor on duty shook his head." this child will die in a few hours."

I went home. By that time it was after midnight, but I couldn't sleep. I called the hospital at eight o'clock the next morning.

A man answered. "That child is still alive but we have few hopes. The mother is next to him all the time. Would you like to speak to her? "

"Yes, Please."
The mother got on. "By the way, would you tell me your name", I asked.

"My name is Felisa."
"Felisa, pay no attention to what that man says. We are going to save your little boy."

"When I saw the senora walk into my home," she said, "I knew that she was sent to save my Miguelito."

I called again at noon. A different man, but the same answer. by five o'clock in the afternoon, the nuns were not willing to talk to me. I decided to go to the hospital. When I walked into the ward, a young doctor had just finished examining him.

"This is amazing," he said, as he turned to me. "this child came in here, more or less dead, but he is holding on a long time. I don't understand it. But he will die."

That night we had friends coming for dinner, which helped because I had to talk to them and could not call until one in the morning, receiving the same report, "No change."

At eight o'clock the next morning, I was calling. This time the Mother Superior of the hospital got on the telephone herself. I trembled to hear the terrible words. the child had looked so beautiful, so helpless, so fragile in that bed in that pitiful shack."Would you be so kind as to tell me how this little boy that I took to the hospital yesterday is?"

"His condition is remarkable. The child came out of the coma two hours ago. There is no doubt that he is recovering. He was even able to take some nourishment. It has been like a miracle.

"Where is the child's mother?"
"She just left."

"I rushed to dress. I took a thermos of hot coffee, a few pieces of cheese and some bread, all I could find in my Spanish kitchen which never seemed to have any food in the closets or the frigidaire. The cook shopped every day and when I complained that she should shop once a week, she told me that if she bought for several days, everything would be gone by night time each day anyway. So I got into my car with the meager package of foodstuffs and went to Vallecas. The grubby shacks looked even more destitute in the morning light. Women wrapped in old wool shawls and children in rags could be seen in the muddy streets. At first I thought I had lost the way, but finally I found the entrance to the miserable hovel with the old striped cloth blowing in the wind.

I could not knock—there was no door—so I called, "Felisa! Felisa! Since there was no answer I lifted the curtain and entered. In the bed were two brown-eyed children snuggled up next to Felisa, who was asleep. In awed silence, they pulled at her hair. She awoke. "Ah, Senora," she said, pushing back her thick black hair. "I was so tired, but you have saved the life of my Miguelin. I saw his eyes open and look at me and I know he will get well."

I looked at the two children. She understood my questioning gaze. "Encarna and Antonio were not here yesterday, my sister was taking care of them."

"Do you mean to tell me, Felisa, that you live in this mud hut with only one bed for you and three children?"

"Oh yes, Senora. When they are healthy, it is no problem."

The little boy, who looked just like her, was about eight years old, and the girl was perhaps ten. I wanted to leave, and let her sleep, but I had to know one thing.

"Felisa, how did you get this bed inside the hut?" there are no windows or openings big enough."

"Senora, that was easy. the only thing I owned in the world was the bed. We put the bed up, and we built the hut with mud around the bed."

Miguelin got better every day. the doctors discovered that he did not have tubercular menginitis at all. He had Urea. the strong dose of penicillin probably had saved him.

As soon as he began to improve it became obvious that the recovering Miguelin could sing, dance, and imitate the flamenco steps. As soon as he was better, he ran around the hospital entertaining the other sick children. but when he was completely cured and had to leave the hospital , the doctors said Miguelito needed a month of especially good food and a house with central heating. Since my house was already very overcrowded, I tried to find someone among our friends who could take care of him for a month. For a short time we squeezed him in with us at home but soon the pilot assigned to the American Embassy, who came often home to dine with us and who had no children of his own was delighted to have him – he came for Miguelito and took him to his lovely house on the outskirts of Madrid. Here Miguelin recuperated completely with good American milk and healthy food, but the pilot and his wife did not want to part with him when the month was up.

I told Felisa that the Americans wanted to adopt her child. "Felisa, do you know what this would mean for Miguelin? I know that it would be sad for you, but you have no husband, no home and two other children. He would have opportunities you could not give him..."

She listened attentively and after some moments said, "I would like to think about it, and will answer you in a few days. By ths time Felisa had visited Miguelin often at the American's house and had seen how happy he was. I hoped for the best. Time passed and I had no news so I went to Vallecas to her small hut one night and questioned her.

By now I knew that Felisa's husband had been killed during the war, or so she said, by Franco's troops in her home town of Martos in southern Spain. That seemed strange to me since the children were too young to have had a father who was killed in the war. She had no one except herself to support the children.

"but ," she said,"I have a good job cleaning offices in the morning and doing the laundry in a private house in the afternoon. The children eat every day. I also have another source of income. My children, Antonio and Encarna pick up coal from between the railroad tracks and I sell it very well."

"What about school?" I asked.

"Schools? Oh, senora, people like us don't need shcools. I don't know how to read and write. My husband didn't either. There are no schools here in Vallecas. Do you think any of these people ever went to schools?" She lifted her arm in a broad gesture.

I looked about and wondered what could happen to a country where so many people did not know how to read and write, where people were hungry and children grew up in such an atmosphere. Felisa gave me her answer.

"I am grateful to the Americans who have been so kind to my son —and most of all I thank the Senora Condesa, but I cannot give up my Miguelin."

There was no way I could convince her otherwise.

Therefore I looked for other solutions, the best was a newly constructed government school where the two boys were admitted as boarders. I paid a pittance a day for their maintainance and the state paid the rest. Then I found a parochial school for Encarna, run by nuns who were indebted to Luis' Aunt, the Duchess of Pastrana. But my greatest difficulty in getting these children admitted was the birth certificate for each child, which was indispensable. When I questioned Felisa, she just shook her head.

"I don't know anything about papers. I don't think I've ever been in a church, either," she confessed, dropping her head, "except for my wedding," she added hastily.

"But Felisa, how old are your children?"
"Well, she said, "I don't know. Maybe Encarna is nine or ten or twelve."

"You mean to say you do not know her age?"
"No, those are unimportant details."
"Well, she must have a birth certificate so I can get her into this school, so we will have to put down something."

I looked at the child and decided that she was probably about twelve. "Felisa," I said, "what date was she born if you do not know the year?"

"Oh, the day? I don't have any idea."
"What month then?"
"Why would I remember that?"

Since I had to fill out a birth certificate, I decided to invent a birthday, why not the fourth of July – a great American holiday."

"Look Felisa, let's do this a little better for your two sons. I must have at least the years correct to fill out this certificate. What about Antonio's birthday?"

"Oh, no, I don't remember at all."
"Was it cold or was it hot the day you gave birth.? Just try to remember."

"It was very cold," she said. "I had just come to Madrid and it was very cold. I was living in my sister´s hut - fortunately there were many in that room, and that's how we kept warm."

So I gave Antonio the age of eight, and named the first of January for his birthday. We got to Miguelin. I was sure she would remember his birthday, he was so young, but no, she had no idea. When I asked her about the time of year, well she wasn't even certain—it was spring, or it was fall: it was cold, but not so cold as when Antonio was born. So I decided on George Washington's birthday, the twenty-second of February, and made him four years old.

Once the children were taken care of, I offered Felisa the job of being my children's maid, to live up on the third floor with her own room and bathroom. I thought she would be ecstatic, but she was not pleased at all. She shook her head vehemently. "No, I will be pleased to work in the Senora Condesa's house, and I will begin tomorrow, but I will not sleep away from my own home." I could not understand how she could prefer to live in her miserable mud hut, but my pleading did not make her change her mind.

One day when I came home in the afternoon, Pepe informed me that Felisa had not come to work and that she had sent a message that she was ill. I rushed to her miserable shack and found her twisting in pain. the doctor diagnosed apendicitis and I took her to the hospital.

When she got out of the hospital, even she realized that she was too weak to travel the two hours a day to her hut and to my house as well, therefore she began living in my house. I felt relieved that at last for the time being she was living in proper conditions.

About a year later, my maid, Maria Luisa. woke me in the morning saying that Felisa was ill. I ran upstairs, she looked pale, and told me that she had been sick all night and all morning. I thought perhaps she'd eaten something that didn't agree with her, but when after the third day she still seemed to do a lot of vomiting, I called the doctor. this time his verdict was,"She's pregnant".

"She doesn't have a husband," innocent me said in disbelief.
"Well, " the doctor said , "those things happen."
"I went upstairs and told Felisa as gently as I could.
She sat up in bed. "What a "calumnia"! (lie). Nothing could be further from the truth. That´s impossible."

I told the doctor that I believed her."She only goes out on Saturday afternoons to visit her children in school. She is a hard-working serious woman. You must be mistaken."

"Well, senora condesa, perhaps you are right. I have no definite proof and at least I'm sure that her condition is not serious."

Two weeks passed, and although Felisa would get up and try to work, I saw that she felt very low, so I called the doctor again.

"This time", he said, " we will take an x-ray."
"The following day, the doctor called. "well, I would like to have the pleasure of delivering to you the picture of the fetus your maid is carrying in her abdomen."

I went to Felisa's room with the negative in my hand. Even with the pictures in front of her, she continued to deny the story. Finally, she admitted, "It's just bad luck. Other women are fresh and carry on with men, but I don't , and then something like this happens to me."

There was no way she would tell me who the father was. For twenty-four hours I had been wondering if Pepe or my other man-servant would be the culprit, but they were much younger than Felisa and had plenty of girlfriends their own ages. My maid, Maria Luisa, told me that an old man, fully twenty years Felisa's senior had come to see her frequently when she was ill, that one day he had brought some pink material for her to make a dress, and another day a bottle of red wine to open up her appetite. I never let on to any of the servants what Felisa's problem was. In those days, such a situation for any maid was as scandalous as it would have been for the daughter of the best family in Madrid, and she had pleaded with me not to tell anyone.

Little by little, the true story of Felisa's life revealed itself to me. After her husband had been killed in the civil war, if she had ever had one, she had come to Madrid with her lover who was a man from her own village. However he was married, and already the father of five chldren. As a profession, he was a rag picker. but he, as any spanish Duke might do, established his wife and chldren on one street and his mistress, Felisa and her children, on the next. Antonio and Miguelin were his children: Encarna was the daughter of her late unknown husband. Now I understood why she had never wanted to live in my house. But Felisa and the ragpicker had continued to meet every Saturday on the corner of my street. Together they visited the children and then went to her old mud hut in Vallecas. It seemed to me quite a love story. What woman would love a man enough to live in such miserable conditions, and what man would remain faithful throughout supporting the rantings of a jealous wife, total poverty, and the problems of so many children!

I learned that Felisa had been attacked many times by the wife of her ragpicker lover, who jealous of her rival's black-haired beauty often accosted her when she appeared in the neighborhood on her way to her hut on Saturdays. The women often had to be separated and evidently these fights had occurred between them frequently. In true spanish style, it never occcurred to the ragpicker to give up his mistress, nor to abandon his legal wife and children either.

Every day I perceived more clearly how similar were the traits of these Spaniards. It seemed to me that they had the same moral principles and standards, no matter what their rank. The dignity of the most humble workman or farmer was as marked as that of a Grandee. There was no servile attitude amongst the destitute men or women of Spain.

I told Felisa that before she began to show her pregnancy I would send her to a finca of Luis's father where the employees had no contact with our servants or our house - there she could stay until she gave birth, and later, we would bring the baby home saying it was the child of a distant family employee who had died in child birth and would ask her to take charge of it. In this way, I explained, she could care of her own child with noone being the wiser. However, Luis and I left for America about this time and when we returned three weeks later, I was horrified to discover that Felisa without any of my servants being aware had had a woman friend perform an abortion.... she explained proudly that it had been done by a specialist in Vallecas who used knitting needles. Miraculously Felisa lived through the dangerous operation, so she never had the baby I had so carefully arranged for.

But Felisa was smart. Gradually she learned from my chefs to become an excellent cook and thus remained with me 41 years in that capacity. When she did not need to work any longer and her children had graduated from school and had their own jobs, we helped her obtain a nice modern apartment where she lived with her daughter Encarna until she died –at what age noone ,not even herself had any idea. Felisa had no more pregnancies and I never was able to meet or see the man she had loved.

Miguelin married and had five daughters, he also had his own tailoring shop. Antonio became one of our chauffeurs for several years, then he married the daughter of Primitivo and Maria – they , had three children, one a beautiful girl resembling her grandmother Felisa.

PEPE

Pepe had come to us looking for a job as a chauffeur or man servant when we first returned from our honeymoon in '48. He was a good-looking young fellow with no experience, but he impressed me with his dignified bearing and good manners. Luis' old servant who came to interview him said that he would learn quickly. "Senora condesa, he will need new clothes, he has absolutely nothing. His shoes have no soles and the suit he wears is borrowed."

Pepe was smart, and in no time became an excellent butler, chauffeur, cook and even nursemaid— the children loved him. Unfortunately the maids also, both those in Pascualete and in Madrid. They followed him around, and whenever I mentioned his name they began to stutter and blush. Their jealousies would make them quarrelsome and I began to lose some of the girls because of Pepe's charms. Whenever I called his attention to this problem, he would answer with a shrug of his shoulders. "I'm sorry senora condesa, but what can I do? The women pursue me. It's not my fault." Each day he became more useful as a plumber, painter , carpenter, anything that had to be done and in Pascualete he was especially useful. Pepe could do anything..

Pepe decided that Felisa should learn how to read and write – she asked him to do her accounts for the kitchen and to read the newspaper for her. One day I heard Pepe telling her.

"Felisa, I understand that it would be boring to go to the school that the Countess wants to send you to in the afternoons. But look, I can teach you. Where are you going to find a better looking teacher than me?"

Felisa would laugh at him; he was only twenty three and she treated him like a child. "I don't think somebody as young as you would be a very good teacher. Anyhow I've gotten along very well until now, and I don't see any reason why I should learn to read and write."

And although she managed finally to do her own kitchen accounts and even became amazingly capable with numbers, she never learned how to read or write.

Pepe often took papers to Don Jose in Luis office and there he met a pretty blond secretary who with time he married, leaving the maids at home heart-broken. He became successful and finally owned a gas station, ánd a good car of his own .

MARIA LUISA

But the one who ruled the house was my personal maid, Maria Luisa. She had been born in Santander in the north of Spain on the coast - she had strong convictions and a loyalty to us which isolated her from everything else. In fact she became as dedicated to the family as a nun to a convent and cared for our home and everything in it as if it was her own, which indeed became her failing.

Despite Maria Luisa's many advantages and qualities soon I realized that she had opinions and pretensions that astounded me . I had been one of six children brought up in a small house in a little town where we were lucky to have one servant off and on. But Maria Luisa, despite her humble family and home in Santander considered any family with less than six servants was not of a quality up to her standards. Also she had her own analytical opinion of all those who entered our house, whether guests or servants - she has been the most snobbish person I ever knew. She looked down upon servants who worked for families she didn't consider distinguished and never admitted them to her own small group of friends. Also somehow she was more aware of gossip or scandal in popular Spanish families than any columnist. She considered herself a necessary guest of any wedding, baptism, or funeral in our home or those in other branches of Luis's large family- this custom had always been practiced in Luis'' family .

Somehow she made a point of gaining the approval especially of our most famous guests and with time was well known and could make contact by telephone with the most popular or important personalities in the country. Often I was amazed to notice that she could call people who normally would not get on the phone personally. She could reach any minister, writer, flamenco dancer, bullfighter or duke with no effort. These persons seemed pleased and sometimes even amused to attend to her requests which I would hear about later. She understood thoroughly spanish protocol and manners and if some of our guests did not come up to her standards, although she was correct and polite, she did not shower them with the same aimiability as her favorites. She had the greatest disdain for those who did not meet her measurements.

She learned to accept my behavior of working and spending time with persons she considered unimportant , but she preferred my time spent going to dressmakers and fitting clothes or going to the hairdresser. She herself dressed with great care when she went on errands or accompanied me on a trip. Yet there were certain household jobs she just refused to do, such as anything in the kitchen; although she would wash our breakfast dishes in the butler's pantry. Also she would not iron anything so vulgar as a sheet, but my custom made dresses and Luis' starched shirts she would take care of at any hour.

When undoing the luggage of guests in Pascualete, if a lady arrived without tissue paper in between each layer of clothes, Maria Luisa could not resist making a side remark to me that senora so and so was not really a distinguished lady- she didn´t even know how to teach her servants the proper way to pack a suitcase.

Maria Luisa came to our house the night before my third son was born and stayed forty-two years, about the same amount of time as Felisa. She knew how to read and write although with many errors, but because of that ability she considered herself superior to Felisa and often made it evident in the tone in which she addressed her. Felisa was not pleased at all and sometimes I could hear her answering Maria Luisa in a theatrically pompous voice.

"Look who's talking—so I don't know how write ! But do I know how to starch the Count's collars! And what does the Duchess Maria Luisa know about getting a husband? Don't come to me with those airs of yours."

Nevertheless at other times they laughed and joked, they were always the two oldest women on the staff. Maria Luisa soon took upon herself to give orders to the newcomers who often were ignorant young country girls.

"Who could believe that a girl eighteen years old could be so dumb that she doesn't know even what a vacuum cleaner is?" Maria Luisa would ask, forgetting that she had never heard of such a machine herself several years before. "What kind of a miserable pueblo do you come from?"

Maria Luisa claimed to be a religious woman, but seldom went to Mass, she was a good seamstress, and as honest as the day is long. she had high standards and principals, and had obviously been brought up in a righteous household.

The flirtations between the menservants and the girls downstairs would meet with her instant disapproval. She once came to my room, puffing with indignance, looking up at the ceiling, I could only see the whites of her eyes.

"Oh, senora condesa, I have seen the most revolting sight." I expected anything. By now I was accustomed to her exaggerations and tendency to create trouble for the other servants. "In the

laundry, "she went on, "there was Pepe with his arms around Maruja and his hand on her bare right thigh."

The servant's part of the house was also the noisiest. The six or seven of them would have their dinners and luncheons after ours no matter what hour we dined and often sat up laughing and talking and quarreling until one thirty in the morning. Now and then, when guests from America would ask for breakfast at seven thirty I would have to explain that there was no way I could get my servants up at such an hour, the earliest would be about eight-thirty or nine.

But when we came back from our trips they would greet us with smiles, the house filled with flowers and our favorite dishes would be prepared, and the place where I was happiest was in our own home.

In Pascualete our children played with the twenty or so children of the shepherds and I invited those country people to our celebrations, especially the American celebrations. Years later one of the children whose father had been one of our shepherds contacted me from a town near Granada. He reminded me of our Easter celebrations and Easter egg hunts and said his greatest dream was to return to see Pascualete just for a short few hours. Miraculously I remembered him well – their "chozo" had been one I visited often on horseback and in fact he had been one of the most amusing and smartest of those children. He told me he was married and now had two grown children, that he owned a shop in the town where he lived. I invited him and his wife to spend a weekend in Pascualete and received them as I would any foreign ambassador. We had a wonderful two days together – he had grown to be a handsome successful man, and told me that his most precious memories were of those years living with his parents in the chozo in Pascualete.

I have never forgotten any of those wonderful persons nor their families. For me they represent the basic examples of the warmth and deep humanity of the spanish people and they formed one of the principal reasons why I came to love and admire Spain.

CHAPTER TWENTY-ONE

FIRST TRIP TO LAS DUEÑAS

Around the middle of April about a week after Easter we usually went to Sevilla to enjoy the Feria which is undoubtedly one of the most glamorous and unique festivities that I have known. It also has the advantage of being available to everyone. My first visit had been in 1945 during the war years when I was working for OSS but at that time I was too involved in espionage and too ignorant of Spanish customs to appreciate or understand this joyful unique week of flamenco and bullfights. Juanito Belmonte's mother had invited me – Juanito was then bullfighting in South America. When his mother took me to the Fair Grounds I was astounded by the elaborate decorations covering all the narrow streets of the Fair area, the horse-drawn carriages, the people dressed in gypsy costumes and dancing in the streets. However the other guests in the house were elderly ladies, noone went to the bullfights and although they did take me at night to the small casetas in the fairgrounds where I saw wonderful flamenco, I met no one near my age with whom to enjoy it.

But when a close friend, Cayetana, the Duchess of Alba, invited us to her beautiful palace, Las Dueñas, the Fair was fun and glamorous. After that first visit we were invited many times and the Fair in Sevilla in April became a yearly delight. Apart from the flamenco and the bullfights, there were dinners with the most interesting vistors in Las Dueñas and parties in other palaces. I need a host of luggage. Since riding was my favorite sport, I took the special riding costumes for this affair- the wide brimmed black hat ,(sombrero cordobes), the short jacket and three-quarter length pants over high leather boots. For the bullfights in the afternoons I liked to wear the classic high comb and black lace mantilla – that was not easy – it necessitated a large chignon and tight pins to hook the high comb in place. And sometimes I wore a flattering gypsy dress which also would be useful at night in the "casetas". One long ball gown would be included in case there was a Ball. palace.

    Luis refused to arrive at the airport with so many big boxes and suitcases , so we usually sent everything ahead by car and went by plane. Pepe who would be in the airport waiting but the drive to the city was never easy during Fair days. Children and grownups were dancing and singing in the streets - their long ruffled dresses grazed the sides of our car as we passed . A carriage drawn by four horses bedecked in colorful ribbons often appeared from a side street – Pepe would have to stop and our way was constantly blocked. The route took us along the Guadalquivir River and past the "Torre de Oro", (Tower of Gold), so-named four hundred years before when the gold arriving from the New World would be deposited there. Today we had to stop first at the Hotel Alfonso XIII to pick up a friend - tall palm trees graced the entrance where elegant ancient Rolls Royces were parked near horse carriages. Hotel doormen in elaborate livery with ropes of golden braid draped over their shoulders shouted orders to the porters.

Then we proceeded to Cayetana's palace, Las Dueñas - as we threaded our way through the crowded streets the clip-clop of the horses' hooves, the jingle of the carriage bells, and the castañets resounded through the narrow streets heighthening our anticipation of all that was to follow . When we arrived at Las Dueñas Juan, the guard, with his usual welcoming smile opened the hugh iron double gate. At this time of year, middle April, the driveway was flanked by rows of blossoming orange trees and the facade and balconies of the palace were covered with flaming red bougainvilla. On one side of the entrance, in front of the stables, two carriages, a landau and a break, were stationed – their impatient horses thumping their hooves, anxious to get moving – The horses were perfectly matched, pure bred Spanish-Cartusian horses bedecked in pompoms and silk ribbons for the Fair - the coachmen in costumes of the period of Goya in the Alba family colors of blue and yellow. But next to those was another carriage, decorated in blue and white, the colors of Tomas Terry, a popular Andalusian and another customary guest who obviously had already arrived.

Immediately the enchantment of the old palace cast its spell. I jumped out of the car – in front of me was the large beautiful central patio with tall graceful columns bordered by arabic arches. For a moment I stood enthralled in the silence enjoying the exquisite artistry of the Arabic architecture, listening to the fountain where sparkling streams of water sprouted high in the air.

Then Luis and I turned toward the narrow side stairway, which went up to the main floor where the guests rooms, the dining room, the veranda terrace and several salons were located. As my heels clicked on the ancient tiled floors, I thought of the many famous personalities that had stepped on these same stones in centuries past. I knew from historical acounts that five hundred years before, Hernan Cortez on his return from the New World after having conquered Mexico had mounted these same stairs when he came to this palace to visit his daughter who was the wife of the owner – that was onehundred and fifty years before the palace came into the Alba family. But only fifty years before our visit, the Spanish-born Empress Eugénie of France had mounted these steps when she visited her sister, the Duchess of Alba, my hostess´s grandmother.

Juan, the gateman had alerted Cayetana who was waiting for us on the terrace. We sat down with her as she told us who had already arrived and who would be coming later – then she went over the plans for the dinners in her house and other dinners elsewhere.When I finally proceeded to the high-ceilinged Victorian bedroom which I was familiar with from the last visit, my clothes were already hanging in the old-fashioned armoire - my boots and chaps were placed next to the sofa at the foot of the canopied bed. From the open balcony, I looked down at the flower-choked garden and breathed in the scent of orange blossoms. Life could be so beautiful.

Cayetana in those days had long honey-colored hair, a clear golden skin, an upturned nose, warm brown eyes, a perfect figure and a spirit that was shy and daring at the same time. She danced flamenco as well as the gypsies, was an experienced horsewoman, a connoisseur of art, an *aficionada* of bullfights, in short - a Duchess who preserved Spanish customs and traditions, and who understood and loved her *pueblo.* Her husband was tall, handsome, and distinguished. With their five young sons and baby daughter, they made an impressive family.

A bit later a maid brought a message from Cayetana reminding us that Tomas Terry would take us in his carriage to the bullfight if we could get ready quckly. So we rushed to change and joined Tomas just in time. Luis enjoyed as much as I did riding in those landaus with the harness bells jingling and echoing through the narrow, twisting streets. The clatter of the horses' hoofs clip-clopped in rhythmic cadence over the cobble-stones while people waved as we went by- everybody enjoyed the sight of the magnificent carriage with its five perfectly matched pure-bred Andalusian horses. The coachmen also commanded admiration, sitting straight and correct -- superb in blue silk bandanas, colorful short jackets, and glossy boots and chaps. All Spaniards took pride in their appearance and especially when they were in costume or uniform.

The pair of lead horses were sleek dark gray and the three wheelers behind almost identical. This type of harnessing typical of southern Spain and was called *"Media Potencia"* - words and customs which no longer existed in any other part of Europe, but which in Sevilla, during the Feria, gave the nostalgic atmosphere of times long gone by.

A bit before six o'clock, we entered the Maestranza, Sevilla's famous ancient bullring. The sandy arena glistened like gold in the hot sun as we stepped down to the ringside. Over the *barrera* in front of me, I stretched my red and black embroidered *manton de Manila*, silk shawl, and looked around the plaza. What a glorious spectacle! Above, crowning the round arena under a narrow, red-tiled roof, was a circle of lovely aged granite columns where in one, next to of the mayor's box, I recognized Cayetana who had arrived at almost the same time to the "palco", box, as I had to my "barrera", ringside seat. She looked especially dramatic in her high comb and mantilla – she saw me at the same time and waved. I had not had time to fix my hair and place the high comb and regretted not wearing a mantilla myself. In the other high boxes surrounding the ring there were many other women with mantillas and carnations in their hair - as was customary - and due to the hot afternoon many were fluttering their "abanicos", (fans). Also in the boxes above draped over the railings of the boxes were many bright colored silk shawls adding splashes of color to the plaza. Behind the ladies in the boxes stood their companions in dark suits also waving and calling to friends while sipping sherry in long narrow glasses. The plaza was packed and the atmosphere was electric. In a few moments, the greatest matadors of the season would enter the ring - the bulls for today's fight were said to be over five hundred kilos each- very impressive and frightening.

Near us ringside was the famous flamenco star, Lola Flores. I remembered the first time I had seen her in January 1944 as Edmundo Lasalle and I had walked into the Teatro Albeniz in Madrid– then she was a curvacious raven haired beauty twisting and gyrating in a fiery dance to "Niña de Fuego", the wailing song, of a tall gypsy whose strange gutural sounds seemed to incite her more with each note. I had read her name in the program that night. Later Lola Flores became a close personal friend. That flamenco show had been the perfect beginning for my espionage - not only because my activities in the future were to be closely connected with Madrid's nightlife but also because flamenco then was a main source of entertainment for all social levels in the country. As yet in the forties there had been no football stadiums and no amplifiers for the voices of the singers who were obliged to perform without loudspeakers.

But today in our bullring seats I was barely able to exchange a few words with Lola Flores when the booming gong rang out indicating the fight was about to begin. Silence abruptly overtook the entire plaza as everyone hastily sat down.

Flamenco contains a rich variety of dance forms. The "buleria" exhuberates wild gaiety, the "tarantula" is dramatic, "soleares" are solemn and stately. Gypsy "rumbas" and "alegrias" are extremely sensous. Surrounded by the whitewashed walls and the arched ceilings of the gypsy caves of Granada enhances this music - the "palmas" hand-beating) echos and resounds until one becomes drunk with the tantalizing rythmns. Those flamenco sessions usually end only when artists and spectators collapse from fatigue. Flamenco is more effective if there are not many more spectators than artists - limited space is an advantage also since it enables the rythmns beat out by the artists' clapping hands and tapping feet to cast their spell.

The works of two famous Spaniards born in that Granada at the beginning of this century reveal the enormous influence flamenco can have on those who understand its enchantment. Garcia Lorca, the poet, produced a classic on flamenco, "Elegia del Cante Hondo" and Manuel de Falla composed his musical masterpiece "Amor Brujo" in Granada - both men knew well the spell flamenco produced when endulged in by those gypsies living inside the Albaicin mountain –many consider this the most pure flamenco.

Many Spanish girls from Sevilla and Jerez de la Frontera dance the "Sevillana", but pure flamenco is difficult for one not born to it - the steps, the gestures, the posture and body movements are unique. During the seventies apart from Cayetana Alba, only a few other women in the social world could really dance flamenco . The "duende",(mystery of flamenco) is such that even old and fat women can become beautiful when they are inspired – when they reach their arms artistically into the air, arch their backs and strut to the tune of the guitar and the "palmas" (the hand-clapping). This perhaps is the secret of flamenco's fascination—it enables those who partake in it to become intoxicated by its complex musical rythmns. It is an art which opens a magic window to beauty.

Arthur Rubenstien, the famous musician, was a flamenco fan – he knew well the atmosphere of night-long flamenco parties and the excentricities of the gypsies. He told me that once in Sevilla after many hours of listening to mediocre singing and dancing, when he got up to leave one of the gypsy men grabbed him , " Don't leave, don't leave - I will kill myself if you do." Then the man grabbed him tighter, saying, " Fatima (the gypsy female star) is just going to begin her famous dance". Rubenstein said that although he sat down again and remained another hour, the flamenco did not improve. He knew well that flamenco is not always gripping. Rubenstein was fun to be seated next to at dinner even when he was 93 years old - his sense of humor and his conversation remain vibrant in my memory.

    A few years after Pastora Imperio and her son-in-law, Gitanillo de Triana, had opened their flamenco nightclub in Madrid, other flamenco "boites" began to appear - El Corral de la Moreria" and "Las Chinitas" , but this more theatrical flamenco lacks the fire of the small flamenco sessions we had been accustomed to. Originally flamenco was an inspired gypsy art form passed on from one generation to the other, the real gypsy artist moves and sings according to his or her inspiration, absorbed in the gestures learned from living in a family where flamenco was a daily passtime - this is the type of flamenco that eclectrifies.

    Apart from the flamenco in the Feria of Sevilla, in the forties and the fifties, it was also often the main after dinner entertainment in private parties in Madrid. Chairs were placed in a huge semicircle; rugs and carpets were removed. Then in came the arrogant flamenco artists. First they shook hands with each guest and after that ceremony had been completed, they stamped on the wooden floor - testing its resonance. Finally they took their places in a line of chairs and the guitarists began to tune in their instruments. A few "Sevillanas" would be initiated to get the festivities started. Even proper old dowagers remained like statues in their chairs until daybreak, apparently not slightly scandalized by the dancer's sensuous movements or the suggestive words of the songs. During my first years in Spain the social world's calm acceptance of the sensuous flamenco dancing amazed me since in those days on the beaches, men were obliged by law to wear tops on their bathing suits and women had to have skirts covering theirs.

Bullfighters and gypsies were closely linked - not many pure gypsies became matadors, nevertheless Gitanillo de Triana was a great matador and gypsy dancers sometimes married bullfighters - today families like the Ordoñez, the Vegas, the Albaicin sometimes produced matadors or dancers.

My friend Ayesha, the Maharajah of Jaipur in Malaga told me that once when she was in a bullfight in Malaga, a gypsy woman approached her asking what tribe she belonged to. Ayesha laughed as she told me, "Gypsies in Spain often think I am one of them because we have similar features and skin color. Perhaps you are unaware that all gypsies came originally from a corner of northern India."

I asked her about the gypsies in central Europe and she explained. "They also originated in India but intermarried much more with other peoples which influenced their music and appearance. The gypsies who emigrated to Spain came through Egypt - those rarely intermarried and although their music contains some Arab strains,it remains the most pure."

Not all gypsies can dance flamenco or sing "cante hondo", (pure flamenco). I had learned this years before when against the advice of my shepherds, I invited a caravan of gypsies into the patio of Pascualete to dance- they were travelling through our ranch on their way to the fair in Trujillo. In those days I was so ignorant that I thought all gypsies knew how to dance and sing flamenco. While some of them were jumping around and howling in a miserable imitation of flamenco, their relatives were robbing my employees of their chickens and donkeys. None of those gypsies had the slightest knowledge of flamenco.

During the incomparable display of Sevilla in costume and the Fair parade of magnificent carriages and horses, foreigners are often unaware of the importance of the flamenco music and dancing at night in the casetas. Sometimes the tourists are too tired or too hungry to look for the flamenco. Years ago

Elsa Maxwell decided to find out if a Fair in Sevilla was as amusing as we had described it. One night she was sitting in a caseta where a group of gypsies were in the midst of a really good flamenco session, but Elsa was looking desperate. "When does one eat in this city? It's already one in the morning," she declared. Beltran Domecq, (the spaniard who took me up to my room in the Hotel Palace the first day I arrived in Madrid) was sitting at her side - he looked at her indignantly. "Eat?" he had to shout in order to be heard over the "palmas" (hand clapping) and the stamping feet of the dancer, "who thinks of eating when you have this," gesturing toward the girl who was performing a "solares" about three feet away.

At "Las Dueñas" during the Fair we would catch a few hours of sleep at odd times between the many events - usually one can squeeze in about three hours after the bullfight which ends at eight in the evening until dressing for dinner at midnight. We then leave for the Fair around one thrity A.M. which is the hour flamenco is in full swing in the small improvised wooden shacks , the "casetas" which cover about six blocks of the fairgrounds. We begin by going from one caseta to another to decide which has the best flamenco - then remain in the one we liked best although some continue to wander all night to other casetas. To choose the caseta with the best flamenco is a gamble and requires patience because flamenco artists are moody, emotional and unreliable. They may perform with little enthusiasm or artistry at two a.m. but by four can become inspired and sublime. All visitors milling around the fairgrounds, if there is room are welcome in any caseta for a "copita" and to enjoy the flamenco. This camaraderie is an example of how democratic and friendly Spaniards are. Strangers from all over the country, laborers, grandees, shepherds, farmers, politicians from the left and from the right—squeeze into the casetas side by side, joking and drinking together, enjoying the flamenco - around six in the morning , survivors go to small street vendors who sell *churros and chocolate* , a sort of fried donuts, the classic early morning repast and then go to their homes to grab another few hours sleep. If anyone leaves the fair before five A.M. he is bound to hear the next day that he missed the best flamenco of the week.

CHAPTER TWENTY-TWO

PRIMITIVO COMES TO MADRID
MARIA & CHICKENS

During these years we continued to vist Pascaulete regularly. The differences in life in Madrid and during our frequent trips abroad with the days we lived on our isolated finca in Extremadura were dramatic. As yet electricity had not arrived, although we had installed a small generator to provide light in the house at night for a few hours. But the shepherds who lived in the "chozos", (straw huts), in far away parts of the property still used oil lamps. However this electric generator necessitated a man to maintain it and turn it off. For the hours I would spend reading in bed at night I continued to keep nine candles (I discovered that nine candles supplied the light of one normal electric bulb) burning on my bedside table rather than oblige Primitivo to stay awake in a small hut near the palacio waiting for me to finish. The town of Santa Marta did not have electricity either –this contributed to the country people maintaining their centuries old customs of a very early bedtime much longer than those who lived in the cities. Without television or telephones their contact with the outer world was limited, nor did they receive newspapers. Well - newspapers never interested them – in those days most did not know how to read and now although all can read, they are only interested in the television. At first many of those over forty did not want to learn how to read despite the good new school in Santa Marta with classes at night for grown-ups. Motorcycles for some years had replacded burros but in the sixties even when salaries permitted the luxury of a car, few residents of Santa Marta were capable of passing the driving tests because of their illiteracy.

However there were other improvements we could make despite the lack of modern advantages.

"Aline, you must do something about Primitivo," Luis insisted. "He is a "guarda jurado", a sworn legal guard, and is supposed to be in uniform. Surely you must have noticed that in other fincas around Spain the guards are in uniform."

Indeed I did remember how fine the guards looked in Luis' father's properties and those of his uncles - I had been impressed with their brown or grey uniforms with reveres and cuffs of red, green or blue, depending on the family colours, also some of these uniforms had wide leather straps from shoulder to waist carrying in the middle a large brass medallion on which was inscribed, "Sworn Guard of----" whoever was the owner of that particular property. They also had gold buttons with the family crest, our butlers in Madrid also had those buttons on their uniforms as did the servants in Luis' father's house. Also all the guards in family country fincas wore leather leggings and a broad brimmed andalusian type hat. "Very attractive" I had thought when I first saw them.

When I told Maria that I intended to get a uniform for Primitivo, she beamed. She said Primitivo's father had had one made in 1914 when he and other guards had been invited to the wedding of Luis'' mother in Madrid – all had attended the wedding dressed in new uniforms. Maria told me , "We have a photograph of those nineteen guards of Pascualete and the adjoining family properties – Primitivo's father is in the photo looks very elegant." Maria informed me that the best tailor for guard's uniforms was in Caceres but that Trujillo also would have a tailor. So I looked into the family archives to find the family colors – I didn't like the colors Luis' grandparents had used- a dark brown with dark green reveres, similar to the guards in the Retiro, Madrid's central public park, but I kept investigating – reading the old paleography until I found the grey with red reveres that we use today, this represented the colors of the Loaisa family a couple of centuries before –then I went to Trujillo, found the exact color grey which seemed most attractive and a nice red for the collar and cuffs. I took Primitivo to a tailor – thus our first guards uniforms were made. Several weeks later he proudly appeared in the patio for my inspection. I had to admit that he made a thoroughly impressive guard. But alas, after all this trouble, he rarely wore the uniform. Whenever he had any work to do he removed it, and I was certain that when we were not in the finca, he never put it on at all.

Of course, I thought, how foolish I am. Naturally he needs two uniforms. When I told Maria to order another one from the tailor in Trujillo she was genuinely upset.

"But Senora Condesa, that is a terrible extravagance. I thought I had taken such good care of Primitivo's uniform, it will last for at least ten years. God will punish us for such indulgences. Two uniforms, indeed!"

About this time Luis made me a gift of a beautiful new riding horse - a three and a half year old black arab mare, called Chiquita which he bought from our friend, the matador, Luis Miguel Dominguin, with the idea of schooling her in Madrid and then shipping her to the finca.

When we sent Chiquita to the Madrid country club, Puerta de Hierro, for training, the grooms there said that they would train her but she would undoubtedly be spoiled as soon as she had been a few months at the finca and ridden in the sloppy fashion of farm employees - so it was that Luis decided

Primitivo should come to Madrid to learn how to ride a horse properly.

This was Primitivo's first visit to Madrid and as it was an important event in any man's life, the entire population of Pascualete turned out to say good-bye to the voyager. For days Maria had planned for this trip. What she prepared, I will never know, for I had never seen Primitivo in anything except his guard's uniform and his farmer's smock.

For his trip to Madrid, Primitivo wore neither. As he got into our jeep, I recognized he was wearing one of Luis' grey old suits which I had given him long ago. He wore no tie, no collar and was very self-conscious in his unfamiliar attire. But the people of the finca beamed with admiration and Maria packed him into the back of the jeep with a large cloth sack, its four corners tied together - his luggage for the trip.

He was greeted warmly by Pepe and the other servants in Madrid - the next day I drove him to the country club to begin his training.

"Now, Primitivo,' I explained. "Out here I want you to learn how to comb and curry a horse, I expect you to learn all the details of grooming and in addition they have new adavanced theories about weighing a horse's food and so forth."

"But does the Senora Condesa think that Primnitvo does not know how to take care of animals" he said trying to restrain his righteous indignation. "My mule and my burro are the best cared for animals in Pascualete, and there are another dozen horses I take care of.   . Maybe I do not know about weighing out a horse's food, but I certainly know when a horse has had enough to eat."

"Yes, I realize that, Primitivo, but Chiquita is a delicate mare and needs special handling. That is why you are also going to learn to ride here."

"Ride? Why the Senora Condesa surely knows that I can ride anything under the sun ".

Although contemptuous of these newfangled city notions, Primitivo got through his first morning at the club without incident. As I drove him back to the house I told him:

"Now Primitivo, every morning you must go to the Club around ten o'clock. Watch how we come back. You must take the bus which leaves from the street near our house which will take you to within a kilometer of the club."

"If the Senora Condesa will allow me," he answered, "I would prefer to walk to the stables. I do not trust these busses that are always having accidents and killing innocent people. No, no, if the Senora Condesa will permit, I will walk."

"Primitivo that's more than six kilometers a day, two miles each way!"

"Si, Senora Condesa, But that is nothing. A strong man like me does not mind a little walk."

The first indication I had that things were not going so well in the servants' quarters was from Maria Luisa, when she brought me my breakfast tray looking tired and wan.

"Primitivo is such a nice man, Senora Condesa, that I hate to complain, " she said, "but he wakes up at five-thirty in the morning and walks about with his noisy boots, opening and shutting doors and waking us all. It upsets him to see us sleeping. He thinks we are oversleeping and that he must stir us to get us up and do the work of the house. Please would the Senora Condesa tell Primitivo that we have her permission to sleep until eight o'clock."

Primitivo found the central heating unbearable, also he did not know what to do with himself when he was not in the club taking his lessons. 'Televsion was late in becoming a normal asset in houses in Spain and there was no TV in Pascualete until years later. I suggested to Pepe that he take Primitivo for a night on the town so he would amuse himself a bit and discover some of the advantages of the city. The next day I asked Pepe how the evening had prospered.

"Well, Senora Condesa, all I can say is that I hope I never have to go anywhere in this city again with that country yokel. When I told him we were going to the theater he decided he had to get all dressed up. He put on his guard's unform—boots, hat and all—and of course, everyone in the bus stared at him and at me. One or two people asked me if he was a special guard of the park."

"That's not so bad, Pepe. You really should be more tolerant," I admonished.

"Senora Condesa, that's not the worst of it. Every time a girl appeared on the stage—and these girls were dancing with very short skirts - Primitivo started shuffling his feet and making such a noise that everyone turned round to stare at us. I guess he'd never seen a woman with so little clothes on."

When Chiquita and Primitivo had finished their schooling, we planned to ship them to Extremadura in a truck. But Primitivo was opposed to this modern means of transporting a perfectly healthy horse.

"It would be much safer to ride the mare to Pascualete," he insisted, not at all dismayed at the prospect of a one hundred and fifty five mile ride on horseback. "It might take a bit of time, but she would arrive in good condition."

We sent her by truck, but as it turned out, Primitivo was right. When we finally saw the mare again , she was covered with cuts and bruises and the trip almost lamed her.

After that, I rarely argued with Primnitivo about the horses, but with Maria, I still tried to maintain a facade of knowledge. Her greatest worry was spending a peseta and she filled entire rooms with things I had thrown out, saying that perhaps one day we would need them. She even ironed the tissue paper in which my maid packed my clothes. So it was not a surprise to me when one day she said:

"Really, if the Senores Condes are going to have so many house guests every week-end, then we must do something about the eggs. It is a shame the fortune we are spending on eggs."

I had noticed that somehow we managed to consume around sixteen dozen eggs in a weekend and agreed with her.

"What shall I do about it, Maria?"
"Well, the Senora Condesa could raise chickens of her own. And I will be able to help her tremendously, for if I do say so myself, I have a magic hand with chickens. Primitivo says it is something one is born with. You see how strong my chickens are and how they produce!"

This seemed a wonderful idea to me and so from my american agriculture books I planned a glamorous modern chicken coop to hold about one hundred laying chickens.

As I had to spend so much time elsewhere since we were now building a house on the coast in Marbella, most of this new endeavor had to be done by mail. Of course there were no telephones in Pascualete until years later. After returning to Madrid, I received the following letter from Maria, written for her by Primitivo in his laborious script. Although the wording may be tiresome for the reader, it is an exact translation: I have carefully preserved all her letters.

"My excellent Senora, of all my consideration, I take the pen in hand to communicate to the Senora Condesa that the house of the chickens is almost finished. It is indeed very pretty and the bricklayer says it is fine enough for people to live in. It gives me pain to inform the Senora Condesa that the bill for the construction of this chicken house is 'una barbaridad', tremendous. I have refused to pay it, as it is 12,000 pesetas, I

do not permit the money of the Senores Condes to be taken by thieves. I hope the children are well and Senor Conde enjoys good health.

Affectionate remembrances from she who has the honour to serve your Excellency.

Your affectionate and Faithful Servant who kisses your hand.

Maria Maestre, Pascualete 10 February

Grudgingly, Maria was persuaded to pay the bill for 12,000 pesetas, plus another for 8,000 for the furnishings and materials. I told her to prepare for the arrival of some wonderful white laying chickens, one hundred in all, which I had ordered at the huge price of l95 pesetas apiece. but I had heard that these chickens were famous for producing more eggs than ordinary ones. I explained to Maria that each of these chickens would have a metal number around its foot and from this she could record the number of eggs each chicken produced. But Maria was not impressed and several weeks later wrote again:

"My Excellent Senora, of all my consideration, I take the pen in hand to communicate to the Senora Condesa that the pretty white chickens arrived. They match very nicely the white house of the chickens. But it gives me much sadness to inform the Senora Condesa that many chickens have died. 22 in number. The veterinarian says that these are very delicate Madrid chickens and it is too cold for them here in Pascualete. He also says that if the others are to survive they must have a special food and they must take many vaccines against the sickness..."

Affectionate remembrances, etc.

Maria Maestre Pasacualete, 2 April.

Maria's letter was indeed a blow, but even after a bill from the vet for 15,000 pesetas for the vaccinations, vitamins and services, I was still undaunted. Indeed, I was told to send to France for a particular oyster shell which was supposed to be especially appetizing to these chickens and I wrote Maria detailed instructions as to the mixing of the food and the feeding of the chickens. Faithfully, Maria kept me posted on their progress.:

"My excellent Senora etc...We received the food and your instructions are followed very carefully. But we feel it is necessary to inform you that as of today only sixteen of the chickens are still with us. The doctor says it was the pneumonia. It is very strange indeed that they should die because my own chickens are very well this year and so far, Gracias a Dios, thanks to God, none have been ill..."

Maria Maestre, Pascualete 7 October

Madrid
Dear Maria,
You will be happy to know that I have bought another 100 chickens, but this time I have not made the same mistake. They will not be sent until they are a little older and they will have all their vaccinations before they arrive. It was explained to me very carefully that the best laying chickens are the most delicate and that one must be prepared for a few disasters in the beginning. Let us hope we have better fortune this time etc...

La Senora Condesa

"My Excellent Senora, etc... I take the pen in hand to inform you that of the 50 surviving chickens we have managed to

collect one dozen eggs. I knew this would give the Senora Condesa great pleasure. They are smaller in size than usual but this is just the beginning. If the Senroa Condesa would not mind, perhaps these very elegant white lchickens may have a happier and longer life if I could cross them with my own simple but strong chickens. Would the Senora Condesa permit me to try this? Affectionate remembrances etc...."

Maria Maestre, Pascualete

Madrid
Dear Maria,
I have discussed with all the experts about crossing the chickens and they advises against it, since our chickens are such a pure breed. However, the Senor conde estimates that each egg that we finally collected has cost him something like 6,000 pesetas a piece and he says not only do you have his permmission to cross your chickens with mine, but that he ORDERS that it should be done instantly or he will end a ruined man. In fact, I have noticed that recently at the mere sight of an egg the senor Conde becomes very upset, so I urge you, the next time we are at Pascualete, not to discuss the matter in front of him, and try to avoid servings eggs for a while please....

La Senora Condesa

"Excellent Senora, etc....I take pen in hand to inform you that the chickens are laying very well. We have no illnesses. The cross between the Senora Condesa's white chickens and my own is the envy of all Santa Marta. Primitivo took 27 dozen eggs to sell to Don Federico last Saturday. I am sure the Senor Conde will be pleased. I hope that he will have his appetite back again as we have so many eggs, God will punish us for not eating them. Your Affectionate, etc..."

Maria Maestre, Pascualete, April 30

Some letters of this correspondence have been eliminated because our exchange of letters took over a year. I have carefully preserved all the original letters and made an effort to translalte her answers word for word.

During these years my mother and father often came to visit us. They would spend a couple of months in Madrid and would also go frequently with us to Pascualete. Sometimes the house would be filled with other guests at the same time - most frequently for shooting parties. One afternoon I was on the terrace with my mother when Maria brought a tray with the tea that she had asked for. As my mother took the first sip, she made a repulsive grimace. "Aline, this tea is pure poison."

"Mother, don't say that too loud. Someone might hear you.. There is nothing worse than these foreigners who come to Spain and complain about Spanish food, saying that they can't eat this or that, they critize the olive oil, they criticize the amount of fried foods."

"Please Aline don't ask me to drink this horrible spanish tea...."

"Look mother, you must drink that tea. Everybody in this house drinks the same tea and no one else has complained. I don't want my Spanish guests to see that you refuse it," I said as I nodded towards those seated nearby. ""Also it's embarrassing that my own mother insults Spanish food"".

Gingerly she lifted the cup again. "It's going to poison me. I'm sure it can ... kill me."

That evening when I was dressimg before dinner the Countess of Rose, a French guest, came into my room. "Aline, I'm going mad looking for Francois' tobacco. It was in our luggage and it's disappeared."

"What did it look like? Was it in the form of a carton of cigarettes?"

"No. It was pipe tobacco and it was in one of our suitcases ... in a green tea can."

Immediately I rushed to the kitchen. I had taught Maria, who by was the head of the servants how to unpack each guests luggage and to carefully and neatly locate eeverything in its proper place. "Maria who undid the Count and Countess of Rose's luggage this afternoon?"

"I did , Senora Condesa."
"When you unpacked their things, did you see any tobacco."
"No, no tobacco at all, Senora Condesa"
"Did you not see a tea can?"
"What color was it?"
"Green."

"Oh, that can. Yes, I saw a green tea can. Since so many guests bring gifts for the Countess in their luggage, I realized the tea was a gift, so I took it to the kitchen."

Thus I learned that I had obliged my mother to drink pipe tobacco tea. Fortunately before anyone else had a chance to try it we were able to return Francois' tobacco in the green tea can to his room.

One day after the guests had left , I took advantage of a lengthy conversation with Maria, to ask her something that had been puzzling me for a long time. Maria so far only had three children, the youngest was already twelve years old and it did not look as if she planned to have any more. According to the priest in Santa Marta, the main problem for the town was that all the families had too many children and needed too much money to pay for their food . This he had informed me kept the people of the town in a state of poverty. Most of the women in the town had at least ten children and sometimes more.

So on this day since we were alone I asked Maria how she managed to have had only three children .

My question made her a bit nervous. For a few moments she merely looked at the floor and then she answered abruptly, , chair."

CHAPTER TWENTY – THREE

TYRONE POWER
AMERICAN STARS IN MADRID

Spain attracted many famous American film producers during the sixties - the sunny climate which permitted filming daily and above all - everything was cheap. Many of these producers were sent to us by Jack Warner or by the Paleys - through them Luis and became close friends with Deborah Kerr and her husband, Peter Viertel, also Audrey Hepburn and Mel ferrer. Then our bullfighter friend, Luis Miguel Dominguin had a romance with Ava Gardner and we came to be intimate friends with her as well. The Viertels and the Ferrers both loved Spain and eventually bought homes near ours in Marbella. All these stars liked Spain´s climate, the flamenco and the bullfights.

Another movie star friendship ended in tragedy. While visiting Jack 'Warner in Los angeles in 1948, we had met Tyrone Power, an outstanding handsome, swashbuckling star of the twentieth century - his career spanned thirty years and he starred in some sixty films. Ty had come several times to Madrid and each time we went with him to bullfights, flamencos and restaurants. In 1958, he was in Madrid making a film called "Salomon and the Queen of Saba".

He was then married for the third time to a girl called Debbie who was pregnant the night he invited us for dinner at Jockey, the "in" restaurant . But that night none of us had an enjoyable evening - Debbie spent the entire two hours insulting Ty and making disagreeable remarks to him. When as usual we left the reataurant about one a.m. , Ty dropped us off at our house. Luis was so indignant with Debbie's shocking behavior that he quickly rushed up the stairs and disappeared. Ty jumped out of the car to say goodbye to me at my door, whispering, "Aline. I apologize for Debbie. Since she's pregnant, she's not in a good mood these days." He was a charming sweet man, always considerate of everyone. During the dinner he had told me that he had just spent several days in the U.S.A. military hospital in Torrejon on the outskirts of Madrid, checking his health. "My father who was also an actor died at exactly my age, forty-five, of a heart attack while on stage. I don't want the same thing to happen to me. I'm going through a lot of stress during the filming of this picture because I'm not only playing the leading role but I'm also the producer and all my money is tied up in it. Fortunately, the doctors said I'm fine."

The next morning my Maria Luisa awoke me early, "The Senor Dominguin is on the phone and says it is urgent."

Dominguin, apart from being the most famous bullfighter at that moment was also a close friend. Aware that he would not call at such an hour if it were not important, I reached for the phone.

"Aline, sit down, or hang on to something. You might fall down when I give you the news."

"Don't be ridiculous, Luis Miguel. You know you've awakened me. How can I fall down if I'm in bed. Where would I be at..." looking at my clock I saw it was nine-thirty in the morning. Luis was still sound asleep next to me.

" You sleep too late but you'll soon forget the hour. I saw you and Luis in Jockey last night with Tyrone Power."

"Yes, what about it."

"He's dead. I'm coming by to pick you up and take you to the hospital where he was just delivered to the morgue. You and Luis are his only spanish friends, and should do something so the press do not get pictures of him in the state he must be right now."

"How could he be dead? Only a few hours ago, he was fine. He's only 46 years old."

"Well, he's dead. A heart attack on the set a half hour ago. They're taking him to the Clinica Ruber right now. It's near your house and I'll pick you up in twenty minutes."

Luis said he would join us later - to call him if there was something special he could help out with. But I was ready when Dominguin arrived and went to the hospital where we were taken into the morgue - a body covered with a white sheet was laid out on a table.

As Luis Miguel and I took places on either side of the table, the doctor whipped off the covering. I was overwhelmed. Ty was dressed in the Roman toga he had been wearing for the day's filming. It seemed I was looking at someone else. This face was pale, no remembrance of Ty's healthy tanned complexion. The legs protuding from the knee length Roman toga were skinny and white, not the legs of the man who had always been such a treat to dance with. My matador friend was already talking with the young doctor. But I couldn't pronounce a word. My state of shock increased as I stood looking down at this weak, small figure , so different from the handsome sturdy man of a few hours before. Then I noticed a bloody scratch over his nose and questioned the doctor about it - he informed that it was caused when the nose makeup was yanked of while they had tried to revive him. Then I asked why his chin and ears were dark bluish-black. "That" said the doctor, " is the usual result of a massive heart attack."

Luis Miguel now was silently staring down at Ty. He no longer chatted amicably with the intern. Then abruptly he reached out, almost in an involuntary mov ement and flipped Ty's head from one side to the other. I found his gesture shocking, a lack of respect for my dead friend. Then the doctor also began in the same way to toss Ty's head back and forth.

The doctor spoke again . " You see, rigor mortis has not yet set in " as he continued flipping the head back and forth.

For me their gestures were disrespectful and apalling. I realized then that once one is dead, we are all no more than a piece of furniture for hospitals and doctors, but I was surprised that Luis Miguel would react like that as well. For me it was an unforgettable moment. I would have liked to touch gently the face so recently alive and filled with charm and kindness.

But Luis Miguel remained absorbed a few more silent moments observing the dead body, isolated, it seemed from us. When he spoke again he shocked me still more. "How long does it take for decomposition?" The doctor offered a few explanations. I started towards the door. In the hallway as we exited, the press flashed photos of the famous matador who was now a short distance ahead of us . While the doctor and I traversed the long hall, he said - "I often have treated matadors wounded in the ring. Always I've noticed that they are obsessed with death. Dominguin is the greatest matador nowadays - he faces death each day when he walks into the ring. The sight of Tyrone Power suddenly dead, as might happen to him today or tomorrow, has naturally had a substantial effect on him. Bullfighters are not like anybody else. Their lives are constantly plagued with the reality of sudden death."

While I remained at home, depressed and ruminating about Ty's terrible end, Luis was helping with the arrangements for the complicated transferr of the body to America. We both felt certain that Ty's rude wife Debbie had been in great part responsible.

Neither the Viertels nor the Ferrers, were in Madrid when Tyrone died, both couples lived part time in Switzerland. However they were shocked and sad when they learned the sad news, They had known Ty well and agreed that he had been a specially wonderful person. These couples came often as the years progressed, sometimes to make a film.

Deborah and Audrey were kind, unassuming and rarely talked about their work- both were among the best real friends I ever had. In fact I forgot that Deborah was a great actress until I saw her on stage for the first time a couple of years later in London in "Day After The Fair." When she walked onto the stage at the beginning of the play, I sensed the enormous presence she emanated - then after the great applause subsided , she began the play totally transformed into the personage. I was very impressed as was the entire large audience. In the same manner, Audrey was so shy that it was hard to believe she had already become a famous star. Both women were much in love with their husbands which was understandable. Peter Viertel was an author and script writer of many famous films and attractive and much fun. He had a special enchantment for children, my three sons adored him - he taught them to ski, to surf, and though he was a great player himself, even had the patience to play tennis with them. The Viertels lived part time in Klosters where Peter was an avid skier. Deborah did not ski but she certainly looked great in a bathing suit on his boat in Marbella.

Audrey was a unique person. It was not merely her good looks, nor was she especially out-going, but she had such kindness and love for everyone, such truthfulness in her friendships plus a bewitching sense of humor. One cold grey day in February I drove out to her house on the outskirts of Madrid to have lunch with her. Mel was working on a film in Madrid at the time. "Aline,"she said, before we sat down, I want to show you a surprise I've prepared for Mel and then tell me what you think of it."She led me into their bathroom and pointed out the window. Despite the cold wintry day, a huge patch of bright colored flowers were blooming in the brown frozen earth as if they had just sprouted.

"Mel looks out this window every day when he shaves. Don't you think he'll be surprised when he looks out tomorrow morning," she giggled. "It's his birthday. That looks like summer doesn't it?"

Mel Ferrer spoke spanish fluently - his grandparents had come from Barcelona to Cuba and then to the USA. Audrey had a flair for languages; she spoke French, English, Italian, Dutch and picked up Spanish in weeks. Mel was handsome, debonair - all women were charmed by him, and he was a delight to be with. I was astounded when they divorced several years later.

Both the Viertels and the Ferrers soon made Spain their center of activities. When in Madrid together we went to the elegant popular restaurants of Jockey and Horcher's. But more often we went to bistros such as Valentin's, "el Botin" and "Lucio", all in the old part of the city. Some of those places had been familiar to me since my first OSS days in Madrid.

In the sixties when nightclubs and restaurants with flamenco shows began to open in Madrid, I became so enthralled with the gypsy music and dancing, that I started taking lessons. Pastora Imperio was already over seventy but she was the most famous singer and dancer of those times and an long-time friend of Luis' - she came to our home to give me lessons. Although I tried for several days, there was no way I could learn the steps - each time she did the steps differently. Pastora had picked up the complicated dance forms from seeing her mother and grandmother perform but she also improvised her own steps according to her inspiration of the moment, as is the case with great interpretors of flamenco.

Pastora's daughter had married the gypsy bullfighter, Gitanillo de Triana, and they opened the first flamenco nightclub, "El Duende" which became very popular. One night we took Lauren Bacall there when she was visiting us. Bacall, a good dancer herself, couldn't resist attempting the flamenco – after an hour or so and a few "copas" of anis, she jumped up on the small stage. The gypsies were delighted but changed immediately to a rumba which is an easier rythmn - she spent much time on the stage twisting and twirling but she was not able to imitate the flamenco steps and gestures. It demands magical gesticulations and movements totally unrelated to any other kind of dancing movements.

Several years later Gitanillo was killed in a car accident at six A.M. while returning from a wild flamenco party at Luis Miguel Dominguin's country estate outside Madrid.

During the seventies on a visit Frank Sinatra made to see Ava Gardner who was then living in Madrid, Ava invited us and a few other friends to a Madrid restaurant with a flamenco show. Before we had finished dinner, she whispered to me, "I'm going to ask your husband to accompany me to find better dancers. These gypsies aren't good enough for Frank. Don't say we're leaving. I want to surprise him and anyhow we'll be right back." Ava had been preparing for Frank's visit for weeks—spending days cleaning her apartment herself and studying the recipes of his favorite dishes which she intended to cook for him. But unfortunately this visit was to end badly just like many of the flamenco ballads where love affairs are usually doomed.

A few minutes after she had left, Frank turned to me with an irritated tone of voice , "Where's Ava?" I explained that she had gone to find better flamencos. "The hell she has. She's gone off with some man," he growled.

I tried to calm him, "She's with my husband and there's no reason to worry. They'll be back as soon as they find the gypsies."

After cursing and complaining for about twenty minutes, he left the table in a fury. Only minutes later Ava arrived, radiant, accompanied by five great dancers. When she discovered Frank had left , she went out herself and looked for him in every bar and hotel in the city . Finally she went home where she spent the next two weeks drinking away her sorrows.

Mel Ferrer enjoyed bullfights but Audrey did not - that was the one spectacle she refused to attend. However Peter and Deborah were real fans and went often. When the season began in April, if they were in Spain , we would go with them to the Madrid bullring. We always bought "barreras", ringside seats, although those tickets were and still are expensive, but for us any price was worth being close to the drama. During the Fair of San Isidro in May, the feast of Madrid's patron saint, there are fights every day for almost a month and seats in the "tendidos", higher rows, are less expensive, but one enjoys the excitement much more seated in the "barreras." It was exciting to exchange a glance with our matador friends during the fight. Ever since the days when Juanito Belmonte was fighting I had known the top bullfighters and when I married Luis, I continued to have many matador friends. Of course the bullfighters loved having famous stars in the ringside seats during their "corridas" . Deborah Kerr and Ava Gardner sometimes accompanied us so we were often favored with the matadors bright capes thrown over the railing in front of out seats. On those days, if the matador was especially successful and if he received an ear as prize, he often threw it up as was customary, to one of our group . Although Spaniards considered this a great honor, most of our foreign women friends were horrified with the gruesome gift.

In the fifties and the sixties Luis MIguel Dominguin and Antonio Ordonez were the main attractions in the big Madrid arena; both were tall and handsome - often one of our visiting women friends would fall for one of them. After Ava Gardner´s romance with Dominguin , Lauren Bacall became infatuated with him. Even after Luis Miguel married Lucia Bose, a beautiful Italian actress, his "conquistas" continued to pursue him and they finally destroyed his marriage. It was difficult for an attractive top bullfighter to escape the adulation and pursuit of many women. In Spain in the forties and the fifties and sixties a matador held more charisma than any other star in the country.

CHAPTER TWENTY – FOUR

PUPPY, FELIPE 2, EBOLI

One day Luis' elderly Aunt, the Duchess of Pastrana came to have tea with me.- she was of medium height, had a prominent nose like her father, the abuelo, lively but squinting blue eyes under gilt rimmed glasses. Her long square face with pale skin had been briefly powdered - her grey hair was swept up into a bun under a smallish black hat encircled with a narrow brown ribbon. She must have been sixty-eight then, which to me made her seem a very old lady. Her black crepe dress was long, although above the ankles, obviously custom-madeand adorned with white lace down the front, the long sleeves had cuffs of the same lace. The hour was exactly six - fifteen, the normal time for tea in Madrid - I realized that as usual by now Tia Casilda's chauffeur had already run up our steps from the street and was probably seated at the kitchen table chatting with Felisa who would offer him a cup of coffee..

"Tia" (aunt) Casilda was not typical of Spanish ladies of her age, She lacked their coquetish mannner, in contrast she appeared austere. Probably because she was not beautiful she was less apt to dress fashionably, but she was known to be extremely intelligent and had the respect and admiration of the entire family. After I had the opportunity of knowing her for several years, I became aware that she was especially liberal in her points of view and not at all austere as most people believed.

As we made ourselves comfortable on the yellow damask sofa Luis had inherited from his grandmother Torre Arias, I became aware of Aunt Casilda's light fragrance, a lavender scent, popular with ladies of her generation. The walls of the room were yellow to compliment Luis' collection of blue and white china and above our heads was the portrait of an ancestor attributed to Goya's assistant, Agustin Esteve. In other parts of the room, were three Goya paintings, also a Tiepolo and a Teniers, all of which Luis had inherited – other more modern paintings surrounded us as well - my husband constantly added contemporary and modern paintings to his collection.

As we began to talk, I told her about a story I had just read by Theophile Gautier.

"Imagine, Tia Casilda," I said, "what this Frenchman wrote about his trip to Spain in 1840. That's more than one hundred years ago. He was travelling from the French-Spanish frontier to Madrid."

Pepe, in his grey uniform, white gloves and best manner appeared to serve the tea as I continued to explain. "Gautier was in a stagecoach which stopped in towns along the way where they would hook up fresh horses and sometimes pass the night. In a roadside Inn. One night when the carriage made its regular stop near Burgos, Teophile Gautier noticed a young woman with a wicker basket on her arm descending from the carriage. As she passed by him, from the basket Gautier heard a whimpering sound, similar to that of a baby. He watched the red-cheeked girl as she walked to the back of the room to sit at an isolated table and proceeded to open the basket, and take out a small puppy. Then, to his astonishment, he saw her unbutton the blouse of her dress, lift the puppy to her breast, and begin to nurse it."

Tia Casilda was listening attentively as she took one of Felisa's cookies. I continued. "A fellow traveller at the same table, noticing Gautier's surprise, informed him that in Spain such scenes were customary. "That young girl", the other traveler told him, "is undoubtedly from the Basque country. Basque women are known to have especially good milk, and she's probably on her way to Madrid to fullfill a job as wet-nurse in some well-to-do family."

Tia Casilda smiled. "Well, Aline, I'm going to tell you a secret I've not divulged to anyone. But you must not repeat it," she said. Furtively she glanced towards the door, her expression making clear that she wanted to be sure neither Pepe nor anyone else was within hearing distance.

"My dear," her soft voice went on as she patted my arm. "Nothing amazing about that at all." A short pause. I sensed she was deliberating how she would word her next sentence. " About forty years ago I had an illness, I don't remember what it was—during the time I was nursing my first child. On one of the doctor's visits to my house -in those days we never went to hospitals - he brought a cardboard box with him which as he entered my bedroom he placed on a chair. Then he approached my bed."

""Now, Duchess," he said, "Today I have a little gift for you. Something especially advantageous for your baby too." The doctor was not his usual self, he was obviously uneasy, his thick white eyebrows were twitching - I wondered why. Then he continued. "Since it is detrimental for your child to partake of your milk while you are sick," his voice bec ame very solemn, "but it is also important that you do not lose your milk which will happen if your milk is not kept flowing - I have brought you a remedy." Then the doctor turned around and picked a small puppy from the box. I can still see it—tan with black spots. Such a cute little spaniel. He placed the soft furry thing in my arms."Duchess, if you nurse this puppy just as you did your daughter, you will not lose your milk, and when you are well, you will be able to feed your child again. I beg of you, Duchess, to heed my advice and to pardon my suggesting something that might be offensive to you."

Aunt Casilda grinned. "Well my dear Aline, that is exactly what I did. And it was a practial system. I became very fond of that puppy and when my illness disappeared I could return to feeding my baby. Now remember, child, I count on you not to tell anyone."

Having nursed three children of my own, I could appreciate the common sense of such a method and even wondered how it was that in France a century ago this system had not been the general practice too. Or perhaps, I thought, Theophile Gautier had no small children in his family and was ignorant of such matters. Gautier evidently traveled frequently – he also went in 1869 to Egypt for the opeining of the Suez Canal. I had made a point of reading more of his books.

Having satisfied my curiosity about Gautier's story, there was another topic I wanted to find out about. In the family it was known that Tia Casilda was particularly well informed on historical matters. And in this case, she was the direct descendant of the woman I wanted to know about - the famous sixteenth century beauty, the Princess of Eboli. In fact, she, tia Casilda, carried that woman's title today. That first Duchess of Pastrana had used more often the title of Princess of Eboli which title had been given to her husband by the Pope when he was sent as Ambassador to Eboli in Italy, a post in those days belonging to the Spanish Monarch, Felipe the Second. Grandees often have many titles, but use most frequently the one they prefer or which sounds best socially at that moment. The Eboli title, being a papal title and therefore not inheritable, was not continued on by the family, they, in future generations used the Duke of Pastrana title. Ever since I'd read the tragic story of the woman who was usually referred to as the Princess of Eboli, I had wanted to question Tia Casilda about her famous ancestor whose life had been extremely dramatic.

When still young and beautiful, she was left a widow and at the time considered the most alluring lady of the aristocracy - she was also very wealthy and known to possess a spirited personality. Unfortunately these outstanding attributes led the great spanish King Phillip the Second, the most powerful man in the western world at that time, about 1575, to fall in love with her. King Phillip was married for the fourth time, old and not attractive. The young Princess consistently rejected his attentions. Meanwhile the King's handsome young secretary of State, Antonio Perez, had also become enraptured with the Princess and his advances were more successful: soon a secret love affair existed between the two. Before long a malicious colleague informed the king that he had been duped by Antonio Perez, his closest confident, and by the much admired Princess of Eboli , that they were having a romance. The King's fury was immediate; Antonio Perez was put in a dungeon - the princess was emprisoned in an ancient tower in one of her extensive properties in Pinto, a town near Madrid. Only a year later when she was almost dying of the cold in the tower did the King give permission to her relatives to allow her to be moved to her palace in the town of Pastrana.

When I asked Aunt Casilda to tell me what she knew of the story , she told me that the two palaces where the Princess had been imprisoned were hers today. These propertieis had never left the family in the four and a half centuries since the Princess' emprisonment. Aunt Casilda added that she visited both properties regularly because they produced part of her income, both were valuable farms with sheep and wheat.

"Is there any chance I could visit either Pinto or Pastrana?"

"Nothing could be easier, my dear. It just happens that tomorrow I'm going to Pinto with my daughter Teresa, and you could come with us." Aunt Casilda looked at her watch. "Oh, but I have been here too long. The story of my ancestor, the first Duchess of Pastrana, is a long complicated one, my dear. Tomorrow I will tell you more. This ancestor was an unusually beautiful woman. Perhaps you have seen her painting in the Prado Museum. You couldn't forget it. She has a black patch over one eye. Yet strangely enough the patch does not detract from her attractions. It is said in the family that she lost her eye when she was eleven playing with her brother. Fencing, I believe was what they were doing. Her tragic story has been passed down in the family from generation to generation so I am aware of most of the details."

The next day I was thrilled to be on my way with Tia Casilda and her daughter to see the tower where the poor princess had been imprisoned. We took the main highway to Andalucia, a route to Aranjuez, where my husband had some property so I had often been there. I well remembered the romantic surroundings and the view of the river Tajo amid gardens and tall forests - in the Spring the tall trees bordering the river change color and provide one of the few autumn scenes of orange, red and yellow falling leaves in a country where few trees exist –and where in the early eighteenth century Spanish kings and their guests used to stroll. Spanish King Felipe the Fifth, grandson of King Louis the fourteenth of France, had built a palace and formal gardens there - it is also a place to step back into history. An important historical drama occurred in Aranjuez when Napoleon's troops in 1808 kidnapped the main assistant of the spanish king Carlos the fourth which led to his exile in France and four years of war while Napoleon attempted to anex Spain. All this is only ten miles from the tower in Pinto where the Princess of Eboli was imprisoned.

As we drove that day Aunt Casilda provided more details of the drama. "Antonio Perez, "she started, "was already married and therefore could not marry her, so they maintained a love affair as secretly as possible. The Princess' husband had been much older than she; she had been married when she was thirteen, a custom normal in the sixteenth century. In her ten years of marriage while still almost a child, she had given birth to ten children. Perez was her own age, brilliant and charming;

and she was probably in love for the first time. They did their best to be loyal to the king, making every effort to keep him and everyone else in ignorance of their romance. But when rumor reached the King that they had become lovers, he had them followed and realized their alliance was a fact. Also later they both admitted the truth." Aunt Casilda sighed. "Then King Felipe acused them of heresy and betrayal to the country. It was easy for him to accuse them of this since he was a defender of the terrifying Inquisition. This accusation appears to me to have been an effort to hide his jealousy and his punishing them for personal motives."

"You never told me all this, Mama", interrupted Teresa.

"You never asked me, my child." Teresa was the Duchess of Andria, another title of the Princess' family.

By now the car was stopping at a gate. Through the iron grated entrance I could see the impressive stone tower standing alone in the middle of a barren field. We had passed through the town of Pinto without even noticing it - a small village in those days with few houses and shops. An employee in a wide brimmed dark hat, a brown cordoroy uniform and a broad smile appeared to open the arched iron grilled entrance. The car continued towards the large austere stone tower, impressive because of its ancient origin and impregnable appearance. In front of the building two men bowed profusely as Aunt Casilda descended. A short conversation ensued about the number of lambs that had been born that month. Teresa and I stood to one side until the explanations came to an end, then one of the shepherds proceeded to open the thick wooden door of the tower with old enormous keys like those of Pascualete. All ancient buildings in Spain seemed to require huge keys. A circular stone stairway led upwards. As we mounted I could see that each floor comprised one room, the size and form of the tower with one small window. There was no indication that any of the floors we passed had ever been been used as living quarters. The building was simply one round tower of stone, four stories high, typical of the middle ages when these towers had served as watchtowers. It was difficult to imagine that anyone had ever inhabited this inhospitable building. I shivered. It had been warm in the car but here it was damp and cold.

Aunt Casilda noticed my gesture. "Well, my dear, the temperature here is nothing compared to that up above in the top floor where my poor ancestor was imprisoned for eighteen months. Come we must go up where you can see for yourself."

Out of breath we arrived at the last stone step. Here there was a wall and a door. The guard produced another huge iron key with which he unlocked the door, then he slid aside an iron bolt and the rustic wooden portal squeaked open. From a long narrow window only a gloomy grey light entered the room. No fireplace, no furniture and the room was smaller than the others.

Tia Casilda stepped inside and we followed. "Well, my dear, here we are. That climb always tires me. From this window I can see all my property, but I must admit I do not come often."

One battered rustic stool was located next to the lone narrow barred window as if someone had been standing on it to look out. A wooden table and three chairs were scattered helter skelter, two were turned over. A metal arabic brazier with some dead grey ashes in one corner.

"Sometimes I've done accounts at this table with my administrator," Aunt Casilda mumbled as she sat down to recover her breath. "But I do not intend to do any such thing today; it's too cold." She shivered as she looked around. "I've often wondered how my fragile ancestor could have resisted this temperture and terrible isolation. She was said to be twenty six years old, small and slight yet a very good horsewoman. But she must have been strong to have resisted living here."

Teresa and I picked up the fallen chairs of thick wood, with straight backs and no cushion or even a straw mat to improve their uncomfortable appearance. "Take into account, my dear," Aunt Casilda was saying, "this lady had been pampered and had lived in luxury all her life. Imagine her emotions the day she was brought here."

There was nothing that invited investigation. I went to the window. The view outside was desolate – only flat open country with many sheep grazing on a sparse field. Very little of the small town of Pinto could be seen above the stone wall of the property.

"But" I asked, "was there no chimney? And what about furnishings? Where did they cook her food."

"She must have brought from her luxurious palace in Madrid carpets and warm clothes and as much furniture as could be fitted into this small space. At that stage of her torture she was still permitted a few minor comforts and if you think this is bad, it was great comfort in comparisom to what happened to her later on. There was never a chimney in this building. Certainly she must have used a brazier or two or three for heat. The guards probably brought burning embers up the stairs from fires maintained outside the tower. Probably her food was cooked outside as well. But she herself was not allowed out of this room. What I have often wondered is how frequently was she given water to wash? We have no idea. The family archives did not include any mention of those details. The cruelty of that king terrified everyone to such an extent that no one dared put in writing something that could be held against him - although we do have a letter in our archives that one of her daughters had written saying that the King had a repellent odor. Remember those were the days of the Inquisition, and it was prohibited to bathe."

We did not stay long. On the way back to Madrid, I pestered Aunt Casilda until she promised to take me to

Pastrana, the other place where the Princess of Eboli had been imprisoned. She promised to do so on her next visit to that property which would be in the month of February. I kept reminding her until we finally went a few months later - this time we left Madrid in the opposite direction. We took the road to Guadalajara. I knew this province quite well since the abuelo Romanones had much property there and most of the family titles carried names of villages in this province. Titles in Spain are different from last names, usually they are the name of the town where the nobleman owned large extensions of land.

The town of Pastrana was larger and much further away from Madrid than Pinto. Although here it was still winter, the countryside was beautiful, beginning to show green with rolling hills, valleys and mountains in the distance. Already a few almond trees were in blossom making a pink and white splotch of color in the landscape. As we went through the town of Pastrana, Aunt Casilda had the car stop in front of an ancient granite two story building, the home of her farm administrator. She left the message that she was on her way to the house in the finca; then we drove a mile further on to the center of her property. When the car pulled up in front of an old stone palace, I asked if this was the palace where the Princess of Eboli was imprisoned the second time and where she had died.

"No, my dear, she was never imprisoned in this house. When she was allowed to leave Pinto because of ill health, the King's orders were that she could live in this palace with the condition that she did not leave the property surrounding it. I suspect the King felt she would have long since forgotten about Antonio Perez who had been all that time in a dungeon."

Tia Casilda gestured towards the house and the surrounding property, "this place must have seemed like heaven after that freezing damp tower. She was ill when she arrived but with the companionship of her family and children and their care and affection, she soon improved enough to be able to go for walks and ride her horses again."

By now we were entering the ancient palace. Although the large rooms were furnished, the house had an abandoned air. It was obvious that Tia Casilda spent little time here. "We only use this house to put up family and friends when they come here for a partridge shoot", she commented as an excuse for the baren atmosphere.

A maid appeared, probably the wife of the guard, asking Aunt Casilda if she would like some tea. Then we continued on to a smaller room where warm yellow rays of sunlight were dancing on a worn carpet giving a slight feeling of coziness. Aunt Casilda indicated that we sit at a round table in one corner. A floor-length dark green velvet cloth covered the "mesa camilla" and as customary we lifted it over our knees and felt the warmth of the burning coals in the "brasero" underneath. The warmth rising from the hot embers kept us snug while aunt Casilda contined the story about her famous ancestor.

"The truth about the first Duchess of Pastrana, who you, Aline, call the Princess of Eboli, is tragic," began Aunt Casilda. "I am always unhappy when I recall that poor woman. The famous Antonio Perez, evidently was handsome, charming and very clever - also had friends willing to risk their lives for him, a real leader with a manner that impressed men. Even when he had been imprisoned by the King, those who had worked for him still held him in high esteem and maintained a true affection for him. And when the time was ripe his jailors helped him plot his escape."

The guardesa appeared with tea and cookies which Aunt Casilda explained were cookies from the adjoining convent where for centuries the nuns had made them from an ancient recipe. "Surely the Princess of Eboli also ate these same cookies," she added. The delicious cookies of honey and almonds were very similar to those I often bought in a convent in Trujillo. Aunt Casilda continued as we munched on them.

"My ancestor's tragedies were not over." Tia Casilda stopped to take another bite. "Months after the King gave the Princess the right to live on her own properties, Antonio Perez managed his escape. Unfortunately that valorous man was so enamored of my ancestor that he made the mistake of going to see her on his way to liberty. He waited for nightfall, thinking noone other than his two companions would follow him. Of course, he was putting his own life in great danger by prolonging his trip to France and freedom but he probably did not realize he was also endangering her. This property was a short deviation from his route to Andorra, a province near the French border over which King Felipe had no jurisdiction and where he could not apprehend him. Antonio Perez managed the short detour and then was able to spend a brief two hours with the princess of Eboli. If anything proves that this man was in love with her, that visit certainly does. But he had to race off, knowing that by this time the King would have learned of his escape and would place hundreds of soldiers on his trail."

I interrupted her, "I read that Antonio Perez' exile eventually took him to France and to England, and that he lived for many years after that."

"Yes," said Tia Casilda, "in fact he lived four years longer than King Phillip, but meanwhile my poor ancestor had a terrible destiny. When the King learned that Antonio Perez had visited her on his successful trip to freedom, his fury became still greater. Probably he was even more incensed because of having been outwitted again by Perez. At any rate since King Felipe could not apprehend Perez, he took his revenge out on my poor ancestor. This time he ordered her to be imprisoned in another palace, one she owned in the middle of the town of Pastrana."

Aunt Casilda now stood up. "Since we have finished our tea, after I take care of a few errands with my employees, we will go to that palace and I will show you exactly where she ended her days. Unless you see the place, you will not appreciate the full horror."

   A half hour later we were in the middle of the town looking up at the ancient fifteenth century stone palace. When we entered the abandoned stone building, the rooms inside were empty and had the damp chill of a church. No one spoke as I followed "Tia" Casilda through one room after another, up one floor and then up another until we reached a narrow stone spiral stairway which led to a small tower room. The entire building held an atmoshphere of gloom. It appeared that noone of the family had lived in this palace since the Princess of Eboli had died there four hundred years before. Now and then someone pushed a button on a wall and a pale light would illuminate our way, so the building must have been used for something. But electricity was the only scant sign of modernity in the desolate edifice. Deep shadows added to the aura of gloom. Already I knew much of what Auint Casilda was going to tell me. When we reached the tower, the door was ajar, here the abandonment and decay were similar— shutters were falling off the open windows of a balcony window which provided the only light.

"Come in, come in, my dear," said Tia Casilda as I stood in the doorway observing the dismal surroundings. "come in and just try to imagine a woman locked in here, as she was, in this cold barren room. It was as you see it now—no chairs, no bed, no carpets. Even worse, the King had ordered that she be locked in alone, that the window be blocked out so she could not see even the sky. A hole was made in the door through which her food was passed. No one was permimtted to talk to her.And here she had to remain until death."

I swallowed as I listened. The truth was hard to absorb, even though I had read those same facts. Tia Casilda had more to say. "One of her daughters, a young girl sixteen years old, prevailed on friends to influence the King to allow her to be locked up with her mother; they were cemented in - more or less. Permission for the daughter was conceded. The balcony window was allowed open only for one hour a day, the door was cemented closed so that noone could enter. That woman, still very young and her little daughter lived here some two years. She was only thirty-six years old when she died; her first child had been born when she was fourteen."

I listened in silence as the Duchess continued, "The daughter who had chosen to remain with her mother entered a convent after her mother died. Antonio Perez spent the rest of his life trying to invent plots - first to free the Princess and after she died to damage the reputation of King Felipe."

"Yes" I interrupted, "Antonio Perez made contact with Queen Elizabeth of England and with Henry the fourth of France. He spent several years in London and made various trips there from Paris where he lived his many years of exile. During this time he attacked King Felipe the Second in books and published articles encouraging other Spanish exiles to maneuver against the throne. Felilpe Segundo declared Perez a traitor to his country, and had him condemned for heresy in absence, using as an excuse Perez's jewish ancestry."

Tia Casilda interrupted me. "Aline, did you know that even after King Felipe the Second died, which was several years before Antonio Perez, the family never dared to note in our archives any details of this terrible family tragedy. Most historians gave the version demanded by the monarchy, that both the Princess and Perez were traitors and heretics. But what I have told you is as exact as anyone could know. You'll not find all the truth in any history book written in that period. During those years everyone was afraid of the King and of the Inquisition."

King Felipe the Second, began to interest me more than ever after my visits to Pinto and to Pastrana. Despite my dislike for him after learning about his treatment of the Princess of Eboli, I became aware that his reign for Spaniards remains one of the most important periods in Spanish history. Felipe Segundo had become King when his father Charles the fifth died in 1556; he inherited and ruled the largest empire in the world for forty-two years until his own death in 1598. Spain's territories covered the globe—including a great part of Europe, what is today Germany, Belgium, Holland, much of Italy, colonies in the Far East, and central and south America,, and in Africa. Felipe considered himself defender of catholicism and the Inquisition. The monastery of El Escorial was constructed by him, and there he died. He was reputed to be cautious and undetermined in making decisions although he took seriously his duties as King. He married four times, the second of which was with Queen Mary Stuart of England; if she had not died childless, he could have added England to his empire.

Felipe the second is recognized as having been a wise and competent ruler in many aspects. During his reign Spain's holdings in the new World were augmented. But he also embarked on disastrous undertakings such as the "Armada" in 1588 in an attempt to conquer England by sea. In that disastrous operation the admiral of the fleet was my husband's ancestor, Perez de Guzman el Bueno, descendant of the man who defended the castle of Tarifa in 1338. In the family archives today we can read his notes written in the fancy scrawl of those times on thick yellowed parchment revealing that this Perez de Guzman el Bueno tried to elude the responsibility of directing that attack on England. He stated that he told the King he considered himself incompetent for such a post and that in his opinion the assault on England would be a perilous uncertain endeavor. He also told the king that he hated the sea, that he knew nothing about ships, that he got seasick the minute he stepped into even a small boat. But

King Felipe did not accept his refusal – that Guzman El Bueno's name and fortune would enhance the operation, that it would encourage other wealthy grandees to contribute to the Armada against England which was necessary to enrich Spain and to add to her power. During one whole year all over the country trees were cut down to build the many ships necessary for the project.

Once while driving through a landscape of barren fields, I commented to my husband about how few trees there were in Spain. Luis was quick to answer "King Felipe Segundo had too many trees cut down to construct the fleet for the Armada against England." So I gather that is the opinion of most Spaniards but personally I never believed that was the reason for Spain's lack of trees. Fortunately Franco's government planted many trees all over the country. The Duke of de Medina Sidonia until the last moment continued to refuse to head the naval assault on England, but King Felipe insisted. The shocking failure of the expedition resulted in the loss of almost the entire spanish fleet and seventy-five percent of the men. Most of the Spaniards who managed to swim to the shores of western Ireland were hacked to pieces by the natives - those who landed in Scotland received the same fate. A few, who their captors believed could bring ransoms, managed to return to Spain several years later when their ransoms were paid, but the majority of the men on the ships were lost. It was the greatest sea disaster in the world at that time and a disgrace for Spain. The English lost few ships and only a small percentage of men. Meanwhile in the NewWorld King Felipe's countrymen continued to found new colonies and bring gold back to Spain but the financial loss and that of the cream of spain's manpower caused by the disaster of the Armada must have made king Felipe's last years sad ones. Also he was suffering from gout, wrapped in a cape, sitting in a large chair in his bedroom next to a window which looked down onto the main altar of the monastery of El Escorial. It is said he prayed for his soul and to redeem his sins. Did he include in his prayers a request of forgiveness for having tortured so cruelly the Princess of Eboli and for having so arrogantly sent the cream of Spanish youth to their deaths in the catastrophic Armada despite the warnings that the operation could not succeed?

There were other indications of King Felipe Segundo's jealousy which contributed to my dislike for him as a person. He had a handsome younger illegtimate brother, Juan de Austria. This young prince behaved very courageously and brought victory to Spain in the famous sea battle of Lepanto – as a result Juan de Austria became the popular hero of the day. The King repeatedly refused him permission to marry and also refused him permission to return to his country after military successes during battles in northern Flanders had enhanced his fame. Juan de Austria died in faraway Flanders while serving his country in war at the age of thirty-three. His tomb is in the Monastery of El Escorial; his bier carries the handsome prince's likeness carved in stone - the stone lips appear worn thin - it is said, due to women's kisses over the centuries.

CHAPTER TWENTY- FIVE

ROMAN ORIGINS OF PASCUALETE

Among my friends in the early fifities was a French Monseigneur who I had known in my OSS days - he had been a brave Free French intelligence agent who provided OSS with information on German troop movements. Despite his pompous ecclesiatic dress –the long black robe and bright red cummerbund, Monseigneur was fun and a stimulating conversationalist. Also he was an avid sportsman and was anxious to shoot an "abutarda", a royal bustard, an enormous game bird that had become extinct in the rest of Europe, but was still abundant in our area – that was the reason we had invited him to Pascualete.

When his big black limousine rolled into Pascualete's dusty patio, Primitivo ran out to stand at attention, trying desperately to look dignified in his new uniform in the midst of curious country children, barking dogs and scattering chickens. An immaculately dressed chauffeur in shiny black boots and fancy gold-embroidered hat stepped out and with a great flourish opened the door, revealing a beaming round red face looking out towards us. Radiating his usual charm, Monseigneur emerged with outstretched hands.

"My dear Aline and Luis, what a treat to be able to visit you here in your beautiful country place."

He made a grand gesture at the bedraggled patio as if he were viewing the gardens of Versailles, his tri-cornered shiny black hat under his left arm, his immaculate black cassock swishing in the wind, the long crimson bands of his wide cummerbund making flashes of colour all around him. Even the patio animals—to say nothing of the children—stood back in awe.

As Luis and I led our elderly friend into the house he glanced up at the stone escudo above the door.

"This house has a marvellous atmosphere," he said. "One can feel the strong unbending character of the Spaniards typified by that escudo which has obviously been here for centuries."

Later, as he was sipping a glass of sherry in front of the fireplace, he looked down at the cobble-stone floor.

"But what is this I am stepping on? Do bring the light closer."

Heedless of his flowing skirts he dropped to his knees and began to rub the stones with his fingers to remove the dust.

"How remarkable! Why, this is an ancient Roman tombstone and very legible at that!"

With his contaigous love of drama, in a solemn voice he began to translate the worn inscription on the stone slab:

CAENUS, SON OF CAVCIRIUS, HERE LIES BURIED. MAY THE EARTH REST LIGHTLY ON YOU. HIS DAUGHTER VALERIA SET UP THIS MONUMENT.

When Monseigneur stood up, he declared, "This really is an ancient home you have here. That tombstone is two thousand years old."

As I listened to his words once again I was enticed by the mystery of the building. More and more, it seemed, the ghosts of yesterday were trying to lure me back into an ancient world.

"Monseigneur, I have seen these stones, even in the cattle barns. I never dreamed they might have been here since the Roman colonization of Spain."

"My dear Aline, wherever you find Roman tombstones you can be certain there was Roman life in that very spot. Show me some of these other stones."

Leaving our sherry glasses forgotten on the table, he ran after me into a back room. Even Luis, who susually reserved his enthusiasm for his flower garden or the sight of a bevy of flying partridge, ran behind us. It was difficult to place a flashlight so that the Abbey could read the lettering in the dark window opening; he was obliged to lie on his back on a table with his head resting on the stone ledge to see the inscription which he read to us in a specially solemn tone of voice:

"PUBLIUS RUTILIUS MUNUS, 55 YEARS OLD, HERE LIES BURIED. MAY THE EARTH REST LIGHTLY ON YOU. HIS SON HAD THIS MONUMENT SET UP."

We all exchanged amazed glances. "Everything in this palacio shows the origin as being Roman of the first century. What incredible fortune to own a home two thousand years old."

That evening I took Monseigneur to one of the dark cattle sheds. As Isidora's husband, Paco, lit our way with an oil lamp, Monseigneur began to tell us more about the Roman conquest of Spain.

"After almost two hundred turbulent years of warfare, the Romans settled down to an intensive agricultural exploitation of this hitherto savage country. They cleared entire forests, preparing the land for cultivation, wells were dug and seeds and equipment were brought from Italy. By the second century A.D.," Monseigneur continued, "this spanish colony of Rome was at the peak of her civilization. Spain even provided Rome with great emperors such as Trajan, philosophers such as Seneca and many writers and poets. Extremadura was one of the most important agricultural sources , since it provided a wealth of wool and wheat."

We followed Paco who led us along the line of oxen munching on hay to the end of the long narrow building Monseigneur continued, "The main Roman houses were built around a rectangular patio, exactly like you have here, with the same type of a strong stone center building with small windows and high ceilings."

In the tunnel-like vaulted cow-shed Paco, who until then had been silent, began to speak, the light in his trembling hand making jagged flashes and shadows - Paco was shy but tonight he was excited to find himself addressing such an important personage.

"Pardon me, Your Excellency, but does Your Excellency think Pascualete might once upon a time have been a farm of these Roman people?"

"Yes, my son, there are certainly many indications. These feed troughs, for example, of hard granite are the identical shape the Romans used. You can easily see by the deep grooves on the side where the cattle fed that they are worn by many centuries' use."

"After the Romans lost their control over Spain in the middle of the fifth century, barbarian tribes came in from the north and began to fight each other - these Roman buildings fell into disrepair. Many were occupied by the Arabs when they invaded Spain in the seventh century. All who farmed here in the following centuries profited from the walls and buildings of those first Romans and constructed on top of what remained. The capital of all Roman Spain and Portugal was Merida, which is near here. the amphitheater of Merida is considered the second most important Roman construction left in the world today."

The next day, after shooting a magnificent 30 pound royal bustard, when Monseigneur, before leaving, remarked about the beauty of our house, I knew he meant it.

As we watched him leave, I commented to Luis, "It must be thrilling for you to know that you had ancestors living here centuries ago!"

"I have no idea how long my ancestors lived here. And what´s exciting about that. You also had ancestors living someplace hundreds of years ago."

"But mine were probably peasants who lived in shacks and I don´t even know where they lived." Luis´s lack of pride for his many unusual advantages always amazed me.

Padre Remigio

During most of my trips to the finca in those days I would receive a visit from Padre Remigio, the old priest of Santa Marta. His arrival as I watched from the small medieval window of my bedroom was unique. In hot weather he would be seated backwards on a grey burro, a tattered black umbrella in one hand tottering over his head to protect him from the sun and the folds of his long black frock clutched in the other. The burro would be kicking up puffs of yellow dust along the path that wound in broad curves down the hill from the direction of the village.

But two years after one of these visits ~~one day~~ the racket of a motor cycle surprised us echoing from the direction of Santa Marta. The unusual noise brought all of us running to see what was happening. Within minutes a young priest, his black cossack skirts blowing in the wind, his new round hat of shiny thick velour covered with a thin coat of dust, burst into the patio. He smiled as he jumped off the shiny machine and announced that he was the replacement for Father Remigio who had been retired to a residence for elderly religious persons in Leon in northern Spain.

On my next visit to Santa Marta the young priest invited me to see his improvements on the old priests' house. . His mother and sister were sitting under a lemon tree in the little patio busily crocheting and sewing his socks. What a change! Everything was clean and neat. but in a corner of his simple study there was a pile of dirty torn old yellowed papers which when he saw me looking at them, he went over and picked up some, handing them to me.

"These papers, senora condesa, I found in a damp corner of the old priests's bedroom, buried in filth and falling apart from decay. They are obviously what's left of the archives of the church , but I cannot read the script. It's letters mean nothing to me, I have only been able to discern that a family named Loaisa owned Pascualete in the fifteenth and sixteenth centuries. These papers are very damaged from the dampness of the old church. Perhaps the countess would have some interest in them."

I turned the tattered pages over. Indeed they were in bad condition. some pages had been loosely sewn together in book form with thick yellow cord, but others were just loose, they appeared very anicent indeed, certainly hundreds of years old. I thanked the young priest, grateful that at least I could learn the name of some of Pascualete's past inhabitants. Who knows what those dirty manuscripts would tell me. I was glad to take the pack of torn papers home with me. Placing all back into the worn envelope, I looked forward to studying them. Monseigneur had fomented my curiosity in the history of our ancient but that night when I tried to read the tattered manuscripts I could not make head nor tails of them. I decided to get someone to help me. Early the next morning I started off early to Trujillo. Now that I knew Pascualete had Roman origins and that parts of our house had been constructed in the thirteenth century, I wanted to know what and who filled in the gap between until those Loaisas appeared in the fifteenth century. Only Pillete would be able to advise me how to go about this.

When I found Pillete in the plaza he had no doubts."the only person in Trujillo who knows about history is the old priest, Father Juan Tena, head of the municapal archives. He can read anything."

"Pillete, please take me to him immediately."

"Oh no. That's not possible. Padre Tena does not like to be interrupted in the midst of his reading. Anyhow I don't know where he is now. He may be in one of the convents where he has daily religious obligations. Or in the house of the widow Ramirez, who has been dying for a week now and finds solace in the Padre's prayers. Or he might be in the castle up on the hill, copying some strange markings on the old stones."

Padre Tena was indeed a busy and important person, and it would be very difficult to find him.

"But if the senora condesa just stays here at this little table in the bar near the window, and has a cafe con leche, sooner or later we will see him crossing the plaza, and then I will introduce you."

I had no choice but to resign myself to what seemed to me Pillete's inefficient method of introducing me to Father Tena.

The cafe con leche appeared. The usual bootblack , when he spotted me sitting down, came running carrying his wooden stool in one hand and his box of shoe polishes in the other. "I cannot permit the Senora Condesa to walk about Trujillo with those dusty shoes. Even at my own expense, I will take upon myself this obligation."

I looked down to see what dust could have collected upon my old country Oxfords which Maria had polished to shining brilliance five minutes before I left. As usual neither the ride nor the twenty or so steps from the car through the plaza had impaired Maria's work, but it was such fun to listen to his conversation, that I put up a shiny foot and he went to work.

Just as I was wondering how many cafes con leche it would take for Father Tena to appear, Pillete came running and pointed towards a lone figure in long black skirts crossing the plaza. I nearly knocked over the bootblack in my haste and we both ran out into the bright sunny town square.

Padre Tena's crinkled sparkling blue eyes regarded me quizzically as Pillete explained that I had an urgent matter to discuss with him. Although tall, his back was as bent as any of the farmers, his lined pale face was kind and pleasant. With few words he indicated that I should follow him and we continued through the narrow streets to the old palace which held the city archives.

"Well, Condesa," said the companion at my side. "so you are interested in finding out something about the history of Pascualete. I know your old palace well, I stop there each year on my way to Santa Marta when I go to say mass on the day of their patron saint. You have many interesting things to uncover in that ancient house. I suspect its origin is thirteenth century or even before. The palacio must be intimately linked with that of this noble city of Trujillo."

His voice was soft and warm and I was charmed by his picutresque appearance. His long, white hair hung untidily from under the round straight-brimmed black priest's hat and his ample black skirts revealed many years wear. He glanced at me now and then out of the corner of his eye as he walked along with an amused glint that disturbed me. I could not tell whether he was pleased or annoyed by my inquisitiveness.

"Unfortunately Trujillo's noble families have long since left, but their mark is still here. Some of the greatest names in the history of our country came from Trujillo – this was once a very rich important city- few towns that can boast so many palaces. What do you have in Madrid? Nothing but modern buildings. There is no real history in a city like Madrid that was founded only four hundred years ago."

We mounted two flights of wide stone steps and then a narrow winding wooden staircase which creaked ominously. My new friend pulled out of the deep pockets of his cossack a conglomeration of old keys of enormus size and poceeded to open several doors , all of which led into rooms crowded with shelves bent under the weight of yellowed manuscripts. I followed his shuffling footsteps as he placed two chairs at a table near the window and offered me a seat. This window looked out upon ancient red-tiled rooftops and down into an old patio where scraggly chickens were pecking about the ruins of some beautiful columns.

When I handed father Tena the tattered manuscripts the young priest of Santa Marta had given me, I told him I was having difficulty reading them and asked if he would help me. I wanted to discover the history of my house of Pascualete. He gestured towards the shelves lining the walls. "All these cases contain similar manuscripts of the past centuries. It is impossible for me to read all these papers, child. In these archives you will learn much more than in those papers from Santa Marta. But you will have to attempt to do so by yourself. I will gladly provide you with some manuscripts that I know would be of interest to you." He stood up and went to a shelf at the end of the room, returning with a stack of yellowed pages. "These refer to your property and you can begin with them, they are seventeenth century and may be easier to read than those that you have."

Then he sat down again next to me and told me much about the history of the city from the time of the Romans up to the French invasion—"which," he said, destroyed our notable city forever."

He also told me that the Loaisa family had owned Pascualete and large tracts of land between Trujillo and Caceres for many centuries. "They were one of the ancient families of this city. Their palace was the oldest in the villa. It was called the Casa de la Boveda. Alas...also destroyed by the French."

At home that night, struggle as I may I could not make any sense of the strange markings on the papers Padre Tena had given me. They were as illegible as those from Santa Marta. So the next morning I was back in Trujillo again. This time I waited at the entrance to the archives until the priest appeared. "Father" , I said as soon as he appeared, "How am I going to learn about the history of my house if I cannot maake any sense out of these papers. I cannot read one letter.

I waved the manuscripts in front of him as he proceeded to open the door. While we climbed the old steps he seemed thoroughly amused by my misery. I began to think that he was not so nice after all. He glanced up at me now with his usual fatherly smile.

"Really , child, you are getting into deep water when you aspire to decipher documents unread for centuries. I am the only one in Trujillo who understands this science and I would gladly help you, but I have not the time. I fear neither your american energy nor your american belief that all secrets can be unravelled are sufficient to provide you with the patience you will need to learn to read these manuscripts."

"Father, I cannot understand even the dates on these papers. Is there someone who could teach me how to read these things?"

He laughed out loud. then he said:

"I wondered what you would do when you got face to face with "paleography". Of course you cannot read it, it is ancient script and only people who have studied this science are able to translate those documents."

Now he sat down and took a piece of paper from the table and began to scribble something that looked like an address. Glancing up at me with his usual fatherly smile, he said.

"You will need patience to learn."
"How long will it take?" I was always impatient.
He handed me his little piece of paper.
"I suppose it is useless for me to waste my time discouraging you. Here you have the address of the Conde de Canilleros, a distinguished historian who lives in Caceres. He may find someone to give you lessons."

With the address of the historian in my hand, I felt I was on my way, and determined to see the Count the following day. But Luis had to be back in Madrid and I had to leave with him - that was a big disappointment but I was determined not to rest until I discovered who these Loaisas were and how long the property had been in my husband's family.

CHAPTER TWENTY – SIX

THE WINDSORS

I had met the Duchess of Windsor during my honeymoon in New York in the dinner parties arranged by Elsa Maxwell. The Windsors had become the couple most pursued and commented upon by the world press ever since the Duke´s abdication in 1936. His declaration that he could not fullfill his obligatons as King without the companionship of "the woman I love" had been publicized in every country by radio and press repeatedly ever since. The fact that the handsome young Duke, the most loved of the royal family in England and the most popular royal personality world wide was giving up his throne for a twice divorced american woman, called Mrs. Simpson created one of the greatest international love stories ever known. The Duke had been king of England eight months , although not yet coronated, when he made his formal declaration and it became immediately an event of enormous world importance.

Snce Luis and I were usually the only titled foreigners in these formal dinners we were almost always seated at the same table. After the first encounter we met yearly in New York in the month of November when the social life in the city was at its peak. Maybe because we both were Americans living in Europe or that we had few intimate friends in these parties, the Duchess was always especially kind and affectionate with me. After several years being together in New York she invited Luis and me to visit them in Paris. This began almost thirty years of visits to that lovely house in the Bois de Boulogne.

The arrival was always the same. Martin, the chauffeur, would be waiting at the airport and would drive us in the Duchess' old Packard along his customary route across Paris through the Bois de Boulogne to the Rue de Champs d'Entrainment. At the gate he stopped the car and got out to ring the bell for Germaine, who appeared a few moments later, a short navy cape clasped tightly over her shoulders to protect her from the cold gusts of wind. She opened the huge black iron gilt-spiked gates and the car followed the slightly curving driveway past the line of barren sycamore trees and the low dahlia bushes the duke had planted years before, up to the classic, small turn-of- the century palace which they had rented from the city government when they moved in twenty years before.

Georges, the butler, in gray pants and blue-black tails stood waiting at the bottom of the steps to open the car door. Just behind him was Olegario, a young footman we had sent from Pasculete, proud and self-conscious in his grand uniform – a far cry from the worn cap and corduroy pants he had worn when working in our fields. The Duchess had asked me several years before if I could find a servant for them in Spain and I had sent several from the small town of Santa Marta. They had been delighted with each young man. The Duke said they were far superior to those in France and similar to the old servants he was accustomed to in Buckingham Palace. This particular fellow's father still worked for us in Pascualete as an "alimañero", a gamekeeper to eliminate predatory animals, and I had sent him to the Windsors about six months before.

"Madame la Comtesse" – Georges bowed – "Monsieur le Comte." Georges was smiling as usual.   "Their Royal Highnesses are waiting for you upstairs,"

The Duke and Duchess were standing at the top of the curved marble stairway looking over the railing. "Aline, Luis, come up," the Duchess called out. "We're so glad you've arrived."

The pug dogs were barking, as always. "Oooh, these dogs, David," complained the Duchess. "What a racket! I can't stand it."

"Diamante, shut up! Gin-Seng!" The Duke sounded exasperated. "Shut up, I said!"

The Duchess called out. "Oh, how good to see you."

The pugs continued to bark.

There was an elevator, but we ran up the stairs and, as always, they waited for us on the landing.

His Royal Highness wore a blue checked suit and she a Chanel suit, also blue, with just the right jewelry for daytime, what they called their "sentimental jewelry"---small things they designed together, often in remembrance of trips or special shared occasions, and made by Cartier or Van Cleef.

I curtsied to the Duke and then kissed him hello. I did not curtsy to the Duchess. I never did. They would have appreciated that, but I was too American at the beginning, and then it became a habit.

From the early days of our marriage Luis had informed me that the rules about treatment of members of a royal family are unwavering. A lady always curtsies to members of a royal family, be they man, woman, or child, even though she may be so close a friend as to follow the curtsy with a kiss. The kiss is for the friend and the curtsy is for the ancestry, for the royal blood. So, I always curtsied to the Duke when first seeing him in the morning and when kissing him good-night.

We had arrived at tea time and they led us into the room between their bedrooms, "the boudoir," they called it, a cozy room with a fireplace and French windows overlooking the garden, and with comfortable upholstered armchairs, a sofa, a piano on top of which were masses of photographs of friends, I remember in particular a picture of C.Z. Guest – she was a friend of mine also. A footman set up individual tea tables for us, and Georges brought in the tray. The Duchess went to her chair while the Duke sat in his, next to which the footmen placed a silver tray with tea things.   The Duchess never poured the tea, and in the last years the Duke had arthritis in his hip, which made it a painful effort to get up from a soft chair, so I always stood up to do it, but I never succeeded.

The Duke would stop me. "Aline, Aline, let me do the tea."

"Sir," I said, "don't bother to get up."

"But don't be silly, Aline." He strained painfully to get to his feet and hold the teacup out to me.

"Sir, that's hurting your hip."

"Oh," he said, as if the word were *Bah!* "I never pay any attention to that."

The first time we stayed with the Windsors, in my excitement I called him "Your Majesty. That was, of course, after his abdication. "Aline," he said, "It's not 'Your Majesty.' "If it's anything, it's 'Your Highness', but defintely not 'Your Majesty.'" So I usually addressed him as "sir" and spoke to him in the third person, as we do in Spain with royal personages.

I must have embarrassed my kind patient husband many times with my lack of social awarenesses but life with Luis provided me with the opportunity to make up for my ignorances.

The Duke enjoyed his tea, but the Duchess never took anything – there were many little things, tiny puffs of something with cheese on top, or bacon, some were so tiny they dissolved in your mouth instantly.

The Duke took two or three cups, with milk. After a few mintues he looked at my cup. "That tea must be cold." Taking it from my hand, he studied the tea service. "Where's the slop bowl? Georges! You've forgotten the slop bowl! Ah, no, sorry, it is right here on the tray."

Georges never forgot anything. The slop bowl was an antique silver bowl into which the Duke emptied the cold tea from our cups. "I can understand iced tea if it appeals to one, but there is not use for cold hot tea." With a fresh cup of hot tea, he sat back in the armchair and lit a pipe. He smoked relentlessly—the only thing he did which infuriated the Duchess. Every day he finished a tin of pipe tobacco and two packages of cigarettes, and every night he had two cigars.

"What's happening in Spain these day, Aline?" he asked, comfortably puffing on his pipe.

"Things seem to look better every day, sir," I answered. "Luis and I have just bought a piece of property on the southern coast in a place called Marbella that Alfonso Hohenlohe has been developing. It'a a marvelous spot. One can see across the Mediterranean and distinguish not only the Rock of Gibraltar but beyond that the two hills of Ceuta in Morocco. Also, the climate is always good. Alfonso tells us that this is bound to be a good investment, and anyway, it's a nice place for the children, on the coast with our own beach, and the sea is not rough."

"How much do you expect to spend on the building of that house, if you don't mind telling me? he asked.

"We think we can build the house for one and a half million dollars, including, of course, a good-sized swimming pool. The terrace and the inside of the house will be in white marble. Marble is cheap in Spain.

"Do you really think you can build it for that? It's becoming very expensive in France." He turned to her, "Darling, how would you like to have a house in Marbella?"

The Duchess pulled her chair closer. "I would love that, David. You know how I like the sun and the warm weather. I can't bear these gloomy summers in Paris, where it's always raining." She interrupted herself to address her maid, who was passing through the room. "Please press my blue satin for this evening, Ofelia." Then she went on. "You know, we are simply not as rich as the Rothschilds, and we will have to go someplace where it is inexpensive if we want to take on the added expense of a summer house."

They did eventually buy a piece of property next to ours in Marbella and made plans to build there a copy of her favorite seaside house, one she had visited in Hammamet, in Tunisia, belonging to a man named Georges Sebastian. But just as they were about to begin construction, the Duke had to be operated on for an aneurysm in Houston. That was one of the Duchess's few plane trips. They always traveled by train, boat or car, because she was terrified of flying. As for the house in Marbella, they never built it.

"Is life getting as expensive for you in Spain as it is for us in France, Luis?" as the Duke, leaning toward Luis to light his cigarette.

"Not so much, sir. Also, everyone's income is larger than before. There is little unemployment, as a lot of construction is going on. Apartment buildings are shooting up all around Madrid."

"I remember well," said the Duke, "going to your country when I was young. There is probably no country in the world, Luis, where protocol is as strict as in Spain. Did you know that?"

"That surprises me, sir. I thought in England the protocol was much more rigid."

"Not at all. When I was young, I went to Spain to have a good time. I understood that for my first dinner it was perhaps natural that I had an elderly lady next to me, whom I made a point of saying good night to pleasantly; but unfortunately it was not good-bye, because the next day at luncheon I was given the honor again of being her companion. This went on for an entire week. Then finally I was able to go to the Sevilla for the famous F*eria- in Sevilla*. I had some lovely girls in mind that I had seen in photographs. I was still a young lad and wanted to flirt, but what was my dismay when I attended the first dinner in Sevilla to find that I was seated to the very same dowager duchess as had been my companion at every meal in Madrid.."

"I know," said Luis.

"You do?"

"She was my grandmother, sir."

We all roared with laughter.

"She was the first *dama* in the court at that time," explained Luis.

Looking annoyed at the clouds of smoke, the Duchess glanced in my direction nodding to me and when the two men began to discuss racehorses, the Duchess gave me a knowing glance. "Aline, while our beaus talk, I want to show you what I´m wearing to the Rothschilds' ball on Saturday. Givenchy made the dress. The headdress was an idea of Raimundo Larrain, who is a genius. The whole thing cost a fortune and I´m not sure I should have spent so much."

When we reached her room her pug followed and when she sat down he jumped up on the sofa at the foot of her bed.

"I've planned a quiet dinner for you and Luis at home tonight. Two tables of eight. Edouard, my hairdresser, will be here for me at six, Aline. Of course you want him to come up and do our hair also, don't you?"

Every day of her life, the Duchess had Edouard, from Alexandre's, come to the house in the Bois de Boulogne and do her hair. Once a week she went to Elizabeth Arden to have it washed. Her hair was rich and full and long, and her wonderful skin was a major beauty asset. "Aline," she told me, "the most important thing is to take care of your face. The other end you sit on. My mother used to tell me that."

The Duchess never took a nap. Occasionally she would rest on her chaise longue, but she really relaxed only while having her hair, face, and nails done. Every afternoon a makeup artist came to the house to do her face. The tones he used varied with the color of what she was wearing, and he applied false eyelashes so discreetly that people didn't realize she wore them. She had a manicurist come in three times a week, and she rarely altered the color of her polish, which was bright red.

After tea she said, "You children go upstairs to your dreary attic." She grimaced. "I wish that we could do better for you, but it's all we have. That's why we never have houseguests."

Their guest rooms were on the third floor, and they were not bad by any standards. The suite was composed of two bedrooms separated by a bathroom. Luis's room was decorated with miniature soldiers, models of troops which the Duke had commanded as King of England, and which his ancestors had commanded since England began. The room was in red, white and blue, like the British flag. Neither bedroom was large. The Porthault sheets and pillowcases matched the flowers in the room, which were changed every day.

While we had been at tea, the servants had attended to our bags. Luis's closets had been unpacked by the Duke's valet, Sidney, a black man they had hired when the Duke was governor of the Bahamas, in the early forties. Sidney had also found out from Georges that the dinner that evening was to be black-tie and he had ironed and returned the appropriate suit and shirt.

One of the Duchess's maids, Marie, looked after me. By the time I got to my room she had hung my long dresses in a closet with a high rod, and the shorter dresses in another closet, each dress or suit with its shoes placed below and the corresponding hat on the shelf above. Before she left, she asked me what dress I would be wearing for dinner, and took it away to touch it up.

In those days we didn't concern ourselves about overweight luggage, and dinners were never informal. I had brought what I needed for a week with the Windsors—dinner dresses and ball gowns with matching capes or coats, daytime clothes for Paris, all with hats and shoes, plus shooting clothes for a weekend which we were spending with the Rothschilds.

I used suitcases only for small things; my dresses, capes, and coats were folded in large cardboard boxes so they would not be too wrinkled.

The bathroom was cozy and comfortable. The toilet paper was always removed from the roll, cut with scissors in lengths of two squares, and piled up on a small tray on a table near the toilet. A Guerlain perfume burner filled the room with the most marvelous scent.

The bath had been drawn, and the water was the perfect temperature. I really don't know how they managed that. There was always Elizabeth Arden't Fluffy Milk Bath, which the Duchess loved, as well as five or six bath oils to choose from.

There were also a thermos bottle of ice-cold water, a plate of ginger cookies made by Lucien, the Windsor's chef, and a tray with whiskey, Coca-Cola, and ice, which they knew were what we liked to drink.

A blue cardboard folder was waiting for us on the desk. It contained the plan for the week, including the list of luncheons and dinners and indicating those which had been accepted for us. The Duchess always telephoned me in Madrid before our visits. "Aline, would you mind going to dinners with us on Monday and Tuesday?" Or "Listen, Aline, on Wednesday we're stuck for dinner at Lady Iris's, and of course you're invited, but you and Luis should go off to the theater or something. Why should you young people want to be bored by that old bag?"

"But, Duchess," I said, "she's not so old. She's your age."

"Aline, I can't *stand* people my age! Old people like me are such bores, the way they forget things."

Whatever we had agreed upon by phone was then arranged and written down and waiting for us in the blue folder. For example:

Tuesday, December 2, 1969, Madame la Comtesse de Romanones,
Tuesday, December 2: Dinner at "Cris de Paris" at 9:00
Wednesday, December 3: Lunch with Her Royal Highness and Baron de Rosnay at Maxim's at 1:15; Dinner at Mrs. Bory's at 9:00 and Dance at the Duchesse de Liancort's.
Friday, December 5: Dinner here at 9:15 before the Baron de Rede's ball.

There were also messages received for us and typed out by one of their secretaries.

Tuesday, December 2
Madame la comtesse,
Eduourd at Alexandre's (Tel. ELY.42.90) would like to speak with
you about your hairdo for December 5. The Baron de Rothschild
(Guy) would like to know if Monsieur le Comte needs some
cartridges for shooting. You are expected on Saturday at tea-time
until Sunday after dinner.

When the dinner was to be at home, we got an advance notice of the seating arrangement. Even for dinners in other homes we usually had guest lists, a special courtesy extended to the Duke because he had been King. Beside some names would be a note about what he or she did, as an aid in conversation. The blue folder also contained reminders and bits of information relative to our stay or our departure:

May I have your ticket. Please!

Monday, December 17, 1962
Madam,
The car will leave from the house tonight at about 8:45 PM.
The
dinner will take place in a Restaurant called "Cercle Rive Gauche."
> *The guests will be:*
> *Their Royal Highnesses*
> *Le Baron de Rede (Gentleman of leisure)*
> *M. Alexander Böker, German political Director, attached to N.A.T.O.*

Your seat is reserved and definitely confirmed on Air France, Flight 515 leaving from Orly Airport at 5:20 PM. Arriving in Madrid at 7:10 PM. The reporting time at the Airport is 4:40 PM at the very latest.

I was bathed and waiting for Edouard when Marie came in with my dress. As always at the Windsors', my dress looked almost better than new. And the matching embroidered silk shoes, which were a bit worn, appeared fresh and spotless. I once asked Ofelia, "How is it possible to do better than professional cleaning and pressing in a private house?"

"Señora Condesa, the Duchess knows everything about cleaning every kind of fabric, exactly what removes every kind or spot. She has taught us just the type of an iron to use for pressing every material, and we have marvelous equipment. We rarely send anything to a dry cleaner."

She really was the Best-Dressed Woman. There will never be another one like her. And being immaculate was the hallmark of her personal style: "Aline, you can wear a dress that's twenty years old, but it must be immaculate. And it cannot have a wrinkle. You must always look like you just stepped out of a bandbox."

She always carried an extra pair of white gloves in her bag when she left for lunch. "One pair to go, one pair to come back." Her shoes were always shined underneath, on the instep and inside the heel, which can be seen when you cross your legs.

Her clothes were the epitome of simplicity in line, and of highest quality in materials and workmanship. She did not believe in busy shoes, busy handbags, busy anything. The Duke was famous for being just the opposite, able to mix colors and three different kinds of stripes or plaids. "I could never mingle things together like my roommate does, Aline. He's incredible. I have to do it by being simple. And immaculate. Everything has to be spotless and shiny."

She liked the fact that I enjoyed dressing up, and that I was careful about my hair and makeup and clothes. It made her terribly nervous when people weren't soigné; it was like bad manners to her. She liked people to be expressive, to have a sense of humor, to be attractive and extroverted. For her dinner parties she looked for outstanding people—the best novelist of the moment, or what ever scientist or musician or explorer happened to be interesting at a given time. The Duke liked political people, military personalities, and sportsmen. They both maintained that of all the women they had known, Princess Ann-Mari von Bismarck was without question the most beautiful. They had met her in London in the thirties when Bismarck had been German Ambassador.

Dinner guests were invited to arrive at eight o'clock, and dinner was served at 8:30. the Duke and Duchess were punctual to an extreme. Coming from Spain, where we did not dine until ten P.M. at the earliest, I was always out of breath getting ready in time.

I left my room at a quarter to eight. On the floor below, four maids were carrying a bed sheet, each of them holding a corner. The first time I had seen them do this, I asked was was happening.

"Señora Condesa, we're making Her Royal Highness's bed. We don't make it until evening, because the spread would cause wrinkles. Her Royal Highness would never think of having a wrinkle in her bed. When she goes down to dinner, we remove the spread and bring up her sheets, which have just come off the ironing table. After it's made, we always do a final touch-up and press the sheet again on the bed." I knew, however, that she slept with a huge transparent plastic covering on top of the bed so that the pugs could sleep with her.

Walking through that house was a sensuous experience, because every room had its own perfume burner with its own distinct perfume. When we got downstairs, the younger of the two footmen said, "Buenas noches, Señora Condesa," and smiled proudly. I was also proud of him. Another one of the boys I had sent to the Duchess from our ranch in Trujillo . The son of one of our shepherds, he'd had little formal education, and he had poor posture; but the *cura*, the priest of Santa Marta, had recommended him as a boy with potential. Now he stood elegantly erect, immaculate, well groomed, and confident, informing me that his new uniform had been fitted and made by President de Gaulle's tailor. Over the years I sent five boys to work for them as footmen. Three of them returned to us again after the Duke died. They were all deeply affected by His Royal Highness's death, and told me that no man could compare to him in kindness and generosity.

As guests arrived, a pair of footmen opened the car doors on both sides so that no one had to slide across a seat getting out. When they entered the front hall, they saw the Duke's banner hanging in the curve of the staircase. These royal banners had rested on the biers of english kings while they lay in state, before the Duke's time, just as one day this one would on his coffin. On a table in the hall was the "red box," which as King of England he had used exclusively for correspondence between him and his Prime Minister. The red box had belonged to his father, George V, and it was one of the few things he kept when he abdicated. Beside it was the book which arriving guests were asked to sign, as well as a chart with the evenings seating arrangement. Beside each place at dinner was the menu, handwritten by Georges.

    After dinner we retired to the salon for coffee and drinks. Amid the magnificent furniture was a grand piano, and often they hired a pianist to play from ten until midnight. Standing leaning on the piano, the Duke would sing "Alexander's Ragtime Band." With no coaxing at all, the guests joined in, and I was often fascinated to see some of the world's most famous political leaders belting out, "Come on along and hear, come on along and hear –Alexander's Ragtime Band."

    Sometimes the Duke said, "Georges, where's the gramophone?" and with that the butler would bring in an ancient portable phonograph and play a record of one of Winston Churchill's speeches. The Duke loved Churchill, who had defended him in the House of Commons. He loathed Baldwin, the prime minister in the thirties- oh, how he loathed Baldwin.

    People began leaving at eleven o'clock. Dinner parties were a nightly affair for most of these guests, so they could not end very late. By midnight everyone had gone. After all had left the Duchess waited while a plastic slipcover was put on the antique sofa in the entrance hall, and then we all went upstairs to the boudoir for a nightcap.

    "It was a marvelous dinner," I said. "Everyone had the best time. Why, you even had Lockjaw talking." (That was her nickname for one notoriously closemouthed man.)

    "Did you see that?" she asked, delighted that I had noticed. "Did you see how I had him giggling and laughing like nobody ever has? He's just shy. I tell you, Aline, if there's one thing I can do well, it's to get people talking. I'll always find something that can get them going." Her pleasure changed to annoyance as she mentioned the name of another of the guests. "Now, he's *not* shy but he sat there thoughout the entire dinner and didn't say a solitary word. What nerve. How dare he? Nobody has the right to come to a party and sit there like a piece of furniture. You're invited to contribute to the party. If I'd been closer to him, I'd have told him that the sphinxes are in Egypt, not in the Bois. What a bore. I'm never going to invite him again. I resent intelligent, wordly people who won't make an effort. They're just parasites, relaxing while other people entertain them."

The Duke said, "Aline certainly wasn't bored. What was Lord Harris going on about? He never let you get a word in."

"Well, sir, he's speaks such aristocratic english that I could hardly understand what he was saying."

"You know, Aline," said the Duke, "that is not aristocratic at all. It is quite a false sound, or accent. Nobody in my family has ever spoken that hot-potato-in-the-mouth type of English."

Listening to him, I realized that the Duke's accent was mild in comparison with that of many Englishmen.

"That funny sound which some Englishmen make instead of speaking started just before the turn of the century in certain good schools, like Eton, where it became the style to speak like that—a bit like wearing a school tie. The graduates carried that dreadful sound away from school with them. And then, as one might expect, people who hadn't been to those schools began affecting that accent."

He went to a little table in the corner and poured himself another whiskey."Recently, an important matter came up, and I phoned my solicitor in London. A woman answered, and I asked if Mr. Allen was in.

" Who's calling him please?"

" the Duke of Windsor. "

" Oh, I'm sorry, but he's not in."

" 'Well, would you kindly ask him to call me?"

" 'All right,' she said,' I'll tell him'."

"A week passed, and I didn't hear from Mr. Allen. I called him again, and again he wasn't in, and I left the same message. Still I didn't hear from him. Something must be quite wrong, I thought, and I called again. The same woman answered. I said, 'Now look, I have called Mr. Allen several times, and I recognize your voice as the person to whom I have spoken. Mr. Allen has not yet returned my calls, and it is urgent that I speak with him immediately.'

" 'Who did you say is calling?' "

" 'The Duke of Windsor' "

" She said, 'Now, you look, whoever you are. I have never had the pleasure of a chat-up with the Duke of Windsor, but I can tell you that it's a sure thing he doesn't have an American accent such as you've got.' And she hung up."

The next day Luis and the Duke went to Saint-Cloud to play golf, and the Duchess and I had lunch on the terrace. I commented on how beautiful the garden looked. "Yes," she said, "it gets better every year. Everything gets better with age except women."

I asked how she had slept. "I hardly slept at all last night." She told me. "I was awake worrying about the servants breaking the dishes we used for dinner. I just know that when they wash them and put them down, they don't bother to put two towels under them, and one towel really isn't enough."

It was just the two of us, so lunch was served by Georges and a footman. The Duchess ate almost nothing. She never needed to diet, and the Duke had his own regimen. He awoke between eight and nine in the morning. His breakfast was cold water; then nothing else until around 11:30, when a tray was delivered to his bathroom. There he had a large brunch while he shaved; his favorite dishes were smoked haddock and small white sausages, which he had sent to him from England. He usually skipped lunch. Often he played golf during the lunch hour, as he was doing that day.

In the afternoon we went to an art gallery on the Faubourg St-Honore to see a new exhibition. From there the Duchess went to a fitting at Givenchy, and I returned home.

The Duke was standing in the driveway with some gardening tools in his hands, and he waved for my car to stop. "Aline, where's the Duchess?"

"At Givenchy, sir, having a fitting."

"She shouldn't be doing that. She had a cold this morning. I'm worried to death about the Duchess, Aline. She's really doing too much. She's going to become ill."

"Oh, sir, I don't think there is cause to worry. She seemed very happy and comfortable. And she has her car with her."

I continued up to the house, and he went on with this gardening. He was not the kind of country gentleman who loves gardening as long as somebody else does the dirty work. He employed three gardeners, but he had planted dozens of the trees on the grounds with his own hands. He did not, however, dress for role of gardener. That particular afternoon he was wearing a tweed suit with knickers which I knew he had inherited from his father, George V.

About 5:30 he called to me from the boudoir. "Aline, the Duchess still hasn't come back." Just then the front door opened and she walked in. "Ah," he said "darling." I never heard him call her Wallis, always "darling." He put his wrist to her forehead and seemed pleased. "You should have a hot bath and get into bed and rest. I've had your tub drawn."

As they walked toward her room, the Duchess called up to me, "Aline, dear, be sure to stop in before you go out. I want to see how you look."

Luis and I were dining at the Spanish Embassy. Their Royal Highnesses had been invited, but they had declined, and were going to spend a quiet night at home.

We were expected for dinner at nine o'clock. At 8:30 we stopped off in the boudoir. A table had been set up, and they were going to dine there. They always dressed for dinner as if they were dining out or giving a party downstairs. She was wearing a long gown and was combed, made up, and bejeweled. The Duke was in black tie and a velvet smoking jacket. He was freshly shaved; he shaved twice a day even if they were not seeing anyone.

After leaving the embassy, Luis and I went to some nightclubs, and it was nearly three A.M. when our car arrived at the gates. At night there was always a guard because the Duchess was frightened of intruders. Her fear had originated in England before the abdication, when mobs of curious and angry subjects of Edward VIII had swarmed around her residence to "have a look at Mrs. Simpson."

We tiptoed upstairs. On their floor we heard bursts of laughter coming from her room, then low voices, then more laughter.

Long ago she had told me. "You know, Aline, we're not as young as you and Luis, and we don't sleep very much. Of course, David wouldn't think of going to bed all the way over there in his own room; he always comes here into my bed and we sit up talking all night."

In a few hours we left to go shooting with Guy and Marie-Helene de Rothschild at their palace, Ferrieres, outside of Paris. The Duchess said, "You're leaving the poor for the rich, and misery for luxury."

The Windsors had a household staff of well over twenty: the chef and four footmen, four maids, three chauffeurs, three secretaries, a switchboard operator, the concierge, several laundresses, and three gardeners.

I told the Duchess. "We'll be back on Monday."

"But how are you going to come back here from the marvelous Ferrieres, back to your miserable little attic?"

We were in the boudoir, and she was studying a large, extremely amateurish portrait of herself, which was propped up against a chair. She made a little face and said playfully, "Now, Aline, where am I going to put his? Even David shudders when he looks at it. That new footman you sent us from your ranch unfortunately has a serious defect. He fancies himself an artist, and has just presented me with this fruit of his labor. I must certainly hang it *somewhere*. Who can afford to lose a good manservant these days?"

CHAPTER TWENTY- SEVEN

THE CHILDREN

By1961 our three sons, Alvaro, Luis and Miguel were twelve eleven and ten years old. Alvaro had brown eyes and dark hair like myself and the other two were blonde and blue-eyed favoring their father. They had been going to school since they were three and a half, the youngest age permitted in Spain. Luis wanted to be sure his children enjoyed the pleasure of the type of schooling he had been denied. The three were strong, healthy and in my opinion the most clever and brilliant children in the world. I remember during those years of my children's childhood feeling motherly towards all children of the same ages that I saw on the street- I was totally absorbed in them and often avoided taking part in other activities during those brief years of their childhood – my sense of protection and love of my children absorbed and fascinated me.

As in the homes of our friends, our children had a foreign language governess –since we spoke English at home – their governess was French - Luis wanted to be certain her accent was correct, so he interviewed her. I couldn't tell if she had a good or bad accent -in Pearl River I was the only student who spoke French due to a french maid we had for some years when I was small but Luis told me my American accent in french was horrible. My OSS trainers had not realized that and during the first month of my training I had hoped I would be dropped by parachute in France behind enemy lines – the prospect thrilled me -when OSS advised me later on that I would be going to Madrid I was despondent – a neutral country – so far from the actual fighting – no excitement there. But undoubtedly if I had been dropped in France with my accent of which my instructors had been unaware, the enemy would have realized I was American immediately.

Luis had suffered three governesses, an English nanny, a German Fraulein and a French mademoiselle- they all lived in his grandmother's palace at the same time with him and his two sisters making their lives insupportable with their jealousies of each other.

Since Spanish schools were exclusive for either boys or girls, my sons missed the companionship of girls – everything was so different from my upbringing in Pearl River where I had to oversee walking five brothers and one sister to school every day and help take care of them. But precisely because there had been no luxuries in Pearl River, I made a point of taking advantage of the many worthwhile things my children could learn in Spain . Lessons in tennis, riding, golf were inexpensive so they had all three, also added to those lessons

Luis taught them how to shoot at age eight. As of age eight I also arranged daily lessons in piano and guitar for them, later I even added flamenco lessons. Years later I overheard my eldest son Alvaro say, "I had a miserable childhood – we took lessons non-stop – we arrived home from school and then began lessons every day in all kinds of things until dinner time and then went to bed. Never time to play."

My children also enjoyed the kindnesses of our friends like Ava who did not have children of her own -Ava Gardner was especially fond of all our boys – she brought them all sorts of presents. I was strict with the children in everything-neither I nor their father wanted them to be brought up spoiled as he had been. As soon as they were eighteen years old I managed to find them summer jobs in New York city in a bank and once in Madrid for Alvaro in the large department store, the Corte Ingles. No one we knew in Spain had ever considered having their children work during their summer vacations – it was even difficult for me to find summer jobs for them in Spain in those days.

Peter Viertel also was a wonderful friend for my boys -he taught them how to surf in Biarritz in the early sixties and also how to ski in Switzerland. In Marbella during one of Ava's visits with us she played tennis daily with Miguel. At the end of the month when my husband was paying Miguel's monthly bill for the tennis games and his usual soft drinks in the hotel, he was astounded at the price . He asked the hotel employee how a ten year old child could have such a huge bill for drinks at the bar.

"He was very well accompanied, Senor Conde, and both he and his guest ordered several drinks"- was the answer. " He always has a soft drink but his companion does not." So now Luis realized that all during her visit one of the reasons she liked to play tennis with Miguel was that she could get as much booze as she wanted. In our house we tried our best to restrict her access to liquor.

Bringing up three boys was always fun and filled with small dramas.

CHAPTER TWENTY – EIGHT

FERRIERES & ROTHSCHILD

From October to the end of June Luis and I made frequent trips to Paris – we stayed with the Duke and Duchess during the week and then on the weekends with the Rothschilds in Ferrierres. Martin, the Windsor's chauffeur would drive us the twenty one kilometers from the Windsor's home to the Rothschild's famous palace in the town of Ferrieres.

Arriving at the Château of Ferrieres was always a delight. Our car wound through the small town of Ferrieres and entered the walled-in three-thousand acre Rothschild property through a massive iron gate. Then, after following a winding road through a forest of enormous trees, suddenly the large palace became visible -huge and romantic, a fairy-tale palace of turrets and spires, of carved stone embellishments on roofs and balconies and elongated Gothic windows, with a curved double entrance of wide stone steps which led up to a grand portal.

Joseph Fouche, Napoleon's police minister, had been its owner before Guy's great-grandfather had purchased it in 1830 from Fouche's widow. The palace had not been imposing then, not until the famous English architect Paxton—the same man who had done the Crystal Palace in London - enhanced it on orders from the Baron James de Rothschild. In 1860, the Baron James de Rothschild inaugurated the fairy-tale château with a weekend houseparty and pheasant shoot for Napoleon the Third and his Spanish-born Empress Eugenie. Even those visitors must have been astounded by the fabulous collection of art works and museum-like furnishings, an accumulation of the finest Europe had produced during the past centuries. When we arrived for the first time in the middle sixties the château showed the important art additions made by the following three generations of Rothschilds - each had continued to enrich that heritage.

On a normal weekend invitation guests arrived at tea time on a Friday. Instead of entering through the grand front entrance which was used only on special occasions , we entered through a small side door, which was the family custom. Boots were left there if one had been walking in the country - coats also were deposited there on arrival—the luggage for the weekend was being removed from the car by a footman and taken to our rooms where it would be unpacked.

The weekend invitation included dinner on Friday, a pheasant shoot Saturday, a dinner Saturday night including the guests who had come to shoot from Paris who would to return to Paris that night, and a luncheon Sunday for all house guests who would leave about five that afternoon. Marie Helen always invited famous or amusing friends from Paris and usually mixed in peole from other countries. Sometimes the weekend would be concentrated on the pheasant shoot with mostly shooting personalities from France and abroad. Marie Helene did not shoot, but she wanted interesting conversations.

Before and after dinner Marie Helene and some guests would play gin-rummy. Pompidou, who during the first years we went to Ferrieres was President of the Banque Rothschild and later was Prime Minister of France was usually one of the card players - he also liked to shoot. It always pleased me to be shooting in the butt next to him because he was always charming and I could down more pheasants than he did. But nobody could beat Valerie Giscard D'Estaing, another frequent shooting guest – he was an important government Minister and later also became Prime Minister.

So on arrival we would run up the narrow side stairway which led to a large high-ceilinged red salon where the walls were covered with eighteenth-century tapestries plus some Rothschild family portraits. A large square sofa-couch

covered with many cushions was located against the wall in the center of the room , often several guests would be reclining on this, the preferred place to stretch out and chat.
Converation was usually peppy and amusing, especially if our hostess was present. She was daring and often entertained herself by encouraging a guest to divulge a juicy bit of gossip. Under an ornate six-foot-high mantelpiece, a fire glowed, around the room was an assortment of cozy armchairs inviting the latest guests to be comfortable.

    After a brief spell of conversation in the red salon we proceeded to the next salon where tea was being served. Guy had a favorite dog, a mini-tekel which was often in his arms - the sleek, doe-eyed dog, was an important member of the household whom we knew well - we had given it to Guy several years before from our bitch's litter.

    While everyone chatted, I looked around for our dynamic hostess- her artistic genious was the engine behind every Rothschild festivity. Marie- Hélène was seated on a blue sofa talking to Prince dArenberg, one of the shooting friends . Her long-lashed aquamarine eyes smiled up at me. "You're late," she began and then, disregarding that detail, went on to say, "Tell me, did Luis bring the *jabugo*, the Spanish cured ham , I asked for?"

    After assuring her he had, we moved on to the bufffet table which was loaded. The cheese board always had a selection of choice cheeses from every part of France and the fruit was from all over the world. Mangos from India, oranges from Morroco. Added to this were tiny sandwiches, petits fours, small sausages, cakes, and a special brioche—all prepared in the enormous kitchen below, where on other visits I'd seen four chefs working. In the time of Guy's grandparents, the kitchen had been in a separate building two hundred meters away from the palace, with a small underground train to deliver meals to the main house – Guy explained this had been done to avoid cooking odors to reach the dining salons. That bit of information astounded me since the rooms we dined were distant from the huge kitchen in the cellar. Guy admitted that such exaggerations had been an unnecessary out-dated custom.

    Breakfast would be served downstairs on shooting weekends in one of the large salons at 10:00 a.m. Otherwise breakfast was in our bedrooms. Before the shoot the buffet breakfast with four menservants in attendance was enormous - besides ham and eggs and other normal breakfast items, there was spaghetti with meat sauce, little steaks, roast haddock, croissants, Danish pastry and all kinds of French pastry made in the house.

  A general fluster went through the room when Pompidou came in. He knew everyone or they all knew him as he came many weekends and was an asset with his wit and jolly unassuming manner .

From where I was standing in front of one of the high arched windows, I looked down at the magnificent view. On the lake on the other side of the lawn, white swans floated majestically, and in the woods beyond, wide expanses of spectacular trees with myriad colored leaves were in view. Guy had told me that his great-grandfather had brought those trees from the many different countries to provide a variety of leaves of different color to the rolling landscape. A wide granite staircase led from the palace to the park, where long avenues of lawn, not very green in this month stretched out on either side. In the distance the last rays of the winter sun revealed a path leading to a small Victorian gazebo on a hill.

    After tea guests started to move up to their rooms on the floor above while a few stayed below to play cards. By the time I reached our suite, I saw that my clothes had been unpacked, pressed, and placed in a closet in the hallway which led into our large bedroom. Luis' clothes and our shooting gear were in a closet on the other side. The guns for the shoot had been left downstairs. Instead of a maid asking "Which dress for tonight?" at the Rothschilds', everything had already been pressed and hung in the closets ready to be worn - this custom was usual for guests in most large homes, the same as in the Windsors. However in some houses the maids who pressed the clothes were more professional than others.

Usually we were placed in the rooms that had often been occupied by Napoleon the third and his spanish Empress Eugenie one hundred years before. This sumptuous bedroom had enormous proportions and incredibly high ceilings - two canopied beds faced an ornate chimney mantel flanked by windows leading out to a balcony. In a far corner was a large desk with all kinds of writing paper, postcards of the château, and pens and pencils. On the opposite side of the chamber was a ladies' dressing table - on either side of the fireplace were comfortable armchairs.

Luis was still downstairs engrossed in a game of backgammon, so I decided to bathe and be out of his way when he arrived. In the bathroom a deep old-fashioned zinc tub encased in time-polished mahagony was drawn and waiting. Luxuriously, I settled into the warm water and enjoyed the smooth feeling of the polished metal, even warmer than the water, enjoying the awareness that this same sumptuous tub had been one of the first to be installed in France.

By the time Luis appeared, I was at the dressing table where a maid had prearranged my makeup. Every kind of famous cosmetic product was on the table, plus masses of small details. Marie Helene prided herself on having the most luxurious guest quarters and she did – she wanted to be the most outstanding hostess and she was.

At nine we were seated at the large oval table in the dining room. Six liveried footmen served the eighteen guests. The menu in front of my place was lengthy. The table at Ferrieres was set and served the same for twelve as for two hundred.

The menu had always been prepared by Marie-Héléne with her chef, the best in France. She seated the table according to her own protocol, much more agreeable than our strict Spanish custom - here guests were matched for their mutual interests and ages, at any rate all Ferrieres guests were witty or attractive or famous - sometimes the mixture of nationalities gave a spicy touch when political differences existed. The stimulating atmosphere encouraged people to be amusing and sometimes brilliant.

After dinner Marie-Hélène and her attractive mother, Maggie van Zuylen, Pompidou and Luis, played gin at one end of the large blue salon. At the opposite end of the room, Guy and the then Minister of Finance, Giscard d'Estaing, and the rest of us chatted, laughed, and helped ourselves to drinks from a table nearby. Some of us would go to bed early to be ready for the next day's shoot.

For me, accustomed to rough hilly terrain and Spanish customs, shooting at Ferrieres seemed almost like shooting in a large garden. Everything was surprisingly pristine and neat—the beaters were dressed in white jackets to avoid being shot, trucks transferred them from one drive to another. Our beaters in Pascualete were dressed in whatever raggedy cothes they happened to own and went by foot to the drives. In France it seemed to me that even the pheasants contribute to the orderly atomosphere - they flew on straight lines and made a convenient racket, so one was alerted in advancde and ready to shoot. Nothing was similar to our silent sneaky partridges darting in at all angles with such speed that one had to be very quick to get any. Nevertheless I was surprised when I tried to shoot my first phaesant – those big noisy birds were not at all easy to down and I missed many.

Guy was generous about giving me a butt, unlike the English who stick to only eight butts and rarely offer a stand to wives. That first time, I found myself next to stiff, formal Giscard d'Estaing, whose good looks charmed many women-he was also a top shot and I felt embarrassed to miss so many. Pompidou was on my other side. I wasn't as good a shot as some Spanish women, but I still downed more birds than Pompidou - we both laughed about that. Pompidou was charming always.

Luis and Teddy Vicuna, a Spanish guest from Madrid, were both accustomed to the competitive Spanish custom of noting the number of birds each gun had downed after every drive - but here no one asked. This French lack of competition eliminated part of their fun since they were top guns. As we walked to the next drive I kidded Luis about nobody being aware that he had downed twice as many birds as any Frenchman - maybe not Giscard but certainly more than the others. Of course Luis just laughed, but he got in his jab at me – "Lucky for you - at least they won´t know how many you missed."

When the group was about to break for the small midday snack out in the field - some of the women who had slept late were just arriving to join us. Jacqueline de Ribes appeared in a glamorous long dark suede coat lined in mink, a matching hat, an elegant walking stick and high fur-bordered boots. Since we were not supposed to spoil our appetites for the high tea, the snack was restricted to steamy consomme, tiny sausages, and hot red wine spiced with cinnamon to ward off the chill of the day.
 Everyone made an effort to wear especially attractive shoot apparel. I liked showing off my spanish hand-embroidered leather chaps, my custom-made divided skirt, and my carefully fitted leather "polainas" leggings, snug around my legs. Naturally I wore the Austrian shooter´s hat, classic for everyone. In Spain sometimes when it was cold, we wore the classic Portuguese fur collared cape-coat. Nevertheless nothing could beat the elegance of Jacqueline´s attire when she appeared for the snack, but her outfit would have been impossible for shooting.

When Guy came to Pacualete to shoot with us, he was equally surprised to see the differences - the Spanish picking up their own birds, the men comparing notes of how many each had downed. Spaniards consider themselves the best shots in Europe and as Guy comfided to me, "they should be, they've been shooting more birds more days a week than any other hunter in Europe."

Years later, about the beginning of the nineties, I was invited by Francois de Grossouvre, a top French secret intelligence official, to a shoot at the impressive government palace of Rambouillet. Everything about that beautiful royal palace was exceptional - the ceremonious reception by the military Guard on arrival, the salons, my bedroom, and the meals. Since I had coincided with Francois Grossouvre several times in secret meetings of intelligence agents in Washington where I was the only female - I suppose Grossouvre expected me to be a top shot. But my shooting was not at its best - it was a rainy day in Rambouillet - I wore my best spanish shooting gear, but it got wet and didn´t look like much the second day. Grossouvre was assassinated shortly afterwards, so I was not invited again. His death was published as a suicide but my "inside" informant assured me he had been assassinated and gave me all the details. This invitation was during the presidency of Mitterand, so before dinner that night I telephoned Guy from Rambouillet to give him my impressions. He was pleased to learn that I found the men I was shooting with, who were principally members of Mitterand's cabinet less amusing than those at the Ferrieres shoots.

Marie Helene's favorite activity were the Balls she gave once every year in Ferrieres – they are considered the last great Balls given in Paris. The theme and décor for each Ball was different and always dazzling. About twenty special guests were invited to reside in the palace during a Ball weekend and almost two hundred would come Saturday evening for the Ball.

On one of the Ball weekends while those house guests who had just arrived were in the salon partaking of the delicious buffet, Elizabeth Taylor and Richard Burton appeared —a fun addition to the guest list, I thought when I saw them walk in. I had never met them before. Burton was attractive, but I was surprised to see that his face was badly marred by what looked like pockmarks: I wondered if this had been evident in his movies. They did not advance to join the rest of us around the buffet table, they appeared uncertain, uncomfortable – obviously they did not know anyone of the group. Unfortunately Maire Helene was not at hand to take care of them. We were all anxious to meet them but they did not come closer to say hello. They remained talking to each other leaning against the back of a sofa. I was anxious to meet Elizabeth because both Ava Gardner and Deborah Kerr had told me she was very nice and a wonderful friend. They had made a film with her a short time before in Mexico in Puerto Vallarta, so I went over to chat with them and found both very friendly- in fact they seemed quite relieved and came to the buffet with me. Elizabeth explained that she was currently involved in a film in Paris and complained of working too many hours.

A few minutes later Marie Helene entered the room with my beloved friend Audrey Hepburn – I was surprised not having been aware that Audrey was going to be at the house party.

"I'm so excited," Audrey exclaimed when she rushed over to join me. "Do you know, I've never been to a ball before?"

Both Marie- Hélène and I were astounded. "How's that possible?" You of all people. Why, I've seen you in so many balls—in *War and Peace*, and *My Fair Lady* and..."
She laughed,. "That was only in the movies- and that doesn't count – that´s not like a real ball- it´s just work and repeats.

I've never been to a real ball in my life." Audrey was, as always, totally honest and unpretentious

"Well, Audrey" I said. "You are lucky. Your first Ball tomorrow will be the most glamorous Ball in the world.

No one in Paris had ever given anything to compare to the magnificence of Marie Helene's fancy dress balls. Sometimes it would be a Ball in Oriental costume, another a Romanesque theme of an Eighteenth century ball. Tomorrow was to be a Sur-realist Ball – the costumes and entrees of the guests would be extraordinary. The French especially enjoy costume balls in which they give vent to their love of dress and artistic talents. Every year no matter what type of Ball Marie Helene gave, the next day the entire French press would declare it to have been the best.

Considering some of the guests I had just seen, this weekend was going to be especially glamorous . Already, now the day before, twenty house-guests had arrived - we had been informed that hairdressers, masseurs, and make-up artists, were available for us in the chateau. Meanwhile trunks and suitcases of all sizes were continuing to arrive and decorators and carpenters were still working in the main entrance and main ballroom. Tomorrow two hundred guests would arrive at eight in the evening – the hour the Ball was scheduled to begin. It was customary for each guest to make a separate entrée. Always there was much secrecy and competition- everyone was aware that all the costumes would be outstanding –some guests had spent months choosing their costumes after lengthy discussions with designers – each guest wanted to create a spectacular entrée.

On saturday just before eight o´clock , we house guests took a stand near the entrance to see the guests as they made their "grandes entrées". One of the first to arrive that night was a group of four dressed in undertakers top hats and black suits carrying a coffin made of painted sugar with a life-size nude woman stretched out on top.......she was also made of sugar and decorated in candy flowers. During the next hour each entrée was more spectacular than the one before – each outstanding in originality and magnificence. Table decorations were equally impressive - each table was different, decorators had created tables with individual themes of artistic beauty and ingenuity. The anticipation and excitement seemed to augment even before the dancing and dining began. The unbounded gaiety made it difficult for guests to leave before five or six in the morning.

    Guy was a brilliant business man and had presided his bank for many years - he was considered the most outstanding member of the large European Rothschild family. He was also looked upon as the most elegant man in Paris. Nevertheless he was cozy and his conversation charming. One evening while dining in a small Parisian bistro, he told us that the origin of the word "bistro" was actually Russian. " The word", he said, "became current after World War One when the city began to receive masses of people escaping from Russia´s Bolshevik revolution. When these Russian exiles went to a bar and asked for a drink or something to eat they referred to the bar as a "bistro" which in Russian means "fast" or "vite" thus those bars started to be called "bistros" even by the Pairisians themselves."

    I remember another of Guy´s amusing stories – this one about the origin of the word for pumpernikel bread. "Did you know", he said , "that Napoleon is responsible for calling dark German bread ´´pumpernickel´´? Of course we were all in doubt about that, but he went on - "During the time when Napoleon was conquering Germany, in a small German town while he was eating, he was given some dark bread. He looked at it disgustedly and pushed it away, saying to his aide, "Give it to Nickel." Nickel was his horse."

    Luis and Guy both liked racing and shared the ownership of several horses in France. Invariably Luis and I went to Paris

for the Grand Prix in June when one of their horses would be competing. I enjoyed not only the races but also chatting with friends in the neighboring boxes. One day I was astonished to see Maria Felix, the beautiful Mexican movie star in the adjoining box – she had often dined with us in Madrid, but I hadn't seen her in years. Guy explained that she was now married to a Frenchman whose horses won many races. When I knew Maria years before she did't even want togo to the races with us in Madrid, but now after a short conversation with her, I realized that she not only owned a top race horse but was even an expert on their geneology. Usually in Paris before the races we lunched in one of the popular restaurants with Guy and Marie Helene – they were always nervous wrecks worrrying about their horse's chances to win the coming race. These weekends we stayed at the Windsors but they never went to the races with us. The Duke liked to ride and had been a top polo player, but he was not fond of racing.
.   Marie-Hélène was extremely versatile about the geneology of race horses, I was totallly ignorant. I would have preferred to be riding on top of one rather than watching a race. Luis' grandfather Torre Arias has started racing in Spain and Luis had been a fan all his life. When we visited Cornelius Vanderbilt Whitney, in Lexington, Kentucky for the yearly "Derby" in the first week of May, Luis knew more about the pedigree of Sonny's horses than he did. During that visit Luis bought seven brood mares there and sent them by plane to Madrid while we travelled tourist but the mares were his main interest. Luis' trips to England also were dedicated to buying race horses. And the purpose of our summers in Deauville staying with the Rothschilds in Meautry, was principally to attend the horse sales and to buy a few. Gradually Luis brought to Pascualete about 64 brood mares and for years we had this large amount of race horses in the "finca" – Luis always cared more them than for our two thousand sheep. But thanks to his knowledge of our mares geneology, we won many spanish races.

During World War II, Guy, who was president of the French jews, with much difficult y had managed to escape from France to the United States. Soon he was able to take a boat to England where he wanted to join General de Gaulle's Free French group. Guy's ship was sunk by a German submarine. but miraculously he was one of the few survivals, eventually arriving in London where he worked with the Free French until the end of the war.

The palace of Ferrieres was occupied by the Germans during the entire war but thanks to Marie- Hélène's unparalleled energy, the château, although having been abandoned twenty years, had been completely restored. Years later Guy made a gift to the city of Paris of the Palace of Ferrieres - he built a modern house nearby, but the luxury and glamour that we had known became a thing of the past. In the "new Ferrieres" there were only three or four guest rooms, not enough space for a Ball or even for a minor party. The glamorous shoots were eliminated. Guy still owned the property that surrounded the palace but the spirit and the glamour was gone.. One afternoon Luis and I left the rambling, California-style "new Ferrieres" to take a walk through the country – we discovered at a short distance a wire fence through which we could see the lonely palace of old Ferrieres, huge and stately in the distance. But Guy's gift of his magnificent home was not appreciated by the French government of Mitterand. Guy had intended it to be used as part of the University of Paris for cultural studies. But although the house, when he donated it was in prime condition, without a flaw in the plumbing, the painting freshly done, the floors impeccable - Mitterand's government made no use of the building whatsoever, nor was any care made to protect its interior or exterior. Nevertheless the beauty of the famous palace remains there in the midst of the huge park to see as a reminder of the glories of past days.

CHAPTER TWENTY – NINE

JAEN, THE SHOOT AND FRANCO

During the fifties at a dinner in the Brazilian embassy in Madrid, Luis and I met Franco's daughter, Carmen, and her husband Cristobal, the Marques de Villaverde. On our way home that night we agreed that the Villaverde's, as they were referred to, were extremely "simpaticos" and surprisingly unassuming. Since Carmen was the dictator's only child, we realized they must have received much adulation and expected them as a result to be pompous and insupportable. After that dinner we <u>coincided</u> in various other places, and each time liked them more..

When a few weeks later I told one of Luis' aunts that I was giving a dinner and had invited the Marqueses de Villaverde along with many relatives, including the Duke of Alburquerque and other relatives and friends, she was shocked. With much firmness she told me, "You can't do that, Aline. Your dinner will be a disaster. Beltran Alburquerque is the aide of our King who as you well know is obliged to live in exile in Portugal . Beltran will never accept meeting the daughter of the man who is responsible for not allowing the king to return to Spain. Most of the others you have mentioned will have the same reaction."

Normally I took great care to do what the previous generation of Luis' family advised, so I was upset. But this time, what could I do. Everyone had already been invited. However, I did not think Beltran Alburquerque, who was a cousin and fond of us both, would not come. To my relief the night of the dinner as the guests entered the room and were introduced to Carmen and Cristobal, not one person showed any reserve, even though I realized that they were surprised to meet this couple in our house. The evening proceeded normally and by the time people were leaving, Luis and I could see that they had been captivated by Carmen and Cristobal's simplicity and charm. Also they were an especially attractive couple - Carmen was intelligent and good-looking - Cristobal was a promising doctor and a superb athlete- and charming . As time passed it was only natural that the Villaverdes became popular and socially sought after. We saw them often in dinners and since they both were good shots invited them to shoot in Pascualete.

Sometime around the beginning of December 1959 Carmen called to ask if we would like to go to Jaen to a partridge shoot in her husband's finca for two days over New Years. She explained that in the finca there was a small farm house with bedrooms only for themselves and for her mother and father so we would have to stay nearby in Jaen at a small hotel. We were accustomed to "rough it" when shooting in the country so a small hotel was no inconvenience. We were especially delighted to realize that we would have the good fortune to finally meet the Generalissimo. This was a treat because Franco did not socialize at all and few persons we knew outside of government ministers had any personal contact with him.

Franco had the reputation of being austere, formal and unapproachable – it was rumored he didn't like bullfights - although he did go on special occasions. But for the most part, the few people we knew who had met him all were in awe of him.

General and Mrs. Franco had chosen not to take up residence in the royal palace in Madrid where the last King, Alfonso the thirteenth, and his family had resided, but lived in a large palace in the open country outside the city called El Pardo which was less pompous. It was a large white building built by Felipe V in the eighteenth century and used thereafter by the Kings of Spain for shoots of big and small game.

Carmen and Cristobal and their seven children lived there as well.

On Fridays Franco's cabinet meetings were held in El Pardo as well. One of the members of Franco's cabinet had told me that these meetings were extremely formal - that the Ministers prepared carefully for the occasion because each was obliged to give a detailed informative speech about the issues and activities of his ministry. Sometimes Franco would ask pertinent questions but for the most part he allowed each minister to make his own decisions. This same cabinet minister told me that they all dreaded the weekly luncheons after the cabinet meetings which were as meager and austere as in a military barracks.

Despite Franco's reputation of lack of carisma, he never hired a public relations company or tried to improve his image as is customary in chiefs of state. But the country's economy was improving with new industrialization. For the first time several automobile factories were functioning as well as many other industries that had never existed in the country. Added to the advantages everyone had to admit that we lived in peace and safety, far different from the situation in Germany, Italy and Ireland where terrorists and strikes during the end of the fifties and the sixties were making life hazardous for the inhabitants. Neither Luis nor I were in favor of a dictatorship, so we were surprised to see that this one was improving the country.

Since I was American I did not have a natural inclination for a monarchy either and although Luis had been born in a monarchist family, he believed, as I did, that a country should have free elections and a leader chosen by the majority. Luis' father was president of the Grandees of Spain, all of whom were openly critical of General Franco. Also during these years of general improvement the wealth of the large landowning class decreased tremendously when Franco's government expropiated properties of numerous landowners, just as it had expropriated Luis' property in Extremadura. Despite this great loss we had to recognize that the results of Franco's different efforts were improving the economic situation for the larger majority of Spain's inhabitants.

    Until now I had only seen Franco on May first when he presided over the parade celebrating the end of the Civil War - we watched from a balcony the abuelo' house on the Castellana. After the Abuelo died, the Abuela continued to live there - Franco presiding in the stand facing us. The parade would begin with the arrival of Franco's magnificent equestrian Moorish Guard, the horses'' hoofs painted in gold and silver, the soldiers wearing white capes with red and gold plumed hats making a beautiful contrast to the white horses. On the platform short plump Franco was resplendent in his General's uniform surrounded by his cabinet members and fine-looking military officers. This parade was one of the infrequent occasions when the public got a glimpse of their leader. Even when televsion became available in Spain in the late fifties, rarely was Franco on the screen except for official speeches. Noone knew the chief of state as he really was. Now I realized I was going to have the opportunity to see just what kind of a person this dictator was.

    .   Jaen is in southern Spain on the way to Granada. One drives through kilometers and kilometers of rolling hills covered by masses of olive trees- as one nears Jaen the snow covered mountains of the Sierra Nevada become visible silhouetted against a deep azure sky. The trip by car from Madrid for the first two hours is unattractive, just flat plains, but once one arrives at Bailen, the endless hills of olive trees and the mountains in the distance make a breathtakingly beautiful view.

    Carmen had told me we were expected for dinner at the farmhouse about nine P.M. - that since it was New Years, dinner would be later than usual, because there would be a Midnight Mass before dinner in the small chapel next to the house. She had said dinner was not black tie, that any short dress would do, that if we arrived early enough, we should come sooner because they played cards in the afternoon. Luis and I arrived about five thirty, so as soon as we had changed, we took the road to their finca, "Arroyovil", which was about fifteen minutes from the hotel. When we arrived at the gate of the finca there were only two Civil guards in their long dark green capes and shiny black hats - we had expected something more important since the Chief of State was present, a man more powerful in Spain at that time than any king or president. Then when the long winding road terminated at the door of the small house, another two Civil Guards were standing at attention there, but nothing more. Accompanying us was an American couple, Winston and C.Z. Guest, who were most disappointed and even shocked not to find some sort of pomp or at least a large number of military guards which would be normal for a Chief of State, not to mention a famous dictator.

The house was a small white washed stucco building, typical of country farm houses in southern Spain... one floor...red tile roofs. Inside one big room about twelve people were seated at three card tables, engrossed in their games. Carmen jumped up from one table where she was playing, welcoming us quickly, telling us to ask for a "copa" and to make ourselves at home, that soon they would be finished with their game. We did not want to interrupt so we went to one corner of the room where there was a small improvised bar and made ourselves a drink. Two of Carmen's small children were running about the room.

At a table in the far corner was the "Generalisimo", as we referred to Franco – he was absorbed in his cards, apparently oblivious to the children running about and ignoring the rest of us as well. Luis had heard that General Franco was a top player of "mus", a classic spanish game in which players use signs and are supposed to cheat as much as possible. Curiosity led Luis little by little to edge up to Franco's table, observing with amusement the game and the men's grimaces and gestures. Luis himself was an excellent player of this particular game as he was of all card games.

Within a short time more guests arrived, Cristobals' parents and brothers and one government minister. Around nine-thirty the card players stood up, Franco disappeared quickly without addressing anyone while the others went to the table in the corner for a drink. Two men servants began to fold and remove the three card tables, and then in the same area they set up one long narrow table for the dinner. Evidently this large room could be rapidly adjusted to whatever activity was going on. Another hour passed and we were advised to put on our coats in order to go to the small chapel outside the house. At this moment General and Mrs. Franco appeared in the doorway with their coats already on. This was my first view close up of the famous leader – no introductions had been made while he and the others had been absorbed in their card game. Franco smiled and one by one he shook hands with each of us. It was cold and there was no fanfare nor were many words exchanged as we stood in the hallway near the door. Later I became aware that this lack of words was due to his shyness -difficult to comprehend in a man with a record as a fearless soldier and forceful leader. As soon as he had met everyone, we all entered the chapel for Midnight Mass.

It was one o'clock by the time we were back in the house and almost one thirty before we twenty guests sat down to dine. General Franco and his wife presided in the middle of the table. Mrs. Franco was tall and slim, her dark hair was coiffed in a simple chignon, her dress was black and elegant but simple.....her manner was quiet, pleasant. Neither of the Francos seemed to be slightly extrovert.

I was astounded to find myself seated on Franco's left. At first I was too impressed to think of much to say but gradually I found myself involved in conversation with him. I had been told that Franco was not easy to talk to or to get along with, so most likely I was slower to converse than usual due to my respect for the great leader. Franco had a rosy smooth complexion, a prominent nose and nice warm brown eyes. His voice was high..I had already heard him speak on the radio so I was aware of that..otherwise his timber of voice would have surprised me... so different from his aspect. He told me that he liked fishing better than shooting and described the exciting salmon fishing in the northern rivers of the country which few people, he said, seemed to know about. Then he asked me about President Kennedy...his remarks revealed that he read profusely about what was happening in my country of birth. I don't remember what I said to him but although we were both making an effort, I think he was more successful than I. Nevertheless the result was that by the end of the dinner I no longer felt at all uncomfortable with him . Years later Carmen told me he had been more at ease with me than with many of the wives of his ministers who were usually seated at his side.

   The American couple, the Winston Guests, were not accustomed to Spanish hours and were not catholics either, nor did they speak Spanish...all told they must have been exhausted by the time we finished dinner at two thirty a.m. A year before when Carmen and Cistobal had made a trip to the USA, I had asked the Winston Guests to take care of them and as a result of their kindnesses in New York, now Carmen and and Cristobal had invited them to shoot in Jaen. If Ceezee Guest had not been seated next to Cristobal who was a charmer and her husband next to Carmen, things might have gone worse.. After all it was New Year's eve and in other countries people were celebrating late as well, at any rate when we got up from the table it appeared to me that the American Winston Guests were as happy as the rest of us. The menu was festive - oysters and smoked salmon, then another three courses and several desserts.

After dinner Carmen's little children were still running around and sometimes sitting on their grandfather's lap. The long improvised dining table was removed, folding chairs were brought in and placed in a semicircle. This indicated that there would be flamenco and sure enough, shortly after a group of gypsies arrived in a taxi. They had been travelling from Sevilla and were the best artists in the country. They piled into the room, removing their coats, the women fluffing out their dresses and smoothing their chignons, the men glancing around the room nervously since they were as anxious as the women to meet Franco. Gypsies can be extremely talkative, and are not shy , so Cristobal cleverly put a quick end to introductions – it was late and he wanted the singing and dancing to begin without delay.

The gypsy women were dolled up in their best polka dot long skirts and began tapping their feet on the floor as soon as the guitarists started to tune their guitars - a general shuffling and the sound of heels resounded - about ten minutes transpired while all this was going on, time enough for the artists and guests to down the whiskies Cristobal was passing out. Soon the first song began and within a few minutes we were witnessing the beginning of a great flamenco evening. The best dancers and singers of Andalucia were before us – all anxious to do their utmost for the Generalissimo who was obviously prepared to enjoy the show as much as the rest of us. General Franco started to take pictures with the new camera the Winston Guests had given him. To my dismay, he joined the others clamoring for me to dance, which I did very badly - then he stayed until four A.M. The flamenco had not begun until two thirty and despite being New Year's eve, even we young people were astounded by the hour.... we were scheduled to meet at nine in the morning for the partridge shoot. Bullfights and shoots are two things that begin on time in Spain. We younger people must have slept a brief three hours that night. But I had learned that the great dictator lived in a simple manner with no luxuries. No special attention had been made for the great dictator, Spain's most famous military general and his stately wife. This impressed me but astounded the Americans, Zeezee and Winston Guest.

The next day we were all on time out in the field taking our places for the shoot at nine A.M. The bright sun, the snow covered peaks of the Sierra Nevada against a deep blue sky, and the excitement surrounding the preparations of a partridge shoot made us forget that we had hardly slept. It was the first day of the year of 1960, and Luis happened to have heard while he was dressing on his transistor radio, which was still a novelty in Spain, a piece of striking international news.

"I wonder if the Generalissimo has heard the news from Cuba," he said as we descended from our jeep. But nothing in the activity surrounding us indicated that anyone knew something unusual had occurred and when a few moments later Luis asked several friends, the answers made it clear that noone had heard anything about Cuba that morning. We were walking towards the first drive which was going to take place near a large field of olive trees where the butts as usual were in a line separated each from the other by about forty meters. Franco was in the middle of the line which was always the best butt, however outside of that no special consideration was given to him. Nothing was done differently for Franco than for any of the other guns and no special care seemed to be taken to protect him. As we approached his butt, two military aides were taking the Generalissimo's guns out of their cases and preparing the cartridges and the seat for Franco's loader, just as was occurring in all the other posts along the line. No bodyguards were present, only his loader and "secretario" – the same as for every other guest – "secretario" is the name for the man responsable for picking up the birds at the end of each drive.

Luis and I walked up to the Generalissimo's butt... not feeling as relaxed as we would have been, had we been approaching any other butt. Despite Franco's unpretentious manner, he inspired respect and though unassuming he was not cozy. It was easy to understand the awe his ministers and officers felt for him. Today the Chief of State was dressed much like the other men in the party, tweed knickers, wool knee socks, a tweed shooting jacket and an Austrian shooting hat. Men never seemed to notice cold weather... Luis was also only in a wool shooting jacket but although the morning was sunny, it was a bit crisp, so I was wearing my my warmest shooting divided skirt and wool jacket plus my long shooting cape pulled tightly around my shoulders and still felt chilly. Franco was testing the feel of his gun when we arrived, lifting one to his shoulder and then lowering it. After the usual "buenos dias", Luis immediately broached the subject that had been on his mind..

"Mi General" - one of the customary manners of addressing Franco, "Has Your Excellency heard the news about Cuba this morning?"

Franco's expression showed that he was immediately interested. "What news, Luis? About Cuba did you say? What's happened over there?"

"The radio announcer stated that Presdent Bautista has been obliged to leave Cuba by plane only a few hours ago and is now in New York City. He was ousted by a group of rebels."

The General looked at Luis for a moment in silence and then shaking his head said, "Well, well. I had not yet been informed. Thank you for this significant information, Luis." Then he paused a few minutes more, glancing at the ground, seemingly turning the news over in his head. Finally looking at Luis again, he added. "I always said, those dictators never come to a good end."

Luis and I walked back to our butt dumbfounded. Franco did not consider himself a dictator. How could that be.? And how was it that he had not been advised of such an important international occurence. We were doubly shocked.

Despite the chill of the January weather the day was glorious in the midst of rolling red fields criss-crossed by endless lines of olive trees – and in the distance were the snow covered mountains of Granada, the usual clear blue sky. the view could not have been more beautiful and invigorating. Although I was not shooting, it was delightful just to sit in Luis´ butt and watch him down one partridge after another, in spectacular twists and turns- Luis was a great shot. I had learned to shoot early in my marriage - mainly because as soon as the shooting season began, Luis would be several days each week someplace shooting partridge and I soon realized that I was faced with spending several months a year without a husband or learning how to shoot myself. Although I'd been taught how to shoot men in the espionage training school in Washington, D.C. it took some time and was much more difficult to learn how to nab those small fast birds. The way we shoot in Pascualete is the same as in Jaen or any other shooting property in Spain. The hunter does not go out with a dog and walk the fields hoping to flush a covey of birds as is the case in Texas. Instead the guns sit in a butt and wait for the birds to fly over. About forty men are beating the bushes, flushing the birds and directing them to fly over the line of guns. In Pascualete our butts are made of retama bushes - we sit in a small cover waiting for the drive to begin.... it takes from half an hour to forty minutes.... meanwhile our country assistants ....secretarios and loaders... are quite talkative and dispense much free advice and local lore. They enjoy the shoot almost as much as we do and are indispensable for restraining the dog, loading the guns and picking up the birds after the drive is over. We had a wonderful time, although different from what I had imagined – it was a surprise to realize that this dictator was so void of pretentions and also a loving family man. I should not have been surprised - really important people are almost always more unpretentious in their private lives than the unimportant ones.

CHAPTER THIRTY

LAWRENCE OF ARABIA

By the time the sixties overtook us, I had become as spanish as any other woman in the penninsula, at least on the surface - their language, customs, literature, clothes, food and hours were mine. I wore a mantilla to the bullfights , I calculated in kilos instead of pounds, kilometers instead of miles. Often I was taken by my own compatriots for Spanish. One night after dinner in the American Embassy the then American Secretary of State approached me - he was visiting the American Ambassador Angier Biddle Duke and the black tie dinner was in his honor.

"Countess, you are the perfect example of how I have always imagined a Spanish woman." I thanked him, but did not consider it was the moment to tell him that I was actually American - he had made such an effort to be polite and agreeable. But he continued - "You Spanish women have something unique. I don't know how to describe it—so feminine , so exotic." I was beginning to feel extremely uncomfortable—now how could I dare tell him that I was not Spanish. But he didn't give me time. "Our american women don't have that mystique." So I remained Spanish for the rest of that evening. Repeatedly foreigners took me for Spanish, yet I continued to be the person visiting americans contacted when they needed a special solution to a problem.

Babe Paley, elegant wife of the powerful owner of CBS, the most important TV channel in the USA in those days, called to say she had given our telephone number to Truman Capote who was coming to Madrid with Cecil Beaton and asked me to take care of them. I didn´t know Truman at all, nor that he had recently become one of the most famous authors in the USA nor did anyone else in Spain. When he entered our salon Luis and I were both startled by his appearance - the bang of blonde hair over his forehead, the wide flowery bowtie and the tone of his voice. Nevertheless after a few minutes we discovered that he was charming and that night we took him and Cecil to Lucio's restaurant for dinner, thoroughly enjoying his clever sense of humor and conversation. But we realized that with Spaniard's old fashioned mentality it was going to be difficult to invite him with friends anyplace. Therefore after showing him the sights of Madrid we decided that the most pleasant way for him to enjoy his visit would be to travel around the country. I suggested he begin in Granada and reserved the train tickets for him and for Cecil, his charming photographer companion and off they went. Many years later I happened to pick up a bedside book in the house of the Windsors in Paris and read for the first time his account of that trip. Later when we went to New York we learned that Truman was the social star of the city, but it was still too soon in Spain for people to accept anyone who dressed and acted like Truman. Spain's coming up to date would take more decades.

 The Paleys continued to ask us to befriend friends visiting Spain - we were delighted to do so because those they recommended were interesting personalities. On one day in early 1962, Bill Paley called asking us to help his friend Sam Spiegel who was coming to Madrid and had a serious problem. He said that Sam was having difficulty getting admitted into the Ritz Hotel in Madrid. Sam Spiegel was a famous movie producer, having made many popular popular films – African Queen, Bridge Over the River Quai and others - we had also met Sam before briefly through Deborah Kerr and Peter Viertel who also telephoned us requesting the same favor. The problem was not an easy one to solve. The woman who ran the hotel Ritz was well known to Luis and to some of his relatives. Many of them had lived there at the end of the Civil War while repairing their homes that had been destroyed or while looking for new living quarters. This respected lady was referred to as "Doña Carmen" and had become famous among

Madrid's aristocracy . Doña Carmen believed that people related to the world of the cinema would detract from the distinguished atmosphere of Madrid's most elegant hotel – in her opinion they attracted photographers and fans would accumulate in front of the hotel crowding the entrance. Nevertheless somehow Luis convinced Doña Carmen to accept Sam in the hotel – thus Sam Spiegel became the first film personality to be admitted to the Hotel Ritz. After that his gracious behavior and generous tips opened the door for others of the cinema world. Nowadays it's difficult to believe such inexplicable prerequisites could ever have existed.

When Sam telephhoned to thank Luis, he asked him to lunch the following Tuesday when he would be in Madrid. "My reason for this visit, Luis, is that I am going to make my next film, a very important one, in Spain and I need your help on various matters ."

The following Tuesday in "Jockey", the top restaurant in those days, Sam revealed the details. "This film's about Lawrence of Arabia. And it just happens that the only place I can find the atmosphere and the Arabic architecture necessary for it is in Sevilla. My scouts have searched throughout the Arab world, in Kuwait, in Saudi Arabia and even in Morocco. It's been useless. The film can not be done anyplace else. Only Sevilla has enough beautiful arabic buildings and can provide the atmosphere Cairo had in those days of Lawrence."

What Sam wanted was to meet Luis' cousin, the Duchess of Medinaceli, who lived in Sevilla. She was the eldest daughter of Luis' uncle who had recently died and since there were no sons, Mimi had inherited the title and many of her father's properties –including "La Casa de Pilatos", the famous and most beautiful arabic palace in Sevilla that Sam's scouts had told him would be ideal as the main building for his film.

Mimi Medinaceli agreed to Luis's request and was actually delighted to have her magnificent palace used for the film and to meet the famous actors who were taking part. In those days it was not yet customary in Spain for owners of famous properties to rent them for public use. Later Mimi became a close friend of many of the stars of that film and told us she had enjoyed enormously their presence in her home. Since we went often to see the filming , we met the stars—Omar Shariff, Peter O'Toole, Alec Guiness, and the great director, David Lean.

During the filming Sam invited me to take my children to witness the battle scenes that were being done in the desert outside Almeria, a Mediterranean city on Spain's south Eastern coast. We boarded Sam's yatch in Malaga and went overnight to the coastal city where the filming was taking place. Luis and Miguel, my two youngest, about ten and twelve, were enthralled watching the mass of actors on horses racing across the desert. I was surprised because I had not known that such a huge desert with dunes and hills and sand storms existed in Spain. Hundreds of extras dressed in chilabas and turbans gave the impression of being in an Arab country. As a gift to my children Sam invited each to choose one of the horses – they were both fond of riding and when the film was finished Sam had the horses shipped to Pascualete. For years after my children enjoyed riding their movie-trained horses which with a mere kick in the plank would fall down and roll over as if dead as they had been trained for the battle scenes. Also Sam had imported one hundred and twenty camels from Morocco. He made us a gift of as many camels as we might want for Pascualete where he thought they might be useful. The idea of having camels in Pascualete sounded wonderful and I accepted immediately – but one of my Moroccan friends advised that camels could make much trouble –that they became wild and extremely difficult to handle – that I would have to find an arab to come over from Morocco to control them - that I would regret having them. So I refused his offer. Today Sam's camels or their descendants are in the Madrid zoo which was the only place they were accepted but I have always regretted not having a few Lawrence of Arabia camels in Pascualete.

In Sevilla that winter during our visits to watch the filming I became friendly with the Hindu wife of David Lean- She loved to shop and since she did not know the city nor where to go, I sometimes accompanied her. She was delighted to discover that Sevilla had shops where she could buy mantones de Manila , antique fans and gypsy dresses. This was in December, the weather was cold and while we walked through the narrow chilly streets, I was suprised to see that she was always dressed in a long chiffon Sari with a wide bare midriff. Sevillians were as surprised as I was and observed her everyplace we went. Although Sevilla weather in winter is not apt to be freezing, it is too cold to be in the street with a bare midriff. When I asked her how she could stand the cold wind on her bare skin , she laughed. "Oh, we Hindus never feel the cold; we massage our skin with oil, I am very comfortable, not cold at all." Then she added, " And if I don't wear my Sari, the gypsies here think I am one of them and accompany me everyplace. You are aware I am sure that their origins come from our part of the world." I told her that the Maharani of Jaipur had already told me this because she had been often mistaken by gypsies as one of them.

CHAPTER THIRTY – ONE

PALEOGRAPHY, CANILLEROS, TIA CARMEN

We were constantly restoring that big ancient stone building of Pascualete - also we tried to make a garden and a swimming pool behind it. We struggled to perk up the barren appearance of the entrance patio as well. Luis had moved his brood mares from Oyarzum in northern Spain near San

Sebastian to Pascualete and each year we had more mares to provide race horses. Meanwhile the house's history persisted to intrigue me- a history full of mysterious people who had lived there over many centuries. But I had not had time free on my trips to Pascualete to visit the historian in Caceres whose address Padre Tena had given me. Now that I knew people had inhabited the house in the thirteenth century and that in the fifteenth their last name was Loaisa, I wanted to know more about them – each year I was more determined to discover when the building had come into Luis' family. When I pestered Luis about going to Caceres to meet the historian, he kept saying "next time". So I still had not learned how to read paleography when one Sunday afternoon at the races in Madrid Luis'Aunt, the same Countess of Yebes came to our box to chat with me. She was an historical biographer and I knew she would be sympathetic to my problem of wanting to uncover the history of our fascinating house. As soon as I told her about my desire to learn paleography, she was helpful .

"Luis inherited Pascualete and many other fincas in Extremadura from his grandfather the Count of Torre Arias, whose family came from Caceres," she began. We were sitting alone in the box during one of the long waits between races while Luis and our other guests had left to see the horses."That family name was Golfin, one of the great families of Extremadura. As you know last names and titles in Spain are different. Titles are useful when investigating the history of a family because in our country only the eldest son inherits the title or all the titles, if there are many - if there is no son then the eldest daughter inherits the titles. Therefore if you learn how to read paleography, you will be able to study the family archives of those past centuries and learn more about tht family."

"The Golfins palace in Caceres is, called the Casa de los Golfines and is perhaps the most beautiful of the old fortress palaces in Extremadura," she went on. "You must meet a friend of mine in Caceres, the Conde de Canilleros – he is the authority on Extremanian history today and he can find someone to teach you paleography."

That was the same name Padre Tena had given me, so during my next visit to Pascualete months later, on one hot day in August , I took the road to Caceres, about thirty minutes distant by car from our finca. I had telephoned before leaving Madrid and Count Canilleros and I had settled on the day and hour convenient. Luis and some friends were shooting "tortolas", doves, which in the month of August fly from their nests in the trees into the fields to glean the remains of the harvest - they are small tasty birds and gather in great bands in Extremadura at this time of year. So while Luis was shooting doves I was finally on my way to Caceres to meet the Count of Canilleros.

    A huge stone archway leads into the ancient part of the city which is referred to in signs on the main road as "The Monumental Medieval City" - my car tires rubbed on either side of the curb of the narrow arched entrance road as I passed through the stone wall which encircles the old part of the city. Now I found myself in a medieval plaza with a Gothic cathedral on the far side and two huge palaces enclosing the other sides. Approaching the first person I saw, I asked if he could tell me where the Conde de Canilleros lived; he pointed towards the impressive granite structure directly in front of me.

On the magnificent facade of the Canilleros palace was the usual family crest, carved in stone over the arched doorway. The windows were covered by intricately designed iron gratings, similar to those in other spanish medieval cities. Entering the open doorway I was immediately in a cool refreshing large paito surrounded by thick granite columns where two maids in black uniforms and white aprons were dusting the leaves of several large green plants. Before I could say anything a door on my right which gave on to the patio opened and a lean, distinguished man with a scholarly air and a warm smile walked towards me. His well-tailored grey suit struck the only modern note in this sixteenth-century setting.

"I am Miguel Canilleros," he said as he kissed my hand. "Welcome to Caceres."

He motioned me to pass before him through the open doorway and I found myself in a dimly lit high-ceilinged library with railings on all sides and ladders leading up to second story bookshelves. My host led me past two large writing tables, when we reached a cosy corner with comfortable armchairs, he invited me to sit down.

In the summer Spanish houses are usually dark inside. There was no air-conditioning and the huge outside shutters were shut to protect the interior from the heat of the strong August sun. The small infrequent windows in this fortress palace made the darkness even more profound and it was several moments before I noticed the many family portraits and illuminated genealogical charts crowding the wall space.

After answering my host's enquiries about Tia Carmen, I proceeded to explain my interest in the history of the Golfin family and my desire to learn paleography, desperately hoping that he was not going to find me an ignorant bore.

However very aimiably he offered me a cigarette and sat back in his chair, saying, "I made our appointment in the afternoon because, since I read and work until four in the morning, I never awake until one o'clock the next day." He paused to tell a maid who had just appeared to bring us some water. Then he went on:

"How satisfying that finally a member of the great Golfin family is interested in its glorious traditions! He paused and settled himself in a more relaxed position in the worn leather chair. "I was born here in this palace, as were all my ancestors since the year 1511 when it was constructed by my forebears. Most of the old palaces of Caceres are still inhabited for certain parts of the year by the descendants of their original owners, but the Casa de los Golfines, your family palace , the most beautiful has been uninhabited and neglected for the past eighty years.

Your visit pleases me for many reasons, but especially because it indicates that you, whose husband and sons are the heirs to the titles and traditions of the Golfins, will receive them with great interest and appreciation. For one who loves the history of this city and who has dedicated his entire life to its study, as I have, anyone who shows an interest in these matters I consider a special friend."

He chatted on about the history of his family and then looking at his watch, exclaimed. "It's almost six o'clock. My mother and I always have tea at this hour. Would you be kind enough to join us?"

We walked back into the patio which now was splattered with late afternoon shadows to the opposite side where an open door revealed a little old lady with sparkling white hair sitting at a round table in a rather barren room. She was dressed in black right to her ankles, with a little narrow white lace band around her neck. I was introduced to the dowager countess and we pulled our chairs closer to the small petticoated table to feast on thick black chocolate and cognac-drenched cakes. I wondered why my hosts referred to this as "tea" and marvelled at the old lady's sturdy liver which had weathered so many afternoons of this Spanish repast. I was aware that many spaniards still partook of a small cup of thick chocolate for breakfast which for centuries had been the usual start of their day, rather than coffee or tea as in other countries, but I was surprised to see that hot thick chocolate was also consumed instead of tea at this hour. .

My distinguished host and his mother began to tell me about my husband's forebears. Each centuries-old Golfin was dragged out of his tomb and discussed in the most intimate and gossipy manner., as if they were friends they saw regularly. They knew which ones were attractive, which had been intelligent, which married well - all sorts of choicy bits.

About an hour later, as I took my leave, I asked my host if he could direct me to the Casa de los Golfines. Since I had never seen it, I did not want to return to Madrid without seeing it. He looked at me in amazement:

"What! You have never seen the Casa de los Golfines? Nothing could be simpler—come with me!"

We took a few steps across the plaza, turned left at the corner of the cathedral and in that instant, right in front of me, I saw the most beautiful palace in Caceres. The last rays of the sun were casting rosy shadows on the carved stone borders of the roof and the old stones of the fortress tower glowed golden in the Estremanian sunset. As I looked up at the facade I saw the careful lettering of an inscription carved deep in stone:

ESTA ES LA CASA DE LOS GOLFINES (THIS IS THE HOUSE OF THE GOLFINS)

The Conde de Canilleros murmured... "How proud that first Golfin must have been when he placed that inscription on his palace....what a daring declaration! He built that palace in 1260 and it was the first palace in this city."

We walked closer to the ancient stone building, Canilleros encouraged me to turn the corner so I could view the depth of the building which he informed me had housed over three hundred people at times, he said that laborers on Golfin's nearby farms had often inhabited the palace with their families when it was dangerous to live in country areas. Canilleros loved to talk about these old buildings. "Since your husband's uncle, who now owns the house, rarely comes to Caceres, and noone of the family has lived in that house since 1873," he went on, "the palacio is completely closed with only a caretaker and his wife to guard it. Look at those shutters. Although they are closed you can see that they are destroyed from lack of care."

I looked up at the balcony windows where some of the shutters were falling off their hinges and one of the windows was broken. What a pity I thought. How will the inside of the house look, if the outside is so obviously neglected.

"You see, in 1873 there was an attempt to bring a Republic to Spain and your husband's great grandfather sold many of his wife's properties to help finance that endeavor." Canilleros shook his head. "A big mistake. The Republic floundered in eleven months time. Not only did your famly lose much land and a great part of its fortune, but also the result of his actions brought him into disgrace with the monarchy for some time after." Canilleros pointed now to his own palace. "Since my family has remained such close neighbors to the Golfins for centuries, we know all the intimate details first hand from our ancestors. One day we must go through this palace's magnificent drawing-rooms and courtyards together."

He took my arm and led me up a steep street constructed entirely of steps - obviously automobiles were not able to navigate in this part of the ancient city ."Before you leave, stroll with me a bit through these old streets, so I can tell you the history of some of these other palaces. Caceres, as you see, is one of the few medieval cities which has remained undestroyed throughout the centuries. Much credit is due to your ancestor Golfin who faced up to Napoleon's troops when they tried to march into our city."

Now we were walking along a street lined on either side by granite palaces. There was a strong resemblance to Trujillo, but here no tumbledown buildings marked the passage of time. the count told me a dramatic story about each one as we passed by.

As I said goodbye, he kissed my hand."To think that it has taken an American to make the family Golfin come back to life!" were his parting words. That night I drove home laden with pamphlets and books the Count had given me and with dreams of the many things I wanted to learn. Fortunately above all Miguel Canilleros had offered to find a teacher for the lessons I wanted in paleography.

My conversation with Canilleros included referances to the battles led by the Duke of Wellington against Napoleon's French troops in 1809 in Talavera de la Reina. "Those English are amazing," Canilleros had commented. " Only a month ago the descendants of those same soldiers came here to Caceres and financed a building to be constructed in memory of their ancestors who had lost their lives in our defense one hundred and fifty years before, and they also contructed a monument in their honor in Talavera."

I told the Count that the actual Duke of Wellington had been shooting "abutardas", royal bustards, in Pascualete with us only a few months before. He was impressed and told me "At least our government made a gift to Wellingon after that important victory of a large property outside Granada - that probably has kept the family's attachments to Spain alive." I told him that Luis and I had spent a weekend in that property invited by Valerian Wellington to a partridge shoot, that the Wellingtons came often to Spain for their vacations. I remembered the lovely view of the snow covered mountains of Granada and the nice house which was large but quite modern since it had been built about 1860.

That summer Canilleros arranged lessons in paleography for me in his library with his secretary. I returned daily to Caceres for the lessons and thanks to this man who became a great friend, I learned paleography so well that I was able to translate any ancient documents in Trujillo's archives.

CHAPTER THIRTY – TWO

THE FOUR SISTERS

    During that summer in the sweltering month of August almost every afternoon I drove to Caceres, taking the narrow dusty dirt road through Santa Marta and wound down scary turns to the river, then many twisting curves back up again. Since it seldom rains in Extremadura from May until October or sometimes until November , the river was almost dry and the dust so thick that I could barely see through the windshield. On the second trip I devised the solution of wearing my polo hat which I often used for riding in hot months, with a chiffon scarf tied over that around my head and face which avoided the layers of dust from collecting on my eyelashes and making me choke. I had to keep the windshield working constantly to remove the dust so I could see where I was going.

    Luis was still shooting with friends again who had come to Pascualete for the dove passes so he was happy, and I was equally so sitting in Miguel Canilleros' library taking lessons in paleography from the teacher.

    Partly through Luis' family archives which went back to the year eight hundred and partly through archives borrowed from the Caceres "ayuntamiento" (town hall), I learned not only how to read spanish paleography but also much about Pascualete's history, including the Napoleonic wars that destroyed Trujillo in 1808. At the same time I became aware of some incredible family dramas that Luis had never heard of.

The last ancestor with the name Golfin y Colon was born in 1760 when the title Torre Arias entered the family . The first last name, Golfin, was of the father and the second last name, Colon, was the mother's.- she was the direct descendant of

Christopher Columbus or Cristobal Colon as he is called in Spanish.

I remember one day in Madrid when I came downstairs looking for Luis and found his secretary standing in the library, apparently absorbed in studying a document from the Spanish Ministry of Justice. The secretary was a history buff, and especially interested in Luis's many famous ancestors. "This is really fascinating," he said, fingering a framed genealogical chart. "You never told me Luis was descended from Christopher Columbus. It says here that Luis's great-grandfather was Columbus's direct and principal heir – that ancestor had only one son and one daughter."

"And that daughter was Luis's great-grandmother," I told him. "These things impress me, too, but Luis gives no importance whatsoever to his family's history. Columbus's male heir, Luis' cousin, carries the title of Duke of Veragua, (which translates to the amusing title of Duke of See Water), which was bestowed upon him by Isabel the Catholic in 1496. That title, of course, always went to the male heir, but Luis's great-grandmother inherited Colon's archives and papers - she also inherited our ranch Pascualete in southwestern Spain where you've visited."

Jerry nodded. "I didn't know I'd been in a property belonging to Christopher Columbus."

"Let's say to his descendants. That ranch has been in Luis's family since 1231, way before Columbus discovered America. The amusing thing is, the archives show the family was not especially impressed with Colon's main descendant when he married Golfin's daughter."

"He probably had less money or properties. That was what counted in those centuries," Jerry answered.

This particular Golfin was an only child and therefore the sole heir to the huge Golfin fortune and properties. This fortune he had enlarged in 1788 by marrying the only child of a noble

Trujillian family, called Maria de las Casas y Mendoza, Marquesa de Santa Marta, Condesa de Quintanilla and several other titles. Most important for me was the fact that she had inherited Pascualete which added to the Golfin properties making them one of the largest landowners in the province.

Since Pedro Golfin y Colon's father was still alive when he married, he had not yet inherited the family title of Torre Arias and began his married life using his wife's title of Marques de Santa Marta, which they continued to use throughout their lives.

Four daughters were born to this couple. In 1806 the eldest, seventeen years old, married the son of a Caceres family who at that time was Spanish Ambassador in London. Don Pedro Cayetano Golfin prepared a fabulous wedding feast for his daughter to which the entire population of Caceres was invited and which lasted seven days. An enormous fountain of wine was set up in the plaza in front of the Casa de los Golfines and there were bullfights and dancing in the streets daily. At night the old palace reverberated with the sounds of theatrical representations and fancy galas.

However, tragedy was not far off. A year later, word arrived from London that this daughter had died in childbirth.

Two years later the newly-married second daughter and her child also died in the same manner. The family doctors held a consultation and advised Pedro Golfin and his wife that it was very possible all four sisters had the same physical malformation and there was little hope that the other two girls could survive childbirth.

As is often the case, sorrows never come singly - a few months later the city of Caceres was threatened by the advancing French troops which in 1808 had broken through the ancient walls of Trujillo which they had reduced to rubble, slaughtering many of its inhabitants and looting everything of value.

Pedro Golfin, now a man of forty-eight, highly respected by his fellow citizens and looked upon as their leader and protector, put his personal sorrow aside and studied the manner of saving the people and the city of Caceres from the savagery and destruction as had occurred in Trujillo. However, there were no troops nor enough people in Caceres to attempt a defence against the invasion of the seasoned French army, nor could mercy be expected from Napoleon's troops if they entered the town. All the Spanish cities hitherto occupied by the French had been sacked heedlessly, as had been the case with Napoleon's troups in the rest of Europe.

Pedro Golfin y Colon, Marques de Santa Marta, employed the only means in his power to prevent Napoleon's armies from entering the city. When the French troops were visible approaching Caceres from Trujillo, Pedro Golfin directed the citizens to remain within the city's fortress walls, to close the four great entrance gates, while he set out alone on horseback to meet the advancing enemy troops. The Caceres populace watching from behind the powerful city walls, saw Pedro Golfin, Marques de Santa Marta advance alone to meet the officers in charge of the marching columns of thousands of French troops. Both stopped. They saluted each other. Five minutes later the people of Caceres were astonished to see the French officers give orders to their troops to remain in place - then they saw Pedro Golfin, Marques de Santa Marta accompanied by General Soult, the head of the French troops and three other French officers turn their horses towards the city gates and slowly approach.

The four men entered a silent city; most inhabitants were now hiding in their homes while the French troops remained outside the town walls. Those watching from behind the "almenas" the stone protectors, on the stone wall surrounding the city saw the French officers and Pedro Golfin proceed up to the door of the Casa de los Golfines and disappear inside.

That day, by the time General Soult left Pedro Golfin y Colon had been able to negotiate an agreement by which Caceres became one of the few cities in the wake of Napoleon's troops to avoid all contact and destruction. Not one French soldier ever set foot in the city, and in return Golfin, at his own expense, provided supplies and food to maintain the French garrison in Trujillo. Golfin even became friendly with the enemy officers, who often came from Trujillo to dine at the Casa de los Golfines.

The small town of Santa Marta also was affected by the French invasion –only five families and a widow remained alive in the town which had inhabited over eighty families previous to the arrival of the French. Also remaining in Santa Marta was the small octagonal church, although partly destroyed, and the "rollo", a stone pillar, as existed in all ancient towns and cities – this one had been placed there in 1438 by Alonso de Loaisa, when he created this village as a living area for the many serfs who worked his fields in those long-ago days.

Probably owing to Pedro Golfin's influence with the French officers, or perhaps because of the fact that Pascualete was far from any highway, the French did not touch the old palacio of Pascualete where the Marquesa retired with her two remaining daughters to live out the rest of the French occupation.

From the archives of the Caceres town hall which I had read in Canilleros' library during that hot month, I learned that the last members of the family to live at Pascualete were this Marquesa de Santa Marta and her daughters. Therefore, over one hundred and fifty years had passsed with noone of the family inhabiting it until the day that Luis and I first set foot there.

When the French soldiers withdrew two years later in 1810, the Marquesa de Santa Marta learned that her palace in Trujillo had been completely destroyed. This house was referred to in the old tourist books as the Casa de la Boveda. The documents said that every piece of furniture, painting and article of value had been burned or pilfered. The Marquesa after the sacking of Trujillo never returned there in her lifetime although she had gone to her home in Trujillo each time she gave birth, and had cared lovingly for that palace of her ancestors, the oldest palace in Trujillo.

After his wife's death, Golfin, Marques de Santa Marta was much affected by the many tragedies and from that time on lived quietly in Caceres. King Fernando V11 returned to the throne in Spain after Napoleon's troops were ousted - that King's behavior had not been very commendable, but that is another story..

Several times Golfin's two remaining daughters wished to marry, but they always encountered their father's opposition. In 1822 Golfin , at the age of sixty-two and beloved by all who knew him, died in Caceres. Four years later the third daughter married and a year after, fulfilled the doctors' fatal prophecies when she died in childbirth. Now only one daughter was left, the youngest Petra, the only remaining Golfin heir and the wealthiest girl in the province in 1832, at the age of thirty-four, fell so in love with a handsome young man called Jorge Gordon and defied her fate marrying him.

When a year later the time came for Petra to give birth, she went to Madrid where the greatest European specialists had been summoned to care for her. When the deilivery began three doctors were carefully following every development. But their efforts were ineffective and the poor girl was three days in labour. As I read the old archives I could imagine the suffering and horrors Petra endured, not only because of the pain but having to put up with so many men practicing their useless treatments on her.

While I was reading this, Miguel Canilleros was sitting at the other end of the silent library, deeply engrossed in his own work. My curiosity was such that I interrupted him and called across the silent room, asking if he knew what had actually happened in that moment to the poor girl. Canilleros lived more in those past centuries than in this one, so I felt certain he would have something interesting to tell me. After all, the two families, Golfin and his Ovando family had been neighbors for the last four centuries. He had to know.

Closing his book he crossed the long room, the paintings of his ancestors looking down upon us as he came over to where I was reading the paleography of the yellowed manuscript.

"Of course, I know what happened. That Golfin fortune was the largest in Extremadura and if this girl, Petra Golfin, Marquesa de Santa Marta, Condesa de Torre Arias, died without issue all those properties would go to my ancestor who was the closest blood relative, not one cent would go to the husband. In fact the outcome would have affected me today."

I asked Migel Canilleros, "what do you know about the husband, that Jorge Gordon."

"Not much. He was related to a Scottish family that had settled in Malaga - he probably married her for her fortune. She was no longer a young girl. In those days age made a big difference in women."

"But do you know any of the details of what happened that day?"

"I certainly do. My ancestor and others of the family had gone to Madrid to be present for the childbirth. Naturally the result would affect them greatly. Outside the sick room my relatives waited. I understand that there were quite a few of them, since the ancestor affected was elderly and had many children who could benefit from the results. After three days and two nights, nerves were at a breaking point. Rumor had spread quietly around the room that the husband was being questioned. His permission for a macabre operation was necessary. It was a terrible decision for the man to make. Evidently the doctors had explained hat her bones had to be chopped with an axe, much as one would do to save a calf."

"Oh, Miguel," I admonished, "you exaggerate. They were probably thinking of a doing a Cesarean operation."

"Not at all. What did doctors know about Cesareans in 1833! Anyway what I'm telling you is the information my ancestors passed on to my grandparents and to my mother. It was believed all over the province that Petra would most certainly die in childbirth as her three sisters had. Since the fortune was so immense, my ancestor and his children were already convinced that they would soon be the richest family in Extremadura."

Miguel sighed while I waited. "But" he went on, "Gordon gave his consent, and his wife was mutilated, suffering the most awful pain. They say her screams were dreadful. And thus your husband's great-grandmother was brought alive into the world."

Later I learned that that girl child born in 1833, who came into the world under such grotesque circumstances married a fellow from Cordoba, Enrique Perez de Guzman el Bueno, descendant of the hero of the castle in Tarifa. Also this same man was the one who some years later in 1871 sold many of his wife's extensive properties to bring a Republic to Spain – which must have necessitated a lot of courage at that time. As a result when the republic failed eleven months later the government expropriated the property next to the Palacio de los Golfines including the family cemetary.

The Guzman el Buenos evidently had not lost their individuality nor their courage, inherited from their famous ancestor of 1338 because this daring descendant , my husband's great grandfather had a courageous brother, one of the few aristocrats to become a top bullfighter. Recently a newspaper article in Madrid recounted this gentleman bullfighter's extraordinary exploits of over a century before when he alone had killed in Sevilla ten huge bulls in 1831. Nevertheless he did not live long because on a trip through the mountains of Toledo in April 1838 he was ambushed in his stagecoach by bandits and slain. The description of the body as copied in the recent newspaper account from the official report of that day describes a man very similar to descriptions of other Perez de Guzman el Buenos that I have been able to find over the years. His cadaver was described as... five feet eleven inches tall... age thirty two, light color hair, red beard , long sideburns, light blue eyes , an athletic body. Added to all that was the description of his boots, blue silk shirt, linen socks, his trousers etc. Even my husband at that age was near that same description.

After reading the history of this family and of Extremadura, I began to have some understanding of why so many noble families abandoned those provincial towns. It was not because they suddenly lost interest in the country that encouraged them to move to Madrid, but the French invasion had left their homes ruined and their properties destroyed. Also many roads and bridges had been demolished by the French troops. During the following years for some time law and order ceased to exist in these areas where bandits took over. At the same time landowners were assessed enormous new taxes which added to their difficulties in rebuilding and reclaiming their ravished properties. Therefore this move to the capital, which began as an interim means to weather the post-war era, with time became a general trend and many old families became isolated from their provincial homesteads.

CHAPTER THIRTY - THREE
JACKIE KENNEDY AT DUEÑAS

As Easter week ended in April 1966, Luis and I prepared to go to Sevilla for the Feria which usually takes place one week after Holy Week. Again we were invited to "Las Duenas" but this year Jackie Kennedy was going to be one of the house guests. Although the Fair lasts for one week beginning on a Sunday with bullfights every day, the most popular festive days are the last three. The Princess of Monaco, the former movie star Grace Kelly, was going to be there as well –she was staying with the Duchess of Medinaceli in the "La Casa de Pilatos" where Sam Spiegel had centralized his film "Lawrence of Arabia" only four years before. Also Audrey Hepburn and her attractive husband Mel Ferrer were going to be in a suite at the Hotel Alfonso Trece - so we were looking forward even more than ususal to these days of The Fair.

 Cayetana had never met Jackie - the Spanish Ambassador in Washington , Antonio Garrigues, had told Jackie about the Feria and had asked Cayetana to invite her. Not yet three years had passed since Jackie´s husband had been assassinated and the Ambassador thought the Fair would cheer her up. Everyone in the houseparty was thrilled to learn that this famous woman was going to be with us. Angier Biddle Duke, the American Ambassador in Madrid and his wife Robin had informed Cayetana that Jackie had requested a hairdresser ...probably because I had told her when she phoned me from New York that there would be many changes in outfits and hairdos during the Fair. Certainly a hairdresser would be necessary if Jackie wanted to wear a mantilla which necessitates a large chignon - I realized she would want to take advantage of all these glamorous Spanish costumes.

News about the presence of the famous guests, especially Jackie, attracted masses of paparatzzi and by the time Luis and I arrived the city was packed not only with the usual fans of the Fair but with press from all over the world.

 Mimi Medinaceli was giving a Ball in her palace in honor of Grace and Rainier - this alone would have attracted the press. An extra large amount of top flamenco artists were expected to be in the casetas every night. The most spectacular carriages and horses would parade every day as well and the matadors were the best of the season.

Mel Ferrer and Audrey had been in Sevilla several days, sightseeing in the nearby towns of Jerez de la Frontera and on the coast in the Puerto de Santa Maria. So we decided to go to Sevilla a day earlier to help with their sight-seeing. We met them at the entrance to the Barrio de Santa Cruz – in medieval times the Jewish section, which has remained one of the picturesque parts of the city. Fortunately they had escaped from the hotel by a side door and no press was following us.

As she greeted us Audrey was saying, "The enchantment of this city is the sounds. During our walk over from the hotel it was so delicious to hear the clip-clop of the horses hoofs on the cobblestones, the rattle of the carriages, and the music of a guitar in a patio."

We were on a narrow curving street which took us to a small plaza with benches and orange trees. A gypsy was sitting there singing a song to the tune he was strumming on his guitar. Enchanted we stopped to listen. When he finished we dropped a few pesetas in his plate and continued wandering through the twisting streets. There were no carriages on this narrow street, but a lone horseman was turning the corner in front of us. The whitewashed two-story houses all had balconies dripping with flowers and vines - the streets were so narrow that some balconies almost touched those of the house on the opposite side. The doors to the old houses were open so that any passersby could view the patios - some had superb gardens, others just a few palm trees - most were private, but now and then among them were a few small "pensions", (boarding houses).

"What a pity," said Audrey. "We could be staying in one of these dream houses instead of a pompous hotel." Audrey was always impressed by authentic simple things, she possessed an ethereal quality, unlike anyone else- with a love for plants, animals, a tune, or just children romping in the street. Mel had once said to me, "she's like an exquisite diamond that sparkles on all sides. I have never known anyone like her."

Through an entrance to a restaurant in the Calle del Agua number six, we saw a garden with small tables. In the center was an old-fashioned well that looked make-believe with purple bougainvilla climbing around an elaborately carved iron arch. A knarled grape arbor provided shade over the tables. Only one corner was occupied by two elderly people. We decided that no matter what the food would be like we couldn't resist the quixotic atmosphere of the place. During lunch Audrey asked me what Sevilla had been like when I first went there. I told her about my first visit in 1944.

"Oh that was during those awful war years", Audrey interrupted. " I was living in Holland with my mother then. I was only thirteen and taking ballet lessons." She glanced for a moment down at her chest, and laughingly added. "In fact we had so little food , that I've always thought those years of starvation when I was developing is the reason my bosoms never filled out more."

In the meantime Luis and Mel had been chatting. "Luis," asked Mel, "at what hour should we go to the Fairgrounds tomorrow? Audrey and I have been offered two spectacular horses which we are going to ride in the "paseo".

Mel knew the "paseo" was the daily parade of horses and carriages during the Fair -he spoke spanish, his parents having been born in Barcelona. The horses he had been offered belonged to two popular Sevillians- Angel Peralta , the greatest "rejoneador" (bullfighter on horseback) and his brother.

"And I'm scared to death," interrupted Audrey. "I was thrown from a horse while filming in Mexico a couple of years ago, and broke a lumbar vertebrae. It really hurt and I was laid up for a month. I don't know how to ride. I'm afraid I'll fall off again."

"Well," Luis said, "don't think about it any longer. There are so many horses and carriages in the "paseo" that the horses hardly move. Even the most spirited ones remain absolutely calm. It has always surprised me that no matter how crowded the streets are and how many people push into them, the horses never make a false move during the parade. You'll be perfectly safe."

From there we took a quick stroll through the Plaza de Espana, an addition made to the city for the 1898 World's Fair. Despite my many visits to Sevilla I had not seen it before. The plaza was fascinating, in a large semicircle were a series of gigantic paintings made entirely of colored mosaic tiles showing all the periods of the history of Spain.

Years later, I was in that same plaza with Malcom Forbes' when he lifted off in his spectacular balloon, a replica of Cristopher Columbus´ flagship the "Santa Maria". That was the ship in which Columbus had discovered America. Malcom had invited me and some friends to come with him in his plane from New York. Naturally Sevilla was the proper place to launch his flight, but as Malcolm rose in his balloon and floated over the city at the mercy of the breezes, suddenly the wind changed direction - the huge globe moved across the city to the bullring – where we saw that it suddenly landed. Fortunately no bullfight was taking place, but getting Malcolm out of the ring became a problem. No one had the key - not until I was able, with Cayetans´s help, to contact the Mayor were we able to get Malcom and his deflated balloon out of the well- locked bullring.

As we turned to leave the plaza a scraggly old gypsy in a red bandana and dirty flowered skirt grabbed Audrey's hand, obviously wanting to read her fortune. I pulled Audrey´s arm. "Don't pay any attention to that gypsy, Audrey. She's a fake .

This city is filled with gypsies during the Fair -they try this trick just to get money," But Audrey, always kind to everyone, stood meekly with the woman's long messy black hair hanging over her arm as she passed her dirty fingers over Audrey's palm.

We continued to move on so I did not hear the gypsy's tale, but when Audrey joined us a few minutes later her normal bright smile was gone. Usually gypsies tell an optimistic story hoping to get more business from others nearby, but I realized that this time the woman had given my friend disagreeable news. Years later Audrey mentioned that fortune teller to me, saying she had been absolutely correct in what she foresaw and had ruined her beautiful day. But that particular day Audrey did not tell me what the bad news had been.

Suddenly Luis realized we would have to hurry back to las Dueñas to be ready to go to the bullfight and we waved to a passing carriage taxi. Audrey and Mel continued their sight seeing – she didn´t want to go to the fight.

The next day, Friday, most of us guests were on the terrace of Las Dueñas when Jackie arrived with the American Ambassador and his wife. The car entered the gates about two thirty, just before lunch. Jackie came up the wide official stairway onto the terrace with Cayetana and one by one every guest was introduced. She was very attractive in a knock-out white suit, designed by the celebrated couturier, Oleg Cassini. Everyone was delighted and looking forward to meeting her. Only Luis and I had met her before, not even Cayetana had ever met Jackie. At first Jackie was shy and very quiet – although she smiled warmly there was little conversation, she seemed shy and said little. Only three years had passed since the assassination in Dallas and we all realized she was still affected by it. Most of us had come back early from the "paseo" in the Fair grounds for this formal luncheon in her honor. Since I had been on horseback, I was still in riding costume and boots. Ambassador Duke approached me, he was an old friend and a charmer – a professional in putting everyone at ease. His wife Robin was also a great social asset and while the introductions were being completed and cocktails served, we continued to chat looking over the railing down at the patio below. The Dukes had never been in Las Dueñas before so I took advantage of the time before lunch to take them through the salons off the terrace.

When we returned Jackie seemed to have become more comfortable and was now talking with some guests. In New York she had the reputation of talking more to the men than to the women and this seemed to be the case today. When we moved into the dining room and took our seats, Jackie was seated next to the Count of Teba, a handsome man, considered the top shot in Europe. During the rest of the luncheon she was in animated conversation with him and appeared to have cheered up.

The rectangular dining room has a carved ceiling of arabic design – in the center wall is a fireplace flanked by a portrait of Cayetana as a child in riding costume and another portrait of her aunt, the Duchess of Santoña also on horse back . Normally on the days of Feria the luncheon was in form of a buffet so each person could arrive at whatever time was convenient between two until five. In this way Cayetana's personal schedule was not interrupted either - usually she had lunch before the guests since she went earlier to the fairgrounds with her children in the carriage and returned before the rest of us. But today because of Jackie, Cayetana had arranged a formal luncheon and we were seated around the large oval table.

Also today the luncheon took more time than usual so there was little time to help Jackie with the hairdresser to put on her high comb and mantilla and to put on my own as well–so I went without. But Jackie was delighted with hers. The mantilla is flattering with its long lace scarf framing the face and flowing down from the high comb to the hem line of the dress.

The combs upon which the mantilla is draped are sometimes six inches high and give the woman heigth. Also I suggested Jackie wear a decorative shawl which I had brought for her. We call the shawl "manton de Manila" – it is customary to take one to the bullfights in Sevilla - these colorful embroidered silk shawls for generations had been imported from Manila and still are. The Phillipines until fifty years before had been one of Spain's favorite colonies.

The next day Jackie and I went riding. We left for the Feria early about one thirty - but had much difficulty - the roads going out from las Dueñas were crowded with press and photographers, - we finally arrived at the Caseta of the Aero Club in the fairgrounds where the grooms were waiting with our mounts.

Cayetana had checked with Fermin Bohorquez, a friend with a great stable – he was also a famous "rejoneador", a matador who fights and kills the bull from horseback. Fermin had sent "Nevada", his most beautiful white mount for the occasion.

My riding habits had been made by two famous couturieres, Herrera Y Ollero- Jackie loved the riding costumes I had brought. She liked to ride as much as I did and was thrilled when I told her that we would have the best pure bred Spanish horses in the fairgrounds. We were the same size so my riding outfit fit her perfectly but her feet were larger so she had to wear Luis' boots. I asked her to choose between a green velvet jacket and a red one . She grabbed the red one - in fact it is now among her things in the clothes section of the Metropolitan Museum in New York as well as Luis embroidered chaps.

One takes a special posture when riding in the Feria -slightly arrogant, chest out, waist in, right hand on the right thigh and reins in the left. Sevillians are exacting about riding outfits and style. Some details are so minute that after making many mistakes I still fail to be on a par with the natives. Spanish ladies on horseback look devasting, especially when they wear the old-fashioned side saddle outfits which are romantic and striking - unfortunately neither Jackie nor I had ever mounted side-saddle, but I had a side-saddle skirt and changed into it when I returned to Las Duenas for lunch - the skirt drapes up on one hip and is extremely glamorous . Jackie was disappointed that I did not have an extra one for her, but she tried mine on and enjoyed just walking around in it. Both of us decided we would have to learn how to ride side-saddle, but of course we never did. Where, outside of the Feria of Sevilla, would we ever be able to ride that way.

Anybody can ride in the Feria if he can find a horse. There are usually a group of Mexicans in their fancy costumes and big hats, American cowboys show up as well - everyone becomes everyone else's friend - people speak freely to each other. Normally speaking to persons one does not know in Europe is considered an Americanism, but during the Fair it is customary and adds pleasure and charm. But that particlar day it seemed the only horse the people wanted to see was Jackie's horse and all of them wanted to talk to her.

The feria grounds consisted of three or four streets of about four blocks, parallel to each other - as we rode we tried to peep into the casetas where flamenco dancing and singing was going on, but we never could get close enough to see inside any of them.

Again the next day somehow Jackie and I managed to get to the fair and mount our horses but the crowds following us were still greater and it soon became impossible to move. Jackie was fun to be with and was no longer shy and quiet- she's a good rider and enjoyed all the fuss, but were not able to do any real riding nor was Jackie ever able to get off the horse to enjoy the flamenco inside the casetas. Nevertheless at least she was able to see the carriages -the landaus and the breaks with four or six or sometimes even eight perfectly matched Cartusian horses bedecked in pompoms and silk ribbons. She was impressed with the coachmen's costumes and admired the men on horseback in their attractive outfits - the short jackets, the straight wide brimmed hats, the vest and cummerbund, the three quarter length trouserss, the leather boots and leather chaps. Many horsemen had a pretty girl in a long colorful ruffled dress perched side-saddle behind on the horse's rump, her arm around his waist, the other clutching the saddle to secure a firm seat. This is called riding "a la grupa".

Mingling in the crowds gypsies in long bright skirts and shawls also followed us, sometimes we had to stop to watch little girls, some just children ,dancing in the middle of the street in long ruffled skirts - bright red rouge on their cheeks and lipstick too. People were dancing at random in all fairground streets unattentive to the traffic and carriages, but when we neared they stopped and crowded around our horses.

Automobiles are not allowed inside the fairgrounds but carriages are inexpensive - any visitor can enjoy the pleasure of riding through the fair to enjoy the view. The streets are dirt or cobblestoned, the "casetas" are merely small canvas improvised coverings with wooden slats and decorated with colorful streamers and Japanese lanterns. The small "casetas" are open to the public - the hospitable Sevillian families allow people at random to enter and sometimes invite to "a copa of jerez." Sherry is made in the nearby city of Jerez de la Frontera - Spaniards prefer the sherry called "Fino la Ina" or "Don Pepe", and they drink it icy cold. They also insist that good "light" sherry should be not more than six months old. On the floor of the private carriages there is usually an ice bucket and a couple of bottles of sherry for the owners to offer to friends who pass by on horseback. When Jackie and I pulled up on horseback in front of a friend's caseta, it was impossible for the host to get through the crowds around us, to offer the usual "copa" de sherry.

Going to the fair at night was even more difficult. After dinner in Las Dueñas instead of leaving around one A.M. for the Feria , our usual hour, we waited another hour hoping the press and photographers would give up and disappear, but no luck- even if Jackie was disguised with scarfs and sunglasses , the press recognized her. As a result it was difficult to enter the casetas where we knew a great show was going on. Jackies'visit spoiled the fun for all of us. It was also a let-down for her. She confessed to me that she was accustomed to this disagreeable pursuit which always spoiled her fun -that wonderful affairs in different parts of the world which she could have enjoyed were all converted into a nightmare by the press. She realized that Sevilla in Feria gives everyone a taste of the happy, wild spirit for which Spaniards are famous but she was not able to enjoy it.

CHAPTER THIRTY-FOUR

HISTORY OF LAS DUENAS

I was more interested than Luis in the history of "Las Duenas"- probably because he was accustomed to living in homes centuries old – in the United States we have nothing that can compare to Europe's ancient palaces. Las Dueñas had been been built around 1460 and the history of its origins and those of the "Casa de Pilatos" the palace of the Duchess of Medinaceli are united. In those years both palaces had belonged to the Pineda family. But the Arabs were still in control in parts of southern Spain and had not given up reconquering their lost territories and belongings. For some years they resorted to kidnapping wealthy personalities to obtain ransoms. Juan de Pineda, the man who owned both palaces, was kidnapped by the Arabs and his wife was obliged to sell both houses to pay the ransom. Then a couple of years later in 1483 both palaces were bought back from the Arabs by a wealthy Spanish woman, Catalina de Enriquez de Rivera.

She gave the Casa de Pilatos to her eldest son and Las Duenas to her second son. The two palaces although similar in style are quite different; both were erected in the mozarabic style- in fact they had been built by "mozarabes", (christians who employed arabic tastes and customs). Mimi Medinaceli´s palace, was larger and more formal but both have the same Islamic aura with plaster carved inscriptions in Arabic forming decorative borders on the walls - arches surrounding the central patios – beautifully carved wooden ceilings.

Almost two hundred years later in 1646 a Duke of Alba married a daughter of the Enriquez de Rivera family and that is when the Albas became owners of Las Dueñas. But about one hundred years before that, when the palace was still owned by the Enriquez de Rivera family, a daughter of Hernan Cortes, the famous conquerer of Mexico, married the eldest son of the owner. It is written that Hernan Cortez, when he returned to Sevilla often went to Las Dueñas to visit his daughter and his grandchildren. I like to imagine the valiant Cortes' sensations – he had been born and brought up in a poor town near Trujillo - when he first walked into the arabic beauty and luxury of his daughter´s home after having spent so many years in the wilds of Mexico as it was in the sixteenth century.

Another ghost that intrigues me and surely roams the old palace is that of the Duke of Alba who inherited the Palace more than a century later through his wife who was an Enriquez de Rivera. He had been sent by the Spanish king on a mission to Rome and during his years there had a love affair with the wife of the King of Rumania. Finally his affair became so public that the scandal spread all over Europe and the Pope was obliged to write to the King of Spain, "will you get your Duke of Alba out of here...he is making a cuckold of the King of Rumania and already has sired two of her children."

Nowadays during Feria before-dinner cocktails are served in a room with red damask walls and a fancy arabic carved ceiling. On the walls are portraits of the Empress Eugenie of France, Cayetana's great aunt who married Napoleon the third - there is also a portrait of him as well as other relatives of that generation.

Eugenie and her sister Paca had been born in Granada. Their mother, an English woman had married the Conde de Teba, was determined to marry both her beautiful daughters well. After Paca had married the Duke of Alba, the Countess of Teba, took Eugenia to Paris where she attracted the attention of Napoleon the third. Many aristocratic mothers were trying to catch Napoleon for their daughters, but it was the spanish Eugenia who became the Empress of France. In Spain Paca, after giving birth to three children died of tubercolosis at any early age, but Eugenie died many years later at age ninety -five in Las Dueñas. She had weathered many tragedies, among them that of losing her only child , a twenty-one year old son in a battle the French were fighting in Morocco. Over the door of one of the guest bedrooms is the inscription "Here the Empress Eugenie of France spent many of her vacations in Spain."

Today in Las Dueñas customs of centuries before continue to exist as if time had not passed. The coachmen sitting up front in the carriages are still dressed in the same short pants and blue silk pirate-like bandanas, and the paintings on the walls of personalities who lived there years before facilitate their ghosts roaming about – the palace maintains an atmosphere that has changed slightly despite the many centuries. Ancient houses have the capacity of reaching you, of capturing your imagination and your emotions. If one lets oneself go, one can almost hear the voices from the past. The presence of those who have lived before us is a delightful cozy quality found today in ancient houses all over Europe.

CHAPTER THIRTY – FIVE

CORDOBA
MONASTERIO DE SAN JERONIMO

Ever since Luis took me to Cordoba to meet his sister a few weeks before our wedding, we had both wanted to return – mainly to see the famous city which we had missed on that first visit. Finally the occasion occurred when his uncle, the Marques del Merito, asked us to spend some days in his fabulous monastery home, "San Jeronimo" which was high up on a mountain outside the city. This unique home actually had been a San Jeronimo monastery built by the San Jeronimo monks in the sixteenth century. Peps Merito's mother had bought the monastery from the San Jeronimo monks at the end of the nineteenth century and had only changed a small part of the enormous structure in order to create comfortable living quarters for her family and guests. Peps Merito had been a pilot in the Spanish Civil war and was wild about airplanes, so below his ancient sixteenth century monastery home he had built a small airport in a huge open field to harbor his five planes.

From the first glimpse the city is intriguing - I had heard and read much about its history. It had been founded on the banks of the Guadalquivir river a thousand years before - the Romans had protected it with thick stone walls. Entering by car over the original Roman bridge, one passes through the Gate of Triumph and is already in another era. Despite the Roman beginnings - inside the atmoshpere is Arabic. For me Cordoba seems closer to the atmosphere of Islam than any other part of southern Spain . Sevilla and Granada also have a large history of Arab control with many important Islamic buildings but the ancient part of Cordoba retains more of the atmosphere of its arab forebearers. The winding twisting streets are too narrow for automobiles but one can walk or take a carriage and there are often a few ass-drawn carts carrying pottery, foodstuffs or even twigs.

But since we were in a hurry after the long trip to arrive at Peps´s home, we passed quickly through the old city and headed for a narrow country road beyond the city in the direction of the mountains. About fifteen minutes further on is the road leading up the mountain to the Monastery home. The narrow dirt road is steep and has many curves, winding higher and higher until one arrives almost at the crest of the mountain. Then suddenly a gigantic stone building seems to jump out of the thick overgrowth, its huge facade so covered with bright red and orange bouganvillea that it almost appears to be on fire. Surrounding the majestic structure is endless dense green underbrush and thickets with the mountains rising wild and isolated high above.

Descending spellbound from the car we entered a patio, which on one side was formed by a large chapel and on the other by thick vines of fat yellow lemons climbing up a high stone wall. The head guard was waiting to give orders about the luggage and lead us to our rooms - soon we were passisng through one large patio after another, five lovely patios in all, each more beautiful than the one before, each had gardens of flowers and frothy green plants plus here and there decorative ancient stones—also tall slim cypresses and more bouganvillea of various shades. The children and the governess were taken to rooms on the second floor near ours. Actually they were much too young to enjoy anything – Alvaro was perhaps three, little Luis was two and Miguel was still in a crib. Peps and his wife Graciela, had been thoughtful enough to include our three little boys in the invitation which made the visit more fun for us since we, like most young parents were fascinated with our children, but I now realized how foolish we had been to bring them.

When we were signing the Guest Book on that first visit, Luis saw that his mother who had died when he was eight years old had been there when she was pregnant with him, thirty four years before. Luis was touched and I decided that I would place a similar book in Pascualete on my next trip there.

Perhaps not only the faith of the monks but also the beauty of the patios had enabled them to support the isolation of this magnificent building so far from the outside world. Undoubtedly a more beautiful place to live would have been difficult to find. Even today the huge stone building maintains an aura of the peace and silence that those holy men who had lived there during three hundred and fifty years must have known.

About twelve other guests made up the rest of the houseparty -

later we all met in a large salon bordering one of the huge patios. As Peps Merito began to introduce us to the other guests, another couple entered the room. The husband was especially handsome and the attractive wife appeared to be pregnant. As I shook the hand of the man, Peps introduced me to "Beltran Domecq". The newcomer smiled and said, "Don't you remember, we have already met." I knew he had to be wrong, I would never have forgotten such a fabulously good looking man. When he realized that I did not remember at all, he went on. "The first day you arrived in Madrid, must have been January 1944 because I was living in the Hotel Palace while taking my University exams. You appeared in the entrance and went to the reception desk. I was very impressed and went to the bellboy who was just going to take your two suitcases, I gave him five pesetas, and told him to disappear. Then I had to struggle with a Mexican looking fellow who tried to pick up your bags which I took and went up in the elevator with you. Now don´t you remember.?"

Suddenly the entire scene those ten years before came back. I remembered clearly how nervous and worried I was in the elevator, suspecting that he was a German agent who had already uncovered me and somehow knew that I was an American spy. He was – so tall –so blonde so German in appearance and so determined to follow me !!! Little did I know then what an important role this young man , the first spaniard I had ever met in my life - was to play many times in my future life. His eldest daughter was to marry my eldest son thirty years later.

The weekend with Peps and Graciela was delightful. We dined in the huge refrectory where for almost four centuries the San Jeronimo monks had dined. Our bedroom on the second floor was ample with a sitting room and windows from which we could look down the mountain to the city and the valley below. The large salon below on the main floor adjoined one of the five patios - it had two huge fireplaces so high that several persons could stand under the canopy . Next to that slaon was the monks´refrectory - a huge dining area planned to seat over one hundred and forty monks; nevertheless it was still used by the Meritos with no alterations. The long rectangular room still possessed twenty of the original thick seventeenth century wooden tables, each table seats twelve, the original high pulpit where one monk used to read prayers while the others dined in silence, remains in the center of the refrectory.

That first night while having dinner – twelve of us seated at one table in one end of the enormous long room, after adjusting ourselves to the fascinating atmosphere- the high ceilings, the enormous space, the heavy silence we all seemed to emerge suddenly from the spell and bombarded Peps with questions—principally about the monastery. He explained that most of the stones used by the monks to build the place in 1546, had been taken from the magnificent arabic palace, "Medina Azahara" ,the ruins of which , he added, we had passed on our way up the mountain, but probably had not noticed, since there was little remaining of what had been the most luxurious of all Islamic palaces in Spain in the tenth century. It had been the center of Islamic Spain since for many centuries the Caliph of Cordoba had been the most important ruler in Arabic controlled Spain. The only known university in all Europe in the ninth century had also been in Cordoba. All the culture of the entire western world was concentrated in Cordoba during those centuries. As in fact had been the case with the Romans before that, both the Emperor Trajan and Seneca the great philosopher had been born in Cordoba.

We all wanted to know more about the city -it was the first visit several guests had made , so Peps proceeded to recount some of the old legends. One, he said was about the year 950 when the Calif of Cordoba went to visit the Calif of Granada. While there he fell in love with his host's beautiful daughter and the wedding was arranged. When the Calif of Cordoba brought his bride back to his magnificent palace, he expected her to be impressed with its grandeur and splendour. However although she admired the delicately carved architecture and the fountains and the size of the palace which was much larger than the Alhambra in Granada, she was sad and admitted that she was homesick. When the calif finally got her to tell him what she missed most, she said that the Alhambra in Granada was surrounded by beautiful snow covered mountains and that she did not feel at home in such a barren green countryside. Her husband told her to have patience, that soon the mountains around Medina Azahara would also be crested in white. Then he ordered thousands of Jara bushes to be planted all along the moutain ridges as far as one could see. In a few months the young princess was happy— the surrounding mountains were covered with large white flowers of the Jara bushes giving the appearance from a distance of snow- Jara blossoms are similar to white dogwood blossoms. Thus Peps´amusingly explained the mass of white blossoms that still remained surrounding the monastery on the neighboring mountains.

The next day on our way to the swimming pool we walked through the many patios again, observing details that we had not noticed —the gardenias and multi colored orchids , the fountains which in each patio were different. The monks had adopted some Islamic customs, perhaps without being aware- since there were fountains in every patio producing the peaceful sounds of splashing water which the Arabs believed contributed to peace and tranquility of spirit.

Emerging from the long monastery building, Peps had made a modern swimming pool on the edge of the mountain; below was the entire valley of Cordoba, the river glistening like a satin ribbon, parts of the ancient Roman walls and spires of many churches and buildings could also be seen there below us.

Our bullfighter friend Luis Miguel Dominguin, who was the star matador for the Cordoba Fair that week, had been invited for lunch; the women guests were looking forward to meeting him. Recently Luis and I had been with him in New York where he had caused a sensation in evening dress with a glamorous spanish cape thrown over his shoulders. He was in New YOrk for a television program and his charm was such that although he spoke very little english, he managed to do the program in English, speaking in broken English fearlessly and somehow making himself understood. Of course his accent and mistakes only made him more appealing - his handsome appearance and debonair bearing helped as well.

    When we arrived at the pool where lunch would be served , Luis Miguel was already in the water. Later while we were eating in bathing suits, suddenly one of the women guests pointed to the scars on Dominguin's body. "look …...horrible wounds from the bulls". The women guests crowded around to get a better look. He entertained them with the names of the cities where he had been gored and described the passes that had caused each wound. The women continued to gaze enraptured with the ugly redish injuries. For a few minutes the discussion continued. "Oh, that big one must have been terrible." "that scar is deeper". "Is that one from the goring in Bilbao?" "In what bullring did you get that". One guest was gently tracing with her finger the curve of some old stitches.

One of the most fascinated was the wife of a diplomat in the U.S. embassy in Madrid. She had seen few bulllfights, maybe none, and so knew much less than the rest of us but she was plying him with questions. At this time Luis Miguel was the matador "numero uno" and his fame had spread even to foreigners. Someone had told this lady that the sign of true bravery in a matador was his ability to go back into the ring after a bad goring. This and more remarks continued to make Luis Miguel the center of attention. Meanwhile my husband was sitting quietly watching and listening. He was also stretched out at the side of the pool in his bathing trunks. Suddenly in a calm deliberate voice he interrupted the discourse.

"Anyone interested may notice that I have a few wounds too," All eyes then turned to Luis --- the one half of his left upper arm had been removed as the result of a severe wound suffered in 1937 during the civil war—then they saw the other huge scar on his right thigh which was from shrapnel when in another battle he had almost lost his leg. His wounds were so much more drastic and impressive than Dominguin's that for a few moments everyone gaped. Then Luis ,as if it had no importance, commented, "Of course mine have only been the result of wounds of a war."

We all laughed heartily. Luis' rapid clever remarks always sparked up any conversation and brought humor to a group. In the afternoon we all went down to Cordoba for some sight seeing. First Peps took us on a stroll through the old quarter to see the patios of the houses which were open to the public. In the summer these interior open patios are covered by huge canvas awnings under which the inhabitants spend hours seated on low wooden chairs; the heat of the middle day leaves the patios empty until evening when the scalding sun has receeded, then the inhabitants, like rabits emerging from their dark holes, again appear to bask in the beauty of this most important part of their homes. In the winter Cordobans also spend much time in their patios which are filled with masses of red, pink and orange geraniums. Each year in the Feria of May a prize is awarded for the most beautiful patio, and strangers during that week are welcome to admire the different ways each group neighboring families had enhanced their patio with plants and flowers.

Peps pushed us on saying "follow me to the most important monument in Cordoba – also it's one spot that is always cool."

We continued along the twisting streets and up some steps into a plaza filled with orange trees and the sweet fragance of the last blossoms of the season. Silently he led us to a large arched entrance. As we walked through, we all stopped – astonished – by the vast incredibly beautiful interior. "This", said Peps ,"is the Mezquita of Cordoba, one of the seven wonders of the world."

Of course I had heard about this famous Aarabic Mosque, but nothing had prepared me for what I now saw - an endless forest of graceful marble columns crowned by hundreds of arches in white and red stripes, combined by an infinite nmber of bovedas, arches and columns. The vastness of the place was as impressive as the awe-inspiring quietness. When I recovered from the shock of the breathtaking sight, I turned to Peps who was at my side.

"So many columns!" I whispered.
"About nine hundred. Once upon a time, there were many more."

Slowly we walked through lines and lines of graceful columns, under endless red and white arches. Only our footsteps resounded on the marble floor. Then the sound of a faint trickle of water sprouting from fountains someplace ahead. As we proceeded, abruptly a catholic altar interrupted the symetry of those columns and arches, like a wrong note, destroying for a brief distance the harmony of the exquisite arabic architecture.

"Too bad," Peps murmurred, " when we Spaniards reconquered Cordoba in 1236, King Ferdinand the third, ordered the Mezquita to be consecrated as a Catholic cathedral but to be maintained in its original state. However in 1489 an over-zealous bishop who claimed that such Islamic beauty might distract the populace from their christian religious obligations began the mutilations which continued off and on until the beginning of the nineteenth century. But much greater destruction had occurred between 1523 and 1607 when hundreds of columns and arches were torn down to build a cathedral and many small chapels along the borders of this great Mosque. Fortunately the destruction stopped around 1882 when this Mezquita was declared a national monument and certain restorations began. Anyone can see today that these gothic constructions of the catholic area, although worthy in themselves, detract from what had been and still is the most beautiful holy temple in the world of Islam."

But as we continued to explore further, the myriad of columns and arches continued and we were once again in a thoroughly arabic cathedral.

Peps told us that the arabs had used many of the columns left by the Romans and that many were of a magnifcent quality carved from marble that in those early centuries had been shipped to Spain from Carthage, Rome or Byzantium. The heavy silence seemed to put a spell on us. It had been an emotional experience never to be forgotten.

Outside in the old city again, it seemed that those ghosts of Romans and Arabs were still accompanying us as we walked by the small hotels built inside the depths of the ancient

Roman walls. The small "Hotel Amistad", and another called "Hotel El Triumfo" maintained the arabic atmosphere with patios containing trickling fountains and geranium blossoms. Nearby we dined in an attractive popular restaurant called "El Churrasco" where the owner claimed that the delicious specialties were from recipes passed down from centuries goneby. The tasty dishes certainly defied any sarcastic comments written by foreign visitors of a century ago criticizing the spanish cuisine.

The next afternoon after lunch in an intriguing restaurant with more delicious food and the atmosphere of a convent mixed with a wine cellar, we went to the "corrida", the bullfight. We had ringside seats which was important since Dominguin was the star that May afternoon. In his second bull, he was was such a success that the president of the arena flipped out his white handkerchief, a sign for the "aguacils" to give the bullfighter one ear which they immediately sliced off the dead black animal and handed to our hero. Luis Miguel began his turn around the ring as is customary , the spectators aclaiming him and tossing flowers and wine bags at his feet. When he arrived in front of our seats, he stopped a moment and most likely remembering the american woman's fascination with his wounds the day before, he threw her the bloody ear. She ducked and shrieked in terror and it was of no avail that we told her she should grab it, that this was a great compliment, but she couldn't even touch it. We were all much amused, but I fear that she was one American woman who never became a bullfighting fan despite her fondness for Dominguin.

When we left the following day I knew that San Jeronimo would always be the most outstanding private home I had ever seen in all Spain.

CHAPTER THIRTY - SIX

THE JEWS AND PEDRO GOLFIN

"Aline", Miguel Canilleros said, it's getting late and I must leave." We were just finishing a long luncheon in my house in Madrid. "If you are so determined to get more intimate information about Christopher Columbus and the persecution of the Jews, may I suggest you look into your husband's family archives." He went on to explain that Luis' ancestor, Pedro Golfin y Colon, had been the closest assistant to Queen Isabel during the second half of the fifteenth century and had accompanied her at all times, that it was during Golfin's occupation of that all important post that the decree to oust the jews from Spain had been issued. I was especially interested in the problem of the Jews because Luis had astounded me once in New York when I heard him telling someone in an arrogant manner that he was jewish. Later when we were alone, I asked him how it was that his family presumed to be catholic and that now he said he was jewish. "Although some of the most important people in New York are jewish", I said, "they don´t brag about it as you were doing".

"Well in Spain we are proud of having a jewish ancestor." Luis answered "All top grandee families have some jewish blood. Of my twenty-four last names, at least two are jewish. "Torres" is a jewish name and so is "Silva" – so I can say that I am jewish -why not". Luis always astounded me – he knew by heart all his last names for the last many cenutiries- I could only name a few of mine. Then Luis went on explaining, "They were very rich jews and my family must have been delighted to have them joined in marriage – of course that was about four hundred years ago, but we admire jews in Spain, why don´t the Americans?"

Canilleros continued telling me he was as fascinated as I was with the history of Spain′s sixteenth century and the shameful persecution of the jews. " Also, Aline, it was during those same years, at the end of the fifteenth century, that Queen Isabel agreed to finance Columbus for his first trip to the New World."

In fact" Canilleros went on , "Pedro Golfin remained with the Queen until she died – you can see the painting in the Prado Museum of him sitting on the chair next to the Queen's death bed." The Count of Canilleros had been standing but suddenly he took another cigarette from his silver case and sat down again. He smoked non-stop and finally died because of it about ten years later. Now he continued with the same subject. "These archives are especially meaningful for you because they show how your husband has come to be the direct descendant and head of family of so many important historical personalities. With marriages, sometimes of daughters, sometimes of sons, your husband today is also the descendant of Perez de Guzman El Bueno, a hero of 1338 whom you will have to learn about in time and also of that Christopher Columbus of 1492 among many other historical characters. And of course he is the direct descendant of this Golfin. Remember titles are passed on to the eldest daughter when there is no son and last names change accordingly. Well, throughout many centuries of our country's history, your husband's ancestors were persons of historical reclaim and through these many centuries and many marriages, he gained the titles and properties you now enjoy.

His cigarette finished, he stood up again, but he encouraged me once more to look into the family archives, telling me that these archives also contained notes accumlated over the centuries about Christopher Columbus. "Evidently by your husband's great grandmother who was the daughter of the head of Cristopher Columbus's family and married the eldest son of Golfin -. this was the second time a direct descendant of Cristopher Columbus had married a Golfin. Remember although her brother inherited the titles and most important properties, she inherited the valuable archives which you will be able to enjoy." He started again to finger his pocket looking for his cigarette case but decided against it and walking towards the door continued, "These archives should eventually belong to your husband when his uncle dies. Now that you can read paleography, you will be able to enjoy them, "were his parting words.

I had no intention of waiting until Luis' uncle died to see those archives. Anyhow Luis had been on bad terms with his uncle since the death of his grandmother but although I tried, his uncle's adminsitrator had refused to let me see the archives personally. Finally the Conde de Canilleros managed to get permission to investigate the archives which occupied an entire floor of a large family building in Madrid that belonged to Luis' uncle. Canilleros had been kind enough to make fotocopies of the manuscripts and sent them to me. "This is the best I could do," his note stated. "The archives are not well catalogued and it's difficult to find the exact dates I was looking for."

With great excitement I glanced through the photocopies. To my dismay some pages went back to the tenth century—but others were dated near 1492; however they did not refer to Colon's discovery of America. None the less as I started to read, I became intrigued. Many pages were written by my husband's ancestor, Pedro Golfin himself around the end of the fifteenth century while he was accompanying the Queen - I had to use a magnifying glass to be able to distinguish the letters. All pages began by identifying the date and place- some had been written in Valladolid, others in Burgos, and they were not consecutive. During all this time he had continued to accompany Queen Isabel on her travels throughout her domain. Everything Golfin had noted absorbed me and I spent hours reading the pages, not able to tear myself away from the flowery ancient script. The sheets I was reading were shiny white fotocopies, not the original yellowed fifteenth century manuscripts, but the contents took me back into another world.

Two were letters Golfin wrote to his wife. One was dated January 1504, "My most dear wife, I take pen in hand to tell you of my great sadness to see that our brave Queen is each day weaker. I fear for her life. We have seen every doctor who is schooled in this part of the realm. I regret that with the declaration that our Queen was obliged by her religious advisors twelve years ago to sign against the Jews, the best doctors who were all jews of the realm have gone. It is ironic that with her own hand perhaps she signed away the one possibility of being saved from this cruel illness that no one seems to undersatnd. There is no doubt in my mind that the son of Don Ezequiel would have understood Her majesty's sickness."

Another letter a few months earlier: "My Most dear wife, I take pen in hand to tell you that I am in deep worry because of what you tell me about our sons' behavior. It is frightening indeed that young people these days do not obey their parents as we used to do. What is going to happen to the country if the youth behave in this disgraceful manner? Who would believe that children brought up as ours to take care of their lands and to respect their elders opinions have decided against my wishes to follow that foreigner Colon to the other side of the earth with his wild ideas and who up until now has brought back only a few pieces of gold, and some bedraggled natives too puny to reach the age of reason. What good can come of a trip into the unknown where the larger part of these crews never return? I am against it. I understand, my dear wife, your prayers and desolation. I am also sad that for these past three months I have not been able to see you and do not think that I do not regret it as do you. When will these interminable trips give me time to go home to Caceres."

While going through these papers, I received a call from Miguel Canilleros. He would be a few days more in Madrid and invited me to join him that afternoon in a literary meeting. "This will be interesting for you, Aline. It's my "tertulia", my group of historian friends who meet regularly to discuss mutual interests. Some of the people you will meet are important intellectuals. No place could you get better answers to some of your historical questions."

As I pulled up before Canilleros' apartment in Madrid a few hours later, I saw him waiting in the doorway with a chubby elderly man in a black suit and thick black-rimmed glasses; I recognized Jose Maria Cossio from newspaper pictures I'd seen - he was an outstanding member of Spain's prestigious Royal Literary Academy. Neither man was able to open my jeep door, so I jumped out and ran around to the other side to let them in. They were not accustomed to women driving jeeps and much less to women opening doors for them, but nevertheless they managed to squeeze into the wide front seat close up beside me. They were men from another era -I felt. I realized they were thinking that American woman are very very strange.

We proceeded on to the Cafe Gijon on the Calle Alcala. Although I had never noticed the place before, I now became aware that it was just across from my dressmaker, Pedro Rodriguez, where I went regularly and who had made for me many sensational hand embroidered long evening gowns that had created much success in New York and in Paris.

On the sidewalk in front of the cafe were several small tables which today were empty; we proceeded inside, I liked immediately the old fashioned atmosphere of the plain bar room. Groups of men were seated around small tables in darkened corners, engulfed in smoke and surrounded by coffee cups. We went towards a banquette facing one of the marble topped tables. When I arrived all the men stood up, and I was introduced with much bowing and handkissing to Antonio

Rodriguez-Moñino, a famous intellectual, Jose Camilo Cela anovel prize winner for his literature, plusthe famous writerJose Maria de Cossio and other less famous historians whose names I have forgotten .

As soon as I had taken my seat and odered a cup of tea, I mentioned that I'd never been to a "tertulia" before. One of my new acquaintances explained that in Spain almost every man had his particular "Tertulia" but that it was a spanish custom that was fading out. When Canilleros told the group that I was interested in details about Cristopher Columbus and also about the eviction of the Jews and when he said that I read paleography and had been reading manuscripts from the archives of the Conde de Torre Arias, they looked at me with more interest.

"You are fortunate," said one of the men, " Pedro Golfin was one of the few aristocrats in the fifteenth century who knew how to read and write, maybe for that reason he preserved a detailed record of his activities. In those days most aristocrats had "escribanos", writers, who did this for them. Golfin was an excellent Secretary of State for Isabel the Catholic and accompanied her everywhere. No one knew more about her character and her opinions."

Another man joined in, "You may not be aware, Countess, that the country in those times did not have a capital, so Queen Isabel governed her domains by travelling on horseback from one province to another, inhabiting the home of the leading aristocrat in each area."

Encouraged by their interest, I explained that some of the manuscripts I had read thanks to having learned to decipher Spanish paleography referred to problems between the Jews and the Inquisition, and told them what I had learned so far. As time went on my access to Golfin's important archives and my interest in historical matters led me to become a regular member of the Tertulia and in the following weeks I learned much about that interesting period of spanish history—partly from the manuscripts Canilleros had obtained and partly from the wealth of knowledge of the members of the Tertulia. The results are the following.

One of Golfin's greatest preoccupations in the year preceeding 1492 was to alleviate the problems of the jews whose land was being confiscated and their fortunes expropriated for the mere reason that they were jews. In some cases these unfortunate Spanish "sefardis" as the jews were referred to, were burned at the stake. Golfin tried to show the Queen how much of this was being done out of jealousy. Nevertheless in november 21st, 1492 Queen Isabel and King Ferdinand signed the edict against the "sefardis".

In one of the many letters Pedro Golfin has written to his wife, I had read, "This edict against the sefardis will begin years of tragedies and injustices." I understood that Golfin did not dare to write even to his wife further details about the matter since the Inquisition had been recently establilshed by the powerful leaders of the catholic church in Spain and they executed anyone who opposed them.

While studying in more detail Golfins archives I kept coming across details about the Jews. Among his papers I found one letter from a jewish friend. "Pedro, do not endanger yourself trying to help us, anyone who may have a grudge against you can use blackmail to hurt you or to get money, just as they are doing to us jews. It is useless to think you can fight the Inquisition and Torquemada."

The truth behind the hypocritical facade of religious unity was explained by one of the members of the tertulia, Antonio Rodriguez Moñino. He told me that the jews composed a wealthy group who kept much to themselves, mainly to observe the strict prerequisites of their religion and standards, which were quite different from that of the christians who represented the majority of the country. The other historians agreed for the most part, that the greater mass of spaniards would never have taken sides if they had not been manipulated and threatened by greedy clerics and mediocre politicians who wanted to eliminate the jews whose influence in the country and especially in the banking world was very strong.

The topic was taken up heatedly by the Tertulia. During those weeks I learned that during the end of the fifteenth and the sixteenth century a well planned campaign had been carried out with money of the church and often with funds obtained from innocent christians, to defame the jews and to convince the populace that their ills and their poverty would disappear with the expulsion of the Sefardis.

It was even known in the tertulia that it was Golfin who had obtained a clause in the edict signed by the Catholic Kings which minimized the drastic rigidity of the royal decree against the jews. This edict permitted those Sefardis who were willing to forsake their religion and become baptised and practice the catholic religion to remain in the country and not have their properties expropriated.

However all other Jews who did not give up their religion were not only expelled from the country but their properties were confiscated as well. For the most part they were only allowed to take out of Spain that which they could carry with them. Therefore many wealthy Jews became destitute overnight.

I had found mention in Pedro Golfin's papers of a close and much admired jewish friend who decided to leave Spain and go to Amsterdam - he sold his properties and bank at great loss and was among the first to leave.

The areas with the most prosperous Jews were Sevilla, Medina del Campo and Toledo. Many ancient synagogues were burned, others were converted into catholic churches, the rest were closed. The Inquisition and those who ran it were in a position to collect large sums of money for the protection which many Jews requested for themselves and their families. The exodus from Spain began in 1492 and all those who did not leave were in danger of being imprisoned, expropriated of their belongings and some of being burned at the stake. There began in Spain a period of "Auto de Fe's," the burning of heretics in the streets and in the plazas of the main cities. Those burned publically were principally Jews but in a much lesser numbers those subjects of the Queen who had been found guilty of not observing the strict requirements of the catholic religion.

During all this time Golfin was actively working with a Sefardi friend called Ezekiel Torres to find means of helping those Jews who decided to accept the catholic religion and remain in the country. Their plan was to convince the Jews to marry into Spanish families whose stature in society was important enough to protect them from any encroachment upon their personal safety or upon their fortune. There were many old aristocrats, grandees who were interested in keeping the Jews inside the country and delighted to obtain the financial alliance which a marriage to a wealthy Sefardic family could bring.

Later when it became clear that all the Jews were not leaving, another government campaign was begun against the Arabs, obliging all arabs who would not accept the christian faith to leave the country. The Arabs who remained after the moslem Califs had lost their power and possessions represented the most ignorant and poorest group in the country – they were farm employees, indispendable for large landowners. Many of these large landowners were Jews who depended almost entirely on the arab farmhands to maintain their olive orchards and wheat fields, so this edict also damaged the few jews who had managed to remain in the country and became another means of destroying their power. As a result extensive areas of vital farmland remained barren for years creating poverty and hunger in those areas.

In Pedro Golfin's manuscripts he complained frequently about the decree expulsing Jews and he also critizied expelling the Arabs, but he gave much less importance to Columbus' impending voyage.

My tertulia friends filled me in about Columbus' return from his first voyage to the New world. The Monarchs, Queen Isabel and her husband, were in Barcelona when word was received of Columbus' arrival in Sevilla and of the great discoveries he had made. They requested him to come by land to Barcelona to recount his findings personally. Colon brought with him to Barcelona six Indians, 40 parrots, quantities of other exotic birds and fruits and plants, plus gold and trinkets worn by the natives. He made his entrance parading through the center of Barcelona on a horse with his retinue of exotic indians and animals and birds preceeding him. The Kings received him with ceremony and gave him a seat next to them, an special honor in those times. During the next few days, there were many festivities celebrated for the new hero who the King and Queen honored with the title of "Admiral of the High Seas" and that of Duke of Veragua as well. Also they gave him other royal privledges, some of which his direct decendant enjoys today. It was easy now for Columbus to obtain money for his second expedition; rumors had spread about gold existing in abundance in the New World and it was also rumored that there was a fountain of youth where all who drank of its water would remain young forever. There were even stories about trees that produced golden apples.

In Golfin's papers of february 1504, I read that one of his sons left for the New World with Hernan Cortes, who was a friend from the neighboring village of Medellin near Trujillo. Hernan Cortes, was to become famous as the conqueror of Mexico. He and Golfin's son had both attended the University of Salamanca together where the stories of Columbus's great discovery and the riches to be found on the other side of the ocean had created enthusiasm among the students. In short order other students began to leave for the New World. Many joined Hernan Cortes later when he made a second trip to conquer Mexico.

These "conquistadores", conquerors, were mostly from Andalucia and Extremadura. In fact King Charles, who became King in 1517 did not allow men from other parts of the country to go to the New World - he was in need of men for his battles in parts of Europe where he was conquering principalities in what is today Germany. He even attacked the Vatican in 1537 - in his era the spanish troops were feared all over Europe.

Queen Isabel died in 1504 in Medina del Campo. Pedro Golfin, the Lord of Torre Arias as he was also known, was one of the witnesses who signed her testament.

In later manuscripts written when Golfin was 71 years of age, he mentioned a meeting he had had with Francisco Pizarro who had come to see him from the neighboring city of Trujillo. Pizarro had just returned from the New World and was searching for people to finance his discovery of a land whch he believed would contain more gold than had as yet been discovered. Later this area was called Peru.

Golfin wrote in his manuscript about his meeting with Pizarro, " "I am struck by the strength of character and fitness of this simple man already over 45 years of age. Despite his many years in the New World and his awareness of the deceptions and the few men who return, he has confidence and valor for this new adventure. It will be more risky and more expensive than any other before."

Golfin by now had changed his attitude about trips to the New World and was so impressed with Pizarro that he contributed a large sum of money for the expedition.

Later through my tertulia friends and through Canilleros I learned that Golfin´s son who accompanied Hernan Cortes never returned but he fathered two of Isabel de Moctezuma's children; she was the daughter of the last emperor of Mexico. Later these children returned to Caceres and made their homes there- one can see the palace they built in the old part of Caceres today. The return of these two young men is not recorded by Pedro Golfin who had died by then, but in other archives of the city of Caceres I saw that their return with gold and Indian servants is registered.

Golfin and his wife had eighteen children who reached adult age, which in that time was extremely unusual. Families then were large, but many children died when they were still infants.

Golfin's activity did not diminish with age. In 1537 a dreadful plague atacked the people of Caceres. One fourth of the city of Caceres was wiped out in three weeks. Two daughters of Golfin, who were nuns in the convent he had built next to his palace also succombed. Golfin shocked the town clerics by demanding that the convent be emptied and scrubbed, all clothes burned and worst of all that the nuns bathe. In those times a bath was considered by the inquistion as cause for heresy, but no one dared to defy Pedro Golfin and all had to admit that his methods helped abate the plague. At the age of 84, he died and his grandson became the mayorazgo, the heir, of the family Golfin.

After the reign and death of Queen Isabel, Golfin continued to act as secretary to her descendants. He , of course, was close to her grandson King Charles the first, but Golfin then became the secretary of King Charles' brother Fernando who was sent to Naples to rule that colony which then was very important in European politics.

CHAPTER THIRTY – SEVEN

WINDSOR AND FRANCO SHOOT

The Duke and Duchess of Windsor used to come often to Spain, usually because they wanted to avoid the "terrible depressing weather in Paris" as the Duchess complained in her letters, written on a variety of pale blue stationery emblazoned with their feather crest in white at the top of the page. I have many of these letters in my files. She protested that the weather there was gloomy all year long, not compararable to the sunny dry weather in Spain. Other times they came merely because we insisted they visit us - in Madrid the Duke liked to play golf with Luis during the winter months when it was cold and raining in Paris, and sometimes there were good partridge shoots which he also enjoyed.

On one of their visits we gave a dinner for them. I knew that the Duke would like to meet the daughter of Franco, despite the fact that Franco was responsible for not permitting the Duke's cousin, our King Don Juan to return to Spain. The Duke was always interested in political matters. Everyday when I would go into "the boudoir", (the Duchess' name for their private salon adjoining her bedroom) to say "good morning" there were always stacks of newspapers from all over the world on the floor next to his armchair. He had asked me often what I thought of General Franco and I could only say that I had not seen him often enough to be able to give a reliable account. Then he suggested "at least you seem to live in peace in Spain - no terrorist upheaval as is now going on in Italy".

Both the Duke and the Duchess always made any party a success; they knew well how to amuse people with their witty conversation. Also during this dinner while we were having coffee in the salon, the Duchess showed us the new dance called the "Twist" that she said was the current rage in New York. I had invited Franco's daughter , Carmen and her hsuband and about one A.M. as the Duke and Duchess were leaving, I overheard Carmen saying to the Duke, "Your highness, I will send all the details about the partridge shoot in Mudela tomorrow morning. My father will be pleased to learn that your highness can join us."

Luis and I were delighted to learn that the Windsors had been invited to that particular shoot. Not only would General Franco be there but Mudela was the best partridge shoot in Spain and has a palace converted into a "parador", (government hotel") rented by the government from the Marques de Mudela. The chief of state, we had heard, gave shoots there once a year, as does today our King Juan Carlos .

But we were still more pleased a few minutes later when Carmen took her leave and in her unpretentious manner, said. "Aline and Luis, I do hope you will be able to shoot with us at Mudela also. You would be such a help. After all, I met the Duke for the first time tonight and when he told me how fond he was of shooting partridge, since they are here and the shoot is next week, it seemed to me a good opportunity."

The next morning the Duke called from the Hotel Ritz. "Aline," he said, " please ask Luis to find a place where you and I can practice shooting clay pidgeons. We don't want Luis to come along, he's too good a shot. Maybe you could come with me instead. But I must prepare for the big event in Mudela. My father used to be the best shot in Europe, but I'm the worst and badly need practice. I've heard about that place Mudela and am delighted to go; the duchess is too. Already she's called Ophelia to send her country clothes and told Sidney to send my shooting gear. The Duchess has some new Wellington boots she's dying to have an opportunity to wear."

There was a shooting range in a section outside Madird called La Moraleja where one could practice and Luis arranged for us to go. When the Duke picked me up, he left his car and chauffeur below in the street and came up the many steps himself to get me. I never ceased to be impressed with the man's kindness and consideration, his determination not to take advantage of his position in any way. This morning he was in a blue wool plaid suit, checked shirt, a contrasting tie in small stripes –don't remember what colors and with a brown tweed cap - since it was November and quite chilly a coat over his shoulders of a different tweed. Today as I am writing I have such a clear picture of him as he was that day. I couldn't help commenting. "What a beautiful shooting suit, sir!"

"Puf," he grumbled. "Just my old country suit, Aline. Perhaps it's been made over from one of my father's. I use many clothes of my father's."

We drove out to the Moraleja, about twelve kilometers outside Madrid. Luis had managed to contact a sort of sports club there and found someone to release the clay plates. When the Duke started shooting he was irritated with himself, saying "damn" whenever he missed, which was most of the time, but then he began to get a few and his humor improved. He was delighted to see that I was doing as badly. This put him more at ease. Noone else was present and we did not have to be embarrassed by all the plates we missed. Despite my training with revolvers and machine guns shooting at plates or flying partridge with a shotgun was much more difficult.

"You know, Aline," the duke said,"I don't know what Franco will think of my bad shooting. I've never met the chap, but we have a few things in common and I'm looking forward to talking with him."

"Franco is a very unassuming man, although most people complain that he is solemn and difficult to talk to." I explained."I think the problem resides with those who criticize his seriousness - they have such respect for the Generalisimo, that they themselves become tongue tied when they meet him. The only time I had the opportunity to talk to him I found him very comfortable – also he has a sense of humor and amused me with of all sorts of stories."

The duke chuckled. "Often the case. What's more difficult when one occupies an important post, Aline, is learning how to put the other person at ease. It's annoying to be talked to as if one were a statue. That's one of the qualities that attracted me to the Duchess. She never wasted time being formal with me and what a sense of humor." he chuckled.

All the guests for the shoot would be staying in Mudela and since that was near the small town of El Viso, where Luis' cousin Casilda, the Maquesa de Santa Cruz owned a famous palace that held relics of the battle of Lepanto of 1571, Luis wanted to visit it. He had been fascinated since his childhood with stories of that battle. Casilda, through her mother, also named Casilda and with the title of Duchess of Santo Mauro, was the direct descendant of the admiral of the famous battle of Lepanto and they had converted the small palace into a museum . Casilda was delighted that we wanted to see it, so just before arriving in Mudela, we spent an hour in the small museum.

Casilda's famous ancestor, Alvaro de Bazan, Marques del Viso, also titled Marques de Santa Cruz had been born there in 1526. (These many names and titles are perhaps irritating for the reader - they were for me also when I first came to Spain- as I have noted before - last names and titles are different in Spain and as if that is not difficult enough, everyone must add the mother's name.) This ancestor was the son of a Captain General of the spanish fleet – he had won battles against the French in the north and also against the famous pirate Barbaroja in the Mediterranean.

On our way down in the car Luis told me about Barbarroja who had been a christian pirate, probably a Greek whose nickname, "Barba Roja", referred to his "red beard" – he was blonde and blue-eyed. After many small successes on his own in the Mediterranean, "Redbeard" joined forces with the Sultan of Estanbul which was then called Constantinople and he was such an excellent admiral of the Otoman fleet that in a few decades he became the terror of the Mediterranean sea. Thanks to Barbarroja, Redbeard, the Sultan's power increased by creating havoc for all Christian ships from Estanbul to Gibraltar. The Turkish fleet was the unbeatable obstacle the great spanish King Carlos the Fifth faced in protecting his terrritores in Italy, in the Mediteranean and northern Africa and kept him from establishing himself as the maximum defender of catholicism. "Redbeard" attacked not only the commerical ships but he also plundered towns in the interior of Mallorca and along the Eastern coast of Spain , taking the natives as captive slaves in his ships to man the oars. Even the great author of "Don Quixote", Cervantes had been captured by Redbeard.

After the death of "Barbaroja" in 1556, and of king Carlos in the same year, his son, Felipe The Second, decided to eliminate the Turkish threat and its harrassment in the Mediterranean. He grouped together his own fleet with that of the ships of the Venitians and the fleet of the Vatican. He named Alvaro de Bazan, the Marques de Santa Cruz, leader of a reserve fleet of thirty galleys and he also named his own young popular bastard brother, Don Juan de Austria, Admiral of the fleet.

That important battle of Lepanto lasted five hours. Of the 300 turkish ships, 250 were captured by the christian troops of the Marques de Santa Cruz and young Don Juan de Austria with their 400 cannons. The christians released the men who had manned the oars of the enemy ships, (3000 were turks and 10,000 were christian slaves. Among them was the author of

"Don Quixote", Miguel de Cervantes, who had been four years captive on one of the Turkish ships. The Spanish fleet lost only fourteen ships of their 210 galleys, 2000 lives were lost, plus 4000 wounded, most of whom died soon after. The battle was going badly for the spaniards when Juan de Austria ordered the fleet manned by Alvaro de Bazan-the Marques de Santa Cruz into action to enter the battle. The action of Alvaro Bazan's thirty ships and the courage of his men marked the turning point in this famous sea combat. This battle also made a hero of Don Juan de Austria, King Felipe's handsome half-brother who despite his youth, maneuvered the ships with courage and intelligence. This is said to have been the bloodiest sea battle in history. The ships smashed into each other, the men boarded those of the enemy and in many cases defeated the enemy in hand to hand combat. The victory shattered the power of the Turks in the Mediterranean and gave glory to the reign of Felipe the Second.

The palace which had been the home of Alvaro Bazan or the Marques de Santa Cruz as he was more known, was small but typical of homes of his period- it was also filled with remnants of his fascinating career at sea. Luis and I didn't have time to study all documents the family had added to the museum-like home but by the time we drove away to continue on to Mudela, both of us were ~~were~~ awed by the remembrances we had just seen of those brave men of four hundred years before.

     The Mudela shoot was more formal in every way than the shoot we had attended with Generalissimo Franco in Jaen - the invitation had stated "black tie" for dinner the night before the shoot. Guests started to assemble about nine in the large salon. The Duchess had asked me days before if manor houses in Spain were as chilly as those she used to go to in England.

"It was always freezing," she had told me. "In those English country palaces they never had much heating, nor other luxuries –especially in the bathrooms." And she had added, "The. Duke tells me that Buckingham Palace was always cold and uninviting, - that's one of the reasons he chose to live at "The Fort".

That night the Duchess was beautifully dressed for the occasion as usual; she was not overdressed or showy but just right for the country palace in which we were, in a long full dark blue satin skirt with a knit sweater embroidered in azabaches. Her black shiny necklace, I knew she had bought in Christian Dior the year before, and although she had beautiful real jewels which the Duke had given her, she loved to pick around on the counters in Paris boutiques to buy a few false earrings or trinkets. Rarely did she change her hairdo and was accustomed to having a hairdresser every evening before going out. Now that I think about it, I wonder how she solved that problem in Mudela where we were far away from such extravagances.

The menu was more elaborate than usual for a shooting group, so we were longer at table. We must have been about twenty-five that night at table, the ten guns –some with their wives, plus a few government officials whose wives were not present. I wondered how Franco and the Duchess who was on his right would get along. He did not speak english and she spoke neither spanish nor French which Franco knew well. it must hve been grim because the dinner was long.

When dinner was over the group retired to the large salon again. The Duke and Franco walked over to a corner where there were two comfortable armchairs; almost immeditaely Franco sent a message across the room asking if I would be kind enough to act as their translator. When I joined them, both men stood up and Franco pulled up a chair for me facing them. They were more or less the same heigth, both short, although the Duke looked taller because he was thinner. Both were in black tie, the duke was smoking, Franco was not. A man-servant in grey wool jacket with dark blue piping and dark blue pants was serving them cognac. Their attitudes seemed relaxed and I sensed that both were looking forward to exchanging impressions.

"Aline," said the Generalissimo, "His highness speaks spanish, but not one I'm capable of understanding." He chuckled slightly.

"I have always presumed to speak a little spanish, Aline," the Duke explained, but I'm obliged to accept that it is not sufficient for a conversation." Amused, he discarded his cigarette. "We have just discovered that we are of the exact same age" he went on "and have many things to discuss."

Then the The Duke who was expert at putting people at ease, added, "His excellency," he began as he took a cigar from his pocket, cut the tip and continued to light it, " has made admirable efforts to understand my dreadful spanish, but ..." He gestured to Franco who was smiling, "the problem is that he speaks French, I do not. So we are at your mercy, Aline."

For almost an hour the two men compared opinions, sometimes concerning serious international crisis of the past years and other times light comments in which each displayed a keen sense of humor. I already knew how amusing the Duke could be, but I was pleased to note General Franco's sense of humor was equal. Few people in Spain had had enough intimacy with Franco to be able to chat with him informally. The government officials who saw him regularly gave the impression that Franco was ultra serious, never given to discussing light matters. These Ministers had been chosen for their abilities and qualifications - therefore Franco had as much respect for them as they for him and since he was accustomed to conduct all matters in a strict military manner, there was rare opportunity to change the atmosphere.

At the beginning of their chat, the Generalissimo and the Duke had discovered that there was only six months difference in their ages. The duke seemed surprised but once that mutual bond had been estalished, they started to speak with less reserve. As their conversation proceeded I sensed a mutual understanding growing between them. As different as they might have seemed to most people, they had similar opinions on many subjects and even on certain personalities. I regretted that both men were too discreet to confess all their opinions. I knew that the Duke of Windsor was not fond of his first cousin, Don Juan, recognized then as the Spanish king in exile in Portugal, but he did not refer to him at all. This mutual lack of confidence in Don Juan would certainly have given vent to more intimate opinions.

Franco confessed that he regretted not having been able to travel outside his country and asked the Duke about different foreign heads of state and personalities; he explained that he had only known some of these people through newspapers and books and sometimes through a representative.

"What is your opinion of ...., and how do you think the war would have ended if ......?"

"Yes, I was lucky. I enjoyed travelling as Prince of Wales, and meeting so many international personalities. In fact I think that has helped me to be at ease with people. Actually when I was young, one of my many defects was my timid character. It was on a trip to Argentina that I became interested in learning spanish. I had been brought up speaking German, but strangely enough no other foreign language. When I was sixteen my parents sent me during the summer vacation to learn French with some freinds who lived outside of Paris. They all spoke English perfectly so I never learned French."

The following morning we had been informed that breakfast would be served at eight-thirty and that the cars would leave for the shoot at nine-thirty. I was not a good shot, but I did have magnificent shooting clothes and gear. Luis' mother had been a top shot and from her photographs I'd copied her classic tweed shooting outfits with split skirts. Luis'brother-in- law, the Duke of Tamanes, had made me a present of my wonderful ~~my~~ custom-made leather chaps in Cordoba years before - my shooting hats were from Austria, and best of all were my custom made leather leggings, so much more flattering to a lady's legs than bulky boots. I took care to have my hair in a neat chignon - and the bullet case tied around my waist held makeup instead of cartridges-noone was ever aware of this . The loaders who accompanied us always had enough cartridges anyway, so I felt it was silly to waste such valuable space.

Since this was a very special shoot for me, I arose early. Luis was astounded when he saw me up before him. I dressed hastily but with care, and descended the wide staircase at eight-fifteen. I wanted to be sure to be on time for breakfast. The men always expected ladies to be late for such things and I certainly did not want anyone of such a special group to be able to accuse me of being late.

When I arrived downstairs, at first I thought no one was yet in the room. Then in the early morning shadows at the opposite end of the room I perceived someone standing alone. Walking in that direction I was astounded to recognize the Chief of State, General Franco . We greeted each other and since for the next twenty minutes no one appeared, we chattted happily –I believe both of us enjoyed our conversation – I know I did. My translating of the night before had made me much more at ease with him. Then when more time passed and no one appeared, Franco took my arm, and led me into the dinning room.

"These lazy spaniards," he quipped, "why should we wait for them? I'm hungry. We can begin and we'll get the best of everything."

Directing me to one end of the long table, we sat down to an immense "desayuno"—mornings before a shoot are the only times spaniards eat anything for breakfast. Usually they have a "cafe con leche", or "cafe solo" and nothing else. I still suffer to notice my three sons and my grandsons indulging in this meager breakfast and not listening to my pleas of having at least some orange juice. This morning in Mudela we were offered the classic "Migas" (fried breadcrumbs -strange for foreigners but delicious) with sausages, jamon serrano (spanish cured ham), fried eggs, croissant, bread, rolls, anis, "tinto" (red wine), cookies and cake. Fruit was more customary as a table decoration, and if one wanted orange juice, it would have to be requested. In a country where oranges abound people do not have the american custom of orange juice for breakfast. While we ate we became so involved in conversation that little by little although people started to fill up the table no one dared to interrupt us. They all had such respect for the Caudillo that they dared not come close to him when they saw he was in deep converation with me.

The Generalissimo was a charming table companion, amusing me with many stories of his days as a military officer in Morocco before the Civil War. He gave me a very humorous account concerning Moroccan customs and General Jordana who had been the Spanish Capitan General in Tangiers about thirty years before. Evidently Jordana had a very unattractive wife and one day when he was receiving an official visit from the Arab sheik of that area, Jordana and his wife greeted the Moroccan official as he arrived at the entrance to the Spanish military palacio. After introductions the two men retired to Jordana's office to talk business. Later when the sultan left, as the two men walked toward the door, the arab dignitary asked him, "My dear General, was the lady you introduced me to when I arrived your wife?"

Jordana nodded his assent.
"And is it true that in your religion you are not allowed to have more than one wife?"

"That's right," answered Jordana.

The Sultan took a long look at Jordana, then patted him on the back. "You are really a very good man, General, a very good man."

Franco and I enjoyed a good laugh as he finished the story, I realized that the commentaries about his being so austere were not true at all.

Since the chief of state told me that he had served thirteen years in Morocco, I was aware that he knew much about that country so I asked him how the Moroccan General Mezian had such an important position in the spanish army. I was curious because Mezian's daughter happened to be one of my best friends.

Franco explained that Mezian had been the only Moroccan cadet ever to attend the spanish military academy which in those days was in Toledo and that Mezian had graduated first in his promotion. (After the Civil War the academy was moved to Zaragoza). Franco added that this unusual situation had come about due to the fact that King Alfonso the thirteenth had made a visit to the spanish province of Melilla in Morocco and in one of the schools he visited where there were both spanish and moroccan students, a young fifteen year old Moroccan boy gave the welcoming address to the King - this was fifteen year old Mezian. When the king who was dressed in military uniform, asked him what he would like to be when he was older, young Mezian answered, "Your majesty, Sir, I'd like to be what you are."

The King was so amused by the child's answer that he arranged special permission for him to enter into the Spanish military Academy when he reached the age.

"And," said Franco. "It just happens that that young man became the great Spanish General Mezian. He was one of the heros in our civil war and later because of his merits became Captain General in several of our provinces. Right now he is sixty and with the exception of vacations has spent his life occupying important military posts in Spain. Only a month ago, his own Moroccan king Hassan, aware of Mezian's many merits, asked him to return to Morocco to become Minister of the Army. We don't want to lose him. As yet I do not know what Mezian will decide to do. Despite Mezian's many years in Spain, he has retained his Mohamedan religion and customs."

I had seen that this was true when I visited the Mezian family in Casablanca - in the privacy of their home , they all lived in an entirely Mohammedan manner although my friend and some of her sisters and brothers had been born and educated in Spain. One day while lunching in their home in Casablanca we were seated on cushions at one side of the large salon with their mother while General Mezian dined alone in the opposite corner of the room, as is the Moroccan custom. Moroccan homes are very cozy –while we girls sat on cushions around the table, their attractive mother was sretched out on the banquette next to us dressed in the usual chilaba with her head wrapped in a turban – the father alone in the opposite corner was completely ignored as he dined alone.

My conversation with Franco that morning showed to what an extent important people rarely resemble their reputations, that they are like anyone else –some are more amusing , more intelligent and kinder than others. I remembered also that even way back during the war years we of OSS intelligence knew that Franco had given orders to his embassies and consulates in central Europe to facilitate Spanish visas to all Jews who were trying to escape Hitler's atrocities – that he was far from the monster the international press had created. This General Franco I was beginning to know now was a kind, normal compassionate man. But of course I, like most persons, had been influenced by the anti-Franco propaganda.

I was especially pleased to become aware of Franco's real personality since he had become a good USA ally ever since

President Eisenhower's visit to Spain in 1953. During that year Franco attracted American industry to Spain by lowering import restrictions for American investors – this gradually gave relief from Spain's poverty and assisted in a rapid leap in Spanish industry which improved the economy - by the end of the sixties Spain's standard of living had become equal to other European nations.

    Later through Carmen and friends I learned more about the Franco family - I was able to visit the home of his parents in El Ferrol where he and his brothers had been born on the coast of Galicia in northern Spain. This unimpressive small house is kept as it was originally and today is a small museum for people to visit. However Franco's entire family was exceptional. His brother Ramon Franco was a pilot - in 1925 he managed to cross the Atlantic flying to Argentina – something hard to believe now since they used hydroplanes in those days and the distance to Argentina from Spain is almost three times that of New York to Paris- where Lindberg landed thirteen years later in a much more modern machine. Franco was short but his brother Nicolas Franco was tall – I met Nicolas when he was Spain's ambassador to Portugal. Franco's sister Pilar married and had ten children- many of whom I met over the years. All of them were unpretentious – never taking advantage of their close relationship to the head of the country during forty years.

    General Jordana about whom Franco had told me such an amusing story had been Minister of Foreign Affairs in Madrid during the forties. When sometimes I encounter his descendants I always remember General Franco's story about the man's wife.

Franco's amusing anecdotes lasted throughout breakfast and it was only when the table was emptying that he stood up. No one had dared to sit near us at the end of the table. I had learned something few Spaniards realized - the Chief of State was not always a serious solemn man.

Later out in the field while places were being determined for the shooters, Carmen told me we would be sharing a butt together next to her father. "What luck," I said. "we'll be in the center of the line then and get lots of birds".

"Don't think, it's going to be a good spot, Aline," she answered. "We will have my father on one side and the Duke of Windsor on the other. We won't get a bird."

"What are you talking about? Maybe I won't get many, but you will, you're a top shot. At least we're bound to see a tremendous number of birds. For the first time in my life, I may have a chance to really shoot. So far I have always been at the end of the line where few birds appear."

"No, no", Carmen shook her head. "Don't be so pleased. The soldiers who accompany my father as his secretarios and his loader, as soon as the drive is over, will pick up every bird they see, no matter who downed them, and they bring all the birds back to him. They'll take all our birds, you'll see."

"But you can tell him. After all he's your father and you can say what you want to him."

"No, I don't dare criticize his soldiers. My father doesn't even know that many of the birds they bring him are from other posts."

"He's a great shot. He's said to be one of the best in Spain and doesn't need those extra birds."

"Yes, that's true, but those soldiers think they are impressing him with how well they work so they bring him as many as they can find."

Carmen was right. Between us we downed 30 birds, I think she got 24 and our "secretarios" were only able to bring back to us about fifteen.

At about this point the Duke of Windsor came walking dejectedly to our butt. He had one partridge dangling from his right hand.

As he reached us he explained, "I'm a terrible shot, I got only five birds. I should have downed fifty." But his voice showed his amazement. "The most amazing thing happened. At the end of the drive, Carmen, one of your father's soldiers came almost into my butt. I hadn't yet had time to pick up my birds. That soldier had the nerve to lean down right in front of my butt and pick up a bird that was obviously mine. And then turned around and started to walk off with it. I screamed at him. "Para". At least I know the word for 'stop" in spanish. He stopped all right, and even gave me a military salute. Then I said to him, in good Spanish, and he understood. "Usted es un ladron", (you are a crook). The fellow looked at me and respectfully said, "Si, senor". Then he brought

me my bird, saluted again and walked away." the Duke shook his

head in disbelief. "Damndest thing I ever saw," he mumbled.

Carmen and I burst out laughing. Then Carmen told him about her father's soldiers annoying habit. "I'm sorry, Senor," she said. "it's very discouraging. Let's see if we can get our butts changed for the next drive. Any butt near my father is bound to have this problem."

I wanted to tell the Generallissimo what had happened - I felt certain that he would like to know. But the minute the drive ended other guests surrounded him and I did not dare push past them. I was sure Franco would have laughed and ordered his soldiers to change their habits.

CHAPTER THIRTY – EIGHT

GLAMOUROUS NEW YORK

Every year in the fifties and the sixties Luis and I jumped from the rustic existence in Pascualete to the super modern life of New York City. Since Elsa Maxwell had introduced us to so many notabales, invitations to balls and festivities poured in every year. Usually these affairs occurred in the month of November, so Luis would give up part of his busy shooting season and we went regularly every year for our New York holiday. Many people we had met seemed to be in New York at that time – the Windsors – Americans from Texas, Chicago and California - movie-picture people - all seemed to appear there for a few days in November. The outstanding social hostess was beautiful Babe Paley, but there were also alluring film openings, operas with formal dinners afterwards, special nights at the theater, benefit balls- an unending amount of glamorous affairs. Also some titled europeans and political personalities came to New York in November and formed part of the social whirl. During the eighties the president of the United Nations, Perez de Cuellar and Marcella, his attractive wife, hosted many interesting affairs with current international politicians.

Clothes were always an important part of social life, therefore before the trip, I attended the Madrid collections, spent hours fitting numerous outfits, selecting the newest hats, looking for chic raincoats – it usually rained in New York, noone ever owned a raincoat in Madrid - I especially spent time choosing my evening dresses – the most useful and admired gowns I took with me to New York were hand embroidered evening gowns from Pedro Rodriguez. My experience years before modeling during summer vacations and for Hattie Carnegie after graduating from the university were excellent useful preparations for the life I was to lead later on. That experience had taught me while still very young much about elegance, make-up and hair-dos – important attributes for any woman. In 1956, I had been named to the International Best Dressed List - the Duchess always was number one, Babe Paley was number two- I don't know who the others were but thanks to my elegant Spanish wardrobe I entered on the eighth spot. My spanish dressmakers were delighted -Luis was also, since the spanish custom houses made me gifts of the clothes.

There were many balls in New York City – but very different from the Balls at Ferrieres or in Venice or those of the Baron Alexis de Rede in Paris or the formal dinners in the house of the Duke and Duchess de la Rochefoucauld. The important balls in New York were Benefit Balls open to the public to obtain large sums of money for worthy causes. However the yearly "Bachelor's Ball", a private party, was the most glamorous with the best band and with selected fun guests. Spaniards do not have the same preparation for dancing as Americans who begin at any early age - even in Pearl River high school we had dances every Saturday night, so all Americans are better dancers than most Europeans.

My initiation to the benefit balls in New York was "The Ball of Seven Crowns" in 1954. Titled ladies from seven different countries were invited and I was the lucky one from Spain- husbands were included in the invitation which covered choice of airplane or passage on the liner "France" , plus a suite in the Waldorf Astoria with car and chauffeur. Again Luis was impressed. "Those incredible Americans" he would comment - they always did things on a scale impossible to imitate in any other country. Those who attended this ball evidently paid enormous entrance fees to cover the expenses and the benefit. The seven titled women, were asked to wear a famous tiara which international jewelers had provided for the occasion. Mine – the tiara of Napoleon the third's wife, the Empress Eugenia was magnificent and I was thrilled.

The Majarani of Jaipur, "Ayesha", was the lady from India. We met during the preparations for the Ball and since all the other women were older than Ayesha and me, we became close friends. Ayesha was the most beautiful and the most unassuming - despite her many royal ancestors. .

We learned that we were expected to rehearse our entrances and to be photographed for many magazines- all of which consumed hours during several days. We were surprised to realize that Americans always rehearse important events – not even weddings are rehearsed in Europe. On the night of the Ball on the large stage the hotels ballroom, each lady was escorted by a distinguished American gentleman and introduced and then taken down the steps to her country's table decorated by her country's flag. When my turn came, I was presented on the stage as the Countess of Quintanilla, which was my title then – and as we went down the steps and crossed the room to my table a band was playing "Valencia, Valencia- Lady of Spain I adore you." As I listened to the music I was surprised to note that I was being considered Spanish now even in my own country –something I would have to get accustomed to.

A short time after sitting at the table, the man sitting next to me commented, "You speak quite good english for a Spaniard."

" But I am American."

"No, I mean real American. One can see that you are Spanish."

"I'm sorry to disappoint you but I have been born and brought up in the United States."

"Then what are you doing here with that crown on your head and the announcement that you are a grandee of Spain? "

"Obviously I married a spaniard. " His remark annoyed me. In my own country I was proud to be real American. I disliked being taken for a foreigner.

Ayesha Jaipur's husband who we called "Jai, was named Ambassador of India to Spain in 1965 and we then resumed our friendship which had begun in New York. They came often to Pascualete – Jai liked to shoot partridge – a far cry from shooting tigers in India. He was a top shot and also a star polo player. Ayesha and Jai became extremely popular with everyone and also with the diplomats = he was the first Indian Ambassador to be sent to Spain.

Although In India the Jaipurs lived in oriental luxury-where their subjects would fall to the floor in front of them whenever they appeared, they were totally unpretentious in Spain. Ayesha seemed delighted with our medieval stone home in Pascualete despite being accustomed to her familys palace in Cooch Bejar, reputed to be the most impressive royal palace in India. When we visited our little village of Santa Marta with them , Jai mixed with the farmers in the village, asking about their sheep and chickens as if he were a simple farmer or shepherd like them. In fact Jai especially liked our village and told Luis that it reminded him of his small towns in Jaipur . I have to laugh when I remember that day because Luis commented to me later "ufh, as if Santa Marta could be as miserable as those small villages in India".

When the Jaipurs spent Easter with us in Pascualete, Ayesha astounded everyone with her fondness for hot spanish sausages. We had never eaten them ourselves or served them to our guests but one day when Ayesha and I were in Trujillo and went into Pillete's bar for a cup of coffee. She saw the men nearby eating sausages and asked for one. I warned her that she would not like them – "this part of Extremadura makes the spiciest sausages in Spain but nobody I know has ever eaten any – they will burn your mouth, Ayesha." Nevertheless to my amazement she consumed the sausage with no difficulty and asked for more. The country workmen sitting in the bar nearby had been observing her and were even more amazed than I. Despite their normal reticence to speak to someone they did not know, they approached Ayesha and expressed their admiration saying that she was the only lady they had ever seen capable of eating these, the spiciest sausages in Spain.

I well knew that her husband was accustomed to very hot food because sitting next to him at dinner in their embassy residence many times I had seen rivulets of perspiration pouring down his cheek as he ate the special dishes his servants prepared for him, but it had never occurred to me that fragile very feminine Ayesha could do the same.

Apart from the intense social whirl, Luis and I spent much time in art galleries in New York. Luis was an artist and when in Madrid spent many hours painting. I could barely get him home for meals while he was preparing a huge fresco in his grandfather's house on the Castellana where he had much more space than at home. Luis had his first exhibit in 1962 in New York and in Palm Beach the next year = this enormous fresco encouraged him to paint more than before – and he couldn't do that in apartment in New York.

Also we had fun in New York in the nightclubs - even elegant restaurants like the Stork Club had good live bands for dancing. .We went almost nightly to El Morocco after dinner or the theater. Normally entrance there was restricted which was probably why the place was so popular with film stars and known personalities. I remember one night when we were there with the Aga Khan and the daughter of President Truman – a strange combination – at the table next to us was Elizabeth Taylor with some celebrities. I recall that night because Aga Khan was such a disappointment despite the glowing reports about him in the press, I did not find him especially entertaining nor attractive. In Washington, sometimes we stayed in the spanish embassy and other times we spent a few days in the house of the Secretary of the Air 'Force, Harold Talbott and his wife. We had met the Talbotts in New York. These invitations always entailed dinners and large balls in Washington. Luis loved to dance and was a much better dancer than most Europeans but he thought the American custom of "cut-ins" was rude and never did it himself. We continued to discover differences between European and American customs.

At Babe and Bill Paley''s dinners we met the most interesting people who happened to be in New York at the time- we had met Jack and Jackie Kennedy there before he was elected President. By now I had become as accustomed as Luis to European customs and often was as impressed as he with differences. Although I had worked in New York city before being recruited by OSS I was a very young and never had gone out at night in the city, so I was completely ignorant about the glamour that later I came to know. Now and then friends with yatchs like Malcom Forbes' would invite us to a dinner onboard while circling the island of Manhattan, always with a group of interesting guests.

When Luis became president of horse racing in Spain we made a point of going to New York yearly to attend the Belmont Races One of our friends, Bill Woodward, owned the two outstanding thoroughbreds of that time , Omaha and Gallant Fox. It was a shock for us when a friend called to say that Anne had just murdered Bill with one of his guns. A huge lawsuit covered daily by the press followed. We knew that Anne was jealous and had a wild temper, but we were astounded when she was accused legally of having killed her husband. Later the Duchess of Windsor told me that she had been at the same dinner in Long Island with Anne and Bill the night Anne shot him and that Bill had told her in confidence during the dinner that he had just informed Anne that he was going to divorce her. However Bill's wonderful mother intervened to protect her two young grandsons from going through life with the stigma of having a mother who was a murderess – her declarations saved Anne from a death penalty. But the drama continued to be a terrible tragedy for all that family. Handsome Bill had met Anne who was a dancer in the Copacabana nightclub during a leave from the Army during World War Two and had married her hastily. If Bill had not been happy with her, he had hidden his feelings for several years very well.

Trips fom New York to Palm Beach for the weekend in friend's planes were frequent – noone had these luxuries in Europe. Guy de Rothschild did for a short time, but hardly any other of our friends – there were still few airports in Europe. Once a friend took us in his plane to California to attend a special football game. Again the extraordinary Americans! Yes, Luis'uncle Peps Merito had come to visit me several times in Pascualete in one of his five small airplanes. But they were just small old fashioned planes –nothing like the fast modern American planes. For all foreigners, the life of the privileged in New York made it the most glamorous city in the world.

CHAPTER THIRTY – NINE

THE WINDSORS AGAIN

After years of visits to the Windsor's house in Paris and many glamorous social affairs together, at the beginnig of the seventies I noticed that he was declining in energy and health. This was not generally known despite the fact that the international press had continued following his and the Duchess' every move as had been customary ever since the Duke's abdication so many years before.

Early in the morning on Sunday, May 28, 1972, a friend phoned me in Madrid saying, "I just heard on the radio that the

Duke of Windsor died an hour ago." Unfortunately the news was no surprise. Since April, only a month before, when Luis and I had stayed with the Windsors and seen the Duke struggling just to putt a golf ball on the lawn in front of their house, we'd both been expecting it.

I waited two hours before dialing Paris. Germaine, the concierge, answered, and a moment later I heard the Duchess's voice with its clear diction. "So good of you to call, Aline"

"I'll leave Madrid on the first flight out."

"No, dear, don't come now. I'm all right. But I will need you badly when I return from England after the burial. Right now the house is surrounded by newspaper people and television cameras. Everything is confusion, and I can hardly realize what has happened. But when I come back from London I will be terribly alone. If you can possibly be here and stay with me for a while then, that's when I'll need you."

I flew to Paris as soon as she returned. Martin, the Spanish chauffeur, met me at the airport, and at first everything seemed just as usual—the drive through the Bois, Germaine in her navy-blue cape running out of the gatehouse to open the huge spiked metal gates, the drive up to the house past trees and bushes the Duke himself had planted twenty years before, Georges in his gray pants and blue-black tails waiting with a footman in front of the house. Even the pugs were making their usual racket as the Duchess called down from the landing at the top of the curved stairway in the high-ceilinged marble entrance hall, "Aline, I'm up here." That was the first change: "I", not "We."

I ran up the stairs, and we embraced. There were no tears; she wouldn't allow tragedy to show. We moved into the "Boudoir," her warm, cheerful salon between their bedrooms. I could not help looking toward the Duke's chair, and then toward his room.

"Yes," she said, following my gaze, "why don't you come and see?"

We walked into the room he had left only a week before. "I haven't changed anything, even those horrible cigarettes. They're still in his closet. He smoked up until the end. I always hated them, and they killed him finally."

She touched his writing table. "He was noting things down here until a few days before he died. He would get up from his bed—thinking I couldn't hear him from the boudoir—and write little notes of what I should do about different things when he ws gone. He pretended up to the last minute that he was in no danger, and I did the same I think we both knew the other knew. How strange it was, trying to fool ourselves, to save the other from suffering."

Photographs of her covered the wall, the tables, the desk. Even his bathroom was filled with pictures of her—only her—not another person in any of them.

"It was two o'clock in the morning, and he'd just had a bad hemorrhage. He'd called for me, and the nurse came into the boudoir, where I was dozing in a chair. I ran in and sat on the side of his bed, and he looked up at me—that adorable, adorable face that I will never see again—and he said my name. She paused, controlling her voice, then continued. "I took him in my arms. His blue eyes looked up at me, and he started to talk. He could only say, "Darling..." Then his eyes closed, and he died in my arms."

She opened his armoire. "Here are all his clothes, those wonderful plaids and checks that he knew how to mix as no other man ever did." On one shelf I could see cartons of cigarettes and boxes of cigars and pipe tobacco. Back in the boudoir, we sat down again. "The Queen was here before he died. On a day when he had just had a terrible hemorrhage. They couldn't operate on him, because it was too late. My poor, dear romance..."

He had always enjoyed her quirky phrases, her twist of words.

"He had no strength at all," she continued. "But when he heard his niece was in Paris and coming to visit him, he was very pleased. He wanted to receive her in the large salon downstairs. The doctor said, "Your Royal Highness must receive the Queen here. You must remain in bed."

"I will certainly not receive Her Majesty the Queen that way—no, no, no"

"Even as he was protesting, he had to lie back and rest from the ordeal of speaking. But nothing could make him remain in bed that day. His respect for the Crown was so profound that I think he would have died then if he'd had to receive the Queen in bed. And so Georges and the nurse and I helped him up and into that chair." She indicated his eighteenth-century French armchair.

"Even he realized then that it was impossible to think of going downstairs. But he refused to receive her in his nightgown and robe." I knew the Duke's nightgowns well, because once when an airline had lost my husband's luggage, His Royal Highness had sent Sidney, his valet, up with a stack of them for Luis to use—knee-length—in pale colored poplins, gray, blue, beige, all piped in another color.

The Duchess went on, as if she were reliving the sad moment. "He had to be dressed properly to receive his Queen." She paused, looking out the window at the tops of the tall elms. Then she turned back to me. "I greeted the Queen at the door downstairs. She was not at all warm to his wife of thirty-five years, but then, I shouldn't complain. She was just as cold to him. I escorted her upstairs. Her expression was hard when she entered the room.

"He was sitting in this chair. As she entered, he began struggling to get to his feet, trying to stand in her presence. I don't know how he managed to do it, but he got himself up, though only for a second. His legs would not support him, and he fell. The Queen's face showed no compassion, no appreciation for his effort, his respect. Her manner as much as stated that she had not intended to honor him with a visit, but that she was simply covering appearances by coming here because he was dying and it was known by all the press that she was in Paris.

"David had thought it would be something of a family reunion. He welcomed that, knowing that he was going to die soon. I thought it would be appropriate that I leave them alone, so I went downstairs. But she stayed only a few minutes. When she had gone, David was deflated, not at all as he had been before she arrived. He understood then that not even death would change anything."

I did not interrupt The Duchess as she told me what had happened. She needed to talk about all she had just gone through. "Alexandre telephoned me as soon as he heard that David had died, and offered to accompnay me to London to do my hair for the ceremonies. I said, "No, thank you," but then I thought, Yes, of course. The last thing David would want would be for me not to look my best. They were going to continue to hate me no matter what I did, but at least I wasn't going to let them see David's wife without every shred of dignity I could muster.

"Givenchy was so kind; he came over immediately to prepare what I needed to wear. And then, too, I thought, But I'm not going to a a ball; I'm going to a funeral: I'll wear anything. I knew I would never care about clothes again, or anything else for that matter. But it gave me strength to think of David looking pleased at seeing me looking my best.

"I had never stayed in Buckingham Palace. David had disliked it enormously because of its inhospitable atmosphere. He said it was cold and stiff, but it was much better than I had expected. My rooms were nice; even the bathroom had details like perfumes and bath oils. As soon as I got settled, I sent word to the Queen that Alexandre was there and at her disposal, but she did not accept. Do you know, Aline, in all the time I was there, no one in the family offered me any real sympathy whatsoever."

I said, "there was a picture in the Madrid paper of you looking out a window from Buckingham palace over the square below. The photographer must have used a strong telescopic lens, because he captured your pathetically sad expression."

"Yes", she said. "There were members of his own regiment of Scots Guards playing his favorite song. They had asked me which one he liked best and I told them "The Flowers of the Forest". Later, at Windsor Castle, I stood for hours looking out at the endless lines of simple people forming day and night to pass his bier to pay their last respect. Years before, I had looked out from St. James's Palace, the day when he was being proclaimed King. And now I was looking down and watching his burial. It was all over."

Finally, just for a moment, one tear welled in the corner of her eye, but it did not fall. Her hands remained clasping the arms of her chair, and she controlled herself by continuing to speak. "All during the ceremonies, even as I stood in the chapel, it was hard for me to realize that I would not see him again, that adorable face with that wonderful upturned nose and those blue eyes and that smile."

Georges came in silently and asked if we would have an aperitif before lunch. She like Lillet, so we both had one. Her voice hardly stopped.

"One must take one's hat off to the English. I'm not fond of them, but they certainly do know how to put on a spectacle better than anybody in the world. In front of me, I could see Cookie standing there...

"Who is Cookie?", I asked.

"The Queen Mother. We called her that because she looked like a pudding dolled up." The Duchess made a face. "My dear! How she was dressed! What would I look like in that dress and hat? I really must copy that outfit. It looked as if she had just opened some old trunk and pulled out a few rags and draped them on herself." She lifted her eyebrows. "And that eternal bag hanging on her arm. A style they all caught from Cookie. But that day she outdid herself. She wore a black hat with the brim rolled up, just plopped on her head, and a white plastic arrow sticking up through it. I thought how David would have laughed. There is a quotation he often repeated: "I shot an arrow into the air. It fell to earth, I know not where." Now, David, I thought, we know where - in Cookie's hat. And I almost laughed. Imagine, at a moment like that , with my dear husband dead in front of me. But then, David and I always had our own jokes, which often made us have to hide a laugh on the most solemn occasions."

The humor left the Duchess's face. "Yes, I remember wanting to burst out laughing. I could not believe what was happening. I had held him in my arms as he died, but I could not really believe that I would never see him again. Then I saw the flowers, white callas, which I had ordered, on top of his bier, which was covered with his flag, and I wanted to weep. But I said to myself that I was going to be as brave and as tough as those English. I wasn't going to let them show me up in any way. They had been so cruel to my husband for so many years, to that wonderful, kind, good, patriotic man, and I maintained that same expression that they all bore – they, who didn't care."

"While I was there, during those days, I never once had a small family talk. After the funeral I had to have lunch with forty people. By royal order. In the long state dining room at Windsor. I was seated with the sun shining in my eyes. I was in pain from it. I sat next to the Duke of Edinburgh, who I had always imagined would be better, kinder, perhaps more human than the others, but you know, Aline, he is just a "four-flusher"- (that was the exact word she used-I had to guess at her meaning). She went on . "Not he, or anyone else, offered me any solicitude or sympathy whatsoever."

"After the burial I was with the Archbishop of Canterbury looking at the place next to where David rested, the place where I will be buried. In his testament he had agreed to be buried at Windsor only with the understanding that I could be buried next to him. Well, they had never accepted me in life, and I could see they were trying not to accept me in death. I was looking at the tiny piece of earth that was left for me—just a sliver, up against a hedge. I looked at the archbishop and said, "I realize that I am a very thin, small woman, but I do not think that even I could fit into that miserable little narrow piece of ground next to His Royal Highnesses's burial plot.

"I don't see that there's much that can be done about it. You'll fit, all right."

"No, I don't think that I will. I think that you should take that hedge away and give me a little more room. After all, I am not a hedgehog, you know."

Now I did interrupt her. "You said *that* to the Archbishop of Canterbury?"

"I most certainly did."

"What did he say?"

"He looked a bit uncomfortable," but said, "Yes, yes, we will have it removed."

"When finally it was all over, and I went to the airport, no member of his family accompanied me."

She touched my hand. "Aline, I've a great favor to ask of you. With David gone...well, I have no family, you know. I would be grateful if when I die you would accompany my body to England and stay with the old hedgehog until you see me safely into my sliver beside David."

She didn't wait for my answer.

"While there, I also picked out the marble for David's tombstone. I didn't like his brother's, the Duke of Kent's, nearby. It was too grey."

Georges came in to announce lunch, and we went down to the first floor in the tiny elevator. A small table had been set for us, looking out on an expanse of green lawn. I wondered if she had chosen the green-and-white Portuguese porcelain in the shapes of cabbage, lettuce, and other vegetables—she usually took care of such details herself. I glanced around the beautiful blue room, up at the small corner gallery with antique musical instruments on it, designed by the Duke himself, and I remembered the many glittering dinners we had enjoyed there. Most often there were two round tables of ten—the Duke presiding at one, she at the other. Occasionally there were three tables, but that was the maximum the room could take, and they liked large dinners less and less as they became older. As the Duchess often said, "Personalities yes, but bores—never."

This day she ate nothing. This worried me, because she was thinner than I had ever seen her. She didn't even try the custard dessert, which she usually enjoyed. She just had a few of the white and green mints she liked so much.

"My doctor has suggested I take some exercise in the garden." she said after lunch, and we went outside and walked around the house and through the three small greenhouses where she raised orchids. But she tired quickly, so we went back upstairs to the boudoir. The only thing that seemed to help her was having someone to talk to. We stayed up late, and she talked incessantly.

"I did not want him to give up the throne. But nobody could make David do anything he didn't want to do, or stop him from doing what he wished. Baldwin knew that. That's why the government wouldn't accept our marriage, why they forced the abdication. They could have arranged it for me to be his wife without being Queen. But Baldwin wasn't concerned with whether or not I was Queen; what concerned him was having as strong a personality as David for King. He had been such a popular and effective Prince of Wales. The people adored him, and with them solidly behind him, well, he was the King who got in Mr. Baldwin's way. I was the excuse Baldwin used to get rid of him. If Winston had become prime minister a few years earlier, history would have been different. He adored David, and respected him. I begged David not to abdicate, begged him not to do it. I would have gone back to America. I did not want him to give up the throne. But he loved me. He really loved me."

Even though she was under the stress of her sadness, she made an effort to speak of other things, and I followed her example. When I confided my distress that my two eldest sons might marry the girls who had moved into their college apartments—which would have been scandalous in Madrid in those days—she replied with her customary wit. "Don't worry, Aline. As my mother always said, "Why buy a cow when milk is so cheap?"

That night I made notes of our conversation, as I had often done before when I stayed with the Windsors, mainly because the Duchess did not have many people in whom she confided, but also because her attitudes and opinions always seemed of significance to me.

The following day Lord Mountbatten called and made an appointment to visit her at three the next afternoon. Lord Mountbatten, the Duchess had informed me had constantly asked the Duke for favors when he was king, and even later when they were living in exile in Paris, he had continued to be a pest. Georges had told me that the Windsors had good reason to dread Mountbatten's visits since he always left with something special he had removed from one of the tables in the salon.

"Aline, please stay here with me. This will be a trial. He's always asking for things. And after my kind husband bestowed all those honors on him! Even Georges dreads his visits. He's so nosey. But what can one expect from a man who threw his wife into the sea?"

I thought I had not understood her, and she, noticing my expression went on. "Yes, poor Edwina. When she died, he took her out to sea and had her burial there. Just dumped her in."

I preferred to beg off. When I returned to the house about five, Mountbatten was just leaving.

"It was awful," she told me. "He wanted me to make out a will right there and then, giving everything to David's family and, or course, some to himself. He had it all worked out, just where everything should go. Well, I did my best to stick up for my rights. After all, I do want to be fair, and what should go to the royal family will go. But they did David out of properties which were his own."

She toyed with a charm bracelet that she wore almost constantly. When she saw me looking at it, she said, "I love this little thing more than all the marvelous jewels my romance gave me. You know, David added a trinket every now and then as a memento of some special occasion in our life together. This one in the shape of a star with a ruby in the middle—that's for our journey to Turkey. Atatürk was the ruler of that country then and a most fascinating charming person. He put himself out to make certain that we enjoyed our visit to his country."

There were all sorts of charms: a telephone, to recall the long months when that was their only means of communication; a boat, for another trip they had taken; and many hearts, in a variety of precious stones.

Later that week the English lawyers came, and the Swiss ones too. She dreaded their visits, she said, because they were always asking her to sign things and she was not certain what they meant. She asked me to stay with her during these visits, but I preferred not to get involved in her legal affairs.

She told me she disliked her secretary. "She tries to boss my servants around. I really must replace her, but I'm too upset to face such problems now. I'm not up to it yet."

The house continued to be well run, however, thanks mostly to Georges and Ofélia, his wife, who had been with the Duke and Duchess over seventeen years. They were a great source of comfort and affection for her now.

The Duchess had many friends in Paris, like Margot Bory and Ghislaine de Polignac and a few other French women but she was always homesick for her own country. She had never learned to speak French, really, and there was not a French book in her house. The Duke never spoke it either. He told me he had been taught German all during his childhood, and that he enjoyed knowing at least one foreign language well. His Royal Highness's upbringing, which was strongly German due to his German relatives gave him a natural fondness for Germany which was interpreted during World War II by some to portray him as pro-Hitler in his attitudes—a most unjust criticism of this honorable and patriotic man.

Despite all the years the Duchess had spent abroad, she had remained thoroughly American. She wanted to go home after the Duke's death, but her lawyers advised against it. She told me, "It has something to do with taxes. I must stay here without going to America for at least two years. My Aunt Bessie lived until she was a hundred years old, and David and I visited her every year, even when she was too old to recognize us. Do you suppose I'll live that long, Aline? I hope not."

CHAPTER FORTY

MARBELLA AND THE ARABS

In 1962 Luis and I built a house on the Mediteranean coast in a picturesque fishing village called Marbella, a spot halfway between Malaga and Cadiz. The first time I had seen that coast was during World War Two in 1944 when I was involved in espionage for OSS. My orders had been to deliver microfilm to an agent who had come from Algiers across the Mediteranean to Malaga – the message would enable him to go through Spain and contact the resistance in France. My boss knew the mission was difficult since only Germans and persons allied with the Nazis could travel freely, but he speculated I could pretend I did not know about this regulation. I took the night train from Madrid to Malaga, but since I did not have the necessary "travel permit", I was taken to the police station and put in jail on arrival. But thanks to Barnaby Conrad, the young American vice consul in Malaga, I was released the next day and able to make the delivery - that was not easy since it became almost impossible for me to get rid of Conrad so I could deliver the micro film – which feat I barely managed to complete in time for the last and third appointment. Of course I could not inform Conrad that I was an American agent -we had been trained to be as secretive and cautious with our compatriots as with the enemy.

During that visit charming Barnaby Conrad drove me along the coast and we stopped to take a swim at a lovely beach in a small village called Torremolinos not far from Malaga - only two or three fishermen's small boats were pulled up on the sand. However, when Luis and I went there twenty years later, this formerly paradisical beach was covered with high rise hotels and apartment buildings. We were looking for a place to construct a summer house, so we went further up the coast to another beach that was still unspoiled and looking much as the coast must have appeared centuries before.

During the first years of our marriage we had spent summers on Spain's northern coast in San Sebastian and in Biarritz, a few miles over the border in France. We had also spent several summers with the children in Mallorca visiting Peps Merito and Graciela, but when Peps died suddenly of a heart attack we decided to look for a place of our own. In those years few people we knew went to southern Spain, but Ignacio Coca, a close friend, who owned a large area on that southern coast in Marbella suggested we visit him – his property reached from the sea to the mountain and he had just finished a large golf course - he knew Luis would enjoy that plus the wide safe beach for the children. Eventually we built a house there on the beach where we could look across the great expanse of the blue Mediterranean and see the coast of Africa - to the right was the view of the gigantic rock of Gibraltar looming gray and majestic. Squeezed up close to that, a bit to the left, jutting up over the sea line we could see the two hazy round bumps of Ceuta's mountains, the closest land in Africa, only seven miles distant across the straits of Gibraltar on Morocco's coast.

All along the coast the influence of Romans, Arabs and Turks who at different periods had colonized this part of the Mediteranean is apparent. From two centuries before the birth of Christ until four centuries after, the Romans controlled a large part of Spain and Portugal. After the Romans came the Arabs in the seventh century and their colonization lasted seven hundred years.

    The village of Marbella in 1962 was merely a quaint fisherman's town but when a large modern port was created masses of tourists soon spoiled its charm. Nevertheless with the background of the peaks of the Sierra Blanca mountains and the year round sunny weather the entire coast far surpasses the resorts in the north and people from all over Europe began to discover its appeal – many others arrived in luxurious yatchs. In those days the natural beauty of the area made it easy for us to encourage friends to visit us – most were charmed with the sunny dry weather and the picturesque scenery of Arab lookout towers and castles - many of our closest friends decided to buy homes near us. The Windsors bought a property next to ours - then Arthur Rubenstein and his wife Nella bought in another area, as did Deborah Kerr and her husband, Peter Viertel - also Audrey and Mel bought a house and spent many months every year there. Finally Guy and Marie Helene Rothschild visited us and bought a lovely house from Alfonso Hohenlohe who had been the one to first discover the idealic zone.

One day during a luncheon with Audrey and Mel someone mentioned that there was a small Arab-like village deep in the mountain range about an hour from Marbella which had remained out of contact with the rest of Spain for centuries and still maintained arabic customs and traditions - that in fact until a few years before, the town had remained isolated. This was part of the same mountains that Alexandre Dumas and other writers had described as the home of the famous bandits of the past centuries - I was curious to see what the descendants of these romantic types were doing today. When I suggested we visit the place, the idea caught on and we decided to visit it that very afternoon. Audrey was always inclined to any adventure and Mel too: Luis golf game had just been cancelled so he decided to take us.

As Luis drove us along the highway bordering the sea in the direction of Algeciras, Mel gestured towards an ancient castle perched on a hill above the beach. "What a romantic sight. I've not seen any ruins along this coast as captivating."

The ancient building was high on a hill silhouetted against the sea and the sky. Luis glanced for a moment at the half demolished towers and turrets.

"That's the castle of Tarifa. It belonged to a man called Guzman. He sacrificed his son for his country and the King added to his name "El Bueno", (the Good One), so his name from then on became Guzman el Bueno".

I interrpted him. "Luis that´s your name."

Luis ignored my remark. "In fact", he went on, " I'm the last man to carry that name today." As had happened so often, Luis surprised me again with the lack of importance he gave to his many illustrious ancestors. We had passed that castle many times and he had never mentioned his connection with it.

"What do you mean Luis," said Audrey, I never heard anyone add "El Bueno" to Romanones."

"No, Audrey, you don't understand. Romanones is my title, not my name. Anyhow Romanones is from my father's side and Guzman El Bueno, is from my mother. In Spain the title is different from the last name. My full name is Luis Figueroa y (and) Perez de Guzman El Bueno. Figueroa is my father's last name, and Perez de Guzman el Bueno is my mother's. As you know in Spain we are obliged to carry the last name of our father and our mother. The fellow who owned that castle was called at the first one to be called Perez de Guzman (the Good One) "El Bueno."

"Oh, tell us about him." cried Audrey.
"Well , it's a story all spanish school children are familiar with, but since none of you went to school here". He turned his head around for a moment and gave me a smirk. Luis always liked to pull my leg about being a foreigner which he knew annoyed me.

" During the end of the thirteenth century," he went on, "much of Andalucia was still controlled by the Moors. Granada, as you know, remained in the hands of the Arabs until 1492. Well, as I started to say around 1276 , my ancestor, Alonso Perez de Guzman, with his serfs was defending his castle against an attack by the Moors. This town of Tarifa," Luis' gesture encompassed all the area around us, "is the closest spot to Africa on this coast, therefore it was precisely here that attempts were constantly being made by Arabs to gain more territory or to recapture what had previously been theirs.

"For six months my ancestor had been struggling to defend his fortress castle and this coastal area. In those days there was no national army, each large property owner with the help of his serfs was obliged to defend his own area. Thus Guzman was defending his property and the country beyond that at great personal expense, preventing the invaders from conquering that part of the coast.

"One day Perez de Guzman's son was captured by the enemy; the child somehow had run out of the castle to play in the open land surrounding it. Perhaps the invaders had been observing the habits of those in the castle and knew that sooner or later one of the children might stray and be easy to apprehend. It is said that with the child clutched in his hand, the Arab leader shouted up to the defenders of the castle. "Senores! Advise your master to look down below. Tell Perez de Guzman that we have captured his son and we will kill him , if the castle is not given to us."

Perez de Guzman rushed to the parapet and saw the little ten year old boy, his eldest son, in the hands of the Moorish arab leader.

"...Surrender your fortress, Guzman, " the Arab leader cried. "If you do , we will spare the life of your son. All of you can walk away in safety. But if you fight on, we will cut his throat."

"Perez de Guzman, it is said, did not doubt. He drew his sword from the belt at his waist and lifted it high over his head, calling down to the boy, "My dearest son, who I love more than anything in this world, Be brave. You must die like a man with honor for God, for your country and for your King." Then Don Alonso Perez de Guzman hurled his sword down to the moors. "Use my own blade, if you must kill him, but this fortress will never surrender."

"I think he could have thought of something a bit more helpful to say to the poor kid," Mel intervened.

"The story is that the Moors killed the boy. But at least Perez de Guzman and his people fought on and defeated them, chasing them back into the Mediterranean and across the sea. But King Sancho el Bravo sent a document to Perez de Guzman stating that from then on "El Bueno" would be added to his name, for himself and all his descendants."

"Luis," I asked. "Is that the framed parchment you placed on the wall in the entrance to Pascualete?" Listening to his explanation I was still more astounded that he had never explained this story to me before.

"After six centuries, today Guzman el Bueno as a name has died out. The only male descendant carrying the name is myself - my sisters and one female cousin, have that name. There are many people with the name of Perez de Guzman, but only the descendants of this man are called "El Bueno". My mother and her father, my grandfather Torre Arias were the last to carry that name as their first last name. Remember Torre Arias was his title, not his name. And since you seem to be interested in these details, my dear," he turned for a moment towards me in the back seat. "Perhaps you would like to know that on the crest of our title of Quintanilla, which as you know came from my mother, the design of a fellow in a helmet holding a sword over his head, is that same Guzman el Bueno. The sword over his helmet indicates what he did that day and the reason that sword was added to his family crest."

"Was it that same Guzman el Bueno's descendant who was the admiral of the Armada against England?" asked Audrey.

"Yes, it was this man's great great great great grandson. In 1588 Felipe the Segundo obliged him to head the largest float until then in existence to attack England."

Since Luis did not remember exactly what the framed document in Pascualete stated, I take advantage of adding here that when I went the next time to Pascualete, I rushed to look at the framed document located on the wall of the "zaguan", entrance hall. The exact words of the yellowed parchment translated by me from old Spanish are below:

"Cousin Don Alonso Perez de Guzman, aware of what you have done in defense of the Villa of Tarifa, having suffered seige for six months while being in dangerous and painful state, and having given your blood for my service and offered to God, and who showed the blood of your first born son to the service of Country and God and for your honor, according to Padre lbrabau who is in the service of God, and you showed the blood from which you came, and for which reason you deserve to be called El Bueno, and thus I name you, and thus you will name yourself in the future and thus will your descendants name themselves. I call you by this name, and this is just, because he who does kindness and braveness, he who makes such great example of loyalty such as you have given to me deserves the name of "the good one",

El Bueno. And I ask you to come to see me because I would do for you other services and favors as you have done for me.

Remembrances to your good wife from mine, and I and God are with you,

        I, the King"

Our conversation about the castle of Tarifa lasted until the turn off where we drove up into the mountains for some miles through barren country without ever passing an animal or human being. The road was narrow and had so many twisty sharp curves that we could well understand how the town could have remained isolated. It seemed we would never arrive, but finally after surmounting another mountainous path, we distinguished way down in a gorge a white village, with small stucco houses with red tiled roofs piled one on the other up the side of the mountain. The view was intriguing, but as we drew closer the inhabitants were dressed as in any other pueblo and a catholic church in the center was similar to other southern villages. We walked up the narrow winding hillside streets where it became obvious that there was still no electricity or telephones but we were disappointed not to find women wearing veils and chilabas. And I saw nothing that reminded me of the handsome bandits of yore.

"These people look like those in any other old Andulasian town," Luis said.

"And it took us so long to get here," protested Audrey. "We'll never be back in Marbella in time for that dinner."

"Don't worry I promised to take you to your favorite restaurant in the Puerto tonight and we will make it, no matter how late it is," said Mel.

In Pepe's restaurant in the Puerto de Banus which was on our way back we discussed the village we had just visited and wondered how long it had been there unknown to others. We came to the conclusion that those living there today had to be descendants not only of the Arabs but also of the bandits who had descended into the villages to rob. In fact with so little sign of farming in that rocky terrain, and not much pasture for sheep, Mel jested that perhaps some of the inhabitants still practiced that occupation.

The port being built by Jose Banus was not yet finished but while we sat there looking out over the water an enormous luxury yatch manuvered into the quay just in front of us. Almost immediately four chilaba garbed Arabs walked down the gangplank. Also at the next table, people were speaking in arabic. "We didn't have to go so far away to find real Arabs" commented Audrey.

Although the Arab domination of Andalucia ended four centuries before, today many Arabs from Lebanon, Iran and

Algiers who are harrassed by terrorism in their own countries are returning to Andalucia again, this time to enjoy the security of a coast and a climate similar to their own.

CHAPTER FORTY - ONE
MARCOS - TRIPS TO FILIPINAS

I first met Imelda Marcos when she came to dinner in Madrid in 1972 on the occasion of the wedding of General Franco's eldest grandaughter to H.R.H. the Duke of Cadiz. Carmen Franco had asked me to give a party in my house after the wedding dinner which was to be in Franco's official residence in the Pardo on the outskirts of the city so that the guests would leave early to enable her father whose health was waning in his later years to retire at a comfortable hour.

Prince Rainier and Grace of Monaco and the Begun Aga Kahn were the first to arrive, not counting the Cornelius Vanderbilt Whitneys who were our house guests during that week. Sonny had been the founder of Pan-American airlines. Also he had been one of the four producers of the film "Gone With the Wind" which he claimed had provided one of his largest sources of income.

Imelda entered with her usual aura of an Empress of two thousand years ago. She attracted all eyes as Dr. Denton Cooley, the famous heart surgeon from Houston Texas approached her. Near the entrance was Cristina Ford, recently divorced from Henry, and Ava Gardner with Luis Miguel Dominguin –they stopped chatting as did the others to observe her and wait for introductions.

The Spanish Minister of Foreign Affairs approached me, "Aline, please introduce me– she is here representing a foreign Chief of State and I must be attentive. Of course he was interested, but I suspected not because of international politics

- more likely because in those days Imelda was extremely beautiful. She had arrived later than the others, probably due to having changed from her wedding outfit to a long glimmering Phillipine gown – she was tall, slim with enormous eyes, flawless skin, no lipstick, her makeup was hardly visible, just a bit of pale pink on her cheeks -all done with care. Her fingernails were painted bright red with tips and moons very white. I had heard that she travelled with a manicurst. She was then one of the great beauties of the world and noone was disappointed. A hush fell upon the room as she greeted me. Her quiet manner was alluring , her clear voice was low yet made everyone immediatley aware of her presence. Despite the other celebrities present, she upstaged them all.

During the following week in Madrid there were many luncheons and dinners for the First Lady of the Phillipines and when she left each hotess received a beautifully wrapped package containing a set of earrings and a ring of yellow pearls set in gold and miniscule diamonds. Needless to say we were enthralled - the charm and generosity of Imelda was discussed for some time.

When Luis and I received the first invitation to visit the Phillipines, we had to refuse because my husband did not want to miss the heigth of the racing season. But when the invitation was repeated a year later I was adamant. "Luis we cannot refuse again, so many friends are going and it's a door-to-door invitation, plane tickets, everything. They've even asked for our measurements and shoe sizes. What could that be for?"

When the day to leave arrived, two men from the Phillipine Embassy came to take us to the airport. We were surprised watching them tie lavender ribbons on each piece of our luggage - when we got to the airport we saw that the Duchess of Alba's luggage had pink ribbons and the Marqueses of Villaverde had red. In Rome we changed planes and met up with other guests—their Royal Highnesses, the Prince and Princess of Naples, also Princess Luciana Pignatelli, the actress Virna Litzi and her husband. Mrs. Henry Ford, the famous pianist Van Cliburn, the banker Mario D'Urzo, the American born Duchess D'Ussez and a few others.

Twenty-five hours to Manila with stops in Karachi and Thailand. Nothing luxurious about that. But when we arrived at Manila airport about one A.M., Manila time, our reception was spectacular. Standing at the foot of the steps to receive us was Imelda flanked by two lines of Phillipine beauties in long colorful dresses carrying masses of sweet smelling leys of sampaguita flowers. They placed two or three leys around our necks and then handed each lady a huge bouquet of flowers. Beautiful girls in orange, pink and red dresses threw rose petals in our path. Other groups were singing, a band was playing.

When we arrived at the entrance of the Malacanang Palace, the garden was illuminated by Japanese lanterns, some hanging from plam trees, others on the ample lawn. The building was large and sprawling with many terraces and porches. But inside the lighting and the wide center hallway bordered by a series of small conventional sitting rooms gave the feeling of a modern hotel. Therefore I was surprised when I heard our hostess saying, "This palace has been the seat of the government since the last days of the Spanish viceroys."

President Fernando Marcos was waiting for us in black trousers, and a white transparent embroidered shirt which I learned later was the Phillipine "borong". He was short, thin, wiry, dark brown skin, agreeable features and a dignified friendly manner. After shaking hands with all of us, we were directed into a dining room .

"Please, sit anywhere," Imelda said. "There is no protocol tonight."

Nobody was hungry. We had just finished dinner on the plane and anyway we were too excited to pay attention to the eight course banquet. From the first moment a comfortable informality was established; tactfully we were made to realize that we were to address the President as close friends. "Do not bother with that "Mr. President" or "Sir", he answered to someone at the table. "I am Ferdinand to all of you, though Imelda calls me Fernando – you can address me as you wish."

Then Imelda told us, "Tomorrow and all the time you are here, you will each have a Blue Lady to assist you," I asked her or someone else did, what a Blue Lady was. "Friends of ours who helped in the campaigns and because they wore blue dresses, they were referred to that way - the name has stuck. They will be like big sisters to tell you where to shop, what to wear—anything you might want to know about our country."

My neighbor leaned close and whispered, "they say those ladies form a sort of court for her, similar to Marie Antoinette."

Some of the guests were housed in a hotel; Cayetana Alba and the Villaverdes were put in the Malacanang Palace - Imelda herself took us and three other couples to the fabulous Guest House, called the Antique Palace, a small two story white palace on the edge of the river that bordered the Malacanang garden. The facade was quaint and lovely; a veranda embellished by an intricate wrought iron border shaped in arches and hung with brightly lit Japanese lanterns stretching across the entire length of the building. As we passed through the doorway onto the black and white checkered marble floor, the enchanting oriental interior made me catch my breath. It was much more beautiful than Malacanang Palace. Thousands of pieces of paper-thin mother-of-pearl chandeliers tinkled as the breeze from the open door passed through, the soft chandelier lighting giving a warm glow to the oriental statues, the blue and white Chinese porcelain vases, the delicate dark chairs and tables inlaid with ivory. Mixed with this were gemlike pieces of French Louis seize furniture.

"The pottery you see in the vitrines was made many centuries before Christ, some of the most ancient pieces in the Eastern world," Imelda waved her hand, "all this was ours before Fernando became president. There was no ideal place to put up state visitors, so Fernando and I donated this house and all that is in it to the country." She took a few steps, talking as she moved. "This little palace was built by the Spaniards who were here from the middle of the 16th century until the Americans helped us liberate ourselves at the end of the 19th. It is probably the oldest house in the city and for that reason we call it The Antique Palace."

For us it was now about four in the morning and, exhausted, I took a seat while some of the others examined the objets d'art.

Imelda gestured to the chair on which I was sitting, "These eighteenth century chairs are made of jade, completely, all of jade".

I leapt to my feet.

"Aline, please sit down. Don't worry about those chairs. They're very strong."

Nevertheless I remained standing.

"Before we go upstairs let me show you where the hairdresser is". She opened a door to a full sized beauty salon. "There will always be girls here to attend you at any hour. "Try the masseuses. They are especially good for "siatsu". That's my favorite. I have insomnia and siatsu is worth three hours' sleep.

At the top of the very wide curving stairway was a large open salon with two tables set with glistening vermeil plates and flatware on starched damask. A chef and four white jacketed waiters stood bowing to us next to a long buffet table stacked with delicacies- it was impossible that any one of us could still be interested in more food.. Imelda enjoyed showing us around, rightfully proud of the luxury and refinement of their gem-like palace.

"At any hour of the day or night there is a staff here to serve you," she continued as we followed her down the hall. "Each of you will have a military aide, the ladies a woman and the men a male officer, who will accompany you at all times and act as translators when necessary. You know our language is Tagalog and not everyone speaks English.

I don't think anyone said a word. We were too overwhelmed by the extent and quality of what we were seeing.

She turned her head around towards us, "Now I'll take you to your rooms. You must be very tired."

There were four suites. One was more fabulous than the other and each was different. Large airy rooms with exquisite antique beds, d'Aubusson carpets, magnificent furniture—a mixture of Oriental and French furniture. The rooms at the back of the house had balcony windows looking out on the river. When she opened the door to ours, I thought it was the most beautiful of all.

Probably because she knew we were dying to go to bed, she did not go in but before leaving, she said, "Each couple has automobiles on duty permanently for their use. Your car, Aline, is number four and Luis' is number five. The morning is free for you to relax but please be at the main house for lunch at twelve-thirty. Have a good rest."

When she closed the door we looked around. Four maids in black organdy uniforms with white collars and cuffs were opening our suitcases. I told them they could unpack the next day and asked if they would bring our breakfast at ten-thirty. They bowed repeatedly and smiled. "We are here only to serve the Count and Countess, of course, anything the Count and Countess wish...." Finally they left and despite our fatigue, we couldn't resist looking at the beautiful objects around us.

The room was enormous with two double beds decorated in richly embroidered silk and masses of yellowed antique lace. From above the high bedposts a fine mosquito netting flowed. The air-conditioning was so cold I couldn't understand what the mosquito netting was for but that lacy awning over the beds looked wonderfully old-fashioned and added glamor. On the other side of the room was a antique French eighteenth century desk, behind that against the wall shelves of books contained a collection on oriental art and the history of the Phillipines. An exotic arrangement of guavas, mangosteens, mangoes, granadas—all sorts of fresh fruit were located invitingly on a table next to a silver plate of tiny fresh sandwiches cut in artistic shapes.

Luis was staring at me, eyes widening. "Aline! You just got up from the table."

"But these mangoes are too delicious..."

While he studied the table-bar stocked with alcoholic beverages and decanters of vividly colored fruit juices which would have served for decoration alone, I parted the gauzy tent over one of the beds and threw myself down, revelling in the silky softness of the pillows which seemed to be made in heaven. Later I learned that that was almost true. The down had been shipped in from some mountainous area in the Far East famous for birds with a unique down quality. On the night table was a Sevres porcelain clock, two dainty handkerchiefs, an eye-mask for sleeping, a small box of ear plugs and a pair of reading glasses set in rhinestones.

The spacious bathroom had an assortment of the best internationally known perfumes, soaps, bathoils, creams - hanging on the wall were two Pierre Cardin terry cloth robes, one with Luis' name embroidered on it and the other with mine. We put them on immediately and they were just the right size. Of course, there were all the normal amenities such as aspirin, clippers, cotton-everything, but on the dressing table apart from every important name of cosmetics, a fancy hairdryer, electric Carmen curlers, all the make-up Estee Lauder had ever produced, there was also in a small crystal box... on opening it - I saw to my amazement - false eyelashes. I laughed. I realized that Marie Helene would be annoyed when I told her that Imelda had outdone her with something she had not thought of - fake eyelashes!

I took out of a suitcase what I planned to wear in the morning and opened the closet to hang it up.

"Luis! Look at this closet. It's filled with clothes."

Hanging there were several outfits, a beautiful silk dressing gown with my name embroidered on it, handbags with my initials, also sandals, shoes and slippers – all made in the Phillipines, many labeled with French couturiers' names. I slipped a foot into one and that fit also. Now I understood why the Embassy had requested our sizes.

Luis was opening the closets on his side of the room. Aline...I've got things too." He had trousers, shoes and several borongs like the silk shirt the President had worn. I stood amidst the luxury, the generosity, the beauty of the room - suddenly we were consumed with exhaustion which excitement had staved off. Luis groaned, "I must take a hot bath before I can go to sleep..."

We looked all over but couldn't find a tub. Fatigue was really cratering me. "Luis, let's just take showers and we'll look for it tomorrow."

"Aline have you ever seen me take a shower?"

It was true. Spaniards are much more accustomed to baths. He was suffering. "I've just travelled more than my ancestor Christopher Columbus, and I need a tub to relax..."

There was a knock on the door.

The Prince of Naples came in wearing a blue Pierre Cardin robe. His face and tone were apologetic. "You know, we're having a bit of trouble. After twenty some odd hours of travel, it's hard to go to bed without a hot bath. Do you suppose you could let us use your tub? We have the most beautiful suite of rooms...marvelous...every luxury imaginable...but..."

Luis answered, "I was just about to come to your room and ask you..."

Nobody had a tub. The Europeans were desperate. Days later as soon as I felt I knew my Blue Lady well enough, I asked about that.

She looked surprised. "We Orientals wouldn't think of sitting in a tub that someone else had been in. It would be extremely unsanitary. We always take showers. You will not find a tub in any private home anyplace in the Orient. "

The purpose of the luncheon the next day seemed to be for us to meet the leading government and business people and also all the other Blue Ladies. In a huge modern room containing a piano and a large platform, about thirty round tables with beautiful floral center pieces had been set up. My Blue Lady was chic and charming and as she took me to my table, she explained. "The tables are small and for six people. Our First Lady believes that eight at a table often makes it difficult for all to get to know each other because they are too far apart to talk comfortably."

A choir of children between the ages of nine and twelve, dressed in pink tunics entertained us with songs. Music was to become an important part of every affair. At the huge buffet the many waiters, most of whom spoke English, explained the details of the great variety of Chinese, Japanese and Indonesian dishes which composed this example of Phillipine cuisine. The tablecloths were 18th century hand embroidered, silk fringed "mantones de Manila (Manila shawls) which astounded those of us who came from Spain, because for hundreds of years these shawls had been used in our country only as evening wraps or to go to the bullfights on a feast day - they are still passed down from one generation to another. Never had we ever seen such a huge valuable collection...some had little hand painted Chinese faces made of white shell. The thought of perhaps spilling wine or food on such priceless antiques was terrifying. When we commented on this to Imelda later, she said. "Oh, I have many more. Exactly one hundred and twenty."

After lunch Luis who had been seated with Phillipine men interested in horse-racing, went off to the races - my Blue Lady took me shopping. With one automobile following and another escorting us with its sirens never ceasing, we raced through red lights in the most crowded sections of the city. The experience gives a shock when one sees people and cars scattering in haste. Yet after travelling this way for a few days, one becomes easily accustomed and I must admit, it is very agreeable.

Imelda had called to us as we left. "Be sure to buy stockings." It seemed a strange suggestion until I saw why. Nylon stockings which were expensive in Europe and the USA in 1974 here those of every color and style did not cost more than ten cents a pair. Everything else was also extremely cheap. Dresses from famous French designers, but made in Manila, were perhaps one fifth the price of the same garments in Western countries. The beautiful high backed manila wicker or bamboo chairs one saw in Paris or New York for about one hundred dollars were only $25. I told my Blue Lady that I regretted not being able to buy some of the marvellous fruniture because of travelling by air.

"Don't let that stop you. Our First Lady will certainly not allow you to be charged overweight."

Looking at her I was impressed with her flawless skin and while she was occupied talking to the salesgirl, I mentioned to a friend who was accompanying us it was remarkable that so many ladies I had met in the Phillipines had such wonderful skin.

"Well, said the friend in a voice that intimated confidence, "The truth is Imelda looked around for doctors who specialize in injections to remove the little wrinkles that cannot be erased by cosmetic surgery. The best she found were a Japanese surgeon and an American doctor. She had some of the Blue Ladies try them out first to make sure which technique was the best."

"Oh, that's hard to believe."

"Not at all. When the First Lady here commands, everyone is delighted to oblige. It may be admiration, devotion or fear. Whatever...she wields a power, a respect, an admiration no western Queen or President's wife could dream of."

Dinner was black tie and long evening dress in the gardens of Malacanang. Regional dancers, the best from some of the seven thousand islands that compose the Phillipines, dressed in exotic costumes, entertained us while we were served. Again there were many tables - I was seated with the President as was to occur often from then on. Carmen Franco, and the Princess of Naples were on either side of him, because they outranked me, but I was facing him and due to the fact that those two ladies did not speak English and he did not speak Spanish or French, I had the advantage of his attention. He was a charming conversationalist—worldly and sophisticated, with a sense of humor and an easy grace.

After watching the dancers for a while, I commented to Fernando about the difference in the color of the skin of the Phillipine people.

"People from Ilocos, which is my part of the country, are usually darker like me, he said. "We have our explanation for that." Now he was smiling. "When God made man He took some clay and shaped him as perfectly as He could. Then He took the little clay firgure and put it in an oven. After a while he took it out to see if it was right, but at first it was too pale and sickly looking, so He put it back again. After a while He took it out again. Now it was only pink and He didn't like that either. He put it back again and again until the figure was a beautiful dark brown, just the perfect color. Then He brought it to life." He chuckled. "Just my color." Fernando was a charmer.

When a band started to play, he excused himself and got up to dance with his wife, which he did well and seemed to enjoy immensely. He disappeared shortly after and a Phillipine guest explained that the president was an early riser who spent at least twelve hours a day in his office and one hour of strong exercise as well, so he always went to bed early. After he left there was a spectacular display of fireworks and more dance music but the First Lady never seemed to be ready to retire. Although we all were having a good time, even the Spaniards were ready for bed about three A.M., but Imelda didn't budge - we realized it would be extremely rude to leave before she did. When she came to tell us that the next day was the Phillipine Independence day and that there would be a ceremony and parade, I took courage and suggested that then perhaps we should go to bed in order to be able to enjoy it properly.

"Yes, if you would like to but please wear long evening dress—the most important one you have brought with you because this will be one of our most outstanding festivities. And you must all be seated at noon in the parade stands."

The next day I was on a reviewing stand in the sunny July mid-day in my best ball gown. The parade was a spectacular choreographed show of magnitude and beauty—

completely created and organized by Imelda, we were told. It depicted the history of the Phillipines beginning with the moslems and hindus in elaborate costumes dancing past us to the accompaniment of musical instruments or on floats carrying replicas of their primitive boats. Each group represented a different historical period up through the centures including the end of the Spanish colonization, then another of World War Two with General MacArthur's governorship.

When the breathtaking two hour show ended, we were driven to the impressive recently finished Cultural Center, a building of excellent ultra modern architecture. There the President addressed a packed auditorium of 60,000 people whom he held enraptured. Without a note or a paper, without a podium, that small man stood alone on the immense stage and for forty-five minutes he even managed to electrify us foreigners with his speech.

Luis whispered to me, "Why are you so fascinated if you cannot understand that language?"

I couldn't explain –Fernando Marcos had a special power of grasping his audience that I have never known since.

From there we were herded onto the Presidential yacht which we had been told would take us during the night to a sea resort. We had also been told not to take any luggage, which was difficult for any of us to comprehend. As soon as I was on board I rushed to find our stateroom and opened the closet in fear. What a relief! Everything I could possibly need including a beach robe, again with my initials, and bathing suits and caps. Perhaps this was the greatest luxury of all, not having to think about what one had to take when going away for a few days. Even my makeup was already on the shelves in the bathroom.

We dined and danced on a deck decorated with colorful paper lanterns and flowers, retiring late as usual. But the next day it was disappointing to find that the boat had not moved. Mines had been discovered in the port we were headed for and the trip had been cancelled. That was the first indication I had that things were not going so well inside the country.

We were told that we would go the next day to Leyte, about an hour and a half distance by plane—that the ladies would fly with the President and the men with the First Lady. I was delighted to be in Fernando's group because the hour was an early one—six thirty in the morning—and I knew Imelda would keep her group waiting but the President would be punctual.

As we took off Fernando said, "It's Imelda's birthday and Leyte is where she was born." His English was excellent and I commented on that. "Well, he answered, "I spent a short time at Harvard which perhaps improved it, but I had to leave when the Japanese invaded my country in World War II. The person who is really responsable for my English and that of my compatriots is President Taft. Do you know that he sent one thousand one hundred volunteer teachers to the Phillipines in 1901. They spread not only their language but gave us the love for democracy also. We have much to thank the Americans for."

I asked him if he had met his wife in Leyte. "No, we met in Manila where she was studying music in the university. She intended to be a singer. I was a young congressman then and had no thoughts of getting married for a while. When I saw Imelda I changed my mind immediately. We were married eleven days later."

When I commented on how well she had organizd our visit and hosted so many large lunches and dinners for us, he explained. "Imelda's had plenty of experience. Ever since I received my law degree my life has been dedicated to politics. I was elected to our congress and then to our Senate and during those years she often had to prepare breakfast for sixty people and luncheons and dinner for more. In our country a politician is expected to receive many visitors and they expect to be invited to share a meal as well."

When we landed the president apologized for disembarking ahead of us. He was always considerate, polite, smiling and affectionate. It was exciting to arrive with the Chief of State, to watch him review the military honor guard. Then we were in cars staring out at the island natives in endless lines on the sides of the road, waving and throwing flowers in our parth until we arrived at the small beach hotel where we would be staying.

Leyte is a beautiful island and we were lodged this time in a building which we were informed had only been finished the day before. Again our closets contained articles we might want to wear there, things made on that island—straw sandals and clothes made of pineapple silk. Luis' closet even contained a set of golf clubs. Then we attended a mass in honor of the First Lady's birthday followed by an overwhelming luncheon of island delicacies. Our day was spent on the beach but the First Lady strolled among the palm trees dressed in a long pink Phillipine gown with a parasol bound in ruffles to match. I had seen her using parasols in Madrid; she never allowed a ray of sunlight to touch her white skin. The President water-skiied with Cristobal Villaverde and several hours later, he was playing squash.

At dinner when I commented on his strenuous exercise, he said, "I practice sports whenever I have time, but when I was young I was able to do much more. You see, during World War II, I was caught and tortured by the Japanese and that has left its mark. They tied me by my feet and dumped me in a well and when my belly was filled with water, they beat me with rubber hoses. I shouldn't complain, though. They did worse than that with our wives and sisters and mothers. It will take generations to erase those memories."

That night there was a show of local folk dancing and music. Imelda presented with pride her two beautiful young daughters who were students at Princeton University -she explained that her son, Bong Bong, was still in school in England and for that reason could not be present. Then the Phillipine guests begged the First Lady to sing. Van Cliburn volunteered to accompany her on the piano. I expected a mediocre amateurish performance, as did an American businessman recently arrived who was seated next to me. When Imelda burst into song with the voice and assurance of a great professional, my neighbor turned to me, astonished.

	"This woman is unbelievable. The First Lady of a country who can sing like that! It's like an operetta or one of those old films of Jeanette MacDonald and Nelson Eddy."

	"That's not all she can do," said a famous Hong Kong businessman, Sir Y.K. Pao, on my other side. "She has changed the physionomy of Manila. Before Imelda and Fernando, Manila was a third class city. Now the Phillipine people can boast of excellent hospitals, university buildings, parks, hotels and highways with overpasses—things unknown here before. Imelda is impatient, though. She decides that the city needs a new school or theater and then gets the people to work night and day to build it. Why do you know, once when I was visiting in the Guest House," he chuckled, "Imelda telephoned me from Malacanang asking me how I liked the new pool she had just put in. She knew that swimming was my favorite exercise and that I was in a pool every morning. I had to tell her that although the pool was beautiful, frankly the water was too warm."

	"Wait, Y.K.," she said, "please wait, just try it again in a half hour." About twenty minutes later two trucks arrived containing large blocks of ice. The men dumped it all into the pool. It quickly melted and I had a most refreshing swim."

Dragging myself out of bed the next morning, groggy, from lack of sleep, I thought I was seeing things when opening the window and looking down at the lawn surrounding our hotel which the day before had appeared to be yellow now was beautifully green. I called, "Luis..." as he arrived at the window I saw two men in one corner spraying the grass with green paint!

"That must be the golf course Imelda told me about yesterday. She said she knew I liked to play and that the course would be ready today." Luis and I kept watching the men with the sprays painting the grass green. "Since the grass must have been placed here in squares that dried up in places, Imelda wants it to look like a good course."

Now I understood the golf clubs in Luis' CLOSET.

As we stood there looking out, Luis commented. "Last night a man told me that Imelda is trying to attract toursim and industry to this country -that her invitations are done to attract foreigners to begin factories and businesses here . Did you know that Henry got the idea of building a Ford Assembly plant here as a result of his first invitation from the Marcos? What do you suppose she invented to encourage him to do that?"

During that weekend the President heard me mention that I had never been to Hong Kong. By now I felt as if Fernando was an old friend and had told him how anxious I was to see Hong Kong."You must go," he insisted.. "My plane will be going there on Monday and will take you and whoever else may be interested," he said.

When we arrived in Hong Kong, automobiles took up to suites which had been reserved in the Penninsular Hotel - chic Chinese girls were waiting to act as guides for each couple, and a 24 course luncheon awaited us in the best restaurant overlooking the bay. When we started our shopping I began at the jeweler's where Imelda said she had bought her magnificent black pearls - Luis wanted to find a pear shaped South Sea pearl to hang from my necklace. We looked there and many other places, but Luis had to be contented with a black pearl necklace for me instead which is my memento of my first trip to Hong Kong.

On the morning we were leaving to return to Spain, we received a message that the President would not be able to accompany us to the airport but that he would appreciate it if we would stop by his office and say goodbye. Cayetana Alba was not ready in time, but Carmen Franco and I went together with Luis and we were shown into his study. By this time I was thoroughly charmed by the President and would have been very sad to leave without saying goodbye to my charming impressive host.

When we entered Fernando got up from his desk - with a smile he came toward us. "I have little presents for you," he said and handed us each a small box.

I didn't want to waste the last moments opening a box so thanking him, I said, "I'll open it on the plane."

"No, open it now, Aline."

The box contained a large, oval shaped oriental pearl, exactly what Luis and I had been looking for when we had gone to Hong Kong a few days before. I was very impressed and touched.

Then he asked, "Is there anything here that you especially enjoyed, anything you would like to take back with you as a remembrance of the Phillipines?"

Oh yes, I would love to have a box of that fruit called Kalamanzi. I would like my children to taste that wonderful juice."

He nodded. "I'll see to it."

When we arrived in Madrid we found that the maids had packed all the clothes and shoes that had been in our closets, the perfumes, the makeup, the reading glasses, even the books in our room and...in additional crates were four kalamanzi trees with instructions of how to plant them. We placed the kalamanzi trees in our garden in Marbella where they flourished and are still the only kalamanzi trees in Spain.

During the following years, Imelda came to Spain seldom but she did appear in 1975 for General Franco's funeral. She had just returned from a trip to visit Mao Tse Tung in the People's Republic of China and told us about it.

"Making that visit was a serious decision since it is not a secret that we struggle against communism, but things are not going well in our country and China is only a few minutes away by plane. We must maintain good relations with our neighbors." I asked her if she had worn her lovely Phillipine dresses and parasols there.

"Certainly not. I wore a "Mao" like all the women of China are obliged to."

" I can't imagine you, Imelda, in one of those horrible dresses they call a "Mao". I had dinner at the Chinese Embassy in Madrid a few weeks ago and I certainly felt sorry for the wife of the Ambassador. Her Mao was so ugly, so plain , so unfeminine. And the wife of the charge d'affaires wore exactly the same. How could the Chinese women accept Mao Tse Tung's order obliging each one to wear the same cheap ugly cotton dress. Not even fitted, like a rag haníng on them, without any decoration or difference even in color.."

She laughed. "Oh, never would I have been so foolish as to put on one of those factory made numbers. Brfore I went to China, I sent for a Mao and the cap too, and had them copied at home of very good material and properly fitted. I assure you , my Mao was quite attractive."

I always admired and liked Imelda but she was not liked by all women, certainly envied by many -although she was highly admired by men of all ages and those from many different countries. She told me that Ho Chi Minh had promised her that while she was First Lady of the Phillipines, her country had nothing to fear from China. She also said that when she had stopped off in Morocco to visit king Hassan, he had given her a belt of gold and emeralds and had filled her plane with - .of all stramge things -. a ton of dates. I knew in Morocco this was a sign of welcome and friendship .

I arranged for Imelda to speak in Washington to a group of intelligence officials from about twenty different countries. At that moment the ASEAN countries were of international concern. I had convinced the group that Imelda could provide us with useful confidential information. The content of her talk was brilliant, but most fascinating was the manner in which she delivered it. She was calm yet dramatic, the voice was low and sultry, her special perfume wafted through the closed room. Now and then to stress a point her long hypnotic fingers with the red and white nails gestured gracefully, her almond-eyed glance passsed from one man to the other around the long rectangular table. In short she got her husband's message about her country across beautifully .

I didn't see Imelda for several years. Someone told me she had been gaining weight – that it was due, one friend said, to too many injections of silicone. I knew that noone gets fat from silicone. I suspected that most likely she was eating too many bananas again – something I had seen her do frequently during the day, excusing herself on the grounds that "when one doesn't sleep , one gets so hungry."

In 1981 Imelda invited us again to the Phillipines, this time with our children. Luis was considering establishing a factory there for a family business that had existed in Spain during the past century. Despite the fact that it was late at night, we were received by the first lady at the airport with the music, the flowers, the beautiful girls and even the military guards. My two eldest sons had come with their wives, my youngest son was not yet married, but he came as well- of course they were most impressed.. When we arrived in our rooms at the Antique Palace, not only all the same luxuries surrounded us as the last time we had been there but when I rang and asked for some water, a file of men servants marched in carrying three huge bowls of caviar on silver trays and several ice buckets with champagne.

While our children and Luis traveled around the islands visitng factories, banana plantations, travelling in canoes through the white water of scenic rivers, I remained in Manila with Imelda – I wanted to see how she spent her time. It was exhausting. Although Imelda never practiced any sport , that I know of, not even swimming, her energy was unlimited. She was busy then preparing the visit of the Pope for which she had built a house where he was going to stay made entirely from material of the coconut tree.

"We must teach the people to employ the raw material which is abundant in our own counry,"she explained. '"every detail in this building is derived from coconut trees – from the exterior to the floors, including the furnishings, even the most minute detail."

The result was unique and absolutely beautiful. Also the International Film Festival was going to take place in Manila that year and she was at the same time organizing those festivities. If Imelda was extravagant, frivolous she was not.

One morning I went to Malacanang early to meet her before her invitation to a small luncheon with her and the Presdient. The long corridor going into her part of the building was packed with servitors running in and out, fashion designers carrying pictures of dresses, architects with large drawings of buildings under their arms – gardeners in blue uniforms holding potted flowers – just masses of people waiting –

waiting. When I reached the small antichamber, I recognized the masseuse who was emerging from the next room. As I greeted her she explained, "The first Lady had a hectic morning working fast and nonb-stop – she is so cmpetănt but she slept only three hours last night. She usually manages at least four. This is the second massage I have given her today".

By now, I had experienced those wonderfully relaxing massages myself in the beauty salon of the Guest House. Instead of covering the body with oil, they were given over a thin silk robe, the masseuse beginnning at the tip of the toes, massaging each joint and muscle throughout the body. Her fingers moving smoothly over the silk and when the massage was finished, it was like coming out of a deep sleep.

Next to us, in the office waiting room was Imelda's hairdresser seated at a small table with the makeup girl who was occupied in putting small boxes into a suede bag. As I glanced over her working material to catch the name of the cosmetics, she told me that because of the hot climate the First Lady refreshed her makeup frequently during the day. That was hard for me to understand since the air conditioning was so cold I was usually shivering. Several girls who looked like secretaries were seated on chairs or just standing. All told there must have been over thirty people waiting to serve or to be received by or to ask a favor of...the First Lady. The court of Louis Quatorze must have been something like this, I thought, wondering how many others were in the next room, the door of which was barred by a woman I knew to be her private secretary.

Eventually Imelda joined me, looking fresh as a daisy—as if she did nothing except care for her looks, dressed in a stiff banana- silk pale green and blue long gown with butterfly sleeves—the flawless skin, the long hair coiffed into a roll, the red and white nails perfect—not a detail of her majestic appearance was any different from any other moment of her day.

During what they called a diet lunch—vegtables and fruit—seafood was added for me—served in a small study next to the President's office, Fernando said he was very busy and worried about the unrest in the country and for those reasons had seen his guests less often. "To make up for my lack of attention, what about a weekend trip on my yacht to Puerto Azul, a lovely resort? Imelda has just finished a fascinating house there made of bamboo which she calls the Bamboo Palace and you must see it."

On that trip to Puerto Azul while at sea two days later the President mentioned that his favorite masseuse, a specialist in acupressure was on board and asked if anyone wanted to try her out. None of my sons had ever had a massage but when they saw the very pretty little masseuse, they became interested immediately.

"Just lie down on deck and try it out," said the President. You're going to like it."

Encouraged, my eldest son, Alvaro, stretched out, stomach down, as ordered. The small girl took off her sandals, crouched on his back and dug her toes into his back bone. There was much groaning and a scary "crack, crack" sound now and then as she pulled on his shoulders and arms but the results must have been excellent because for the remainder of our visit, my sons asked for this particular masseuse every day. The President must have been longing for us to go back to Spain so he could enjoy his favorite massage again.

It was at the Bamboo Palace one sultry night sitting outside on the bamboo porch, reclining on bamboo sofas, when Imelda showed me her emeralds.

"You know, Aline, I was very impressed with your emerald necklace the night we gave the dinner for Susuki."

(Premier Susuki of Japan had been in Manila on an official dinner a few days before) – I had been seated near him on the dais. Fernando told me before the dinner that it was disagreeable for him to be obliged to invite Suzuki since the Phillipines had suffered terrible tortures from the Japanese during World War Two.

She went on to say ,"I think your emeralds are the best I have ever seen—and much better than mine." She turned to an attendant who was nearby. "Please, tell my maid to bring me my emeralds."

In a few moments a large black suede box was placed on the bamboo table in front of us. Imelda opened it. On the top shelf was a small diamond and emerald necklace. She sort of passed over that and opened the drawer beneath it on which was another necklace or bracelet of emeralds. She passed over that also Then she pulled out the next drawer which contained a quite good emerald choker, but she quickly went to the last drawer and there illuminated by the moonlight and the bamboo lanterns surrounding us was a really grand emerald necklace.

"Oh, Imelda, that's breathtaking. It's much better than mine."

"No," she said, "None of mine sparkle as much as yours. My emeralds are perfect. Yours have flaws. But yours sparkle and the real beauty in stones is the life they have."

I was surprised. Imelda was an authority on jewels as she was on so many other things.

Already I had seen a similar suede box of hers with four or five drawers of pearl and diamond clips, bracelets and necklaces. Evidently each type of jewel was kept in a different large suede box container.

Imelda knew that I would be leaving from Manila directly for Washington to attend the inauguration of President Reagan and asked if I would be willing to take a gift from her to the new Frist lady of the United States. "I'm afraid the package will be quite large because I want to give her the most beautiful dresses that are made in my country. You know,

First Ladies never have enough evening dresses and I'm sure she will be able to use these."

Imelda had asked me before we arrived to obtain from Nancy her measurements and she had put her best designers and seamstresses to work night and day. Barely in time for my departure, the ten or so ravishing gowns were ready. She showed them to me one by one—fabulous embroidery on exquisite lace, hand-painted flowers on the typical Phillipine pineapple silk. She had studied Nancy Reagan's pictures in order to discover her preferences as to style and color.

When I delivered the two huge boxes to Blair House in Washington two days before President Reagan's inauguration, the new First Lady looked at them and with what I consider great willpower said with much regret in her voice, "How kind of Mrs. Marcos, but I couldn't possibly accept such valuable gifts. Aline, I intend to wear only clothes designed by American designers, but they are so so beautiful."

In 198------- there were general elections in the Phillipines which showed a wide victory for Fernando. Nevertheless the opposition orchestrated disburbances in the streets of Manila and thereby convinced certain American Embassy employees that the elections had been a fraud. As a result American airforce officers appeared in the Malacanang palace explaining that for Fernando's safety while these manifestations continued they would take Fernando and Imelda to his home province of Ilocos, the northern part of the island of Luzon of which Manila is the capital. Fernando, not doubting the veracity of their offer, accepted and left with Imelda in the USA plane. Instead of delivering them to Ilocos, they were landed in Guam. Shortly after Fernando and Imelda were moved by the American airplanes from Guam to Hawaii, with the explanation of needing more time to investigate the current situation in the Phillipines. Actually they had been kidnapped by the USA officials under false pretenses.

When I learned these details in the press, I tried to contact them in Hawaii, without succcess. Fortunately Imelda called me from Hawaii a few days later and told me that they had a serious problem, because the American government did not permit them to return to Manila nor to leave Hawaii to go anyplace else. In addition she said that Fernando was ill , that she feared he had the beginning of a cancer. I took a plane to Hawaii immediately, hoping to be able to help them.

Fernando told me he was shocked at the attitude of a country he had always defended and admired. He prepared a letter which he asked me to deliver to President Reagan. When I returned to New York and I had difficultly reaching Reagan by phone and I was told to send the letter to Washington, which I did. Neither I nor the Marcos received an answer, although I telephoned Reagan's secretary repeatedly – I fear it was never delivered to him. I have always blamed myself for not having gone to Washington personally to deliver the letter to President Reagan directly. But I was not able to speak personally to Reagan during the days that followed and had to leave suddenly for Madrid since my husband called saying he was feeling very ill.

Fernando became worse and died without the American government making any effort to assist him. Later I realized that Ragan had never seen Fernando's letter, nor was he made aware of Fernando's seious problem. However after Marcos died the american government allowed his body to be returned and buried in the Phillipines.

      I remembered Imelda´s remarks to me about the Shah of Iran who was refused entrance into the United States while in critically in need of medical assistance.

"What a devastating tragedy that family of the Shah of Iran has gone through," Imelda had commented. "The Shah was such a loyal friend of the United States. While he was in control in his country, no group in the Middle East dared to get out of hand. But the Shah was weak and when Presdient Carter's Ambassador advised him to leave, he complied. Imagine, having all that power—all that importance and losing it—so completely as not to be able to return to his country nor even to be welcome in any other. Can you imagine anything so awful happening to anyone?"

In May of 1984 my alma Mater, the College of Mt. St. Vincent, gave an Honorary Doctorate to two alumnae, Cory Aquino, a Phillipine politician, and myself. We had both been boarders in that catholic women's university and had even occupied the same rooms, although at different times. That day while we waited for the ceremony of the Honary Doctorates to begin, we discussed the political situation in her country. I expressed my admiration for Fernando Marcos, Then she told me that she blamed Marcos for the assassination of her father, something that had occurred several years before, although she had to admit that an officer of the Phillipine Army was the one who had shot him. I told Cory that Fernando had informed me of that disaster, saying that it had been a tragedy for him because people blamed him for trying to eliminate a political adversary through an army officer, but Fernando said the truth was that the officer had a personal grievance against Aquino and had been mentally ill as well. Nevertheless Cory was bitter against Fernando and my explanations did not change her opinion. Several years later Cory Aquino was elected president of the Philllipines but had an unsuccessful short term in office.

Fernando had become president of the Phillipines in 1965 - his tenure in office lasted 21 years until the United States military planes removed him in 1986, taking him under false pretenses first to Guam and then to Hawaii. He was never allowed into his country again , nor permitted to leave Hawaii - his situation and that of the Shah of Iran were very similar.

President Fernando Marcos had always been a loyal friend of the USA - he promoted a sincere admiration for everything American among his countrymen. I knew him to be an untiring worker, a man with no pretentions, always speaking well of his associates. He had always made a sincere effort to help his people, his generosity to all impressed me. Fernando Marcos is the most admirable leader that I have known, despite my having been acquainted with quite a few presidents and kings.

CHAPTER FORTY – TWO

TEA WITH OLD LADIES

One hot summer day about 1981 around six p.m. I went to have tea at the house of another of my husband's elderly aunts. "Tia" (aunt) Casilda was the Duchess of Santo Mauro, a most distinguished title, since among her many famous ancestors was the Marques of Santa Cruz, the heroic admiral who eliminated the Turks and "BarbaRoja" from the Mediterranean in the Battle of Lepanto.

When entering the old palace in Madrid on the Calle San Bernardino by way of a wide curved stairway going up to the second floor, I often had stopped on the landing to admire a huge iron lantern - one of the family's important relics from the flagship of that famous Battle of 1571 - it had been inherited directly through the centuries from Aunt Casilda's ancestor. It was this same ancestor's home that Luis and I had visited in El Viso on our way to the shoot with Franco and the Duke of Windsor in Mudela. And although I had come up this staircase many times before, today I observed this significant memento with greater interest. I now knew much more about that Admiral and that famous battle against the Turks which had changed the history of Europe in that century- the fascinating epoch of the sixteenth century—during which century occurred the warfare against the turks, and also the important discovery and colonization of many areas in the New World—it was a romantic incredible period. And as happens in Spain, one is constantly brought into contact with historical personalities and events of times long gone by. These reminders frequently barged into my life - one of the delights of living in Spain. I had also learned that the more I knew about the past, the more I could enjoy and appreciate the country and its people today.

    Although I had met no descendants of Barbaroja, that I knew of, I had the good fortune of now being related to the descendants of the man who had destroyed his control of the Mediterranean.   The old palace where I was about to have tea had been inhabited for generations by that famous admiral of Lepanto's descendants. When I walked into the long narrow room on the second floor already the rattle of teacups blended with the voices of several elderly ladies. I looked at the group – all were over ninety, only my favorite, Aunt Casilda Pastrana was younger, but she must have been at least 86. Casilda seemed to be the preferred woman's name on both sides of Luis' family- today my favorite was wearing her usual small grey hat - the Duchess of Durcal who was sitting next to her also was wearing a hat, but a larger and more glamorous one; All together there were three duchesses and a Countess - then Luis' cousin, much younger and the daughter of the hostess – she now had the title of Marquesa de Santa Cruz and was entering the room from the opposite side. As we continued to nibble and talk several other elderly ladies entered the group. The colors of the ladies dresses merged with the somber tones of the room – on the wall above the round tea table which adjoined a dark red banquette, was a large painting of a landscape, another family heirloom from generations far back. Behind us in other salons were many works of famous painters of the past four centuries – Teniers, Velazquez, Goya, and Tiepolo, plus others.

    The atmosphere was ideal for what I wanted to accomplish that day. I had already told my hostess that I intended to write an article about the changes in customs since the beginning of the century and that I hoped they could give me some examples. When I sat down I realized that the ladies were intrigued by the topic and pleased with my interest in their lives of so long ago. As I glanced over the group, I calculated that their hey-days had most likely been at the beginning of the century. There was a general buzz of conversation as they exchanged ideas and assured me that they had much to tell because the changes had been gigantic. Each lady wanted to speak of her specific experience – they all began to talk at the same time but our hostess interrupted the chattering by declaring that perhaps they should begin with recounting first the enormous differences women had experienced – that it might be difficult for an American to realize how women had lived in Spain before 1936 when the Civil War began. But when they began to speak I realized these women's memories and experiences went back much further than I had assumed . Finally I said I would listen to them one by one so I would not miss anyone's story. The ladies agreed.

    Meanwhile an elderly butler and his assistant were serving the tea and an assortment of foods – not only croissants and sweets but Spanish ham and croquettes and different cheeses. But again each wanted to tell me her personal story. At first they were all talking about the confusion and terror caused by the "reds" trying to enter their houses in Madrid and in Barcelona during their Civil War. They recalled how diffiult it had been to get information from those who were already on vacation in France or Italy – one lady had been in Madrid in the act of having her child baptized when men with hatchets entered the church from the street and her husband barely had time to escape with the baby by a side door. Nevertheless the priest who had been officiating was caught and beaten - she learned later that he had been killed. Each story outdid the other until I raised my hands in despair.

The Duchess of Durcal took over, " Aline you were interested in the changes in women's lives and customs, we must tell you one by one that nothing has been the same since the Civil War and I think we will all agree," she went on as she looked around the group, "that a good part of these changes has been for the better. We women were too isolated from real life. Before the war even the places people went for summer vacations were different. Today my daughter and her family are going to a beach on the southern coast. In our times no one ever went south in the summer. It was considered too hot and unhealthy. We always went north to San Sebastian, or Santander, or Biarritz. No one went to Mallorca either. It was the English who made Mallorca popular.

Then another piped up ,"And long ago it was the French went to Mallorca, that strange French woman who went with that famous musician, Chopin - not married , of course. He was Polish."

"But it was the foreigners who discovered Mallorca as a resort place. It was not considered an accepted place for us," interrupted another.

" Yes , but we seemed obliged to look for cool resorts - nowadays people prefer that new place, Marbella, on the southern coast or even other islands like Ibiza near Mallorca."

"And what about the bathing suits?" All the ladies sighed and lifted their hands.

Then they began to describe the long skirts and sleeves they had to wear when on the beach.

Another lady told how their street clothes differed – "We never left the house without hat and gloves."

"And a woman companion." Interjected another. "Have you forgotten that before the civil war, no lady went about shopping without a companion."

One of the ladies added, "I never was actually alone with my husband before we were married and that was normal for most of us. Do you agree?" They all nodded and then many began to describe the beautiful long dresses and fancy hats, and the mantillas used for so many affairs - black mantillas on Fridays to Mass and frequently white mantillas for weddings and at the bullfights.

One Duchess interrupted to remind the others about the fans they used to carry and how they used them with different gestures to send messages to their boyfriends – even when in church during the mass. Every tilt of the fan had indicated some message that the boyfriend seemed to understand. But they all agreed that life for women in their day was less amusing, and were in agreement that one of the most serious differences which was a grave mistake was that women were not allowed to study careers or work, nor even go to restauarants. Evidently there was very little a respectable woman was allowed to do outside of certain sports.

"And even then, we had to have chaperones,"interjected one lady."

Later when they married one lady said life was so boring that in the afternoons it was customary sometimes to go in their carriages to drop visiting cards at friends' houses. Corners of the cards would be bent to indicate different messages. Bending the top right corner meant the lady had gone in person, the top left meant she would like the lady to vist her, the lower left meant something else.

Every now and then the hostess , the Duchess of Santo Mauro, would jump up and return with a picture to show me a dress she had been wearing sixty years before or a special carriage with the crest of the family on the door, making sure with a tap of her fingernail that I noticed the grand costumes of the coachmen.

A much younger aunt, the Countess of Yebes, about seventy-five, and famous for her beauty had arrived and entered the room. Carmen Yebes had always been especially affectionate with me, she had put me in touch with the Count of Canilleros and she was always especially lively. Imediately she took an enthusiastic part in the conversation, interrupting the others to remind them how skeptical they had been when about thirty years before they learned that Luis was going to marry an American girl. "It seemed as strange to us, Aline" now she directed herself to me, "as if your son Alvaro came to you today to say he wanted to marry a Chinese girl."

"But why so strange?" I asked.

"We didn't see how you would fit into our way of life at all. After all in those days – it was way back in ′′47 – I remember well, there were no foreigners in Spain then, only a few diplomats...no tourists, no foreign businesses. You seemed so foreign to us. We had all seen you someplace or other...at the bullfights or in a restaurant. You had created quite a sensation because you were beautiful and dressed so well. But we were aware that you lived alone in an apartment and that you were working in something connected to the American embassy. That was enough for us to decide that you were "fast". In those days –well, we thought most American women were immoral. We only knew Americans through the movies and the fact that they divorced and had many liberties scandalized us. You were the only American girl in Madrid then. If there were others we never noticed them."

The other ladies nodded in assent and Carmen Yebes continued. "The Romanones family was especially famous and it's a big family. Until then those who had married into it came from similar families with the same customs and opinions. Nobody cared or mentioned whether your family was poor or rich or known...that was not the issue. The Romanones family was rich and important enough so that noone considered those details. But because of that wealth and importance many others were jealous of you."

At this remark, my hostess who was not from the Romanones side of the family sat up a bit taller in her chair. Carmen Yebes acted as if she did not notice and continued. "But all of us thought that the marriage was not going to turn out so well."

"But," chipped in Tia Casilda Pastrana, "It did. You surprised us all, Aline. You did adapt. And we are delighted to have you as part of the family. You fit in better than other girls from known families here might have."

Then Carmen Yebes spoke to me again. "Even I had to adapt when I married your uncle. My father was an ambassador and I came here after living most of my life in foreign embassies and found myself suddenly a part of this Romanones family. They were special.. much more liberal than most ... And as you know very united, ready to back you up if anything went wrong. That is typical of all Spanish families. Whether we were right or wrong we stuck together. So the fact that you had married into a family such as you did, immediatly gave you a backing and a standing in Madrid you would not have had if you had married into another important family."

"But I was unaware of all this then...of how important Luis' family was." I interrupted. " Completely unaware." Listening to Carmen I was fascinated with what she was telling me.

Carmen Yebes laughed. "I suspected that. But you know if you had been short and fat and boring, you can be certain that not even the "abuelo" Romanones would have accepted you or made any fuss about you. You might have remained isolated from us for the rest of your life in this country."

Tea was still being served by the elderly footman who had been born in the house and for whom all the ladies had shown at one moment or another some indication of their affection. These old servants were accepted as part of the family and were an important part of any occasion. The other ladies who were not part of the Romanones side of Luis' family, but of his mother's side changed the conversation. They described the big parties in the palaces where there were usually one hundred and fifty guests, and on rare occasions there might have been a maximum of three hundred people - if it had been a large wedding. They all agreed that it was a pity their lives had whirled around the same small group because they had little opportunity to meet anyone outside their social circle; they explained that women in all social stratas were restricted in more or less the same manner.

    They were anxious to explain that they had enjoyed some advantages that today's world has lost – they agreed that the manners and the luxury of the world they had lived in had disappeared entirely. One Duchess described the elegant uniforms of the head butlers who in those days in Spain were referred to as "maitres d'hotel" and of the footmen who they said would be selected principally for their heigth and appearance. Men servants who would be at the front door, in the salons, or who served the table, had to be slim and tall. The word "hotel", they explained, was generally used in France and in Spain to indicate a large private home or palace. There were few fine restaurants in the first part of the century in Madrid, but when they did come into existence, the head waiters were referred to as Maitres d'hotel, the public restaurants and hotels copied the customs and wordings that had been customary in the great private houses. Everything had carried the family colors—the carriages which were still very much in use until the civil war, later the automobiles, the uniforms of the servants. As an example, she said that in the Torre Arias family, (the hostess was from that side- my husband's mother's side) the menservants' tailcoats were dark blue and their vests yellow with blue stripes. These colors were used on his jockies' silks, as well as on the uniforms of the guards and shepherds on his ranches and farms. When I heard this, again I became aware that I had picked the wrong family colors for Primitivo's expensive uniforms but I had no intention of changing them now; I wouldn't risk confronting Maria's rightful indignation.

    They continued to explain that even the TorreArias suitcases and trunks were painted yellow with a broad blue stripe which bore the nine-pointed crown of a count, with a curved line joining points to show that it was a grandee title, and usually the letters of the title. the hostess added that Luis' grandfather Torre Arias' cars were the best in Madrid. I had a feeling here that one side of Luis' family was trying to outdo the other. She continued to explain that Torre Arias had several Hispano Suizas, a popular car of those times, but what he liked most were Rolls Royces, of which he had five. then one of the ladies mentioned that an English lord during those years had about fifteen Rolls Royces- that these excesses were not restricted to Spain - that all Europe had been different at the beginning of the century. All the Torre Arias´ Rolls Royce´s were confiscated by the reds as soon as the Civil war broke out, in fact for many years the –Rolls that the Hotel Ritz rented out to its clients was a Torre Arias Rolls and was still painted yellow.

The other ladies spoke out to ascertain that their families also had important automobiles which as soon as they arrived from London were painted in the family colors and with the family crest on the doors exactly as had been on their carriages.

"Oh," I asked, "did you drive around Madrid in those small one horse carriages I saw when I first arrived here, the ones used as taxis?"

"Heavens, no. One horse never. We had to have two horses. only the "kept women" of wealthy men went in one horse carriages. Some of our husbands had mistresses. This unfortunately was an accepted fact."

They told me that ladies before the Civil War did not go to restaurants in Madrid but in France and England customs were more advanced. "One of the reasons we liked to travel with our husbands outside of Spain was that they could take us to restaurants and theaters. We lived a much freer existence outside our country."

Then another added, "But despite our restrictions there were as many dramas in our lives as there are today, and often scandals which were very exciting." She recalled her mother saying that at a royal ball at the beginning of the previous century, the Duchess of Medinaceli had made a spectacular entrance on a litter carried by four black servants, almost naked except for her magnificent jewels which completely covered her body. Her reason was her jealously because the Queen Maria Luisa had dared to flirt with the Duchesss' favorite young army officer.

"But that was almost two hundred years ago," interrupted one lady. "How unfair it is that our great grandmothers had more freedom than we did."

Now again they all began to chat about people who had lived almost two centuries ago. Just like Miguel Canilleros in Caceres although he seemed to live in still more remote periods of history.

"What a pity," I said, "that your lives were so dull."

"It did not seem so to us then, Aline. We had our love affairs and dramas just as much as you young people do today."

"Well," I interupted ,"now that reminds me of Arthur Rubenstein telling me that he used to love giving concerts in Spain when he was a young man, because the women were beautiful and exciting and very daring. He said he remembered especially how stiffly starched their nighties used to be. He confessed that he remembered one night when he was on the over-night train going from Madrid to Barcelona, that he could still recall how the lady's nighty scratched him."

My companions did not laugh as I had expected. In fact there was a silence which made me sense I had put my foot in it. And almost before I had finished my brief story, I felt a small foot tapping mine under the long tablecloth. Then, too late I remembered that years ago Luis had told me that the ninety year old Duchess of Durcal who was sitting on my right, in her youth had been responsable for several scandals - that she had been born in Barcelona, the only daughter of a very wealthy Catalan merchant, and due to her beauty had managed to marry the aristocratic Duke of Durcal from Madrid. I realized that she had to be the lady on the night train going to Barcelona. Later the Duchess of Durcal got up to leave when I did - as we descended the expansive staircase together, grabbing my arm firmly so as not to stumble , she whispered, "Goodness, Aline, what a frightful moment. I was terrified you were going to mention my name. You must be more careful what you say."

CHAPTER FORTY – THREE

MARRIAGES

LUIS AND TERESA

In 1973 my son Luis married a beautiful German Princess, Teresa Sayn-Wittgenstein, in Salzburg. My husband and I had never been to Germany or Austria nor did we have many German friends, but Teresa had come to Spain to learn Spanish and had been introduced to us by Portuguese friends . While plans for the wedding were under way I learned much about the customs of middle European aristocracy which were more festive and pompous than ours in Spain– maybe their seating was less rigorous as the duke of Windsor had told us but their weddings lasted three days and were more glamorous than those in Spain.

   The bride's mother, Princess Marianne Sayn-Wittgenstein came to Madrid to meet us and to explain the wedding details. She said that we were expected to have one hundred guests and that she needed the names of each – the total number of guests in the church would be 350 - each would have a place card – the evenings would be at a castle with a seated dinner and dancing –black tie and long evening gowns, diadems were requested for those who owned one. "Manny" as she was known to friends, a beautiful brilliant woman, also requested the rank of each of our guests. This was necessary because detailed table placements had to be arranged as well as placing people correctly for the cortege to leave the church at the end of the ceremony. Guests were to be seated so that on leaving the wedding ceremony the person coming out of the bench on one side of the aisle would match up with another of equal distinction from the opposite to form a cortege of all guests as they exited the church.

When I saw the bride's list which included several European royalties, I realized that I would have to pep up ours. I asked the bride's mother what persons from Spain were considerd most impressive - she had no doubts about that. "The Duchess of Alba and Dominguin , the bullfighter."

"That's great. They're both intimate friends and are already invited.", I told her. " Would it be allright if I invited a few American movie stars." I had already asked Audrey and Ava and Deborah Kerr and their husbands.

"They would be fine."

The first person I had invited was the Duchess of Windsor who was thrilled and ordered new special outfits for the wedding, but at the last minute she fell ill and could not come.

The day we arrived in the Salzburgh airport , the bride's eldest brother received our group from Spain as we went through customs –he had buses and automobiles awaiting to take us to the castle in Salzburg where rooms had been reserved. Our arrival at the castle was spectacular and fascinated our group of spanish titles and dignataries. Twenty men in the classic Tyrolean costume and in the Sayn-

Wittgenstein family colors gave us a twenty gun salute. Such impressive formalities had long since disappeared in Spain or perhaps had never existed. I was dazed – until now I had been enthralled by the many old – fashioned Spanish customs, but these German princely ones certainly outdid ours.

Since I wanted to give a Spanish atmosphere to our side of the wedding, I had asked our women guests to wear the classic black spanish "peineta" high comb and mantilla which was not only beautiful, but also dramatic – and a customary addition to most spanish weddings. However since I feared that that many of my guests might not comply- perhaps they would consider it too difficult to put on properly, or perhaps they had lost their high combs or their mantillas, I bought in the main department store fifty "peinetas", high combs, and fifty black lace mantillas. And to make certain everyone was able to put on the peineta and mantilla properly, I brought with us in the plane from Madrid two hairdressers who were experts in placing mantillas.

The day of the wedding when our guests descended from the busses in the plaza in front of the church of Mondsee – the hometown of Mozart, very near Salzburg where the wedding was to take place - the spectacle of the fifty Spanish women, all enveloped in the classic black mantillas and high combs made a huge impression- exclamations of admiration resounded from the mobs of onlookers as we walked toward the church. Suddenly a loud voice in the crowd called out, "the Spanish inquisition is here." At least noone in the crowd doubted our nationality.

Ava Gardner wanted to stop off in London to get her "tiara" out of the bank for the dinners in the castles at night, but her trip from Los Angeles where she was filming did not provide enough time. Nevertheless she was delighted to wear her mantilla, an ancient white one which had been a gift years before - she was outstanding and beautiful , the only white mantilla in the group..

Audrey Hepburn was now married to an Italian doctor and came from Rome without a mantilla but she did bring a beautiful "tiara" for the balls at night.. Mrs. Cornelius Vanderbilt Whitney brought another famous tiara that her husband's family had acquired a century before. The European aristocrats recognized immediately that it was the one that had belonged to the Empress Eugenie. But the most spectacular tiara of all was a very inexpensive false one which I had encouraged a spanish guest to buy on the Calle Fuencarral in Madrid in a shop dedicated to selling crowns for beauty contests . It was such a beautiful tiara that noone realized the stones were false - during the Balls in the Castles every night many were the glances of admiration and wonderment about where that lady had found such an extraordinary tiara. The wearer was Mitzou, a brilliant designer friend from Madrid who had designed shooting clothes for me – she did not own a tiara but when I showed her the false one in the shop she was brave enough to buy it and wear it.

Three marvellous days followed with luncheons in the nearby mountains while one day the men had a sensational deer shoot and we all enjoyed the magnificent balls at night. How well those German men danced the waltz and how beautiful were the magnificent gowns and jewels and the fabulous hats at the wedding. Germans celebrate their weddings in the middle of the day before lunch, the spanish at eight o,clock at night, but nevertheless the Germans certainly outdo Spaniards in weddings.

At that wedding in Salzburg my eldest son met the beautiful daughter of Beltran Domecq, the young man who had so confused me that first day as I walked into the Hotel Palace in Madrid and then had met again nine years later at Peps Merito's monastery home in Cordoba. Beltran and his wife, Anne, during the following years had become close friends and we had invited them to the wedding - Since they could not attend , they sent their two daughters instead. My eldest son fell in love with their daughter Lucila and six months later they were married in the Domecq's home in Jerez de la Frontera.

ALVARO AND LUCILA

For Alvaro's wedding with Lucila I was determined to show the Germans that Spanish weddings could be as glamorous as theirs – the true fact was that even Spanish royal weddings did not compare to the glamour and grandness of the German princely weddings. So I described to Beltran all the festivities the Germans had organized only six months before and convinced him that we must not let those German outdo us - that we should use typically spanish festivities, as many as possible and extend our children's wedding to the same time of three days. Beltran, the handsomest of the great Domecq sherry family and the most popular had wonderful ideas. "How about a bullfight and also a top flamenco party with the best artists from Jerez and Sevilla! On one day we can also take the guests to Ronda, the beautiful Arabic town, it's only twenty minutes distant, for lunch in Anne's cousin''s famous castle. That way they will see that we also have castles as beautiful as those in Germany and they will learn that ours are more ancient."

Thus our schedule of an unusual grand Spanish wedding was prepared. The first large black tie dinner was preceeded by a show put on by Beltran's cousin, Alvaro Domecqhow , with his world famous Andalusian horses, his unique horsemen and the girls mounted behind the rider, "a la grupa". Alvaro Domecq had already shown this fabulous horsemanship spectacle in the United States and in London but it had not yet been seen in Germany or Austria. The show was provided for our guests seated in the Domecq amphitheater where cocktails were served there before the dinner and party of the first night of the wedding weekend.

The next day a bullfight took place for the guests in the Jerez bullring with the season's best matadors plus much of the fanfare usually seen only in the yearly Fair of Jerez. Beltram Domecq was the most popular man in Jerez and could get permission for anything he wanted to set up. Then the trip to Ronda was also a success since the Arabic atmosphere of the city is impressive, as is the castle, so high above the Guadalquivir river that one can look down from the terraces to the eagles flyng below. The celebrations terminated with a flamenco party the night of the wedding for which Beltran had hired the best gypsy professionals in southern Spain.

The bride was driven to the church in the Domecq family's famous carriage pulled by nine lead horses - the bride and groom also left the church after the wedding for the dinner in the Domecq palacio in the same carriage amidst shouts of admiration from the crowds. Neither the Germans nor the Austrians nor anyone else had a carriage that could compare, nor a three day wedding celebration that was as amusing.

The entire church, had been luxuriously decorated with masses of white roses, white gardenias and white carnations but the front rows were occupied by uninvited people who had filled the church hours before the wedding. In Germany Manny had been able to reserve the church and avoid anyone not a guest to be allowed to enter, but in Spain that was impossible. Guy and Marie Helen de Rothschild's seats in the front row were occupied by two plump gypsy women with their babies in arms, someone found a seat for Marie Helene but Guy remained standing as did many other guests. To my amazement and relief Guy was favorably impressed – later when we explained that in Spain entrance to churches could not be prohibited to anyone- he commented , "Spain without doubt is the most democratic country in Europe."

At the wedding dinner at the bride and groom's table I stood up and told of the wonderful coincidence that my meeting with the first spaniard I had ever known, thirty years before - I pointed across the table to Beltran – had resulted in this wedding of our children thirty years later. It was a nice ending. And also a great beginning since the marriage produced five wonderful children.

MIGUEL AND MAGDALENA

Ten years later our son Miguel married a beautiful Mexican girl, Magdalena Carral. The bride's attractrive parents were outstanding personalities in that country and they prepared a spectacular wedding in the ancient family home which had been built in 1646 in the center of the city of Mexico. The wedding was identical to large weddings in Spain - the ceremony in the church was at eight at night, the dinner afterwards in the ancient family home included over three hundred guests in black tie and long dress. It was moving for me to realize that Mexico, discovered by spanish "conquistadores" five hundred years before was still similar to the customs of the people in Spain today. Although the Spanish conquerors had made sacrifices in lives and in expense, despite the many centuries gone by, their efforts had resulted in almost an entire continent speaking the same language and sharing the same customs.

CHAPTER FORTY – FOUR

TO GRANADA WITH AUDREY

On one cool day in September when the wind started to blow whitecaps on the sea, Audrey, Luis and I decided to make the trip from Marbella to Granada. Mel was in Italy making a film so he was not with us - the distance is not great, but the road crossing the mountains between Malaga and Granada is filled with curves so the trip takes several hours. Audrey was anxious to see the Arabic palaces in Granada and

Luis enjoyed as I did any excuse to visit the "Alhambra" and the "Generalife" on the mountainside above the city. Many times we had gone to Granada but always for short spells, sometimes in the summer with the children on our way by car from Madrid to Marbella when we would stop overnight at the Parador San Fernando which is within walking distance of the magnificent palace of the Alhambra.

Today on this particular trip, Audrey who was always anxious to learn more about Spain, asked us to tell her something about the history of the city and about the arabic kings who had lived in the Alhambra. As we initiated the winding mountain road leaving the views of the Mediterranean, Luis began.

"As I told you the day we went to Casares, the Arabs controlled most of southern spain for more than seven centuries, since about the year 700. During that time they were constantly in skirmishes with christian spaniards who by the end of the fifteenth century had reconquered one city after another. All these southern cities had been under the jurisdiction of different arabic kings who although they were sometimes related, fought against each other. Often the arabic sultans would be on better terms with christian leaders of nearby cities with whom they preferred to make treaties than with their own relatives. These treaties were made with the arabs to obtain promises not to molest and plunder the christian cities near them. In all southeast Spain the population of the towns and the mountain villages were almost entirely Arabic and governed by the caliph who owned their lands and the nearest city."

Now I questoned Luis. "Please explain, " I said, "why was Granada the last stronghold of the Arabs? I thought Cordoba was the most important center for the Arabs

"Because," he clarified, "Granada was the strongest and the richest area, it included Malaga, Almeria and all the small towns in the southeast which were still under the rule of arabic emirs or sultans or caliphs. They were all related...cousins or uncles."

While he spoke, Luis was navigating the car around one sharp curve after another, and suddenly I remembered something written by Prosper Merimee, the fascinating French author of the middle nineteenth century about his trip through these same mountains one hundred years before. He had chosen to go from Granada to Malaga on horseback to avoid the danger of being attacked by bandits who often robbed the stagecoaches. During that trip he kept a diary. "I have discovered," he noted, "that today in 1846, "horseback is the perfect way to travel. So much better than the perilous speed of those modern stagecoaches that race along so fast that one cannot even enjoy the view."

As we all were swung to one side on the leather seats on the next curve, I recounted Merimee's opinion. Luis who had heard me tell that story before, ignored my remark and continued. "The father of the last sultan of Granada had fallen in love with a christian captive and had a son by her who, it was rumored, he intended to have rule the area after his death. The mother of the legitmate eldest Arabic son zealously guarded his rights which caused fighting to break out among the sultan's followers. Mysteriously the old sultan and his half christian son were assassinated - thus the arabic son became Sultan of Granada. He was shy, thin and small and very much manipulated by his crafty mother who had probably been the one to arrange the assassinations which had made him the undisputed Sultan. "

Luis continued "This new young sultan was called Boabdil by the christians and for some years became the master of the glorious palace of the Alhambra and all the area around Granada; But so much fighting among relatives had weakened the number of Boabdil's followers and his defenses also. At one point Boabdil during these confrontations was captured by some christians and when he escaped, he looked for refuge with the spanish King Fernando in Cordoba where he was treated kindly. There, when Boabdil agreed to a new treaty with the Christians, he was released and went back to his realm in Granada. He had promised the Spanish king in this new treaty to fight against his uncle who was the Caliph of the seaports of Malaga and Almeria. This promise he did accomplish, ousting his uncle Zagal from Malaga in 1488, but he had also promised to give over Granada later on, - this condition he did not fulfill."

Then, finding it difficult to keep quiet so long since I also knew the story, I interrupted. "This was the cause of that last battle between the christians and Boabdil which lasted two years."

By now we were leaving the mountain road and entering the flatter ground near the city. "The spanish troops camped on a hill outside Granada in a small village called Santa Fe" I went on. "this brings in another historical event which occurred in Granada at the same time."

Now I recounted all that I had learned about Columbus from my "tertulia" friends during those meetings in the bar room in Madrid. Evidently he had followed Queen Isabel from one city to another from 1490 to 1492 on her way to join her troops who were struggling to take Granada from the Arabs. Columbus hoped to be able to talk to her to obtain her financial aid in his dream to find a new route to the East. His belief in finding a new route to the Indies interested no one except himself and his concept that the world was round, was generally ridiculed. He had already been refused aid from the Portuguese, the French and Italians. But in Spain Colon had made friends with priests who told him they would intercede with Queen Isabel to get the financiation he needed. It was known that her husband King Ferdinand was not in favor of aiding an expedition to far away lands, but the priests believed they could help get Columbus introduced to the Queen and then he could convince her. They also followed her to Santa

Fe, a small town in the hillsides outside Granada where the troops were camped. Nevertheless the Queen's only interest for months and months was in winning this great final battle against Boabdil and eliminating the last Arab stronghold in Andalucia. Day by day she expected a victory, and Colon's pursuit was of minor importance to her, so she never found time to receive him.

The grandees' troops had been surrounding Granada for two years, providing not only men to fight but also victuals, and weapons. The big landowners were the only source of men for the army which the Spanish monarchs regularly called upon to fight their country's battles. The army in those centuries depended on private people who had troops and employees who tilled their fields - many of these nobles possessed their own navies as well which they offered the Crown when necessary. For months foodstuffs and other necessities for the Arab stonghold in the Alhambra had been intercepted, yet Boadbil despite his people starving did not surrender.

Since the battle for Granada dragged on, eventually two clerics who were the only ones who believed in the logic of Colon's calculations were able to arrange a meeting with the Queen. But just as Colon's meetings were about to take place, Granada capitulated to the Christians and the long conflict was over. Christopher Columbus realizing that his request had been forgotten in the excitement of the great victory, gave up and discouraged left the camp – after following the Queen from town to town for two years, he now had no hope left. He was already two miles away when Queen Isabel recalled him. It was in that historic encounter that he received the aid he needed for his first trip to the New World. Thus Spain became the power responsible for that discovery and the colonizer of another continent which would have the spanish language and customs."

"What a story!" exclaimed Audrey. "I'm so grateful to learn all that. I often am ashamed that I have not had enough formal education. When I should have been learning history and such I was taking dancing classes and putting up with the misery of Holland in wartime. But please tell me what happened to Boabdil."

This time Luis explained "The Spanish Kings treated Boabdil kindly and allowed him and his large royal retinue to leave the great palace with the promise that he would abandon the city and retire to the mountains behind Granada, although eventually he had to go back to Morocco."

Now we had reached the outskirts of the city and in the distance the mountains were visible on the other side. I pointed ahead, "Now you will see his famous palace. Nothing that remains of the Islamic world today can compare to it for beauty and splendor. We will not stop in the city of Granada because although Queen Isabel and her husband Fernando were buried in the cathedral there, we have limited time and the "Alhambra" up on the hill beyond the city is what you should see. Another smaller Arabic palace, "the Generalife", a bit higher up the mountain is worth seeing as well."

As we passed through the city of Granada there was a large sign announcing a bullfight for that same afternoon.

"I certainly don't want to see that," said Audrey, pointing to the sign. "But ever since I read Washington Irving's "Tales of The Alhambra" where he lived for over a year, I've been dying to see it. And now with your stories, I'm ecstatic". It was fun to take Audrey places because she was always enthusiastic and appreciative.

"Washington Irving," I added, was born in an area very near my home town in America– it´s called Tappan and located on the Hudson River.. Irving came to Spain when he was young and made a trip through the country on horseback from 1826 to 1829. Did you know that years later he returned to Spain as United States Ambassador?"

Luis asked for a cigarette and then suggested, "Too bad we won't have time to go to the gypsy caves to have some flamenco. We would have to stay over because no good flamenco begins before one a.M."

Luis and I loved the flamenco of the gypsies who lived in the caves in Granada. Centuries ago their ancestors had dug deep holes for living quarters into the Albaicin mountain, an elevation separated by a deep gorge from the famous Alhambra palace on the mountain just in front. The caves are warm and cozy in the cold winter months and cool during the heat of summer. Inside they are absolutely beautiful and have all sorts of modern advantages, including electricity. Despite being carved into the depths of the mountain these dwellings have beautiful interiors with fireplaces and little chimneys spouting from the earth above them; hanging from the whitewashed walls of their entrances are a multitude of red clay pots filled with bright geraniums. A flamenco session inside one of these caves is a real treat. The arched ceilings provide an echo which is ideal for guitar music and the rythmnic beat of the "palmas", (hand clapping) becomes intoxicating.

Gypsies live in bands or groups and throughout history have been discriminated against, but I have always been charmed by them. Their colorful horse drawn carriages used to appear on the highways all over Spain until the end of the sixties. Then they began to travel in old busses which they painted in bright colors often with fancy ruffled curtains on the windows. But now they travel in modern cars much like anyone else and have lost their picturesque customs. However a few groups of gypsies still camp outside cities like Trujillo when there is a country fair – they live in small tents and huts; the women and even the little girls used to dress in long colorful skirts and often the men in fancy colored silk shirts. But unfortunately the gypsies have lost much of their previous attractiveness.

Sometimes Luis and I had gone to Granada to shoot partridge at the finca of Valerian Wellington. The Duke of Wellington's ancestor had been such a hero in Spain that he was given not only this property outside Granada but also the grandee title of Duke of Ciudad Rodrigo, one of the many spanish cities in Extremadura where he had won a battle against the French. Many of Wellington's most decisive battles were in Extremadura in the area near Pascualete. Too bad he hadn't arrived a bit sooner before the French had sacked Luis' great great grandmother's house in Trujillo . By the time Wellington's troops arrived, Trujillo had aleady been taken by General Soult, the leader of the French troops. They also took back to France some paintings from our ancestors' palace. One of those paintings was a portrait of the Countess of Quintanilla of that time - my title had been Quintanilla when I married for twenty years more. That painting which was confiscated by the French troops in Trujillo in 1808 is now in a museum in Pittsburg Pennsylvania, where I was amazed to discover it during one of my lecture tours. Undoubtedlly one of Soult`s troops had robbed it from the Casa de la Boveda.

When we visited the palace of the Alhambra , Audrey was overwhelmed with the intricately carved arches, the beautiful patios, the fountains, the painted ceilings, the walls paved in colored tiles, the graceful columns, the marble colonnades, the fretwork in stucco forming borders with written quotations from the Coran . The Patio of Lions was her favorite part of the Alhambra with the water spurting from the lions' mouths, the arches, the arabesques and its fairytale atmosphere. We had a very late lunch at the Parador of San Fernando, then walked to the palace of the Generalife further up the mountain.

On leaving we did what every visitor has done for decades - we had our pictures taken in arabic costumes and with a background scene of the Alhambra. Near the exit of the Alhambra are photographer's shops with a profusion of pictorial settings and a large assortment of arab robes. The picture is never a disappointment, this custom has been in vogue there probably for a hundred years. At least I have seen these pictures in houses in France and England that were taken by friends' grandparents at the beginning of the century. In our picture Luis is wearing a magnificent Sultan robe of red and gold with an impressive turban. He is reclining on a silvery oriental chaise lounge while Audrey and I dolled up in shimmering satin tunics and regal Arabic headresses with fancy tassels of glittering coins, are kneeling at his feet while fanning him with large "abanicos".

Audrey had been so delighted with the Alhambra that we almost stayed over, but suddenly we were too tired to face a long night of flamenco and decided to return another time to visit the gypsy caves. "The Alhambra", Audrey declared, "has been the most sensational palace I have ever seen. I'm too emotionally moved to take on flamenco as well."

CHAPTER FORTY- FIVE

EUROPEAN SUMMERS

During the month of August Charlie Beistegui, famous for his luxurious palaces and exceptional taste, usually invited Luis and me to spend the "Grande Semaine" in his famous palace "Labia" in Venice. I had already enjoyed weekend houseparties in Charlie's chateau outside Paris in 1946, but now twenty years later we had the pleasure of spending the glamorous week of the cinema prizes in his palace in Venice. The week was especially delightful not because many film stars were there but mainly because almost every night a huge ball would take place in one of the grand ancient palaces.

The most grand and glorious for me was the Volpi Ball. People usually arrived about ten at night – always in gondolas, the façade of the palace was illuminated by flames of torches revealing the arches and balconies. A long line of gondolas laden with ladies in jewels and glittering evening gowns was always lined up in front of the palace. This sight always reminded me of a Tiepolo painting Luis had inherited from his grandmother - but although the arrivals appeared identical, they had been painted by the artist almost two centuries before.

    I remember the marvelous feeling of arriving at that grand ballroom -the couples swaying in tune to captivating tunes - beautiful women in gorgeous gowns in the arms of elegant men. During the following hours the large band would intoxicate us with their glorious music of Austrian waltzes and every modern popular tunes . I always brought the most glamorous gown I had found in the Spanish collections, usually a magnificent embroidered one of the Pedro Rodriguez - after Pedro died I wore those of Elio Berhanyer . Venice is the most beautiful and glamorous of all ancient European cities and remains an example of the splendor and magnificences of centuries ago.

    Every year on arrival at the Palazzo Labia during this special week Charlie gave us written details of the plans for the following days. If Onassis had his beautiful yatch "The Cristina" in the bay nearby, we would be invited there for lunch. That boat had many special luxuries including an exquisite multi-colored tiled swimming pool, impressive gold fixtures in the bathrooms and startling luxurious bedrooms. To me everything on board looked elegant except Onassis himself. His stocky build in shorts did not add to the décor and his heavy drinking did not improve his conversation. I never understood what the lovely Cristina, his first wife , for whom he had named his yatch , or the very nice Maria Callas,, the famous international opera star, saw in him. But Onassis and Maria Callas were both Greek and therefore shared the same tastes. But Jackie Kennedy was very differeent and although she married him, she never remained with him for any length of time.

Almost every day during that week , Charlie took us in his "motoscafo" motorboat to the beach of the Lido where we would lunch and swim. On this unique beach he had two adjoining beach cabanas with dressing rooms . In front of them under a large awning a table would be set up by Charlie's elegantly groomed menservants. We enjoyed a magnificent luncheon while observing the neighbors or we would go into the sea for a swim. The beach of the Lido had been popular with Italians and European personalities since the beginning of the twentieth century - in fact Venice remained the epitome of elegant summertime social life throughout the seventies especially during the Grand Cinema Week of August.

Another fashionable summer resort in Europe during the middle years of the century was Biarritz - this was more popular with international socialiltes in the month of July. The Hotel du Palais was the rendezvous – its large pool surrounded by small "cabannes" and separated from the mass of people on the beach was where people met to chat and take the sun. For many years the Duke and Duchess of Windsor went there at the same time as many of our Americans friends - Bill and Babe Paley, Diana and Reed Vreeland and other popular friends from European countries. Diana was then the all-important president of Vogue and also extremely witty and popular. The Marquesa de Portago owned a large house in Biarritz –she had been born American - and enjoyed giving dinners and dances for these prominent visitors. Biarritz had the added attraction of the Casino - it was in this nightclub adjoining the Casino that Luis and I often accompanied the Duchess one summer when Jimmy Donahue had joined the Americans at the hotel du Palais. That summer the Duke often went back to the hotel with the excuse of wanting to go to sleep early while Jimmy remained with the Duchess in the nightclub, drinking and giggling until the early hours. She asked Luis and me to remain with them so people would not gossip, but despite the fact that it was generally known that Jimmy was not interested in women, rumours about a romance plagued the Duchess for years after.

Many other details are memorable from those days. Only a few months before Anne Woodward murdered her husband I had seen her rip the chiffon evening gown off the shoulder of the woman with whom her husband Bill was dancing in a big dinner-dance at the house of the Marquesa de Portago.

Deauville was another favorite summer vacation resort, but the majority of prominent people who went regularly there were those interested in race horses. We would spend at least ten days in August in Meautry, Guy and Marie Helene''s stud farm. Horse sales took place every day and at night, in the Deauville Casino often there would be a formal dinner or a large ball.

When there was a let-up in the horse sales Luis would play golf with Guy and Niarccos, the rich Greek owner of tankers, similar to Onassis, while I would be at the pool in Meautry with whatever guests happened to also be present at the time. Queen Elizabeth of England was always fond of horse-races and had come to Meautry to attend the races in Deauville. I was not there then and never met her.

But another summer when we were in Meautry Frank Sinatra appeared with his recent wife, Mia Farrow - she was then a current popular movie star - I think Frank only remained married to her for one year. It didn't look like a romance - she was very silent and her normally beautiful appearance was destroyed by her hair in a sort of "crew-cut" for a movie she had just finished.

Luis usually bought several mares during the horse sales while we were there – although we continued to travel "tourist" he never minded the price of race horses. Even the summer when Sir Y.K. Pao invited me to Japan to christen his new tanker, Luis was not willing to give up the horse sales in Deauville and despite the marvelous invitation with luxurious conditions for an added visit of several weeks to see Japan and China Luis did not forego the horse sales. I went but I regretted making that fabulous trip without him.

CHAPTER FORTY – SIX

MOROCCO

In early 1971 we received an intriguing invitation from King Hassan of Morocco – ten days visit to the most attractive areas of the country, including a wild boar shoot in the Atlas mountains. The visit had been arranged for General Franco but since he did not travel away from Spain, his daughter Carmen would be there in his stead. We were also informed that we would be accompanied by the kings's cabinet members and that every amenity would be at our disposal.

We were met at the airport in Casablanca by the King's brother, Prince Moulay Abdullah and many government officials. The colorful scene gave a festive air to the terminal—the Moroccan men were dressed in their formal glamorous white djellabas with red fezzes, but as customary there were no women in the official reception. Carmen and I and the wife of a Spanish businessman included in the invitation were whisked into a waiting room decorated in true Moroccan style with colorful tiles, carved, hand-painted ceilings and round tables with glittering silver trays holding oriental silver teapots and somovars. While our luggage was being taken care of and the officials with our husbands attended to papers and passports, we women sat on banquettes, eating cookies and drinking mint tea from pink and gilt-etched glasses.

Soon we were on our way to Rabat, the capital of Morocco, escorted by a line of black Mercedes. Sirens resounded from the lead cars, and with flags and lights, they cleared the route - cyclists, donkeys, and vehicles scattered before us as if a giant windstorm were blowing them away. When we reached Rabat, we whisked through traffic and red lights. Too bad for the natives, I thought, astounded at the rapidity with which the clogged highway had been converted into an empty road, but I already had learned that it was a nice feeling to be the guest of a head of state.

That night the Prince and his beautiful Lebanese wife gave a dinner dance in the grand ballroom of the hotel,- the decor outdid any Arabian Nights fantasy, yet tables for eight were set European-style and a band from Paris was playing modern western music. In the room were many international celebrities - Malcolm Forbes who had just bought a palace in Tangiers, Brigitte Bardot, the french movie star with the famous french fashion designer, Yves Saint Laurent, Everywhere I looked, familiar faces were mixed with Moroccans resplendent in glamorous grand kaftans – the women in voluminous evening kaftans sparkling with gold embossed silks of a myriad of tones. In the group was Yul Brynner who I was aware had been doing a film in Moroco – he was talking to Cary Grant who was in the same film.

The Prince when he saw Luis and me entering the room, stopped chatting with other guests and approached – after a warm salutation he gestured to a servant to bring drinks and began introducing us to his nearest countrymen with smooth, carefree charm. The Moroccan women were outstanding, most had been educated in France which evidently was their favorite foreign country , probably due to the fact that all Moroccans spoke French. But finally one lady, when she realized I was American, spoke to me in English – telling me that she had graduated from Harvard which had just begun to accept women -I was astounded. Morocco was certainly changing. But I remembered that my longtime friends, the Mizian sisters who also possessed university degrees, had told me that there were still many legal difficulties in the country for women – that their husbands had mistresses and could divorce them and take the children if they dared to complain..

Later while dancing with my husband, he told me that none of the foreigners in the dinner would be included in our trip starting the next morning, that the group would be composed only of those of us who had come from Spain and a large number of the King's ministers.

The next morning at the main door of the hotel a great bustle of activity greeted me - many cars and groups of people plus military officers filled the entrance - hotel employees were running back and forth with suitcases. As I stood there, Prince Moulay appproached. "Bon jour, belle Comtesse , we have a fine day for the beginning of our trip. Everybody is busy as you can see. I must introduce you to the military aide who will be with you at all times and can take care of any wishes you may have."

As we decended the steps, the Prince waved towards a young officer waiting below near a long line of cars. Immediately the pleasant faced young fellow jumped to attention and rushed toward us, bowing ceremoniously as the Prince announced " This is Captain Omar Khalil- he will be your officer. He is also well informed on the history of the cities we will visit.."

The Prince then excused himself and left to attend others while the Captain led me to the car which had been assigned us. Omar's manner was charming, he had large black laughing eyes, a jaunty air, and exuded the scent of eau de cologne. He was obviously delighted to be part of the excursion, bobbing up and down in a series of stiff bows as he explained the route we were to follow that day. I was surprised to note his perfect Spanish and said so.

"My mother is Spanish, Senora Condesa - I was born in Granada." So we had a half Moroccan and half Spaniard as our private guard

By this time Luis had arrived and Omar announced that the caravan was finally about to leave. "The Count and Countess's automobile is number eleven in the convoy," he announced as he settled in his place in the front seat next to the driver. "There are twenty-one vehicles in the expedition." His voice took on the rhythm of a tourist guide. "The large trucks transport the carpets, tents, and special foods for the trip. There's also an ambulatory hospital with a doctor and a dentist. This trip will be pass throughe the most beautiful towns in the country and we will spend nights in some of the loveliest palaces." Our interpreter was becoming very loquacious – but I liked learning more about the history of this country. Nevertheless I wanted to be able to talk to Luis off and on without being understood. "Do you speak English, Captain?" I asked.

"No, I only speak Arabic, French, and Spanish, Señora Condesa," he answered quite humbly.

This was going to be an advantage if I could keep him quiet long enough for Luis and me to compare notes. Luis pointed to a crowded bus ahead. Our interpreter saw his gesture - "Those are the cooks and extra men servants for the trip."

I was surprised to see that there were no women in the group. And then I realized that I hadn't seen any Moroccan women anyplace during the last half hour. Our car had still not moved, so I looked around, trying to spot one of the minister's wives who had been in the dinner last night, but not one was to be seen...

Carmen Franco, the Spanish Ambassador's wife, and the wife of Barreiros, the Spanish businessman were the only women in the group. When I asked Captain Omar Khalil where the Moroccan wives were, his eyebrows lifted in surprise.

"Oh, there will be no Moroccan women on this trip, Señora Condesa." The answer startled me. I might have asked him "why", but he jumped out at that moment to attend to some last minute problem, I continued to wonder why Moroccan women wouldn't want to go on a excursion which promised to be delightful.

New impediments seemed to have occurred - Carmen Franco descended from her car, which was just in front of ours, and walked over.

"I wonder what the problem is," Carmen said. "My driver thinks two of the ministers forgot their guns".

"I don't think we're going to be shooting the first days," I responded. "I was told we'd be sightseeing. Maybe that's why none of the Moroccan wives are going along. They've probably seen these places over and over again."

Carmen chuckled. "I don't think that's the reason." She was about to say something more when General Mohammad Oufkir joined us. I had heard so many fascinating stories about him the night before that he was the one person I most wanted to know better.

"Good morning, Señoras. We have a beautiful day for beginning our tour." He smiled. "His Majesty has asked me to see that you are well attended to." He bowed, just slightly. "Anything you need will be my command."

General Oufkir, I had learned, was Morocco's national military hero. "He has so many decorations that they cover the entire front of his uniform - twelve gold-and-silver-palm emblems. It would take much time to recount only a few of his famous exploits" , I had been told.

At that moment cars started to move. Carmen rushed to get into hers and Omar opened our car door again and jumped in. "The tour now begins," he announced formally.

The roads inside the city had been blocked off, and the twenty-one vehicles proceeded to the main highway in file. The breeze cooled the sun-heated air inside the car, and through the open window wafted the scent of green grass and wild flowers. It was a perfect day to begin an adventure into the unknown.

"Today we are on our way to Khenifra, a small city in the mountains, where we'll stay in a *parador*, which as you realize the same as in Spain is a government-run hotel for tourists. Tomorrow we'll be at the Governor's palace near Midelt, a small city which is the door to the southeastern part of our country. And since there is no town nearby where we could lunch today, we'll be eating in the open country."wild

As he spoke we were passing great fields where pairs of tall gawky camels hitched to small donkeys were pulling ancient Roman-type plows, each pair guided by a farmer in bloomers with cloth wound into a turban on his head. I'd seen these same plows in Pascualete years before, but our plows had been pulled by oxen and our men wore long pants and a straw-brimmed hat - the view here was more exotic although the country was not much different from southern Spain. Undoubtedly these sights had been the same centuries ago.

When we arrived at our destination we were in the middle of open country. As we piled out of the car, I was astounded to see a huge oriental tent, all red, silver and gold about the size of an American circus tent. A long fringe of multicolored, embroidered material surrounding the roof glistened in the midday sun and gave it a romantic aspect. Flaps were tied back on several sides so people could enter. I stood admiring it - spellbound. Outside but nearby, around an open wood fire, men in dark djellabas and turbans bent over steaming copper pots bubbling in a thick yellow sauce that exuded wafts of saffron and spicy herbs. Over other large open fires, the carcasses of whole lambs and goats were being turned on spits—the dripping juice spattered and hissed as it bounced off the flaming embers. Evidently the cooks had left in advance of the caravan to have our meal ready on time. Omar led me through the open flaps into the Arabian Nights tent. From the delicately woven red-and-blue canvas ceiling, literally hundreds of small, round, coin-shaped pieces of colorful metallic decorations dangled above our heads, tinkling in the breeze passing through the open flaps. The dirt floor had just been covered with the luxurious orange-and-red carpets that had been transported in the vans. Throughout the enormous area were many low, round tables set in a blinding array of sparkling silver on snowy-white embroidered damask cloths. Already some guests were seated, their legs crisscrossed on rich satin pillows. I remained transfixed, enjoying the thought that this scene was probably not unlike the banquets of centuries past, when sultans, sheiks, and kings from remote countries met to enjoy a royal feast in conry areas.

General Oufkir appeared encouraging me and other guests to take places at the different tables. Soon I was reclining on my cushion imitating the posture of the Moroccans - also seated around the table were members of the King's cabinet. Servants appeared with white linen towels on their arms, carrying silver trays with huge glistening pitchers. Although I knew I was supposed to wash my hands, I didn't know that this was done with lots of soapy lather, and that after washing, the menservants would rinse my hands again with water scented with orange blossoms. As soon as this ritual was completed, two more waiters appeared, carrying between them a huge round glistening silver serving dish, which they placed in the center of our table. As they lifted the pyramid-shaped cover, it released a delicious aroma of thyme and rosemary.

"Baby kid," announced someone at my table. My Moroccan neighbor, who seened did not speak English or French, reached into the huge serving dish and pulled off a choice piece, which he handed to me in his fingers with a smile. There were no knives or forks, and soon I, too, was diving into the huge silver dish, pulling out my own pieces, copying the men, who were taking bread and dipping it into the sauce. Just as I was about to dive for the third time, my neighbor restrained me. "But it's so good," I said. "I really would like more."

"No, no," he said. Then, in halting French, he added: "Wait. Many more dishes to come."

I looked on in amazement as that huge serving dish was removed and replaced by another containing several dozen small quail in a bed of rice and olives.

During the fifth course, General Oufkir came to sit at our table. "There are few tents in Morocco as large as this one, Comtesse," he explained. "But what may surprise you still more is to learn that this one probably took several hundred men and women many years to make. Every thread comes from the wool of our sheep, the designs are taken from the Koran. Even the dyes were made by hand and will not run, no matter how much rain falls. The cloth is remarkably thick and protects us from the violent sandstorms that occur in the desert. I might sound immodest, but you'll never find tents as beautiful and as strong as these in any other country."

Fortunately my neighbor moved aside to allow General Oukir to take his place next to me – soon I was under the charm of this famous general, obviously a hero for all those around the table. Yet he was unpretentious and extremely sensitive to my questions about how to tackle the enormous platters of food – he charmingly indicated exactly how I

443

should pick up the food with my left hand and answered all my questions with an enchanting patience . I asked him about the decorative coins dangling from the roof of the tent.

Prince Moulay Abdullah who was just passing by, said, "General Oufkir, tell the countess how much time you've spent in a tent." The prince's tone was light and his expression pleasant, but his eyes were sharp. A bit surpised, I watched Oufkir closely for his reaction.

"In the army we spend whole summers in tents when on exercises, but army tents do not have much similarity with this one, of course," Oufkir replied in his warmest tone.

Then he turned to me. "Prince Moulay Abdullah wants to make clear that this tent is very different from those we of the army have known. The King is providing this group with the most luxurious ones we have."

When the sixth course arrived in larger silver serving dishes loaded with pigeons in rosemary sauce, General Oufkir excused himself, saying he would be taking the next course at another table. I was sorry, so far he was the only minister in the group who was willing to answer my questions and give me more details about customs. One after another, the huge, round, silver serving dishes were removed and another appreared—an entire roast lamb, then cous-cous with barley, and after that a towering almond cake filled with chopped dates and honey. But the luncheon was far from over. Now the festivities were about to begin.

Someone handed a guitar to a fellow at our table whom they called Rachid. Very slowly, he stood up, looking for a more central spot from which to play. He looked around and then went to sit at Carmen's table which was next to ours - then he too squatted down cross-legged with the guitar in hand . He began to tune-in the instrument, but did not play until the applause became insistent. Finally, lifting the guitar in the air in sign of acquiescence, he began to pluck strange plaintive chords. After a few moments he lifted his head, closed his eyes, and began to sing. I wondered if this was a song of the desert people with whom Oufkir had told me a few moments before this Rachid had lived for a long time. As the man's warm deep voice wailed the eerie music, the silence in the tent became such that one could almost hear the breathing of the many listeners. Like statues, the waiters in their blue djellabas and red fez caps stood motionless, as Rachid sang one song after another.

When he stopped Luis got up from his table indicating that he would come to mine. As he walked over, the sound of metallic music and the ring of castanets caused everyone to look toward the entrance. At least fifty women, sparkling in long lamé djellabas and turbans, their faces covered by the sheerest of veils, moving and gyrating to the music of dozens of flutes and the loud boom of drums, danced into the center of the tent. The expressions of the Moroccan men told me in one brief second why they had left their wives at home. Later while we were being served mint tea, the dancing continued in frenzied movement around the center table, where Prince Moulay Abdullah was seated with Carmen Franco. Our luncheon must have lasted at least four hours.

We arrived in Khenifra later than expected, where we spent the night in the ancient palace recently refurbished by the government. Always servants transported carpets from the vans to the hallways and rooms as we entered. Luis and I were delighted to see that our rooms here were as comfortable as those in the hotel in Rabat. General Oufkir sat with us at dinner and told us that the parador had originally been a lovely old palace belonging to the sheik of this area – that Morocco was restoring ancient buildings and converting them into hotels for tourists. Then he went on to remind us that even in Spain a century ago the custom of traveling with carpets for the floors and tapestries to cover the walls had existed – "another example of the many Arabic customs that remained in your country and connect us with you," he added. As General Oufkir explained this, I remembered having heard Luis say that his grandparents had traveled with tapestries and carpets when they visited their country stone palaces . Even Maria in Pascualete had told me that she had heard that when the owners had arrived years ago, they always brought tapestries to cover the walls and carpets for the cold floors.

The next day we traversed the Atlas Mountains, where the cool dry air made my nose tingle. The colors were eye-wateringly bright, the green seemingly greener because of the contrast with the dry bare surrounding land. We arrived at Midelt at one o'clock and drove to the palace of the Governor, where we would be spending the night. After centuries of wind and rain, the color of its thick stone walls was almost pure gold-yellow against the cloudless blue sky. Oufkir had told me that the Governor would be delightful since he was a specially cultured person.

Luis and I were shown to separate rooms, which, much to his displeasure, were on opposite sides of the palace. But I was delighted when I discovered we women guests would be inhabiting the Governor's harem. Although polygamy was no longer practiced formally in Morocco, Oufkir had told me that the Govenor was one of the upper class Moroccans who had maintained the harem as it had been for centuries.

The harem was a cluster of rooms surrounding a large bath called the *hammon*, which resembled a smallish round swimming pool; many of these rooms opened onto a spacious walled-in tropical garden. Originally the bath had been the harem's most important feature, the place where the Governor's young wives were bathed, and where the adjoining rooms were used for rubbing their skins with powders, polishing them with henna, and perfuming them before going to the Governor's quarters. The pool-like *hammon* was lined with tiny, iridescent turquoise dark blue tiles which gave the impression of an undersea grotto.

As I was enjoying this view, suddenly my Moroccan friend Tamy Tazi appeared in the arched doorway. As we embraced she explained that the governor was her uncle and owner of the palace and had asked her to help him entertain the Spanish women guests and when she realized that I was among them, she came immediately. This was a treat for me – Tami would tell me all the inside stories of this harem – she knew Moroccan customs fascinated me and years ago had already told me many things. She had told me the size of the harem depended on the wealth of the owner, that some harems had housed over one hundred women while others might have had only twenty. She also told me that the harem was always ruled over by an older woman who maintained peace and order like a sergeant and enforced the many strict customs.

As we sat down together on the border of the hammon she told me that harem women were not allowed to leave the enclosure of their part of the palace except on special occasions, and then only in groups, chaperoned by the matron, that they were obliged to be covered in white veils with voluminous white togas, called *haiks*, which concealed their shape and age. She also explained that in Morocco Eunuchs were never employed to maintain order in the harems as in other Arab countries. She added that their religion obliged the women to wash meticulously before each of their five daily prayers, also before eating, and before and after every sexual encounter. Laughingly she told me that tonight we women would be allowed to leave the harem for dinner in the large central patio of the palace but would be returned to it when the show ended . Abruptly her face took on a serious expression as she told me that she hated harems because they were an example of the humilities Moroccan women had suffered for centuries – she went on to complain that the current king always invited her husband without her to the palace to take part in parties with elegant prostitutes – she said "wives are never invited to the king's fiestas -We women in Morocco still suffer some of the ancient customs"

After a few moments a maid appeared asking Tami and me to follow her. We went to the Governor's apartments where Luis was comfortably reclining on red cushions, talking to the Governor. Naturally, both stood as we entered. I was amused, remembering Luis's only complaint about sitting on the floor in Morocco was that getting up when ladies came in was a lot more effort. As the Governor kissed my hand, he asked me how I had enjoyed the surprise he had prepared for me, indicating Tamy. After much hugging and kissing we all sat down on the thick carpets and soft pillows.

"You were evidently unaware that your friend Tami is my brother's daughter. She is not only beautiful, but clever and gifted - I remember her as a little girl, pelting the maid with oranges in the garden."

Tami hushed him and then turned to me. She giggled , "I knew you would be amused by your living quarters- I told my uncle that you often asked me about our harems." Although I thought Tami had probably exaggerated her stories about harems to amuse me I told her that I still wanted to know many things – did the women wear special clothes – did they all use that exaggerated makeup – did they play cards or any games for amusement ?

"I knew you would still want to know more", she said, " and there is much to tell you." She pointed the direction I had just come from. "Only fifteen years ago there were over fifty women still housed here, but before that over one hundred."

Luis was astounded that any one man could have so many women, and said so. The Governor chuckled. "The very rich had more than Tami knows."

"But how did they keep those women from killing each other from jealousy?", I asked.

This time Tami jutted in "Oh, they killed each other now and then. We women are the same all over the world, human nature being what it is, of course, it happened- although our grandfathers deny it. The most popular method was poison."

She went on grinning at Luis, "In case your husband gets too frisky, Aline, there'a a flower called *bsibisa* which grows in this part of the country. That was especially popular. Also, a green flower called the *gouza*, which is still easy to find. It's similar to a calla lily, with a long center stem. All you have to do is to put a bit of water in the center and let it become concentrated. It's deadly and tasteless. A few drops into some drink or food, and your victim is dead within minutes. Then there's *kif*, our hashish plant...any of these flowers can also be dried and pounded into a powder, and there you are."

At this point the Govenor interrupted. "Nowadays, the way women are becoming liberated, I suppose soon they'll start using these poisonous herbs on their husbands."

"Don´t try to pretend they didn´t do that years ago and if our husbands tried to install harems in our houses today , perhaps we would," quipped Tamy. "Today none of us would put up with that."

"But the country people still do," piped up Luis. "Our military Captain Omar told me a man can still have four wives."

"But you can't call four wives a harem Count" remonstrated the Govenor with a chuckle.

When we returned to the harem as the doors closed behind us, Carmen Franco was changing her outfit in the communal dressing-room, the Spanish Ambassador's wife was having her nails manicured, Doli Barreiros, the other Spanish guest wrapped in a white towel, had just emerged from the sauna. Two hairdressers stood at the door, waiting to assist us. A long table faced a mirror which stretched across one wall, provided plenty of room to arrange our hairdos and put on makeup. Tami was embracing Carmen who she had also known for many years. As I glanced around the room, the scene reminded me of the models' dressing room at Hattie Carnegie years ago.

About eight o'clock the maid appeared to take us to the lovely patio where all the men were chatting together. The Spaniards were drinking champagne but I wondered what the Moroccans were sipping since they were not supposed to take alcholic beverages. After the usual meal sitting on cushions around a round table, General Oufkir came to sit beside me. I was about to ask him about the shoot when a group of women dancers swept into the patio in swirls of gold lamé, wearing jangling bracelets and beating a contagious rhythm on their castanets. Tables disappeared and guests moved back to make room: suddenly we were squeezed in with others and I dared not detract from his attentive glances at the dancers. Most of the artists directed their greater efforts toward General Oufkir and the Prince who sat cross-legged on the other side of the patio. Oufkir was delighted, smiling his enigmatic smile. Tami saw me observing the men.

"Aline", she said in an undertone, "don't be fooled by the General. He has a way with women, but if they knew what a bloodthirsty fellow he was, they might not be so infatuated."

The evening's activities became more and more spectacular. After the first dancers retired, ten more in bright red-and-orange silk danced into the patio. Their specialty was the *danse du ventre*, their voluptuous movements and sultry glances bringing sounds of pleasure from the men. Again, I was reminded of why the Moroccan men had not brought their wives.

When the glittering women swirled out of the patio, the Governor stood up.and with a gesture towards one of the men, the guitarists began to play soft, plaintive, centuries-old music, and a specialy beautiful woman with long darkhair over her shoulders entered the patio – she did so swaying slowly to the languorous rhythm. At first her movements were hardly discernible, yet I could hear the tinkle of the little gold bells hanging from her belt tassel. But as the music became louder and the tempo increased, the dance began to blossom like a flower. Her hips gyrated, at first slowly, then more quickly, but always in time to the music. She threw back her head and hair, slowly raising her arms in a suggestive caress of her breasts and shoulders, then waving them above her head like twin cobras to the beat of the music. Her entire body moved with sensual fluidity and control; her torso moved independently of the rest of her body, keeping up its rhythmic motion as her arms swayed in graceful, slow arcs. There was none of the wild exhibition of the girls we had just seen. This girl's entire body was twisting, her breasts arching high and her pelvis moving seductively, each gesture transmitting a thrill. On her face was an expression of languorous abandon; her almond-shaped eyes were half-closed but held a sultry fire, and her full lips outed, slightly open. Her intoxicating dance held everone entranced, but the governor and Oufkir who were watching carefully were both smiling with a fasciation that startled me. Never could I have imagined that a dance could transmit such sensuality - although actually the girl had done nothing wrong. She had not stripped off her clothes nor touched any man in the room.

Now she sank to her knees, then arched her back with her long dark hair almost touching the floor. She gathered that massive mane of black hair in her hands and let it tumble over her face as she slid onto her back with a final soft chord from the guitars. For a moment, she lay motionless on the floor. There was not a sound, no one wished to break the spell created by the sensual dance. Finally, she rose to her feet to wild applause -calmly she twisted her hair back into a chignon and disappeared.

When we women retired to our banquette beds in the harem - which were benches against the walls covered with thick mattress cushions – all in the same large room, our husbands were still enjoying the dancing. The next morning I wanted to go to breakfast with Luis, but our gate was locked and I was told by the Moroccan maid that the husbands could not come into the harem. Tami was still asleep, Carmen also , so I dressed and insisted that the maid look for my husband and inform him that I would meet him in the patio. He was already there waiting when I finally convinced her to unlock the gate and was able to go into the sunlit center of the house, where we had dined the night before. Two maids, their ankle-length cotton djellabas covered by long white aprons with crocheted borders, were rolling a round table into a shady corner. The table was filled with enticing foods—at least six different-colored juices in tall, graceful glass goblets, various silver platters containing almond bread, small honey-and-almond cakes, little kernals of something sweet and hard, and a wicker basket of exotic fruit. Luis was curious to learn how we managed in the harem and chatted enthusiastically while we devoured the feast. I wanted to know what happened the night before in his part of the palace, after we women had been shepherded into the harem.

"It was quite amusing but somewhat uncomfortable." Luis grinned. "As soon as you girls had disappeared into your quarters, our host took us to another patio at the other side of the palace and brought the belly dancers back. This time they had practically nothing on, and their dancing was quite erotic and crude. When they had finished, the Governer invited us to take our pick. 'They're untouched.' he said. Luis broke out into a hearty laugh. "I was dying to tell him that I certainly believed him. Who would touch any of them? Seein them in better light up close, some smelled bad, others had no teeth, and many were fat. Not even those long, shimmering gowns could hide all their sins." Luis contined to chuckle. "Cristobal and I had a terrible time refusing without hurting our host's feelings. Of course, the Governor thought he was offering us a great treat - that's why you girls were all placed at the other sie of the house. The govenor assured us repeatedly that you were locked in."

Soon our caravan was ready and we bid goodbye to the Governor and to Tami and ran to our respective cars while they remained on the steps of the palace, waving at our departing caravan. Thus the trip from Midelt to Tinerhir began. It had been decided that we would make a detour to explore the Todra Gorges - something similar to the Grand Canyon, but very narrow roads and deep. Normally it would be impossible to traverse in the cold months , but this winter had been mild - the rivers were low, the roads passable, and of course our cars and drivers were of the highest quality.

In a few hours the long line of sleek black Mercedes was winding its way along the bottom of the Dades Gorges—a gigantic fault in the plateau which separates the High Atlas Mountains from the Jbel Sarhro range. The dirt road followed the river along the bottom of the crack between gigantic slabs of rockface, and as we proceeded, the cliffs on either side became higher until the sky was reduced to a narrow slit.

At the town of Msemrir, we stopped for lunch. The vans had been sent directly there early that morning so that the tent would be already up when we arrived.

General Oufkir had invited us to join him in his car and as we continued he explained the scenery around us. "Some of our most romantic villages are in this area, and dozens of beautiful kasbahs—they're the ancient walled-in sections of the town." We were passing through a vast dessert plateau, where a fortifed city appeared perched high on a hill, dramatic and beautfiul—its crenellated walls outlined against the blue sky.

General Oufkir noticed our fascination. "That's a town noted for its famous kasbahs." He told us that many people inhabited these castlelike buildings. The golden city with adobe walls blended in with the surrounding barren dirt terrain of the same color. A short time later the landscape changed again and we found ourselves entering an avenue of palms.

The General looked at his watch. "We're arriving at our destination, Tinerhir. This tour through the Gorges did not make us lose much time after all."

In Tinerhir the caravan followed an avenue of palms which led to the government hotel. From the outside the building looked modern, but inside, the decor resembled ancient Moroccan homes, with latticework on the windows, colorful tiles, many arches, and intricate plaster-of-Paris carvings on the walls. It was near sunset, the sun smoldered in its last red-and-orange rays. Behind us was the sound of servants carrying luggage up a stairway, and from below, out of the palm trees, came the loud chattering of birds. Such a wondrous beautiful country.

The next morning the hotel was in a whirl of preparation. An hour or so from now we were scheduled to leave Tinerhir and head into the wild countryside, climbing the Atlas Mountains once again, this time to the City of Roses. A rumor was circulating that the King might join us there, and the possiblity had sent tremors of excitement throughout the Moroccans and the guests. Servants were running around at a dizzying speed loading cars and trucks. An extra van had pulled up in front of the *parador* and was being packed with a new assortment of colorful carpets, just delivered by local merchants. Carmen joined me this day in our car while Luis went to their car to ride with Cristobal. By now we were high in the Atlas Mountains, and two hours later we entered the City of Rosás.

Omar could hardly contain his excitement."here we are," he said dramatically. "'We are enteering the city of the most beautiful women in Morocco. And it is here I will take another wife."

Astonished I asked,"How many wives do you have now?"

454

"Semnora Condesa," he answered, " I have only two , but eventually I hope to have four. That is what the law permits."

"Don't tell me that a young man like you can support four wives?" I said. Behind Captain Omar Khalil's back ,Carmen and I exchanged glances. She was shaking her head in amusement.

"The Senora Coindesa doesn't understand our customs," he said with wounded dignity, as politely as he could. "Four wives are necessary for a working man. You see, they help each other. One does the cooking, one takes care of the children..."

I still think that many wives would be expensive." I was pulling his leg now, because I realized that these extra wives were like servants he did not have to pay.

" I never take on another wife until I can afford her."

"But don't they get jealous of each other?"

"Why? They know I'm not marryng each one to take her out in to society. The next one will be useful to take care of the children."

Carmen entered the conversation."Perhaps you are unaware, Aline, that the laws here favor the men only. If they tire of a wife, all they have to do is to announce out loud, "I divorce you" three times, and then clap their hands three times and the marriage is dissolved."

"Ah, but the law forces the man to return the woman to her family with her dowry," Omar interrupted. "She cannot be left on the streets."

"But how can you marry a woman you don't know?"

'That has nothing to do with marriage, senora Condesa. I have a right to four wives and if she is pretty I don't ask for more."

As we were speaking, the caravan was rolling slowly up an incline to a village perched on top of a hill. We came around a turn in the road and saw hundreds women lined up on either side of our narrow highway, all dressed in a completely different manner from those we had seen in other provinces. Many held baskets of flowers, and tossed rose petals of various colors in our path;. Others, the younger ones, hid their faces behind their hands and, at first, peeped at us through their open fingers. They wore multicolored skirts, white blouses, fancy aprons, sleeveless boleros – much like our regional costumes in Spain. Many of the young girls had yellow roses in their jet-black hair or had entwined them into their braids. Captain Omar explained that the women in this city were unaccustomed to having strangers see their faces, that for them to show their visage was like being naked, and usually their faces were covered. But today, in view of the visit of His Royal Highness Prince Moulay Abdoullah and such distinguished foreign visitors, they had been asked to remove the veils.

In any event since they saw few visitors curiosity soon overcame their shyness and they stared openly at us. And it was true – the girls were beautiful: they had very white skin and light blue eyes, and their faces were tattooed, but in a very flattering manner. At the far corner of the eyes were tiny green or blue dots which augmented the size of the eyes and enhanced their color: little round orange-and red-dots accentuated the cheekbones. Omar was enraptured and turned his head from one side of the road to the other - I imagined trying to pick out the girl he would marry. The cars in front of us had slowed down so their passengers also could get a better look at the famous beauties of the City of Roses.

All the way into the town. Omar continued to feast his eyes, like a hungry man in a bakery. "I've seen many beautiful girls," he exclaimed, " and I've already made my choice."

I still did not believe he could simply arrive in an unknown town and expect within the period of one day to have a new wife.

"How are you going to get married here when we're only in this city for one night?" I asked him.

"That's where I need your help, countess."

"What can I possibly do?"

"Ask the prince's permission for me to have another wife. He is the one who can marry me."

When we descended from the car, a violent windstorm swept through the village, fillilng the air with the rose petals from the road. Next to a rambling old bulding of limestone and adobe where Omar informed us we would spend the night, was another huge tent. We ran inside to escape the cold wind. Once everyone had entered, the flaps were dropped and the unique tinkling music of the thousands of tin coins hanging from the ceiling ceased. Course after course of delicacies was served, and it wasn't until almost two hours s later that we finally finished with pastry and mint tea.

Nearby my table General Oufkir and the Prince were in a heated conversation. I asked my neighbor, one of the aides of a minister, what was the problem.

"Something to do with changing plans about staying here for the night. Evidently the General wants to move on, and in a hurry. I don't know why..And the prince thought it would be more comfortable for everyone to stay here."

"I hope we stay. This town must be lovely. And my guide wants to pick a bride here, his third." I remembered Omar Khalil's determined excitement.

"If the general wants to go, You can be sure the order will be to move on. He wields much power in these matters. He has more influence with the King than his brother, the Prince. Did you know that the General never went to school or learned to read or write until he entered the military service. He had many brothers and was not the eldest , but he was recognized as the most intelligent. He's not only the bravest military officer, but he is highly cultured and has an incredible voice."

"A fascinating man, there's no doubt about that, "I said. "And I've found him to be the nicest of the group. Many of your country men, although they are polite, are bored when I ask a question about their country's history, but when I ask General Oufkir, he always takes time to explain."

As we were speaking word arrived at our table that a change in plans had occurred. We were not going to spend the night in the City of Roses but would continue on almost immediately to our next destination. My neighbor gave me a "I-told-you-so' glance. Everybody was disappointed.

Luis approached from the opposite side of the tent and suggested we try to see something of the town before we left, but voices called to us and as we turned around we saw that the cars were preparing to leave.

Before I had taken another step, Omar Khalil came running toward me.

"Countess" He cried. "Please help me. I've found my next wife. I must marry her. Only you can arrange that."

I threw my hands in the air. "Me? Of all people. I can't imagine how. I haven't had a chance to speak to the Prince about your marriage , and now we are leaving almost immediately". I looked at him. "Omar, it is no longer possible."

"Oh, yes. It can still be done." He looked at me imploringly. I remembered all the amusing little favors he had done to make our trip more enjoyable. If possible I had to help him.

458

"If the Senora Condesa will ask the Prince, I'm sure he'll say yes," he insisted. "This is probably the only time in my life I will be able to come to this city."

"But what about the wedding ceremony?" I continued. "There's just no time."

'The ceremony only takes one minute, Senora Condesa.' His voice was pleading. "My bride and her parents are waiting."

I looked for General Oufkir to ask his opinion before bothering the Prince, but no one knew where he was. I gave up, and with Omar at my side, we looked for the Prince, who we found giving orders to the drivers of the many cars for the trip to the next city. Around us, everybody was running helter-skelter from one place to the other: there seemed to be a great haste to leave. People rushed to the bathrooms inside the building: servants piled carpets back into the trucks and luggage into the automobiles. As I squeezed into the group near the Prince, Omar remained close by. Such a hubbub was going on, and the wind still blowing, that I had to raise my voice to make myself heard..

"Your Highness, please forgive me for asking such a silly thing," I began uncomfortabley, I was convinced that Omar had lost his mind. "but Captain Omar Khalil has the crazy idea that he can marry a girl from this city if Your Highness gives his permission. I know that's impossible, but he won't leave me in peace."

"No , that request is not impossible, Aline." Prince Moulay smiled. "Would you like me to arrange it?"

"Yes Sir. He's been such an excellent guide and interpreter.."

My reasons for assuring the Prince I would like Omar's marriage to take place sounded ridiculously inadequate to me for something so monumental, but with the confusion of the moment and time pressing, nothing better occurred to me.

The Prince moved out of the group. "No trouble at all, no trouble," he said. "Where's that Omar Khalil?"

" Here, Your Royal Highness" said Omar, popping up in front of him.

"And where is your proposed bride Omar?" asked the Prince.

"She's right here, Your royal highness." From behind Omar as if by magic, stepped a lovely little girl who could not have been more than fourteen or fifteen. Accompanying her were a man and a woman, obviouysly her parents. The beautiful child had very white skin, her black hair was entwined around her head and adorned with small yellow roses. Her cheeks were very pink and when I looked closer, I saw that she, like the other women in her villge, already had little pink tattoo marks over her cheekbones and that her pale blue eyes were enhanced with tiny spots of blue strategically placed at the corners and more just above the eyebrows. The effect was ravishing. The little girl looked up at us for a moment and then embarrassed by our glances, covered her face with her hands.

The Prince moved closer and placed the hand of the father on the hand of the girl, then the mothers's hand on theirs, and then Omar's hand on top. He mumbled a few words and then turned to me. "well, Aline your request has been granted. Omar and this young girl and are now man and wife."

I was astonished. So this was considered a legal wedding in Morocco! Omar had been right. The parents of the girl appeared delighted – they were smiling when it seemed to me they should have been weeping to lose such a sweet young daughter. The girl stared shyly at the ground acquiesing gracefully to the wishes of her elders, not even stealing a glance at her new husband. My heart went out to her. She was so young and pretty, and now she was a third wife of a complete stranger. But since this custom did not seem to upset them, I tried to look as if I too was pleased with the marriage, I said a few words of congratulation, but the girl's parents did not understand French, so I resorted to shaking their hands and then I was obliged to rush to my car. Omar ran to the car also, without even kissing his brand-new wife. As we got under way he took his usual seat next to the driver. Almost immediately, the caravan started to move.

"Captain Omar Khalil" I said."how is your new bride going to to get to Rabat where you live?"

He turned around and looked at me in surprise. " Oh, that's no problem. She's in the truck with the carpets, senora Condesa."

Just by chance at that moment our car was passing one of he vans. Omar pointed. "See. There she is." In the back of the truck, standing, hanging on to the tailgate, was the little girl, looking wistfully at her village as it disappeared in the distance. Her forlorn expression did not discourage Omar. He was delighted. "She'll be just perfect in my house." He said. "And since I'm still young, I can wait a bit before takng a fourth wife."

"She looks too young to be married," I said , thinking out loud.

"Oh, that makes no difference, Countess . She's not the one I will take to social events."

So this marriage Moroccan-style was the most unusual wedding I ever attended.

The next day we traveled to the area for the shoot. The terrain looked like Extremadura in springtime. In the foothills, the meadows wore an oriental carpet of color—scarlet poppies next to fields of deep purple wild flowers, and there was the smell of lavender and rosemary. The caravan of jeeps climbed through entire slopes covered with the white flowers of the *"jara"* (rockrose) and stopped halfway up the mountain near a smallish tent. Everyone piled out - I looked up the steep incline, where a thick underbrush of retama bushes, like a green prickly blanket, provided cover for the game we would shoot. Silhouetted against the blue sky, a few stray cork trees jutted up above the greenery. Inside the tent, hot mint tea and cookies were being served while we awaited the King's arrival. On the mountain it was colder, and windy too, but the tent was cozy, and as time stretched on, servants brought trays of delicious cheeses and bread.

A bustle of running feet and the sound of automobiles told us that the King was arriving. We jumped up and rushed out. Not until the King jumped from one car was it apparent in which car he had been traveling—there were at least six cars, and all were identical. Prince Moulay Abdullah stepped forward, and the two brothers embraced - the King patting the Prince affectionately on the back. Although we were at a slight distance, and they both spoke in Arabic, the King's gestures and smiles made it clear he was kidding his brother about his fancy outfit. King Hassan was wearing regular army boots, regular-issue army camouflage fatigues, a simple canvas army cap, sunglasses, and, hanging from his shoulder, were his field glasses. Nothing regal or ornate about his attire. The King had a nice caramel skin, extremely white teeth, a strong face, large black eyes, full lips and a wonderful smile. He was not excessively tall, but had the powerful build of a bulldog, obviously a man of great physical strength. Prince Moulay Abdullah was more handsome, but the King was stronger and more impressive.

One by one we were introduced. Carmen had met King Hassan during his visits to Spain, but I had never seen him before and was anxious to talk to this man who was reputed to be the most intelligent and powerful leader of the Arab world. As I looked at him, I wondered if he had donned this simple military uniform for the purpose of protection, since his attire was identical to that of the officers surrounding him. The King's cortege of officers and guards for the shoot continued their activity. Loaders transported equipment; cars were being hidden. The monarch moved easily and graciously through the guests, with a smile and a brief comment for each one. Suddenly I found myself alone with him, standing in the middle of all the bustle, although at his side a long line of country men were one by one kissing the King's hand.

"Shooting in Spain is one of my favorite pastimes," King Hassan said amiably while they men continued to kiss his hand, "although I don't have as much time for it as I would like."

"For me, also, your Majesty," I answered. "That's why it's such a treat to be invited to shoot in your beautiful country."

"And I understand that you are an excellent shot," he went on. "The trophies on that lovely hat attest to your skills." He smiled at me with warmth, and I was engulfed with a feeling of admiration for this powerful man who had such grace and charm.

"Our guests from Spain may be disappointed at the size of our wild boar," the King went on. He looked at me with those formidable black eyes and smiled that special smile. "But we make up for that in quantity. What's the saying? 'Quality over quantity'? Well, here we do it the other way around."

I marveled at his ability to carry on a normal conversation as he turned his hand up and down while so many men kissed it. For me, the proximity of the silent file of over a hundred shabbily dressed countrymen waiting in line to kiss the monarch's hand first on one side, then on other, made it an effort for me to continue conversing properly. I would have preferred, like the King, not to look at them, but since I was at a loss as to what attitude was most correct. I found myself glancing at them. Their awed expressions made me remember that for them the King was not only their monarch but also their religious leader. The ragged men were so close that it would have been easy for any one of them to take a concealed knife from the folds of his djellaba and plunge it into the King's heart, but the ceremony proceeded without mishap.

Later as I walked up the mountain, General Oufkir accompanied me and chatted on about King Hassan being of the Alouite dynasty and a thirty-fifth-generation descendant of Mohammed, the Prophet, which he explained was responsible for the look of religious fervor on the faces of the men kissing His Majesty's hand. He also told me that his King was the seventeenth in that family to reign uninterruptedly since 1666. When Oufkir noticed my interest, he went on to explain that Hassan had been educated in a French university and had participated in his father's governmental affairs since 1957. "During those difficult times of the Spanish and French protectorates," he continued, 'although only seventeen years old, his intelligence and integrity already commanded respect. He became King when Mohammed the Fifth died unexpectedly. That was back in '61."

As we moved on, an officer approached, saying he had been ordered to take me to my post. I followed the man along a grassy trail for a few minutes – then he pointed to a huge green roofless enclosure consisting of three walls of matted green branches, indicating me to enter, explaining that this was to be my butt for the shoot. Then he left. Branches and bushes had been intertwined with live oak to make the thick green walls. The floor of the roomlike enclosure was covered with beautiful red-and-orange carpets. Also masses of colorful plush pillows were strewn about—luxury unheard of in shooting posts in Spain or France or England. For a few moments the unreality of it all amazed me – I stretched out on the thick carpet and leaned back Cleopatra-style on the sumptuous pillows, regretting that I did not have a camera to photograph the incredulous size and decor of my shooting post.

I looked up when I saw two officers with automatic weapons that looked like French MAT 49's appear in the back of my fancy blind, the only open side. They quietly stationed themselves there. Quickly, I stood up, wondering what would happen next and why they had come. Was this special protection provided by the Prince or by General Oufkir? I'd never felt in danger in any wild boar shoot in Spain. Why would all this care be necessary? Peering over the green cover of my stand, I looked down the line of guns—what I could see of it, since it wound around the hill, thick with underbrush. In the other posts I could barely recognize anyone; all were invisible behind similar front walls - they would also be invisible to the game when it was driven toward them. Each enclosure resembled mine, and I presumed that they also had the same ornate interiors. Hoping to involve the officers in conversation, I asked why our stands were so high off the ground.

"That's so the wild boar will not be able to reach the shooter. When wounded, boar are dangerous and are apt to attack."

Before I could ask why he and the other officers were on guard with automatic weapons, Luis appeared, with a loader carrying his shooting gear.

"They're changing almost everybody's post, even the King's. So now we're sharing one."

I was delighted, since the thought of being separated if some problem happened had occurred to me. I would prefer to die fighting beside my husband if we were in danger – but actually I considered all this protection absolutely unnecessary. I had been shooting boar in Spain for over twenty years and our boar were supposed to be much larger. I surmised that the Prince or Oufkir had been responsible for all these luxuries.

"What fun , Luis,," I whispered. "Look at all the space we have , more than enough room for both of us."

Our loaders appeared and took their places on little stools, one next to Luis and one next to me – then we began to practice loading our guns as we always did with new loaders in Spain - passing our rifles to our loaders back and forth several times so we would be prepared to coordinate with them when the shoot began. Then three rifle shots rang out and we jumped to attention. The shoot had begun.

Luis and I leaned out over the leafy green wall, ready to shoot the first animal that appeared as we were accustomed. We always had to carefully scan the underbrush for wild boar. But we needn't have made the effort here. Hundreds of men were already racing down the mountain—screeching and wailing. In front of them, masses of wild board came rushing toward us, running, bumping into each other in their haste to get out of the thicket and away from the shouting beaters. In Spain the boar are aroused by several packs of thirty dogs under the direction of one beater. Here there was such a mingling of men and wild boar that I was afraid to shoot—fearful of hitting a beater instead of an animal—I just stood there with my rifle poised. "Shoot, shoot!" cried the officer, now standing just beside me, with his automatic weapon aimed at the animal coming towards us.

"But I might hit one of those beaters," I screamed.

"No importa" The man's voice was tense with excitement. "Señora Condesa, *tire, tire,* shoot, Shoot."

There was no way I could be certain I would not hit one of the beaters. Suddenly I heard Luis shoot - a small boar very near our butt fell, obviously dead. By now the first onslaught of animals was closer to our platform, and the noise of the gunshots, the beaters' screams, the screeching of the animals, was deafening. As I watched with my shotgun raised, masses more of wild boar materialized on the slope higher up. They looked like an army of gigantic bloated rats gone berserk = they were much smaller than our Spanish boar; also, there were so many—all running so fast.

I glanced questioningly at the young officer. Again he screamed, 'Shoot, Shoot," his voice now reduced to a thin, uptight shout. The other armed officer was next to Luis who was shooting as rapidly as his loader was able to reload and pass the next gun.

"Shoot, Madame la Comtesse, shoot," my officer said desperately for the third time. "Don't be afraid. I'm here to kill any animals you may wound, so you don't have to fear they will get up onto this platform."

So that was why the officers were guarding our stand! Nearby bursts of gunfire resounded like the front line of trench warfare. I breathed deeply – that mass of running men out there! if I missed! Rifle blasts exploded from all directions. Luis was carefully picking off a number of wild boar. Already several lay dead in front of our stand. Some had even managed to reach the very edge of our platforkm. Now I understood why the wall had been laced so carefully with crisscrossing branches. The wild boar kept pouring down the mountain and I realized that if I didn't help Luis, one might get into our blind. The beaters' inhuman screams became louder and louder as they came closer. Of course they were terrified – not of the boar but probably more terrified of one of us making a mistake and shooting him.. The boar—many wounded—squealed frantically—each moment closer.

The racket was incredible and exhilarating. I took careful aim, but as I pulled the trigger, I realized the beasts were going almost as fast as our Spanish partridge. I missed. The officer at my side let off two short bursts from his automatic and stopped two boar from jumping into our blind. Hastily, I grabbed the gun my loader handed me and shot again without aiming, just swinging the barrel, like wing-shooting. I did a fast double, killing two fat little ones. Then my loader handed me the guns quickly, rotating them in almost constant movement. I began to kill wild boar at breakneck speed. It was a slaughter, but exciting . Luis was using a rifle, but I had a twelve gauge gun, using solid shot. My loader soon started to rotate three of my guns because the continuous shooting was burning my hand despite my pigskin glove on the barrel.

The drive stopped just as suddenly as it had begun. For a moment a heavy silence hung in the air. Forty-five minutes, and not one letup in the amount of game that had kept rushing at us down that mountain. In Spain we would have been in our posts for about four or five hours, and with luck would have shot from one to three wild boar. Today we had seen thousands of animals all at once. The ground below us, all around and as far as we could see, was littered with carcasses.

Luis, a top shot, of course had killed many more than I, but nevertheless the officer beside me was enthusiastic with his praise. "Congratulations, Madame la Comtesse," he said. "Once you started, you shot beautifully. You handled those guns with great skill."

Carefully, the men with automatically rifles moved out to ascertain there were no wounded animals alive. I looked around wondering if any of the beaters had been wounded, but all seemed to have disappeared. Soon a loud voice in French announced that we could come down from our stands. I looked at Luis. We were too surprised to speak. Neither of us had any idea how many animals we had downed. It had been a unique experience—the noise, the amount of game—that mass of thousands of raggedy beaters scared to death - but I knew he was thinking, as I, that our shoots in Spain were a different kind of sport.

In the distance we saw General Oufkir and the prince rushing down the hill to where the cars had been concealed under large oak trees. It took a few moments for us to recognize the King running between them. But why the hurry? Had something happenned now that was placing the Kings life in jeopardy? Of course any chief of state always had to be protected. We raced to catch up and barely made it to the Kings cars, where we saw him dive inside in obvious good health. There were no goodbyes. The wheels of his black vehicle spun as the driver slammed the powerful engine into gear and started to move down the mountain. Beaters, servants, chauffeurs, officers, and soldiers ran toward it and tried to accompany the vehicle—running on either side, waving and screaming. Some managed to touch the window where he was sitting. Those who could not reach that touched the King's car any place they could.

Luis and I watched the amazing spectacle, astonished at the evident adoration these men had for their King. They kept running wildly, hysterically, next to their monarch's car, - it was quite staggering to see how long they managed to keep up with his big Mercedes. Like Olympic runners they raced, struggling to keep their balance, many slipping and falling off the steep incline on either side of the road, as the car moved down the curving dirt path. I grabbed Luis's field glasses to follow the scene. When the car took on greater speed, the men were outdistanced, but one lone runner continued for another fifty meters, racing like the wind. Only when the car turned a corner and sped off at the bottom of the hill did the sprinter stop and stand there motionless, watching his monarch's vehicle disappear.

Our trip continued several days more, always with new beautiful places and unusual experiences - we enjoyed an specially glamorous goodbye dinner in Marakesch with General Oufkir and Prince Moulay Abdullah presiding. I was not reminded of Morocco again until several months later when as we were lunching Luis handed me the newspaper. It happened to be Sunday, July 11, 1971, The main Spanish newspaper carried front-page headlines:

SOLDIERS ATTACK MOROCCAN SUMMER PALACE: KING HASSAN CAPTIVE.

. Below that, "King Hassan was held captive for 2 hours- the monarch says 3 generals were killed—he accuses Libya of inciting the uprising."

The coup had been planned for the forty-second birthday of the King, a large celebration with eight hundred guests had to taken place in the Kings Summer palace in Skhirat, near Rabat.

Festivities had begun early in the morning, with golf, tennis, and swimming in the palace pools. Diplomats, government ministers, artists, writers and scientists, and friends from all over the world had been invited, but only men, as customary in Morocco for official affairs. The ambassadors of the USSR, the U.S.A., France, Belgium, Great Britain, and many Arab countries had been there.

A few minutes after two o'clock, while King Hassan was lunching under a large tent in front of the palace, sounds of firing were heard. At first the guests and the King thought the explosions were fireworks. But once the first moment of shock had passed, the King realized it was gunfire. He ran from the tent, accompanied by General Oufkir and ten others, and took refuge in the throne room, where he telephoned some motorized units that were loyal to him and ordered them to intervene. His call got through just before all telephone communications were cut.

Luis asked me when I had finished reading. "What do you think of that attempt to kill King Hassan?" His face had taken on a somber expression."Do you suppose the government suspected something was up when they maintained such careful watch over the king during our boar shoot? In fact," he went on, "there was always careful protection of the King – even two days later when I was playing golf with him in Marakesch, military body-guards were nearby. But at the time I didn´t considered that unsual."

"At least we know the King is safe and that he's placed General Oufkir in charge of things for the time being," I said.

There was not bad news from Morocco until almost a year later and it was devastating. I was in our house in Marbella, looking out at the great expanse of the blue Mediterranean.

My maid interrupted my reveries, "Senor Condesa, the Marquesa de Villaverde is on the phone."

As I picked up the receiver, Carmen Franco's voice was unusually excited."Aline, turn on Radio Nacional. There's another coup taking place in Morocco –right now. ... hurry. It's incredible."

When I found the station, the Spanish commentator was saying

, " at two thirty this afternoon, the Royal Moroccan Air Force fighters from their Air Force base in Kenitra attacked King Hassan's 727 over the strait of Gibraltar on his return from a trip to Paris, after refueling in Barcelona.

"King Hassan´s plane was nearing the strait of Gibraltar, cleared the Spanish coast, and commenced descent to Kenitra, expecting to be on the ground in twelve mnutes. At that moment three Moroccan f-5's appeared about 500 hundred feet above the King's plane- the lead F-5 peeled off and attacked the King's plane and opened fire, making numerous hits."

As I continued to listen I learned that King Hassan was an experienced pilot and had managed to take control of the plane himself, landing it miraculously in Rabat airport despite the many devasting blows it had received.

It was incredible for me that another coup, an attack on the king by his own airforce, had taken place almost one year after the last one. My only sense of relief was in knowing that the King was safe, but I realized that there had to be someone responsible for organizing the coup since it had been made by persons in his own airforce, but no name had been mentioned.

Luis was in Madrid when the news broke and he took for granted, as I did, that the most important news of the coup had already been divulged. Therefore I was still more horrified when he burst into my room the next morning, having just arrived from Madrid, shoving a newspaper before my eyes. On the first page, I read,

KEY MOROCCAN AIDE APPARENT SUICIDE, DEFENSE CHIEF FOUND DEAD AFTER 2ND ATTEMPT ON LIFE OF KING

Since I knew that King Hassan had named General Oufkir Defense Minister a year ago, these words told me that my friend Oufkir was dead! The most courageous officer in the Moroccan army and the most powerful! With a heavy heart I continued to read.

Rabat, Morocco, Aug.17 – King Hassan who yesterday escaped the second attempt on his life in 13 months, lost his principal military supporter early today with the death of Gen. Mohammed Oufkir, the Minister of Defense.

For the next two days we lived in constant contact with radio and newspaper. Telephone communications with Morocco were impossible.

First it was published that Moroccans believed Oufkir had committed suicide because he felt he had failed the king in July of the year before, when he had not been able to avoid the attack in the King's summer palace. But two days later the following story appeared:

Rabat, Aug. 19.—King Hasssan 11, in a radio and television address to the Moroccan people tonight accused Gen. Mohammed Oufkir, his right-hand man, of masterminding the two plots to kill him – that of July 1971 and the plane attack on Aug.16$^{th.}$.

Naturally we were horrified. For me General Oufkir had been the most helpful and kind Moroccan officer during our fascinating visit. I did not learn until years later that King Hassan had punished Oukir's traitorous acts by imprisoning his wife and five children, that the family had lived like animals imprisoned for twenty years- without education for the children, without the assistance of doctors or dentists. Finally after twenty years of inhuman conditions, the eldest daughter managed to escape and through publicity in the French press she was able to get her mother and brothers released. As a result the international publicity obliged Hassan to free them and they went to Paris to live.

CHAPTER FORTY – SEVEN

FRANCO'S DEATH
BLACK AMBASSADOR
ELECTIONS 1977

Spain's placid existence was abruptly disturbed by terrorists in 1974 when a bomb exploded under the car of the vice-president of the government, killing him and his driver. The explosion was not far from my house - so strong and loud that I found myself sitting up in bed - the glass in the window next was still vibrating when Mar ia Luisa came running in to tell me something terrrible had happened, as if I had not heard it ! We soon learned the incredible explanation - a bomb...! This was the first warning that terrorism could come to Spain as it already had to other European countries.

In October of 1975 Franco gave his yearly speech as chief of state from a balcony in the royal palace in the plaza del Oriente to thunderous applause. But within a fortnight he fell gravely ill. There was a general state of distress all over Spain when the news reached the public. Affection for the aged dictator was undeniable. But people also feared what would happen to their recent affluence once he was gone. The dictator's agony was long. Regularly the radio gave reports. A foreign guest in our house at the time observed with amazement that the entire country appeared to be grieving. "How could this be", she exclaimed. "If I did not see this with my own eyes I would never believe that a dictator could be so generally loved by his people."

Despatches appeared in the press with the provisions Franco had made in 1968 when he had issued a decree stating that Prince Juan Carlos would become his successor as chief of State, and would be coronated as King - that free elections would follow. Still the populace was worried. Monarchists were few, and the communists and socialists were strongly against a monarchy. But a large middle class had been created and had grown in strength every year - that mass of people accepted Franco's decision, as they would have accepted any other he made during those last years of his control. However there were doubts whether a peaceful democratic monarchy would be possible once he was gone. Would a new government be able to maintain the country as stable and secure as it now was? Noone knew what political repercussions might take place despite Franco's careful preparations. The Civil War was still a terrifying memory for every social strata in the country.

Franco died november 20th [1975] - His body lay in state for two days and nights while, according to the radio, press and television an average of 100 persons per minute filed by his bier in an endless procession. Masses of spaniards braved the bitter winter night standing four abreast in a queue that curved through Madrid's streets for thirty blocks, thousands were still queued up when time ran out. After my having lived through years when Franco was considered a usurper by some, a despot by others, a hero only by a few, it was surprising to see the reverence and affection the same people now showed him thirty years later.

The following day he was buried in the Basilica of the Valley of the Fallen, at the foot of the Guadarrama mountains, thirty miles from Madrid. During the Civil War there had been bitter fighting and loss of life and Franco had wisely created this large cemetery as a memorial to Spaniards from both sides who had been lost in the war. When the massive structure was completed the bones of more than 40,000 casualties from the two sides were taken from their original graves and buried in a common sepulchre in this Basilica, symbol of a re-united Spain.

Immediately after the funeral , the ceremony to install the new King, Juan Carlos, was performed to colorful perfection, just as had been the dignified burial of the departed leader. The parliamentary ceremony for the enthronement of the new King was filled with the pagaentry and pomp Spanish people had been accustomed to in days goneby. The country now faced the beginning of another epoch in their long history and the television resounded with cheers of "VIVA EL REY , VIVA ESPANA".

So many groups started forming political parties in that year following Franco's death that the confusion led to the existence of 120 different parties when elections took place a year later. The proud spirit of the spaniards, their sense of personal consequence was not conducive to cooperation, they were individualists and reluctant to unite with anyone who had slightly disparate opinions . The country was very different from what it had been at the end of the Civil War. Franco's forty years leading the country had been almost as consequential as the forty-two years of Felipe the Second's reign in the sixteenth century. Both men had affected the country's life, customs and welfare. People at the end of both regimes had been accustomed to a strong government and when that leader had disappeared there were doubts as to what the future would bring.

There was one man who I believed could lead the country – Manuel Fraga. While he was Minister of Information and Tourism, I had seen him bring to the country many modern improvements and when he formed one of the first political parties, I collaborated and campaigned in the pueblos near Pascualete. The meetings began late at night, at about eleven o'clock, because that was when the workmen returned from the fields - when they had finished dinner and were able to take part in political discussions. In my small red Seat I bounced over the rutty country roads and paths with Primitivo sitting next to me. We went to meetings in different pueblos organized by local mayors. An entire parliament had to be filled; we needed senators and congressmen-we were starting from scratch - but it was exhilarating for all of us from every walk of life and every political inclination.

Yet in country towns like Trujillo some people were afraid to show their allegiance to a particular party, they all knew each other and being unaccustomed to political elections, they feared that if they were known to have voted for the party that lost, later those in power might take revenge on them. There was no way I could convince the leading ladies of Trujillo that in a democracy each citizen had to defend openly his beliefs. None of them were willing to be photographed for the television that I had organized - I was desperate - it had not been easy to get the national television channel, nor the BBC to come to Trujillo. I had managed this principally because our town of Trujillo was especially picturesque, its magnificent fifteenth century plaza and ancient stone palaces made a colorful background for any TV program. But now no matter how I pleaded, I could not find women who would collaborate. If Pillete had been alive, I knew he would have helped me, but he had died ten years before.

Exhausted and discouraged I went to my favorite restaurant for lunch. "La Troya" , in the plaza in an ancient palace, the dining room has a domed arched brick ceiling undoubtedly constructed by mozarabs about seven hundred years before. The food is good simple country dishes...gazpacho, baby lambchops, tortilla, a "guisado" of pork, delicious "jamon serrano", roast lamb, salad,"arroz con leche", and the price is so low that the place is always crowded when other restaurants in the plaza have few customers. Concha, the owner, was about fifty or sixty in those days...hard to tell. Her round body looked soft and ample and was always covered by a nondesript grey cotton dress tied around the waist with the narrow string of her white apron. Her face and head were roman, like the sculptures in the Museum of Merida, and her smile was distracting - she lacked three teeth at odd spots. Her hair was neither brown nor black nor grey, slicked flat and tightly pulled back into a knot. Her skin had no color whatsoever, Concha was not a woman who went to the country for long walks, nor took any exercise other than a short visit to the butcher to check on prices. I doubt she ever stepped out of her establishment for other reasons, she was too busy keeping her eye on her five employees and working hard herself.

Often she would be near the door and this day hastened to greet me, grabbing me with kisses on both cheeks. She always passed me ahead of anyone else into the dining room no matter how long the waiting line was, and regardless of how many friends were with me she never let me pay. The reason was that in the early sixties when there had been many unemployed in this agricultural area as a result of the arrival of farm machinery, she had begged me to find a job for Diego, her only son - I found him a job him in an american company in Madrid. Although Concha was pleased at the time, later she told me what she really wanted was for her son to become "un banquero", a banker, and could I please get him a job in a bank, preferrably near home. Diego was conscientious and his employers in the Madrid office were pleased with him; I felt it was a mistake to change his job. But eventually I had the opportunity of getting him admitted to a spanish bank in a minor job in the nearby town of Caceres. I told Concha that Diego would have a more brilliant future in the american company, but she considered any job in a bank made her son "un banquero", (a banker). Nevertheless by then with the success of her restaurant, she herself was a rich woman and Diego could have made more money working for her, but no reasoning of mine could change her mind. She wanted Diego to remain a "banker".

That day, as I consumed my tortilla, I unloaded my problem to Concha. I told her the leading women of Trujillo were not willing to put on their local costumes to be photographed in the plaza with banners of Alianza Popular- something I needed desperately for a TV program .

" Don´t worry about that any longer. I'll take care of it," said Concha. "Just tell me what hour and how many people are needed".

"At least ten to make a good showing. This afternoon at five o'clock the televion cameras will be in the plaza and would be the perfect time."

"There will be many women in our local costumes there for the photographers. Don't give it another thought."

Just before five... I pulled into the plaza in my small Seat, worried to death that my television crews would have nothing I had promised them to film. To my amazement on the steps in front of Concha's restaurant about twenty young women dressed in the picturesque yellow and black Trujillian costume were gathering, their colorful shawls, white crotcheted stockings and black alpargatas, making a colorful addition to the medieval background. I could hardly believe my eyes. The camermen were delighted, and even more so when the same number of young men in costumes of black knickers, white shirts, embroidered vests and caps joined the girls. The young people all waving banners of my party animated the act by dancing their regional "jota". A few minutes later a still larger group appeared with Trujillo's band and chorus. With the background of the statue of Pizarro and the quaint ancient stone palaces and towers, the show became one of the best.

When I thanked Concha for her great efforts and told her that I was unaware she was such a strong backer of Alianza Popular, she chuckled. "Oh, I don't know anything about all those political things, nor do I care, Senora Condesa. But if the countess thinks that's the party we should have, I agree with her."

The epoch of our first elections also contributed to changing customs. When I arrived at any small village where often before the mayor would greet me with a bow and a respectful "Buenos dias Senora Condesa", now he merely grabbed my shoulders and kissed me on both cheeks. Free elections made us all chums and we enjoyed it.

Eventually the great day arrived. There were no mechanized machines to help with the voting - only a wooden box with a slit in it. At each table were seated nine representatives of nine different parties. I had requested an election table in a "controversial" area where the majority of voters were apt to be of leftist parties. Since we were not accustomed to political controversy, it was generally believed that there might be disturbances. My husband and my sons did not want me to choose a leftist area , fearing violence, but I loved all Spaniards and was not slightlty worried about facing persons with different opinions. After all in the United States many of my friends were of the opposite party.

We sat at our tables from eight in the morning until seven the next morning, almost 24 hours - once the voting was over we had to count each small piece of paper. At my table most of my companions represented extreme left parties-including three different communist parties. We were all so leery that our party's votes might be stolen, that no one dared leave the table for a minute, not even to go to the bathroom, unless a volatile officer of one's party came to occupy the seat when one was absent. The sandwiches I had fortunately brought with me, I shared with a young communist neighbor who was determined not to leave his place even though he starved to death. He told me proudly that he had been imprisoned for two months for organizing communist meetings and explained that they and the socialists had been organizing secret meetings during all those Franco years. I was amazed, but he was charming and he liked my sandwiches.

During those many hours, I became friendly with all those seated around my table, and when we got up to leave at about seven A.M., one of my sons who was at another table in the same area, saw that I was packing four communists into my little seat to take the results to headquarters. "No need for you to do that, Mama," he said. "There are other cars that can deliver your table results." But by that time I no longer felt the communists were enemies, and certainly they were not dangerous. So of course I drove them to headquarters. However by then I was aware that all those leftist parties outnumbered our parties of the center and the right and that the future of Spain indeed was going to be different. As I drove along the Castellana, they were vociferously celebrating, while I was trying to hide the tears. How could I have lived in this beautiful country for thirty-four years and been so ignorant of the opinions of my wonderful compatriots! But when I reached home Concha was on the phone to tell me that Trujillo had voted overwhelmingly for Alianza Popular.

The final result of the entire country was that a centrist party won the elections. Four years later the socialists with the communist votes came in for fifteen years. After that in 1996

Alianza Popular became enlarged with the disolution of the centrist party and changed name to Partido Popular and came into power. In 2004 due to a terrorist attack two days before which killed over 250 persons, the socialists won again. But we in Spain were learning little by little how to live in a democracy.

CHAPTER FORTY - EIGHT

WINDSORS THREE

The Duchess was never the same after His Royal Highness died. She made an effort to go to a few parties and always put together a small dinner when Luis and I went to visit her, but she was desperately lonely and could find solace in nothing. She who used to read all the new novels that came out now hardly read at all.

When my son Luis married, since she had not been able to go to the wedding due to an ulcer attack, she convinced the newlyweds to spend some days with her at the end of their honeymoon. During their visit she took them to Maximn's, the most elegant restaurant in Pairs for lunch. They had heard of Maxim's but had never been t here, so they were thrilled. To their dismay, the duchess ordered only a hamburger, and they felt obliged to do the same. They had no way of knowing that she usually ordered even less, or that hamburgers were her favorite because they reminded her of home. She said in her next letter how flattered she had been when "the children" left for a weekend at Ferrierres and then returned the next day because they said they had more fun with her. Those long letters on her bright blue or yellow stationary in her large scrawly script always contained flashes of her customary wit despite her loneliness.

One letter caught the Duchess's character and our relationship to a T. It contained a copy of a letter from the firm of Allen & Overy in London, as well as a rough sketch of the Duke's burial plot. The enclosed letter read:

Madam,

I have now had written confirmation that there is ample room for your own grave next to that of His Royal Highness and I know that this was something which was worrying you.

There is plenty of room between the Duke's grave and the border, approximately 9 yards. There is about 6 yards on the other side to the base of the plane tree which overshadows this bit of the garden, but obviously it would be better if another grave is sited on the other side away from the tree.

I enclose a little sketch which shows the position.

The Duchess's note to me said: *"Looks like the Archbishop of Canterbury's been bitten by the tomb bug. Take a look at the attached sketch, just received. Please make certain when my rock-a-bye time comes and when the wind blows and the bow bends, it won't fall on my romance or your old friend."*

Soon after that, I became aware that a serious problem was menacing my friend. Some of the servants who had been with her for years were suddenly let go, and those remaining were glum and jittery, afraid that they too might lose their employ. They complained to me about the Duchess's secretary: "She wants to get rid of us all." When I asked the Duchess about this, she answered sadly, "Economies, my dear. The secretary tells me I cannot afford them and that they were creating trouble. I really cannot understand it, after all the years they have been here."

It was a hard blow for her to lose the familiar faces. They were her only family. As long as I'd known her, she had never gone on a trip without buying little gifts for her servants.

Each visit I found her weaker and more depresseed. In the beginning it seemed logical to me that a house with only one occupant would not need a full staff, so I felt that the secretary's decisions were in the Duchess's interest. But when some of the Duchess's old friends in Paris told me that when they called they were told she could not receive visitors, I was surprised and told the Duchess. She was furious. "It's true I'm not such a great football player as I used to be," she quipped wryly, "and I do forget names now and then, but I think my friends can put up with that, and I need them. You are way down in Madrid, Aline. I want my Paris friends to come whenever they like. The amusing ones, of course," she added. "No bores—I'm certainly not up to that."

Several months later when the Duchess was convalescing at home, I received a call from her. "Aline, you must come to see me right away. I need you desperately." It was a Thursday, and once she assured me that her health was all right, I asked her if she could wait until Monday. I suppose so," she answered. "My dear, just telephone and tell Martin the hour your plane arrives so that he can meet you at the airport. It is Martin who has put this call through to you for me. Fortunately my secretary has her day off today."

When I called the next day to give the hour of my arrival on Monday, the secretary answered. She told me very firmly that the Duchess's doctor said she could not have any visitors. When I asked if I could speak to the Duchess, she said that was impossible; if I had any messages for Her Royal Highness, she would convey them. I was stunned. "Please let her know that I have called," I said with emphasis, "and that I had made plans to visit her as she requested."

483

After I hung up, I wondered what I could do. Suddenly I remembered the new French lawyer who now represented the Duchess, Mme. Suzanne Blum, of whom Guy de Rothschild had spoken highly. I telephoned her and she said that naturally I could see the Duchess whenever I was able. I told her I would go on Monday – she verified the hours with me and said she would have Martin pick me up – that she wanted him to bring me to her office so we could talk. When I met Madame Blum I was impressed by her kindness and efficiency. Told her my worries about the secretary.

"I was obliged to let that young lady go. I prefer not to discuss the reasons. She was much worse than you could imagine. Now the most important care the Duchess needs is medical. We have nurses around the clock. Now that she is at home and not in the hospital, we must try to keep her there, where she is happier." Madame Blum told me her reason to want to see me personally was to comment about a film that had appeared about the Windsors giving a vicious unfair picture of both of them. She said she was making efforts to protect the Duchess in the future from that sort of publicity. I realized that at last my friend had someone who would take good care of her.

"Do you know that the last letter His Royal Highness wrote was directed to you?" asked Mme. Blum.

"But I never received it."

"No, it is here with all his papers, which I am still going through. I intend to see to it that the true story of His Royal Highness is told one day so that all these preposterous lies about his fondness for Hitler and the Germans can be refuted."

"Yes, I know very well how unfair those reports are", I answered. "The men who were the principal government officials involved in this matter in Spain in 1940 when the Duke and the Duchess arrived in Madrid happen to be friends of mine and they have told me details that clearly prove the anti-German feelings of the Duke."

"Please tell me Countess. This is important information for me."

"Not only am I aware of the Duke being anti-Nazi through my friends information, but the Duke himself told me often how he hated Hitler. He said he was desperate when he could not get permission to join the British forces during the war. Both the Duke and the Duchess told me that during their wedding trip throughout Europe in 1937, three years before his country was at war with Germany, they had the misfortune when arriving in Berlin of Hitler welcoming them and being photographed with them."

By this time Mme Blum was tapping my arm urging me to continue. As I spoke I still could remember the expression on the Duke's face when he told me, "That photograph, Aline, caused me much misery. You may have seen it – it was used years later to accuse me of having been pro-German.. Imagine how that has affected me. I despised Hitler – he was the monster of our epoch. But ironically German was my only foreign language and when I was alone with my mother we always spoke German together , as children we all were taught German just as we were taught English.".

I went on with my explanations for Mme. Blum. I told her that a close friend who I saw often in Madrid, the Count of Montarco, had been political secretary of the Spanish Minister of Foreign Affairs in 1940 and had told me that all the information proving the Duke had been anti-Hitler was in the archives in Madrid and could be checked. Mme Blum seemed especially pleased to hear this. Then I told her Montarco had explained that Spain in those years had been fearful of Hitler because German troops were on the northern frontier threatening to enter Spain to reach Gibraltar. He clarified "this would have been disastrous -we were still suffering much poverty as a result of our recent Civil War."

"How fascinating, Countess, but please tell me exactly what the Count said happened when the Duke arrived in Spain. I think it was June 23, 1940"

"The Count of Monarco said that in order to avoid another war for their poverty stricken country, they felt obliged to help Hitler or at least to appear to help him. After the Windsors checked into the Hotel Ritz, they made a brief tourist visit to Barcelona and to Toledo, dined with friends in the British Embassy and left ten days later for Portugal. "

Mme Blum now pulled her chair closer to mine.

I continued. "The Count of Montarco said that in the Ministry they received requests from Hitler through the German Embassy asking them to convince Windsor to remain in Spain to intercede in favor of Germany. Montarco said he was barely able to mention the subject to the Duke because Windsor was so shocked he would not listen to a word and Montarco realized immediately that Windsor was violently ant-Germany. But when Hitler realized this, his demands became more radical – he wanted the Spaniards to kidnap Windsor so they could take the Duke to Germany. The minister and the Count became desperate when Schellenburg, head of the German SS came to Spain to ordered them further. But by this time the Windsors had already left for Portugal. Nevertheless since the Germans were determined to capture him, Montarco with Schellenburg worked out a plan to enable them to kidnap the Duke. The Count owned a palace presiding a large shooting property on the border of Portugal in a Spanish town, Ciudad Rodrigo. They decided to invite Windsor there for a weekend partridge shoot with the intention of capturing him and sending him to Germany. However Windsor declined the invitation. By this time the Duke was in contact with his good friend Churchill who was

486

trying to convince the royal family to allow the Duke to return to London where he would find himself a position in the war effort in the Army or the Navy. But the Duke's brother, now the King, would not give permission for him to come to England nor be placed in any European war assignment. Meanwhile Churchill learned of the Nazi intention to kidnap the Duke and named him Governor of Nassau which would eliminate the dangers of his being kidnapped by Hitler's spies. Fortunately the King agreed to this post for his brother. The appointment was accompanied with a warning to the Duke that if he remained in Portugal there were many people now trying to kill him.

Since Mme Blum wanted all the details I could supply, I told her another amazing story that had been confirmed to me by another Spaniard - a man who had been a double agent during the war, Angel Alcazar de Velasco. This man had been introduced to me quite recently by Count of Montarco, although I had known of him during my years in OSS. Now this ex-double agent wanted to meet me claiming that he had saved my life several times during the war. From the moment I met him, I considered him unreliable – he was a man of medium height, about ten years older than me, with lots of bushy white hair, and insisted speaking in English with a terrible accent. But his information about Windsor strengthened what Montarco had told me about the attempt to kidnap Windsor. This man gladly admitted to having been a double agent - for the English and the Germans, and then proudly claimed to have been an employee of the Spanish secret service at the same time , a triple agent. It was hard to believe anything he said - he was a wild character – had even been a bullfighter at one time in his youth . Yet he also knew more details, elaborating on the fact that the Germans intended to torture Windsor once they had him in Germany to use him as a weapon against the English.

There was much more I could tell Mme. Blum – I wanted to tell her about another double agent, Philby, who had been in Portugal at the same time and who later I met in Sevilla in 1944, but suddenly I realized I didn't have time - I was desperate to visit the Duchess, so I ended our meeting abruptly.

"And the Duchess, how is she today," I asked as I stood up to leave?

"You will see for yourself when Martin takes you to visit her. It is a pity you don't have more time to continue this important information, Countess, but I realize the Duchess will be so pleased to see you. She is weak and cannot have any excitement - her blood presssure goes up, but I know your visit will be a treat for her."

As Martin drove me though Paris to Neuilly, I thought this might be the last time. He opened the iron gates, and we started up the gravel path. The grounds had never looked more beautiful. At the entrance steps, I jumped out to greet Georges. His hair had whitened around the temples, but he was as handsome and impeccably dressed as always. Just inside the door Ofelia was waiting, slim and straight. The two of them were the perfect reflection of a house in which every detail was an example of the owners' special touch. "Such a long time since we have seen you, Comtesse," Ofelia said, smiling.

Georges escorted me up the staircase to the boudoir.

She was sitting majestically in a high armchair on wheels, dressed in a turquoise brocade robe, which reached to her feet. Her thick, shiny hair was pulled back in a tight chignon, exaggerating the high cheekbones. She wore earrings and a necklace to match the robe. Her violet eyes looked larger, and her expression was slightly detached and sad. Georges announced, "Your Royal Highness, the Countess is here."

She kissed me hello. "I've been waiting too long to see you, my child." There were orchids on the table next to her, and as always, in a small dish, the white and green mints she loved. She looked better than I had expected - she seemed to be almost on a pedestal—grand and glorious. But the wheelchair was a grim reminder that she could no longer walk.

I sat beside her, and she smiled at me. Again she repeated, "I'm so glad you've come." I looked around the room at the photographs of her and the Duke. Of course, I thought, it was natural that they should have gone well together—they were so much alike, both small-boned and thin, as if cut from the same pattern and the same origin. They loved parties, dogs, clothes, and they both had a strong sense of humor. True, he was active in sports and she hated even to walk, but they both liked to travel, to bask in the sun, to entertain, and to live in cozy and beautiful surroundings.

"You look like a Chinese empress today," I said.

"People told me that when I was living in Peking in 1924, and David had the same reaction once."

CHAPTER FORTY – NINE

PRESIDENT NIXON

During a trip to New York in January 1968 Luis and I were invited with several other European and American friends to Nassau for a festive three days to celebrate the opening of a new hotel. It was January 2nd.. I remember the date because it was so cold in New york - Madrid is rarely below zero in the winter - arriving in warm Nassau from freezing New York was like coming back to life. Among the guests were many populr personalities, including the Spanish Ambassadors to Washington, the Marqueses de Merry del Val. Festivities for all the guests began with a black tie dinner and dancing. Mercedes Merry del Val, the wife of the Ambassador was especially well liked - her dinners in the embassy in Washington were known to be the most elegant and amusing. That night Nassau was warm enough to walk outside on the hotel terrace in a strapless evening gown- beyond the ball room was the wide white beach – the illumination made the foam crested waves glimmer in the distance. Inside guests were seated at round tables of eight. At one point, Mercedes came to me, "Aline, please do me a favor. Go over to that table," she pointed to one at a short distance and talk to Senator Richard Nixon."

"Who is Richard Nixon? You mean that bored looking man sitting alone over there? Oh, really, Mercedes, I don't want to . I don't know him at all and I'm having such a good time –it's fun for me to see these American friends again and they're all such good dancers."

"Oh, Please, Aline. He's all alone, nobody is paying any attention to him - he's really a very nice man. You would do me a great favor, please. Just come with me so I can introduce you," Without another word she pulled my arm and led me to the table.

Once I was seated with Senator Nixon, he began to talk pleasantly enough. In the beginning I made an effort to be agreeable wondering how long I would have to stay there. Soon he asked me to dance. Yes, I thought, he doesn't look interesting but he is out of the ordinary, he's quite a good dancer and he's nice. Our dances and conversations lasted until someone took me back to my table where I soon forgot about Mr.Nixon – that is, until ten months later when surprisingly he had just been elected president of the United States.

At that time Luis and I were again in New York staying at the hotel St. Regis – it was November, a few days after the American elections – we had come over with a group of friends to accompany our Prince Juan Carlos, pretender to the throne of Spain. As I left the hotel to go out to the street, I noticed through the revolving glass entrance a mass of people trying to come in and suddenly to my amazement I saw that the confusion was created by photographers following the new president Nixon. Now that only a few days before he had been elected President of the United States, he was being pursued by the press. A very different situation from months before when he had been ignored by everyone. Nixon recognized me just as I saw him. He continued to turn in the door until he caught up with me, grabbing my hand and smiling broadly, "Oh, the Countess in the green dress. How pleased I am to see you again." I had forgotten that I had been wearing my favorite Balenciaga strapless evening gown that night in Nassau. What a surprise that he would remember - the press continued to try to push into the door but Nixon held it firm and attempted to talk to me – however we were soon obliged to continue in opposite directions.

I would not have told this story if there had not been a sequel. A year or so after President Nixon resigned, two magazine reporters convinced my secretary in Madrid that I should receive them. When they arrived I had just returned from my daily ride in the country so without changing my riding habit I joined them in the salon. At first they asked a series of pointless questions but finally they told me their purpose – they said they had letters to prove that I had been maintaining an affair with President Nixon and handed me a three page handwritten letter. As soon as I glanced through it I realized it was a lurid love letter supposedly written to me signed by Nixon. Since I had never received a letter from Nixon, I was indignant and made them leave the house- thinking that was the end of a preposterous interview.

But a few weeks after this encounter, Luis and I were again in New York when a small article appeared in the New York Daily News claiming that a certain Spanish countess had a torrid love affair with President Nixon and that letters existed to prove it. Since my name was not mentioned Luis and I thought it would have no importance but the following day another larger article appeared mentioning my title Countess of Quintanilla- in those days we were still known by that title. Immediately I was beseiged by telephone calls from the press, and at every dinner I attended the press pursued me. Nevertheless I managed to deny their claims and refused to speak about the matter and the press dropped the story.

We left shortly after for Madrid and since there was no basis of truth in these articles we forgot about them - until a month later a popular Spanish magazine published a more detailed version of the story but with the title of Countess of Romanones as the lover of presdient Nixon. At that date the woman referred to was my mother-in law. The day the article appeared in Madrid she happened to be in a large luncheon with us at an embassy. Now Luis and I were really upset - what would his distinguished elegant step–mother, Blanca de Borbon, think when she realized that she had appeared in the spanish press accused of such a thing! Luis and I led her away from the other guests to prepare her for the shock. We explained the details of how this had come about and assured her that the story was all false. Blanca listened attentively and then looked up at us laughing. "Do not worry, children, At my age" – she was eighty-eight – "it is very flattering to be involved in a sex scandal."

All stories should have happy endings. Several years later I was at a small dinner given by Imelda Marcos in her suite in the Waldorf Towers Hotel in New York – it was a dinner for General MacArthur's widow. MacArthur's troops had relieved the Phillipines from the Japanese at the end of World War Two and Imelda and Fernando Marcos had always been especially grateful. One of the guests at Imelda's small dinner of eight was ex-President Nixon. Therefore we had an opportunity to talk together and laugh about our fictious affair.

Still a couple of years after that, I had the good fortune of once again being with ex-president Nixon in a meeting of an international intelligence group where he spoke to us for two hours about foreign affairs. His talk was so brilliant that the forty members of the group, some ex- directors of intelligence services of over twenty countries gave him a resounding long ovation and agreed that he had been the one USA Presdient who had really understood foreign affairs. Then a year or so after that I did receive a letter from President Nixon telling me that I had kept him awake all night reading my book "The Spy Wore Red" and that he considered it his favorite spy story. A happy ending.

CHAPTER FIFTY

LECTURES

After the death of General Franco and the Spanish elections, Spain started to gain the attention of American politicians. Friends in Washington asked me to come there to explain the current situation to a group of congressmen. Since I was always interested in politics, I went to Washington and fortunately my talk was well accepted. The next day I was contacted by Mr. Keedick, president of an important lecture agency - he told me that he would like to offer me a series of lectures for which he would pay me very well. He said he thought I would be a good lecturer and that he could offer me a lecture in two weeks in the city of Coumbus, Ohio.

I asked him how many people attended these lectures.

"This first one in Ohio would be a good beginning," he said – "the theater is large and you would have over three thousand spectators."

"Oh I couldn´t do that- this group in Washington yesterday was only seventy- no, no, such a large group would be impossible for me."

"You are very mistaken. Large audiences are much easier. You will see. If you were able to hold the attention of seventy, you will have no difficulty with my large groups. I would certainly not be offering you the opportunity if I were not certain of your success."

"But what will I talk about?"

"To begin with tell them for five or ten minutes what it was like to be an American girl living in Madrid in the middle of the war. Then you can tell them the same political things you talked about to those congressmen. You will speak forty-five minutes, then fifteen minutes of questions – our assistants will be placed strategically with microphones so you will hear the questions clearly. I´ll pay you ten thousand dollars for each lecture, plus first class airfare and a suite in the best hotel. You are going to enjoy these lectures. Someone will meet you in the airport and take care of you during your visit. You can talk about spanish politics or whatever you like to. Just speak as you did when you spoke to the congressmen. I was in that audience and can assure you, you will be a success." I was astounded by everything he told me.

In my busy social life in New York I had never heard anything about lectures , nor in Spain either. I liked the idea but when I told Luis, he was utterly amazed "How would he pay you so much to talk! I´d pay to keep you quiet" - but he was amused and did not mind. So I accepted Keedick´s offer, thinking that I would try it just once – after all a new experience.

When I arrived at the Columbus airport for my initial lecture, two charming ladies met me and drove me around the city. They took me to the main square and pointed out the theater where my lecture would take place the next morning.

After we had completed one turn around the square I asked my nice driver if she would be kind enough to go around once more.

"Oh you want to look again at the beautiful statue in the middle of the square –that is a famous .."

"No, no." I interrupted. " I would like to take another look at my name on the theater marquee"

In big letters all across the theater façade was COUNTESS OF ROMANONES SPEAKS HERE – never had I seen my name like that before and it was a thrill.

The next morning we entered the theater through the stage door mounting a stairway to a barren area where two men were adjusting the curtains through which I could barely see the huge empty stage with one small podium in the center. After chatting a few minutes with the ladies, I was asked to stand behind a curtain to wait for my introduction. As I did so the mumble of the large audience reached my ears. I had seen long lines of people waiting outside the theater as my driver parked her car so I realized that the three thousand or more audience Keedick had predicted was probably true..

There was a silence as the lady who was to introduce me walked out to the podium - I expected a long introduction and was listening behind the curtain trying to hear what the she was saying , but to my surprise the introduction was extremely short – "I now present the spanish lady, the Countess of ...." What a shock – I certainly did not feel Spanish here in the middle of my own country - to be introduced as "a spanish lady." That sounded so phony to me. Suddenly I realized that I had forgotten what I had intended to say to begin with. But there was no time to think about it. As I walked to the center of the huge barren stage the words were still ringing in my ears- what else had she said about me? I had hardly heard – I continued to walk towards the podium- Then I became aware that the strands of a song were filling the air -- _ " lady of

Spain we adore you ..""- again that lady of Spain, just like in my first benefit ball – that was all wrong.

The music stoppped and I was definitely alone, engulfed in the silence of the gigantic theater – for a moment footlights blinded me - but I could see part of the second floor balcony which was packed .

I might have been laughing - I don't remember but when I started speaking, I told them exactly what I was thinking. "I'm very sorry, I don´t want to be here under false pretenses - I don't want to disappoint you - I'm not at all a lady from Spain – I`m just another american from a small town in New York state – I hate to let you down but I'm one million percent American – just like you. But, yes, if you would like, I can tell you how I became a spanish countess and what it was like to be an American in Spain during World Two."

In those years I could not mention my current intelligence work but I could say that I had been in Spain with OSS during World War Two, since that had been published in several newspapers - and I could tell them how fascinating Spain had been when I arrived almost forty years before, so different from the United States in those days. I spoke to them as if they were a group of close friends – I had fun - they applauded now and then – oohed and aahed frequently – they had the same reactions I had experienced while I was discovering that strange captivating country called Spain. At the end they gave me a standing ovation. I didn´t even know in those days that was unusal but I was delighted. I only regretted that Luis had not been there. In the future he rarely came to my lectures – he said it embarrassed him. I never could understand how it could embarrass him if it didn´t embarrass me.

After that first lecture Keedick offered me as many lectures as I had time for - I was delighted and continued lecturing in the United States during most of the eighties. The experience was very rewarding – it gave me the opportunity to know the country of my birth – I was able to visit large cities in many states and had the opportunity of making friends all over the country. My other lectures seldom included so many people as the three thousand in Columbus - they were usually nearer to fifteen hundred but I learned that Keedick was right - the larger the audience the easier it was.

About six years after that first lecture in Columbus Ohio where I had lectured repeatedly over the years, I was selected as their favorite lecturer and invited with four other persons to the celebration of the first century anniversary of their city. I was to share the honor with ex-President Ford, also with an elderly movie star of the silent films who had been born in Columbus – I think her name was Irene Gish, and with another Ohioan who was leading the orchestra. I had been told that we would have ten minutes each to speak about whatever we wished.

Naturally I wanted to make my ten minutes the best possible –it occurred to me that I could make a gift to the city of a few pages from my husband´s archives of his ancestor ,Cristopher Columbus, for whom the city had been named. Since this was a gala evening I dressed formally in a strapless white evening gown with glamorous white feathers on the shoulders – also I wore my emerald and diamond tiara which I knew the Columbus ladies would appreciate.

That night I remember standing behind the curtains awaiting my turn to go on stage and chatting with ex-president Ford - we exchanged in whispers our impressions about the the elderly movie star who was beautifully making her presentation. Ford asked me what I had in my hands. I showed him the yellowed manuscript from the Cristobal Colon archives which I had finally managed to get from the family archives -I told him that I was going to donate them to the city that carried his name.

Ford smiled. "Now what can I think of to make an impression after you have just given them such a great gift?" He was certainly unassuming and charming.

Of course as President Ford appeared on stage the applause was enormous. I wondered if he was the only person from Columbus who had ever been president of the United States.

During a lecture in Wyoming, I was taken to a large ranch where the owner had forty thousand sheep. That really impressed me- until then I had considered my two thousand sheep in Pascualete quite a large number. In San Francisco - in Chicago - in Dallas - each city had a new treat in store for me.Those lectures gave me with the opportunity of getting to know the great country of my birth and I loved it.. Some days I would go from New York to Seattle and then back to Washington, D.C. where my husband and I had rented an apartment. Other times I would fly from San Francisco to Dallas, then to Chicago and the next day on to another city. In all the cities I visited I met wonderful Americans , some became friends later on- I was taken to their homes, their nearby country areas where I saw the natural beauty of those areas. I was able to actually see places in the middle west where my ancestors had fought and migrated – in Iowa, Oklahoma, Nebraska, North Dakota, -- all that wide rich country- for the first time.

CHAPTER FIFTY – ONE

MEETING REAGAN

It was during a lecture in Los Angeles that I first met Ronald Reagan - on January 21st 1980. The date is important because few people thought he would be elected president ten months later - another experience similar to 1968 and Nixon. I had been dining the night before at the house of Jules Stein, an important film producer, when one of the guests, Marion Jorgensen, who happened to have been in my lecture the day before, asked me if I would be willing to go the following day with her to meet Ronny Reagan whom they hoped would be nominated in July on the republican ticket – she added that she knew Reagan would be interested in the political information I had described in my lectures.

At that time there were four different men being considered as possible candidates for the republican nomination - my opinion was that Reagan had less possibility than others, but since my experience with Nixon, I realized anything could happen. Also American presidents were important contacts for our new democracy in Spain –I did not want to pass up any possibility. Nevertheless I had the problem of having already accepted an invitation of Swifty Lazaar, the top Hollywood film agent, to go to the superbowl football game that afternoon. I called Swifty and apologized, explaining I had to cancel because I was going precisely that afternoon to meet Ronald Reagan.

"What ? You're crazy to give up a great game just to meet that second rate actor?" screamed Swifty indignantly. "We are going with James Mason and Lauren Bacall and we have the best seats in the stadium." Nevertheless I was adamant in my refusal.

The next afternoon my new friend picked me up and took me to the Reagan's house up on a hill someplace near the city . After we had exchanged the normal pleasantries and introductions, Nancy took my arm and led me into a small salon – her husband followed. She pointed to the sofa. "I'm going to leave you and Ronny here," she said –"you have much to discuss and I do not want to interfere - nobody will disturb you here ."

Reagan was the attractive man I had been familiar with from his pictures in the press and television. Until recently he had been governor of California for several years. He had also been working for an important lecture agency giving lectures all over the country on political matters - but his lectures concerned U.S. politics while mine were concentrated on the current problem in Nicaragua and the political situation in central and south America.

From the first moment his attitude was that of a comfortable charming friend, there was no stiffness nor distance in his manner as he patted the sofa and indicated for me to sit down. Nancy had already ascertained that I neither wanted to smoke nor have something to drink nor did he. As soon as we were comfortably facing each other on the sofa he began to speak."I know nothing about foreign affairs, Countess , and mutual friends have told me you are in a position to inform me of what you have been telling your audiences about your visits to Central America."

Our conversation began on the anti-USA activities of the government of Daniel Ortega in Nicaragua. During our two or three hours together many times Ronny – as he had asked me to refer to him - mentioned that he regretted not knowing much about foreign affairs. "I must learn about international issues –our great country has many problems but one principal one – we don't understand the politics outside our borders, nor do our presidents. Just look at our countrymen now hostages of the Iranians." Nancy, without uttering a word, now and then entered with a glass of fruit juice for each of us.

It was most interesting talking with Reagan. He was at ease, so was I, eventually his questions spread to topics related to Europe and Spain. Then he returned to Central America which was constantly on the television those days. I had recently been in that area .

"Tell me what is your opinion of Daniel Ortega in Nicaragua and why is he harboring the communist East Germans." Reagan pumped the sofa cushion under his arm, " I will work hard to be elected, but I must learn so much about foreign affairs."

Our afternoon stretched out. At one point, he called Nancy and asked her to bring out the Iranian caviar they had been saving for a special occasion. When we both started to dive into the delicious fat grey kernels, he encouraged me to take a lot. "This may be the last good caviar we will see for some time, if those Iranians don't release our countrymen."

Nancy came in again suddenly , this time very excited. "Ronnie," she said , "Ronnie junior is on the phone, calling from college". A huge smile illuminated Reagan's face as he jumped up and ran to the phone. I heard him greet his son affectionately - obviously he and Nancy felt the same curiosity and anxiety as we all do when our children call from school. While he was on the phone, I retreated to a terrace looking out over the city, wondering if this very down-to-earth nice man would have any possibilities of becoming president of the United States.

During the following months and after he was nominated, I had time to put him in touch with various key political personalities in England, France, West Germany and other countries who advised him in detail about their current political problems in relations with the United States. By the time he was elected he had close connections with many important political figures around the world.

During the first year of Reagan's presidency a successful attempt had been made to assassinate him. I was lunching that day in Los Angeles with Nancy Reagan and Betsy Bloomingdale. Nancy was suddenly called to the phone and when she returned she fell weak and trembling into her seat saying that her husband was in the hospital – an attempt had been made on his life – but that she had been told he would survive. She made efforts to compose herself and without losing time - she rushed to the airport to go to Washington.

The Reagans enjoyed an unusually happy marriage- probably one of the few presidential marriages that was completely satisfactory. Nancy was small and frail physically but extremely strong and courageous. Her love for her husband enabled her to help him constantly.

One night around 1985 during Reagans' presidency I gave a dinner for Nancy Reagan in my apartment in New York. Unfortunately for my plans that evening, a huge fire broke out in the cellar of my building the morning of the dinner. Firemen and police appeared, ordering us all to leave . I was taken in my shower and put on a robe and quickly descended to the patio. We were all ordered not to return to our apartments until the following day. They said that all electricity and gas for the building had been disconnected. Since I had been obliged to postpone a previous dinner for Nancy, when I saw that the fire was under control, I determined to continue with my dinner plans and did not leave the apartment as had been ordered.

Somehow my cook managed to prepare everything in an apartment a block away. The guests were advised that the dinner would continue as planned and were told to use the back service stairway as the elevator was not functioning. Also they were asked to bring candle sticks and candelabra if they had any available - I bought as many as I could - I realized that the only illumination in the apartment would have to depend on candles. Everyone came. The guest list was only sixteen persons but each was special. They talked for many years after about that unusual candle-lit evening. Actually the lack of electricity had been an advantage - the candle-light provided a more beautiful illumination and gave an air that charmed the guests into stimulating coversations. They said that the darkness of the gloomy back stairway with only the light of a candle had created an air of excitement and mystery to the beginning of a very special evening. Miraculously the dinner was more delicious than usual. The next day the Daily News on the front page carried a picture of the façade of my building with flames and smoke pouring out of the windows - the headlines stated *PRESIDENT REAGAN'S WIFE DINED HERE LAST NIGHT.*

CHAPTER FIFTY – TWO

INTELLIGENCE

    I had begun to work the second time for American intelligence about 1956 when Archibald Roosevelt was head of CIA in the American Embassy in Madrid. After "Archie's many attempts to
persuade me to reenlist and despite my husband being against it, finally my CIA friend convinced me to return to work in espionage. Archie Roosevelt told me that CIA needed agents living in foreign countries with experience - that the CIA was aware of my links with top level politicians, not only in Spain but in other countries where Luis and I made frequent visits – that I was one of the few trained agents who possessed the experience of five years of active war service - that we were now in the middle of a Cold War and that I should support my country, etc. It became difficult to refuse - actually I was delighted to be involved again in espionage. I had missed the it - social life became more stimulating when once again it had a purpose and was a source for gaining useful information for my country.
    Therefore in Spain since that date I provided regular reports on matters the CIA considered relevant. When Luis and I were planning a trip to a foreign country I advised my CIA contact. Always some intelligence information would be requested where we were going. Since in most cases I had access to key personalities in these countries, I was frequently able to be useful.

However my espionage activities became especially interesting when in 1981 President Reagan named William Casey Director General of the CIA. Bill Casey had been a colleague in OSS during World War Two - he had been in London while I had been in Madrid. Our friendship and the confidence we had in each other fomented an ideal basis for my work. Since my friend Ronald Reagan was now president of the country and Nancy, his wife had become a dear friend, Luis and I took an apartment in Washington in Watergate which made it easy for me to meet with Bill Casey alone in his office where we talked in total confidence about the projects in which I would be involved. Bill´s excellent secretary, Betty Murphy, would contact me and arrange our meetings. Often Bill´s wife invited to dine with them and their daughter in their home in ´Georgetown.

Bill and I had been accustomed to the much more secretive wartime intelligence operations of OSS – for us the restrictions put on the CIA in the eighties made intelligence work more difficult and less productive. However I had the advantage of possessing a Spanish passport - this made it possible for me to enter countries where I would not have had safe and easy entrance with an American passport. As a result Bill entrusted me with several especially delicate projects in a variety of anti- american Central and South American countries. These espionage trips sometimes provided me with hazardous experiences which I have not yet dared to recount.

As cover for these espionage trips my lectures became very useful. They facilitated my having an apparent reason to contact top political personalities in the countries I visited. Usually these political leaders liked having the opportunity of their opinions being publicized in the United Statess through my lectures and television - I rarely had difficulty in making even the most difficult contacts. These lectures and my Spanish grandee diplomatic passport also gave me a reliable that it didn't tell people what was most important. For a new company, this was a problem. Julia and the other founder, Alex, decided in the beginning that they needed to make OKRs until survival wasn't an issue.

Julia and Alex both talk about the discipline that comes with OKRs. As the founders, their job had as many goals as anybody else in the company. Alex points out that start-ups are resistant to goal setting as they are changing so fast. Often, they want to figure it out. He says the value of OKRs in the beginning is that they teach leadership. When the company scales up, the processes are set in place to succeed.

As mentioned in previous chapters, OKRs also give voices that wouldn't normally be heard a chance to be heard. OKRs put everything out in the open. This culture creates accountability and better teamwork. If someone says that their OKR is in risk of not being made, another team member will jump in to help them.

Another key to building a culture is having personal relationships and somebody who understands you outside of your current role. Julia and Alex implemented monthly meetings with whoever your supervisor is. They are mandatory, but another rule is that the topic cannot be about work. It is about your personal goals. This can speak to why someone is performing or lagging behind. If you can touch on these issues and tie them into the current position as a stepping stone to larger dreams, it creates a completely different culture. Everyone needs to charge their batteries. This gives insight into where and when that needs to happen so people can recharge and execute. Having a strong culture allows people to succeed and believe in what they do. OKRs are a guiding light in a start-up when so many things are going on.

18. Culture

OKRs catalyze culture; CFRs nourish it.

Without a strong culture, a company will be lost. OKRs are the priorities, but CFRs are what create culture in a workplace. Teachings from Andy Grove create five questions:

1. Structure and clarity: Are goals, roles, and execution plans on our team clear?
2. Psychological safety: Can we take risks on this team without feeling insecure or embarrassed?
3. Meaning of work: Are we working on something that is personally important for each of us?
4. Dependability: Can we count on each other to do high-quality work on time?
5. Impact of work: Do we fundamentally believe that the work we're doing matters?

A study by Teresea Ambile and Steven Kramer found that the two most important elements in high motivation cultures were catalysts and nourishers. Catalysts are "actions that support work" and nourishers are "acts of interpersonal support." The companies that treat employees like valued partners rather than slaves have better output. This should be no surprise.

The OKR culture is one of accountability. Nobody wants to be the one holding their team back. An example of Coursera's culture is given. Coursera's culture strongly believes in inspiring workers rather than doing the carrot and stick approach. The OKRs measured their progress.

Doerr uses an example from business philosopher Dov Siedman to describe just how important having an inclusive, transparent culture is. Dov compiled data which asked about a company's transparency. He found the more transparent, the more innovative the company was. Transparency is key to inspiring and keeping people invested in the company's mission.

19. Culture Change: The Lumeris Story

Overcoming OKR resistance with a culture makeover.

Lumeris is a tech company that aims to organize, with its tools, health care into being more preventative than reactionary. They started to implement OKRs but an HR executive found out that the system was all show. Progress wasn't being tracked, people were filling out the forms to fill out the forms. In order to change the company, big changes needed to be made.

The top executives were not leaders in modeling OKRs, so they were asked to leave. The company underwent a huge change. The new leadership believed in OKRs, transparency, and a culture of accountability from bottom to top and vice versa.

Here are some of the questions that were the cultural agenda that helped change Lumeris:

1. Why is transparency important? Why would you want people across other departments to know your goals? And why does what we're doing matter?
2. What is true accountability? What's the difference between accountability with respect (for others' failings) and accountability with vulnerability (for our own)?
3. How can OKRs help managers get work done through others? (That's a big factor for scalability in a growing company.) How do we engage other teams to adopt our objective as a priority and help assure that we reach it?
4. When is it time to stretch a team's workload—or to ease off on the throttle? When do you shift an

objective to a different team member or rewrite a goal to make it clearer or remove it completely? In building contributors' confidence, timing is everything.

The culture shift happened when executives began to be part of the OKR system. And the biggest difference that was made was when an OKR wasn't being completed, rather than the team blaming an individual, they worked together to see how it could be accomplished.

20. Culture Change: Bono's ONE Campaign Story

The world's greatest rock star deploys OKRs to save lives in Africa.

Bono uses his example of starting U2 to compare starting the ONE Campaign. They weren't the best at what they did, but they had a culture, chemistry, and a mission. With that, they just had to move forward with goals. Fast forward to Bono's success; he decided he wanted to change the world.

He started with addressing the AIDS emergency in Africa. A big turning point for Bono was realizing in the development of his OKRs that he needed to include the people that were being affected by them. Once he included voices from Africa, the OKRs changed into OKRs that were going to create meaningful change. This is an important lesson; what you think is the best for someone or something isn't necessarily the best. It was decided that corruption in Africa needed to be addressed before addressing AIDS.

21. The Goals to Come

In conclusion, John Doerr gives a passionate talk on how OKRs cannot only change the workplace, but the world. From an individual level, all the way to the top, objectives and key results can make a difference.

NinjaReads

Thank you for reading our summary. If you learned something useful from this, please leave us a review.

We chase after the key points and analyze every chapter. With in-depth summary and analysis, we help reach deeper levels of understanding for your favorite books in half-time.

Made in the USA
Middletown, DE
03 January 2020

excuse to roam around the countries in which Casey needed certain information.

I look upon those years of the eighties as the most productive and exciting of my life - they were a mixture of stimulating, sometimes perilous intelligence work combined with lectures all over the USA which gave me the opportunity of becoming familiar with the vast great country of my birth. Also the friendship with President and Nancy Ragan provided me with meetings and friendships with international leaders that enhanced my intense social life in New York and Washington.

During these years I was unable to spend much time in Spain or to join Luis for shoots. And although his painting continued to occupy him more and more, he came regularly to be with me in the USA . We both enjoyed entertaining the many new friends we met in Washington . Since I continued to be busy with trips to central and south America, my visits to Paris to see the Duchess and the weekends with the Rothschilds were no longer possible. At any rate the Duchess by 1980 was suffering Altzheimer´s disease and hardly recognized me when I made a quick escape to see her in 1981.

Many changes were taking place in Spain of which Luis kept me informed when he came from Madrid. We bought an apartment in New York and lived mainly there and in Washington -during these years Spanish politics and Pascualete were far away.

CHAPTER FIFTY – THREE

INTERNATIONAL WOMEN

In 1978 I had been invited to become part of a super-secret international intelligence group - so secret that it had no name. Years later it began to be referred to it as "Le Cercle". I was the only woman member – the others were men who held or had held top positions in their country's intelligence agencies. Among these were some of the contacts I had made for President Reagan while he was preparing his campaign for the presidency.

In the eighties at one of these meetings when it had been planned that we would discuss problems related to the Far East, I suggested to my colleagues that we invite Imelda Marcos to address us. I knew she could provide valuable information on this area. She was glad to accept and was a great success. Her beauty enhanced her excellent delivery, and the men were impressed by her extremely knowledgable information concerning the Far East and China.

Dressed in a chic red suit, elegant hairdo and exquisitely discreet maquillage, she arrived in the large barren room where about forty agents from fourteen different countries were seated around a large rectangular table. The men all stood as she entered. After calmly shaking hands, bestowing a smile and a few softly spoken words with each one, she was led to a large armchair facing the table. As Imelda took her seat, she adjusted the chair – I realized she would have preferred a stage – Imelda was an actress. Then as she sat down and crossed her beautiful long legs, with her long slim fingers adorned by the red and white nails, she adjusted warily the length of her skirt. During these gestures I knew she was studying the men at the table. I had told the members beforehand that Imelda had helped her husband win the elections three times in the Phillipines, that she was extremely intelligent and well informed on political issues, that also she was an accomplished singer accustomed to huge audiences, but even before she began to speak the men were entranced. Then as they observed and listened to her, they became still more impressed. Her speech was brilliant, her voice extremely stirring - the tone neither high nor low, but inflected now and then to give special meanings to certain words. Her long beautifully decorated fingers seemed to hynotize her audience when she used them to stress certain points. None in that room forgot the impression Imelda made that day- for years after many of those men asked me for information about her.

I think I met Alia el Sohl the first time in Marbella but I encountered her again in Washington D.C. a few years later. Alia is one of the five daughters of Mohammed el Sohl, who had been the first vice-president of Lebanon - in fact he had been the person responsable for the separation of Lebanon from Siria. In 1948 the constitution of the new country of Lebanon, stated that the president had to be a Maronite Christian and the vice-president a Muslem. This important Arab leader, Mohammed el Sohl, had no sons, so he educated all five daughters as he would have educated sons - this was extremely unusual in the Arab world. Each daughter had studied a professional career in a university, some had done post graduate studies as well to obtain a doctorate. Alia had specialized in journalism and was already a respected columnist in the principal newspapers of the Arabic world. All five daughters had married outstanding men in different Arab countries - their husbands were as important as Prince Moulay Abdallah, who was married to Alia's sister and who I had met briefly in Morocco. Another sister was married to the president of Kuwait. Alia had been married but was now divorced - this was also unusual for an Arab woman. But Alia is exceptional – extremely attractive and brilliant, when we met she was probably near my age, perhaps a bit younger. During the eighties in Washington and in New York we saw each other off and on for luncheons and sometimes at a dinner party – in those days I thought I already knew much about the customs and restrictions of muslem women due to my friends in Morocco, but I learned much more from Alia. My Moroccan women friends were daughters of General Mezian and had been brought up in Spain and had attended spanish universities so they were similar to many Spanish women I knew.

But Alia was exotic, as was everything about her – her house in Washington was exotic, her apartment in New York also. She was different from any woman I had known - Alia had been born in Lebanon and had also spent much time in Saudi Arabia, so she had lived most of her life accustomed to strict muslim rules for women, although she personally respected few of them .

Alia liked to entertain –her dinners were especially interesting due to the important Arabic political guests. We both moved back and forth during the eighties from Washington to New York and each of us gave frequent dinner parties in both cities. During this time I was maintaining my "cover" but I felt certain Alia was involved in espionage for her country and other Arab countries as well.

Alia´s apartment on Fifth Avenue in New York overwhelmed all who entered. She brought to New York a famous decorator from the Middle East to create a luxurious Arabic décor. The result was unique, No chairs or sofas - instead many satin cushions on the floor , beautiful arches connected the rooms, gauzy draperies fell from the ceilings , many candles wafted a delicious perfume throughout –a general atmosphere of Arabic allure and luxury. Entering that apartment was like stepping into a gorgeous mysterious foreign country - the menu of her dinners was also exceptional, containing Lebanon´s most exquisite dishes which are recognized as the best in the Arab world.

She was exceptionally attractive and especially intelligent – undoubtedly in an arab world, she would have a more interesting life remaining single and free to travel. Her two small children were being educated in the United States.

When I met her I was impressed to learn that she was on friendly terms with most of the Arabic leaders of the middle East countries. She knew Arafat, the powerful leader of Palestine, well and telephoned him frequently. She was also intimate with the government ministers of Saudi Arabia. In fact when during the eighties I gave a lecture in California, I met the president of Boeing who happened to mention that Alia El Solh had been the person with whom he had recently negotiated the first landing strip in Ryahd, the capital of Saudi Arabia. When I told him I knew her well, he was impressed. He said she was the most powerful woman in the middle East. Later when I told Alia this man's comment about her, she merely laughed, saying that the Saudi Minister in charge of negotiations was an intimate friend, that he did not speak English, so she had done the transaction for him. She said she often helped her muslim friends in this way. But she added that she disliked spending much time in Saudi Arabia where women were obliged to wear the haik to cover the face and a long black abaaya reaching to the floor – that she never stayed there long and when she left she would change into normal western clothes as soon as she arrived at the first foreign airport.

In Morocco I had rarely seen women of the upper classes wearing the long black abaaya although I myself had worn a veil and a chilaba when shopping in the souk in Casablanca with my friend Tamy Mizzian - but we had done this merely for our amusement since the abaaya was not obligatory in Casablanca. My friendship with Alia increased my curiosity about women's problems in Islamic countries.

Imelda Marcos told me she had avoided the countries that obliged women to be covered in thick veils and abaayas when she was trying to obtain oil for her country during the oil crisis of the late seventies. When Imelda learned that I knew Alia El Sohl, she asked me to introduce her. She said that she also had met Alia's sister in Morocco – that she had heard Alia was extremely influential in the Muslim world, especially with the ruling family of Saudi Arabia and that Alia's name had been mentioned often during her Middle East trip even though she had not visited Saudi Arabia. "Never would I wear that terrible black abaaya obligatory in that country", Imelda had commented to me. Imelda knew that her power over men depended partly on her attractiveness - that her beauty increased her political power. Soon I realized that Imelda knew more stories about Alia than I did.

Imelda interrupted her chat to inform me about the warm friendship she had begun with King Hassan and her surprise when on leaving Morocco and entered her plane she saw that he had filled it with dates. I was aware that guests were greeted at the entrance to Moroccan homes with dates to portray a warm welcome and friendship, but this gesture of King Hassan certainly showed how much he had enjoyed her visit..

Imelda definitely wanted to meet Alia – therefore on her next trip to New York I planned a meeting. I realized that a reunion of these two outstanding women was bound to be a special occasion. As a result of my suggestion, Alia planned an exquisite dinner in Imelda's honor in her alluring Arabic style apartment – she received Imelda dressed in a specially beautiful middle east gown with red satin full bloomers and a contrasting satin and lace blouse. As we entered, the apartment reeked with the enchanting scent of an exquisite perfume and as we progressed into the salons Alia introducied us to the most important Ambassadors of the Arab world who were visiting the United Nations at that time, plus other famous Arab personalities who had just arrived from Washington. Alia knew Imelda liked to make important political contacts and that Imelda was now also interested in obtaining crude oil at better prices for the Phillipines.

I thought these brilliant women had begun a firm friendship but months later, Alia commented to me, "Your friend Imelda is not a woman I like at all. She was anxious to meet me when she thought I could be useful, but once she met me and my friends and realized I was not going to be a useful asset, I never heard from her again." I was surprised. Alia had been especially nice with Imelda and had given her a gift of a beautiful arab gown and had certainly also been charming and considerate with her the night she came to dine. Imelda herself was always generous with gifts and invitations - her lack of appreciation for Alia's attentions puzzled me. Perhaps Imelda considered Alia too strong a competitor with international political personalities.

Alia sometimes asked me if I could introduce her to certain friends. She knew that Luis and I were close friends of Bill Paley, owner and president of CBS, the most important television channel, and Ahmed Ertegun, a man popular in New York social circles whose father had been Turkish Ambassador to Washington.

"Aline, would you please invite me to a dinner at your apartment with those two important Jews."

I was surprised that she would be interested in meeting those particular men – although they were both outstanding. I knew Bill Paley was Jewish but I didn't know that Ahmed was also. Both men were important in the worlds of business. Bill Paley was super important those days and Ahmed owned a large very successful music disk company as well as the most popular football team - but I was surprised that Alia, a Muslem from Lebanon, would want especially to dine with Jews. I had thought they disliked each other. At the same time I wondered if these Jewish men would want to dine with a Lebanese muslim - therefore I warned them ahead of time and proceeded with the dinner when all accepted.   Alia came attired in her most seductive Lebanese gown, maquillada with the black outlined eyes, which normally I thought unattractive, but that night looked devastating.. I placed her at table between the two men. I noticed from the first moment that both men were charmed - her beauty, her clever conversation and her flirtatious manner. One told me he had heard of her but had never had the opportunity of meeting her. Thus the dinner was a great success on both sides. Was it merely an opportunity for Alia to show that Jews and Muslems can get along? I wondered what kind of intelligence she had been able to pick up? I was certain she had a special purpose in meeting those two famous men. Well, I never found out.

The many intrigues Alia involved me in would make an interesting story which perhaps I will tell one day. Certain women gifted in attributes of seduction can be dangerous when they become involved in politics no matter what may be their nationality.

CHAPTER FIFTY – FOUR

DUCHESS OF WINDSOR FOUR

When the Duchess died, Mme Blum immediately called me. I was in Mexico where my third son Miguel was introducing me to the girl he was going to marry and to her family. Mme. Blum informed me that all the plans had been made for my attendance at the Duchess' funeral as I had promised her many years before. I left immediately for New York and from there took the Concorde to London - a car and chauffeur met me at the airport and took me to a hotel where a room had been reserved so I could rest until the funeral the following day. When we arrived at the wide gate entrance to Windsor Palace, the entire area was packed with photographers and townspeople.

In the lovely cathedral my seat of preferance gave me the opportunity of observing at close hand the ceremony and the reactions of the royal family. Princess Anne Marie von Bismarck, the only other representative of the Duchess, was sitting next to me. Anne Marie and I had been friends for many years – she had a house not far from mine in Marbella. The Duchess had met her around 1933 when her husband had been attached to the German Embassy in London and she had remained a friend of theirs ever since. The Duchess always said that she and the Duke considered Anne Marie the most beautiful woman they had known. Anne Marie and I were both absorbed in the beautiful ceremony which appeared to fulfill the Duké wishes – the royal family was sitting in the places mentioned in the agreement the Duke had obtained from his family so many years ago. The flowers on the bier were those the Duchess had requested and the music was the same as in the Duke's funeral, also according to their requests. My main interest now was to see if the Duchess would be placed next to the Duke, in the spot she had struggled with such determination to obtain in her communications with the Archbishop.

After the ceremony we were directed to a path around the large central patio of Windsor castle which led to the cemetary outside. The route took us along one side of the patio and as I followed the silent group, I was surprised to see scattered on the floor many large bouquets of flowers. As I continued walking I observed more and more flower arrangements – many had cards attached. Quickly I bent down to read one on a specially beautiful bouquet and recognized the name of Diana Vreeland, president of Vogue magazine, an admirer and friend of the Duchess. I realized that Diana would be indignant if she knew that her lovely gift for the Duchess had been thrown on top of many other bouquets scattered helter skelter on the floor. Noone else dared to bend down to read the notes – although I suppose they were admiring the many lovely flowers but noone could tell who were the friends that had sent them. I realized I was holding up the line behind me and hastened on out to the cemetary. For me these gifts for the duchess' funeral lying as if discarded in no special arrangement on the floor showed not only a lack of respect but a lack of politness for those who had sent them. The names and the flowers would have made a proper decor around the burial spot. Anne Marie von Bismarck and I shared knowing glances with each other of our displeasure for this lack of kindness and consideration for the wife of a man who had served eight months as King of the country.

As I entered the cemetary and looked down at the open plot I could remember her soft laughter as she repeated to me what she had said to the Archbishop - "Despite being small and skinny, I can´t fit into that little place if you don't remove that hedge. I'm not a hedge- hog, you know." I looked at the Archbishop who was standing next to me. That remark had been fourteen years before, and I wondered if he was also remembering her words. At least I could see that the hedge had been removed as the 'duchess`coffin was dropped into place.

Mme. Blum had informed me that the Duchess in her Will had left me a gift that she would deliver to me when I was able to go to Paris. So I did make yet another visit to that beautiful house in the Bois. While Georges received me and led me into the house, for a few moments everything seemed similar to the other last times, but today instead of those many years of rushing up to her "boudoir" , I was directed to the small yellow salon where Mme Blum was awaiting. As I walked across the room - the furniture and decor appeared the same - the paintings as well were in the usual places, but as I passed the corner of the piano , I remembered the Duke leaning on it while singing with the guests his favorite "Alexander´s Ragtime Band." I remembered his courtesy and kindness, his courage when he was so ill , trying to hide it from the Duchess. Then I turned around as Mme. Blum came towards me from the yellow room. That day I felt sadder than ever before. Also I was touched to realize that the Duchess had remembered me in her Will and surprised. She had been so vague with Alzheimer during those many last years - how long ago had she thought of giving me this gift?

When Mme Blum presented me with a old jewel box , I opened it and saw the lovely diamond bracelet and wrist watch which I remembered well. The Duchess had worn it often. One day she had told me it contained one of their well kept secrets. I was deeply moved that she had made me prescisely this gift. Later as soon as I was alone in the car returning to the airport, I took the bracelet out of the box and turned it over, placing it in a ray of sunlight coming through the window, trying to see what was their "well-kept secret". There on the back in the Duke's handwriting were three lines of words with dates, but I will not give away their secret now. It has been a gift that I have cherished and worn many times.

CHAPTER FIFTY – FIVE

CHANGES

Luis continued to paint and to have exhibits in New York Paris and Palm Beach with much success. I was busy with lectures and espionage. During the eighties for the first time, I had been living most of the time away from Spain but he travelled back and forth so that we were never separated for long. Meanwhile our children had given us eight grandchildren and we realized we would soon be having more . Everything was going wonderfully for both of us.

But suddenly during my book tour for "The Spy Wore" in july of 1987, Luis called from the Rothschilds house where he was staying saying he was not feeling well – he thought it was due to the rich cooking of Guy's French chef, but the doctors had told him he had a liver problem. I convinced him to come immediately to New York to see the best specialists. Since Luis had always been healthy and energetic, neither of us expected he would be ill for long. The New York doctors diagnosed a serious liver problem but advised that if he maintained the strict diet they had outlined, he would gradually get better. We returned to Madrid together and spent the month of September in Pascualete – during which time he took it easy and I watched his diet. In October I had to return to New York for the contract of my next book but Luis telephoned every day always insisting that he was being careful and getting better. But a couple of weeks later, he called admitting that he was suddenly worse. I returned immediately and when I saw him, I realized for the first time that he was critically ill. Ten days later he went into a coma and never recovered. Although I had been with him every minute, I never believed that he could die – it was a devastating blow.

In Spain it is customary to receive friends for several weeks after a death, to have rosaries in a church repeated every evening at eight p.m. for two weeks and after to receive family and friends at home. I was incapable of following this Spanish custom for long- it was difficult for me even to talk to the people. I felt destroyed and miserable, so I went to Pascualete - alone. Even there I felt lost. The house seemed to have lost its warmth - I missed him still more. I was incapable of riding my favorite horse. It was cold - all I could do was sit in front of the burning fireplace and think of Luis who had been the heart and soul of my life. I had no interest in anything. Not even my children could help me adapt to the terrible void. He had been my love, my friend, my teacher. Thanks to him I had become as Spanish as if I had been born there. He had taken me into new worlds - even the world of art, antiques, and paintings -though I never was able to absorb properly that part of his existence. He was an artist- I was not. And added to that Luis´ character had been the most admirable I had known.

The great sadness that overtook me was like a sickness. For a long time in Pascualete, I did not improve - but I remained there alone for one month. New Year´s came and went. It was 1988 - not only Luis was missing but almost all those I had known in Pascualete were gone as well. Primitivo and Maria had died several years before, Pillete long before them, Maria Luisa was already very ill. Felisa also. But eventually

Pascualete was where I found some peace and gradually I returned to my normal life.

I now was aware that the many changes the old ladies had complained of at the tea party ten years before were still taking place. The Spanish Civil War had only marked the beginning of the changes and the Franco years had given impetus to more radical innovations. Also the mass of tourists had brought new ways of dress and different moral codes. Not only the world in the cities had lost much of the attractiveness that I had enjoyed when I arrived, but it seemed that much of the beauty I had known was gone. In Pascualete no burros could be seen, only a few that I kept for my small grandchildren to ride and for my own pleasure - just to look at. Oxen no longer plowed the fields, and the picturesque "Chozos", the straw huts, which had been the homes of the shepherds for centuries were now part of history. Modern harvestors and tractors had reduced the number of people that I could chat with as I rode on my horse around the property. But fortunately factories were sprouting up in Caceres which gave prosperity to the inhabitants of Santa Marta many of whom now owned large shiny automobiles. A large university now existed in in that city also and good schools were in all the small villages.

It was now difficult to find good shepherds – people no longer wanted to live in the country – even though our shepherds had electricity and televisions in the modern houses we had built for them. They preferred to live in the large cities where they thought life would be more exciting and profitable. Much had improved for some. But I had known Spain when it was still very Spanish – similar to that country as it had been centuries before. I had witnessed – as if by miracle - the transformation from centuries of ancient old customs to a modern mechanized world in the space of only a few years.

We now give wild partridge shoots in Pascualete for American and European sportsmen – this helps maintain the large house and compensates for the loss of agricultural income. Trujillo has grown to twelve thousand inhabitants. Madrid is as modern as any other European capital ... crowded with traffic, bustling with activity... with a population of over five million instead of the 900,000 when I arrived.

But despite the fact that many of those who had formed part of my life in Pascualete have died, something of each remains in the old palacio and in the surrounding fields as well. Maria who stitched the crowns and emblems on my sheets seems to be there at night when I go to bed, - I can still hear the ghosts of the past centuries who had also inhabited the house moving around over my head when I am in my bed at night. Primitivo who had taught Juan how to hitch the mules to the carriage is never far away when we go for a ride. Today Pillete's granddaughter controls a restaurant in Trujillo and runs across the plaza to greet me - the smiling faces in Santa Marta are not very different from their grandparents years before.

Years and thirteen grandchildren and one great grandson help me face a world poles apart from the one I had known with Luis - it seems sometimes that more than a century has gone by. Yet peering under the surface, Spain and its people still retain aspects from other periods in its history. And when I see a partridge flush up from a clump of bushes, like a mirage I see Luis with his shotgun on his shoulder and I realize the years and all the beauty I had known have not disappeared entirely and again I can feel the magic of Spain.

THIS IS THE END.

Made in the USA
Middletown, DE
03 January 2020